THE ABINGDON
PREACHING
ANNUAL
2004

THE ABINGDON PREACHING ANNUAL 2004

COMPILED AND EDITED BY
David N. Mosser

ASSISTANT EDITOR
Karen Dies

ABINGDON PRESS
Nashville

THE ABINGDON PREACHING ANNUAL 2004

ISBN 0-687-02701-2
ISSN 1075-2250

03 04 05 06 07 08 09 10 11 12 —10 9 8 7 6 5 4 3 2 1

MANUFACTURED IN THE UNITED STATES OF AMERICA

CONTENTS

❦

APRIL

MAY

DECEMBER

INTRODUCTION

When people don't know what to do, they often don't do anything. For preachers, planning texts on which to preach can be an arduous task, especially in the first few years of ministry. In every pastor's ministry, times and seasons arrive when we can use a guide to help us. The New Revised Common Lectionary can be of service to plan and implement a preaching schedule for the church. In addition, it can also help pastors bring the Word of God to congregations for whom preachers have spiritual responsibility. Although some preachers do not use the lectionary and others use it only occasionally, the church makes the table of readings available to aid preachers and teachers who desire to present a full treatment of the Holy Scriptures. Therefore, when any preacher endures a season of homiletical drought, the lectionary can provide a refreshing spring of water to an otherwise parched homiletical wasteland. In other words, the lectionary is not binding; it is a practical tool when preachers need an escort through the seasons of the Christian year.

Confession is supposed to be good for the soul, so here is my confession. When I was in fifth grade, my teacher caught me looking on another student's paper during a test. She promptly sent me to the principal's office. Our principal was a pleasant and good woman. She did, however, ask me what I thought I was doing. Fortunately I had good grades, and when I explained that I looked on the other student's paper not for the answers, but rather to see if the other student had gotten the test questions correct—as I knew I had—she believed me. Looking at other people's work does not necessarily mean that we are going to copy, cheat, or plagiarize the other person's answers. Perhaps we simply want to check ourselves against someone else's opinion or knowledge.

I suggest that this application of the work in this volume is one of the most important aspects of the *Abingdon Preaching Annual*. Most readers who purchase, read, and use this book are not looking to steal or pilfer another preacher's ideas. Rather, we merely check our exegetical and interpretive work against those whom the church recognizes as our best and brightest preachers from across the United States. When we read other reliable preachers' works, we measure our understanding against theirs. Perhaps this homiletical measurement may give us confidence in the pulpit, or at the very least, may facilitate our creative preaching juices as we serve the church.

Clearly, most preachers do all the other mundane tasks in ministry, such as administrative toil or raising the budget, in order to preach the word. The reading and study of Scripture is its own reward. Most preachers covet time to study and reflect. At the same time, demands on a pastor's time and energy seem to increase annually. We do not have the absolute freedom of time we want or need each week to explore biblical texts and commentaries thoroughly enough. Many preachers feel too harried to do the kind of pulpit work for which the church has trained us. Yet preaching remains the chief requirement for a church to move forward into the world according to God's claim on God's people. Therefore, it is to be hoped that the *Abingdon Preaching Annual* can assist preachers in increasing and advancing their imaginative creativeness.

We have designed the *Abingdon Preaching Annual* to cover all the lectionary texts from the Hebrew Bible, Epistles, and Gospels for the Sundays of the church year. In addition, writers have provided a call to worship from the Psalter for each Sunday. Further, the *Abingdon Preaching Annual* furnishes both an overall worship theme and a pastoral prayer for each day. We have also included a three-sermon series at the book's beginning.

I encourage you to use those portions of the *Abingdon Preaching Annual* that meet your needs. I want to thank our many writers who have worked long and hard to provide this resource for preachers in order that the preaching of our churches may thrive. May our preaching find a home in the hearts of our congregations. We value your comments and suggestions that might make subsequent annual editions even more beneficial to our reader-preachers. May the *Abingdon Preaching Annual* assist you in the important work of preaching the good news of Jesus Christ to the world.

David Mosser

SERMON SERIES

BEGINNING WELL:
MAKING A GOOD START

[Editor's note: the three sermons included in this series were designed to open a new year. Thus the theme "Beginning Well." They take their theme from the three appeals of classic rhetoric: the mind, the heart, and the will. Of course, these three sermons could be adapted to any part of the year when set in a different context.]

ON YOUR MARK: THE MIND

"But he turned and said to Peter, 'Get behind me, Satan! You are a stumbling block to me; for you are setting your mind not on divine things but on human thing.' " (Matt. 16:23)

When the late Supreme Court Justice Thurgood Marshall retired, reporters asked him what he would like for people to say about him after he was gone. "So many accomplishments have been a part of your legal career. You are recognized as 'Mr. Civil Rights.' You won thirty-two of thirty-five cases argued before the United States Supreme Court. In Maryland, they called you the 'little man's lawyer.' Many of your clients were poor and without means to pay for your services, but you defended them anyhow." Retired Justice Thurgood Marshall mused momentarily and delivered a powerful one liner on how he wanted to be remembered. "Tell them," said Marshall, "He did the best he could with what he had."

Everyone has various gifts that God has put into our lives. Clearly, God endows some people more fully with gifts than others. Yet, no person is devoid of gifts. We all have them. In fact, some people define us by our gifts and graces. For example someone might say, "She is an artist" or "he is a fine athlete." This sermon begins a three-part sermon series on "Beginning Well" that has to do with starting a new year, but it could just as well mark the beginning of any new adventure in good living. These sermons examine three gifts that every human creature brings to faith: our mind, our heart, and our will. These are gifts that if developed will serve people well as they become followers of God and as they journey with Christ. God gives us these gifts to use in the building up of God's kingdom. We also possess these gifts to enhance our lives. Over the next three weeks we will examine mind, heart, and will to help us make a good start on a new year. Hear today's lesson:

From that time on, Jesus began to show his disciples that he must go to Jerusalem and undergo great suffering at the hands of the elders and chief priests and scribes, and be killed, and on the third day be raised. And Peter took him aside and began to rebuke him, saying, "God forbid it, Lord! This must never happen to you." But he turned and said to Peter, "Get behind me, Satan! You are a stumbling block to me; for you are setting your mind not on divine things but on human things." (Matt. 16:21-23)

Prior to today's lesson, Peter is at the top of his game, or should we say, "his discipleship." Let us not forget that as a rabbi Jesus was a master teacher. Jesus asks the twelve, "Who do you say that I am?" And Peter gives an A+ answer when he says: "You are the Messiah, the Son of the living God." From Jesus' point of view this is a brilliant answer. Peter got it right! Jesus even goes on to say, "You are Peter, and on this rock I will build my church, and the gates of Hades will not prevail against it." If you could think of higher praise than this from Jesus, then you are among the elite. Few places in the Gospels does Jesus lavish such high praise on a human creature.

I don't suppose any of us enjoy praise any more than when we receive it from a teacher. Most people I know really light up when a teacher says, "That is a very good question," or "Very good, Johnny, you've certainly done your homework." Do you remember when someone heaped praise on you this way? If you do then perhaps you can relate to how Peter felt when Jesus, the ultimate teacher, praised him. It was as if Jesus said to him, "Peter, come on up to the head of the class." Unfortunately, we all know that Peter's brilliance was short-lived. Too soon the other shoe dropped.

It happened like this, according to Matthew's Gospel. After Peter's correct answer, Jesus, after a short interval of time, explained exactly what "The Messiah, the Son of the living God" really meant. In fact, Jesus did not exactly tell the gathered disciples, rather we read: "Jesus began *to show* his disciples." Perhaps Jesus demonstrated exactly what it meant to undergo "great suffering at the hands of the elders and chief priests and scribes." Evidently this dose of Jesus' reality was too much for Peter, because "Peter took [Jesus] aside and began to rebuke him, saying, 'God forbid it, Lord! This must never happen to you.' " No doubt, Peter had begun to realize what was going to happen to those who follow such a Messiah.

I once officiated a wedding in which the bride informed me that her ex-boyfriend was a violent drunk who opposed her getting married. My ears perked up when she then told me, "And he told me that he was really mad and that he might show up at my wedding, now that he has been released from prison on a weapons charge." She asked me if this kind of information was helpful to ministers who did weddings. I thanked her and thereupon reflected that if the mean spirited ex-boyfriend did show up, then I would be standing in the worst possible place at the wedding—between the bride and groom. Our helpful sheriff gave me a bulletproof vest to wear under my vestments. But I do know that Peter was concerned about standing too close to one who would suffer in the ways Jesus predicted. Thus, when Peter blurts out, "God forbid it, Lord! This must never happen to you," I think he really meant, "God forbid it, Lord! This must never happen to *us*."

Clearly, Jesus reads through his intention because Jesus chastises his "rock" with another geological metaphor. Jesus describes Peter as a "stumbling block." The great rock that is to be the church's foundation is now reduced to something of a nuisance stone guaranteed to trip up others. What do you suppose is the reason for Peter's apparent fall from grace? My best guess is that he is setting his "mind not on divine things but on human things." Jesus' statement is the crucial punch line of the passage. It serves as a warning against double-mindedness.

F. Scott Fitzgerald remarked that, "The test of a first-rate intelligence is the ability to hold two opposed ideas in the mind at the same time, and still retain the ability to function." However, this intelligence test is not an adequate test for first-rate discipleship. To be a disciple is to be a person without a divided mind. We are as we think. To be of divided mind is to sit on the fence, and fence-sitting creates second-rate disciples. To be a good and faithful disciple, one must make up his or her mind about who the Messiah is. Then we follow Jesus on Jesus' term and not our own. This is what Jesus meant when he said to Peter, the rock turned stumbling block: "You are setting your mind not in divine things but on human things." There is no alternative to following

Jesus. One either follows Jesus where he leads, or one does not. And in a remarkably concise statement quipped in another context, Henry Kissinger said, "The absence of alternatives clears the mind marvelously." We cannot be double-minded about a decision for Christ and the life of faith (see James 1:7, 4:8).

I like this idea of avoiding double-mindedness. Many of us remember saying at our ceremony celebrating the marriage covenant, "I take you to be my husband/wife, to have and to hold from this day forward, for better, for worse, for richer, for poorer, in sickness and in health, to love and to cherish, until we are parted by death. This is my solemn vow." If we truly hold to this promise, then we don't have to make the decision every time we meet an attractive person of the opposite gender. We make our declaration and promise and then we live by it. In reality it becomes a once in a lifetime decision and we do not need to repeat it hourly. There are many other examples I could drag out, but I hope and believe that you get the idea. Through a discerning mind, we can appreciate the promises and pledges that we make to be the people God wants us to be, and perhaps the kinds of people we want to become.

In the New Testament the mind has always played an important role in faith. Jesus emphasized the new law by teaching, "You shall love the Lord your God with all your heart, and with all your soul, and with all your strength, and with all your mind; and your neighbor as yourself" (Luke 10:27). Paul too alerted his readers, "Let the same mind be in you that was in Christ Jesus" (Phil. 2:5). In addition Paul alluded to the dangers of having a split or divided mind when he wrote to the Christians at Rome "To set the mind on the flesh is death, but to set the mind on the Spirit is life and peace" (Rom. 8:6).

God created human beings with free will, and that includes free choice. Our mind helps us look at facts, weigh evidence gained through experience, and then make decisions that reflect faith in God or faith in something else. If all else fails in your walk of faith or if life's decisions constantly befuddle you, then remember this simple little maxim: Let the mind of the Master be the master of your mind. (David Mosser)

GET SET:
THE HEART

"Do not let loyalty and faithfulness forsake you;
bind them around your neck,
write them on the tablet of your heart." (Prov. 3:3)

Last week I suggested, as we began a new sermon series, "Beginning Well: Making a Good Start," that every person has some gifts that God has put into your life. Although gifts and talents are not absolutely equally distributed, nonetheless, we all have them. Our three-part sermon series on "Beginning Well" has to do with new beginnings. As we contemplate any new beginning, we may look at these three gifts from God Almighty: our mind, our heart, and our will. This sermon explores the gift of the heart.

The greatest danger in talking about our faith is that often when people speak about the heart and the mind we lose sight of a danger that lurks in this combination. Most of us aspire to be "hardheaded and softhearted." Yet, we all know far too many Christians who are "softheaded and hard-hearted." When we say hardheaded we mean that we know how to think dispassionately and with a cool reason. We need to make some decisions with a calculated rationality. For example, your doctor will tell you not to let your desires for certain kinds of "bad foods" dictate what you eat. If you do, then your diet may well "do you in." On the other hand, being hard-hearted is never the aim of a person who is concerned with God or God's creatures. Being softhearted means that we feel for and with another person and his or her circumstance in life. Having a soft heart simply means that we have feeling and passion for life and others. Without passion or zeal we become merely human robots.

Scripture reminds us that being hard-hearted is no good thing. In Exodus, Pharaoh, an example of one who opposes God's will, is regularly described as hard-hearted. We read in Exodus that

21

"the heart of Pharaoh was hardened, and he would not let the people go" (Exod. 9:7). Who hardened Pharaoh's heart? We are not told, but later we find out that at least on some occasions, "The LORD hardened the heart of Pharaoh" (Exod. 14:8). Thus, we are locked in a mystery. God sometimes hardens the heart, while other times the Bible discloses no such source. Either way, however, Pharaoh comes across as God's enemy. J. Stowell writes convincingly of the Bible's use of the term *heart:*

> *Heart* is used in Scripture as the most comprehensive term for the authentic person. It is the part of our being where we desire, deliberate, and decide. It has been described as "the place of conscious and decisive spiritual activity," "the comprehensive term for a person as a whole: his feelings, desires, passions, thought, understanding and will," and "the center of a person. The place to which God turns." (Joseph M. Stowell, *Fan the Flame: Living Out Your First Love for Christ* [Chicago: Moody Bible Institute, 1986], 13)

We see this understanding at work in David's call to become Israel's new king in 1 Samuel 16. Samuel visits Jesse near Bethlehem and asks to see all of Jesse's sons from which Samuel will choose Saul's replacement as Israel's king. Eliab and Abinadab and Shammah each pass before Samuel, and Samuel said to Jesse, "The LORD has not chosen any of these" (1 Sam. 16:10*b*). Finally, David comes in from keeping sheep, and without delay "The LORD said, 'Rise and anoint him; for this is the one' " (1 Sam. 16:12). Why, we wonder, is this the one? The story tells us something key not only for choosing kings but also for our own lives: "The LORD does not see as mortals see; they look on the outward appearance, but the LORD looks on the heart" (1 Sam. 16:7).

God "knows the secrets of the heart" (Ps. 44:21). Therefore, if one wants to get right with God then one had best begin with getting his or her heart right first. But if you are like me, this is a proposition that strikes fear into the hearts of rational people. We all know and know all too well the dangers of combining religion and passion. We want to stick closely with what we can think and therefore control. Wild passion out of control—passion not checked by cool reason—furnishes circumstances like Jim Jones's jungle cocktails in Jonestown, Guyana, or David Koresh's fiery end, along with his flock, in Waco. Hitler's emotional appeal and scapegoated Jews provided his ascension to power. Hitler built his power without any sort of solid logic. We all have good and recent historic reasons to distrust emotional manipulation—no matter how convincing this emotional appeal may be.

All this being said, however, our own passion for the gospel and zeal for our faith is at the heart of our relationship with God. Our enthusiasm and fervor define the depth of our commitments to the things we love. Can you imagine not being passionate about your family or your life's work or even your faith? We are passionate about the things we love. Passion and a heart disposed toward God define the intensity and vitality of our faith. Without it each of us is nothing more than a walking and breathing human wasteland.

On the first Easter Sunday evening, two disciples "were going to a village called Emmaus, about seven miles from Jerusalem, and talking with each other about all these things that had happened" (Luke 24:13-14). As they trudged along, no doubt bewildered by recent events, Jesus drew alongside them and began to talk with them as they walked. "Then beginning with Moses and all the prophets, he interpreted to them the things about himself in all the scriptures" (Luke 24:27). Later (and this is the most telling part of the story), they said, "Were not our hearts burning within us while he was talking to us on the road, while he was opening the scriptures to us?" (Luke 24:32). Because their hearts burned they understood the significance of the encounter. My question for all of us is this: Does your faith in Jesus cause your heart and passion to burn within you? I am not suggesting that you shout or handle snakes or speak in tongues. Rather, I only ask you in the quietness of your heart, are you convinced that Jesus is the Lord of your life?

Søren Kierkegaard once wrote, "Purity of heart is to will one thing." Do you will to have a relationship with Jesus on a personal and heartfelt level? In your heart of hearts do you desire to be a faithful disciple? Do you wish to remove all the impediments in your heart that keep you from a personally satisfying relationship with God? Are you willing to forgive others and yourself for the failure to bind your heart to God? If so, I ask you to decide today to give your whole heart to God through the mercy of Jesus Christ. Remember, "Happiness is in the heart, not in the circumstances." Amen. (David Mosser)

GO!
THE WILL

"Whoever does the will of God is my brother and sister and mother." (Mark 3:35)

We conclude our sermon series on the mind, heart, and will with our exploration of the human will. The will is basically human volition, or in more down to earth terms, a "diligent purposefulness or determination" as understood by the sentence, "She was an athlete with the will to win." Some of our youth might describe the will or human volition as "want to."

Our human will is the third part of our sermon triology that makes up what human beings bring to faith. First we considered the mind and its relationship to the Christian faith. Then we examined the heart and how passion for faith was essential to faith's practice. This sermon investigates the will and how it helps human beings express in action that which they think and feel about the faith we have in the God of Jesus Christ. Sixteen hundred years ago Augustine taught the church how to preach so as to be persuasive: Appeal to the mind, the heart, and the will (see Augustine's *On Christian Doctrine*). Persuasive proclamation asks these questions:

What is the message? (Appeal to the mind)
How does it affect my life? (Appeal to the heart)
What am I to do? (Appeal to the will)

Thus, the mind *thinks* through faith's implications as the heart *feels* through them, but it is the will that puts faith into action. The human will is the engine that drives all of faith's decisions and actions based on the logic of the mind and the passion of the heart. All three elements are needed for an authentic understanding of faith that acts for good in the world. The will is none other than the mental faculty by which a person deliberately chooses or decides upon a course of action. The belief in the effectiveness of human volition champions freedom of will against a doctrine of predetermination. Our human will is our desire, purpose, or determination in light of faith's authority over us.

If all this seems too over the top, let me give you a concrete illustration. Dr. Dick Murray taught for twenty-nine years at Southern Methodist University's Perkins School of Theology, and was quite a funny guy. He once said that the coffeepot was the sacramental altar table in most Protestant Sunday school classrooms. You have to admit this may be truer than we ever imagined.

Dick Murray was a master and genius at helping young seminarians learn how to teach the Bible to congregations. Murray once said something that really made a lot of sense to me in terms of people learning the Bible. "Most modern Christians do not want to learn the Bible. Rather, what they want to do is 'want to want to' learn the Bible." Whether or not he knew it, Dick Murray made the distinction between the heart and the will with respect to learning the Bible. The wanting to want to learn the Bible has to do with our heart. We desire to learn about it, but we are not willing to put the time and energy into the pursuit to bring it to completion. We feel like learning the Bible, but we don't have the discipline to actually pull it off. If we do learn more of the Bible, then it will only be because we made a conscious decision to put forth effort and time in the project. This is the human will at work. We *decide* to learn!

I have often said I wish I could learn how to cook or to play the piano. Have I lifted a finger to bring my wishes to fulfillment? In a word, no. This means that I want to play the piano or cook but I do not want to take the time or put forth the effort to learn these skills. I do not want to learn; I only "want to want to" learn these pursuits.

Let me provide a fleeting notion of how people often imagine human will. A woman tells of the time when she and her husband accompanied their son and his fiancée to meet the priest to sign some prewedding ceremony papers.

While filling out the form, our son read aloud a few questions. When he got to the last one, which read: "Are you entering this marriage at your own will?" He looked over at his fiancée. "Put down 'Yes,' " she said. (Lilyan van Almelo, "Wholly Matrimony," *Reader's Digest* [May 1993]: 138)

Clearly, however, when Jesus speaks of doing God's will he means that our decision is free and clear of constraint. This is because we cannot be coerced or pressured into God's kingdom. Rather, we can only enter God's realm by accepting God's invitation through Jesus. Hear our lesson for the day from Mark's Gospel:

Then [Jesus] went home; and the crowd came together again, so that they could not even eat. When his family heard it, they went out to restrain him, for people were saying, "He has gone out of his mind." . . .

Then his mother and his brothers came; and standing outside, they sent to him and called him. A crowd was sitting around him; and they said to him, "Your mother and your brothers and sisters are outside, asking for you." And he replied, "Who are my mother and my brothers?" And looking at those who sat around him, he said, "Here are my mother and my brothers! Whoever does the will of God is my brother and sister and mother." (Mark 3:19*b*-21; 31-35)

Jesus here suggests that those who align their will to God's will are his brother and sister and mother. What does this mean? It is interesting that the one of whom people say, "He has gone out of his mind," is now the one who defines who his new family is. Jesus' family, according to Jesus, consists of those people who do the will of God. Thus, we have a decision to make. Either Jesus or others have misread the situation. With Jesus' statement, Jesus revolutionized the understanding of the Jewish family, which, next to God, is itself a most sacred association. Jesus essentially points out that one chooses either to be in God's family or falls by default into a "natural family." Jesus calls forth an exercise of the will. Listen to how Henrietta Mears describes the will:

Will is the whole man active. I cannot give up my will; I must exercise it. I must will to obey. When God gives a command or a vision of truth, it is never a question of what [God] will do, but what we will do. To be successful in [God's] work is to fall in line with [God's] will and to do it [God's] way. All that is pleasing to [God] is a success. ("My Will, God's Will," *Christianity Today* [June 21, 1993]: 41)

During his days as guest lecturer at Calvin Seminary, R. B. Kuiper likened God's sovereignty and human responsibility to two ropes. "I [imagine them] going through two holes in the ceiling and over a pulley above. If I wish to support myself by them, I must cling to them both. If I cling only to one and not the other, I go down. . . . With childlike faith, I cling to both ropes, fully confident that in eternity I will see that both strands of truth are, after all, of one piece."

I like Colin Morris's description of a man named Fred who failed to exercise his human will or human volition by making a definitive decision for Christ. Fred was not a bad person, but without using his God-given gift to choose good over evil, Fred became, at best, only a half-person. He lived alone in a couple of rooms on a dreary London street. He was not a man of shining goodness. He was not politically active. He suffered from neither wealth nor poverty. "If anyone loved him, they didn't declare themselves at the funeral."

Dr. Morris described Fred with these words: "Fred's position in the silent majority was dead-center in the back row, biting his fingernails. . . . He died of an indeterminate disease and did not suffer with any marked heroism" (*The Hammer of the Lord* [Nashville: Abingdon Press, 1973], p. 143). In short, Fred never did anything worthwhile in his whole life. He just breathed. He just took up space. He was there, and then he was not there, and no one ever really noticed or cared. No one wants this as the residue at the end of life. Commonly, people would rather have their life stand for something beautiful and make a difference in God's precious gift of life.

Thus, the question before all of us today is simply this: Do you "want to want to" become a disciple of Jesus Christ or do you want to become a disciple of Jesus Christ? If you only want to want to, then at least your heart is in the right place. However, it is only your will that can move your whole being into the realm of authentic and faithful believers. What kind of willpower or faith power will you bring to God today?

Make a decision for Christ today. Do not put yourself into the mode of making decisions for Christ as the need arises. Rather, make one decision and stick to it every day for the rest of your life. When we align our will with the will of God, then we become Jesus' mother and sisters and brothers. Amen. (David Mosser)

REFLECTIONS

Introduction to Monthly Meditations

The *Abingdon Preaching Annual* offers to its readers a series of monthly meditations, or reflections, on Scripture texts. These meditations are for the use of preachers in their own spiritual lives. As most preachers know, it is an occupational hazard to handle sacred things so often and so much that we too habitually miss the scriptural guidance that we offer to others. As intermediaries between God and the congregations of God we serve as pastors and preachers, we routinely find ourselves missing the good news that we pass along. Therefore, the *Abingdon Preaching Annual* offers these monthly meditations to pastors and preachers as a handy way to steer us toward our own spiritual lives. These reflections allow the word of Scripture to bathe our souls as we hope our sermons bathe our congregations in God's sacred word. Rather than reading these meditations, as we too often read books and the Bible (that is, for sermon ideas), I encourage readers to muse over them only for your good pleasure. May these humble offerings of scripture reflections be of use to you in the privacy of your own life in God's spirit.

I selected from among the texts of the twelve so-called Minor Prophets for the 2004 edition of the *Abingdon Preaching Annual* meditations. Too regularly these prophetic writings receive short shrift in the church's preaching with the possible exception of Amos, Hosea, Joel, and Jonah. A rapid perusal through the three-year lectionary cycle brings to light that these twelve Minor Prophets are not nearly as prominent as perhaps they should be in their representation in the lectionary. Like everything, however, the nature of selection from among many alternatives obligates those who design our New Revised Common Lectionary to settle on which texts are included and which texts are not.

Conceivably these meditations will inspire a closer inspection of these prophetic writings that we too commonly overlook.

29

Another advantage concerning these prophetic texts is that many of us will not have to unlearn incorrect, or at least inadequate, interpretations that hover over the church as a result of constant handling and interpretation. In this sense our minds become like palimpsests, which are parchments that artists use again and again for manuscripts or painting. We do not need to erase our previous understandings of these prophetic texts so that we can come to newer and fresher interpretations. For the reason that many of us have such limited interpretive experience with the Minor Prophets, we do not need to relearn what they say to us. Rather we can read with rapt attention to what their words suggest to us (and the church today) without the prejudice that years of excessive contact tends to generate.

Carving out a time for reflection, prayer, and meditation is among pastors' most difficult tasks. Some feel guilty for protecting their own time when people in the church and larger society have so many unmet needs. Other pastors form time management patterns for their own lives that simply do not include sufficient time and space to create a life of the spirit. Habits, either good or bad, are difficult to break. As Charles Reade once quipped with great wisdom, however, "Sow an act and you reap a habit. Sow a habit and you reap a character. Sow a character and you reap a destiny." In God's mercy may we all sow the habit of spending private time with God each day.

My prayer for all who take up this book and read it is simply that it may enhance not only your preaching life but also your life in the spirit. In order to lead people toward God and in God, preachers and pastors in addition need time to develop the inner life that so many people in our churches depend on. We cannot give to others what we ourselves have not received. May God be with us as we continue to move closer and closer to becoming the people God created us to be.

David Mosser

REFLECTIONS

JANUARY

Reflection Verse: *"When the LORD first spoke through Hosea, the LORD said to Hosea, 'Go, take to yourself a wife of harlotry and have children of harlotry, for the land commits great harlotry by forsaking the LORD.' So he went and took Gomer the daughter of Diblaim, and she conceived and bore him a son." (Hosea 1:2-3 RSV)*

Let us preachers not kid ourselves. If there is one thing that we all need, it is encouragement. Life in the modern church for typical pastors is difficult. We juggle a lot of other people's agendas while we strive to find some balance in our own lives. We each know the sinking feeling when the phone rings during that precious moment we call family dinner. Junior, who answered before anyone could stop him, calls out, "Mom, it's the funeral home and they want to know if the preacher is here. What should I say?" Junior, of course, asks this question directly into the receiver. Few of us have either the incivility or courage to tell others to put their tragic lives on hold so that we can eat as a family. Many times we would not want to.

However, we also know all too well that other people can govern our time and life with something I call "trivial pursuit." This involves us because too often people assume that our task is simply to "be there" for people. Whether or not we perceive another person's crisis as invalid or genuine, many people call on us to complete the "crisis circle." You and I have both heard a hundred times, "Better call the preacher." In our hearts most pastors discern that our call to ministry runs much deeper than mere hand-holding or conflict management. Yet, these duties too are part of the pastoral office. We all know that these duties of pastoral reality play out far beyond the gift of technical theological thinking our professors urged on us in seminary instruction.

31

For these reasons and many others, we need encouragement. God has given us a task in ministry complete with its associated expectations that indicate to most preachers that we are in over our heads before we preach our first sermon. Let us not forget who brought us to this ministry location. If we forget about God, then our pastoral duties assure us of a life full of misery, under-achievement, and pain.

What the prophet Hosea experienced in his personal life is beyond scripture's witness. We do know that Hosea prophesied about a host of sins for which God took the people of the Northern Kingdom to task. Among the high points of their collective low life were the sins of adultery, drunkenness, idolatry, and licentiousness. Hardly a nice group of church folks with whom to work! But we know Hosea best and remember him most perhaps for the odd request God makes of him at the beginning of his prophetic career. God tells Hosea, "Go, take to yourself a wife of harlotry and have children of harlotry, for the land commits great harlotry by forsaking the LORD." In other words, the Lord asks Hosea to make his life a living symbol of the harlotry of Israel. More searing yet is the New Revised Standard Version of this verse which tartly reads: "Go, take for yourself a wife of whore-dom and have children of whoredom, for the land commits great whoredom by forsaking the LORD" (Hos. 1:2). Harlot or whore, take your pick and judge accordingly. Whatever the choice, Hosea's prophetic call consumed his whole life—both private and public. One could hardly imagine God issuing a graver beckoning.

If that were not enough of a heavy burden, the Lord calls on Hosea to name his children in peculiar fashion. The children's names will deliver God's message of judgment upon those who hear Hosea's prophecy or, at least, encounter the prophet's family. Various translations render the names of the three children born to Hosea and Gomer as "God sows," "no pity," "not my people." Chiefly the names' consequence means that God will sow judg-ment upon Israel. God will also abandon the Lord's forgiveness and will cease the covenant relationship that God declared to enter with God's people, Israel. We can conceive no judgment more unfavorable to Israel than the symbolic naming of these prophetic children of Hosea and Gomer.

As pastors we find ourselves often at odds with contemporary society. Whether we consider ourselves liberal or conservative, Democratic or Republican, progressive or traditional, young or old, experienced or inexperienced, it matters little. We all face a world in which we often deliver "bad news" as a preamble to God's "good news." Delivering a prophetic word to a people who feel self-sufficient eventually takes its toll. What we need as pastors is a constant and steady stream of encouragement. We receive encouragement from sources that hark back to why and to whom God calls us at the outset.

As we stand with our toes curled over the gateway of a new year, we have built into our Christian tradition a way to seek necessary encouragement. I urge each of us to take our new clean calendars for the year 2004 and block out large segments of time for us to be with the Lord. Perhaps we need to read scripture for our own soul's edification and not simply as a place to begin to "get up a sermon." Maybe we need quiet time away from the phone and constant demands of hurting, needy people to attend to our own prayer life. Whatever way we find encouragement and however we strategize to pull off this time away, practicing spiritual disciplines will both nourish and encourage. Once, when some pressed him about eating with tax collectors and sinners, Jesus observed, "Those who are well have no need of a physician, but those who are sick" (Matt. 9:12). Jesus understood that those called by God must attend to their own human foibles and address them honestly before they can attend to other people's shortcomings. In other words, Jesus prayed. Too many preachers recommend prayer and the spiritual life but forget to "practice what they preach." Perhaps, we preachers are guilty of the phenomenon that James Moore's book title suggests: *Yes Lord, I Have Sinned, But I Have Several Excellent Excuses*.

Few of us function under the burden of Hosea. Yet even with the burden God imposed on him, God guided Hosea. Moreover, Hosea kept his connection with the Almighty unbroken. As we enter a new year, although we anticipate it with hope, we also need to be realistic enough to prepare for the stormy times. We do this by practicing the spiritual disciplines as if God were calling us for the very first time. Amen. (David Mosser)

JANUARY 4, 2004

New Year

Worship Theme: The human desire for eternal life begins in humankind's awareness of God's time. God gives humankind the days and seasons of life to prepare for eternity that is beyond the temporal.

Readings: Ecclesiastes 3:1-13; Revelation 21:1-6*a*; Matthew 25:31-46

Call to Worship (Psalm 8, selected verses RSV)

Leader: O Lord, our Lord, how majestic is thy name in all the earth!

People: **When I look at thy heavens, the work of thy fingers, the moon and the stars which thou hast established**

Leader: What is man that thou art mindful of him?

People: **Yet thou hast made him little less than God**

Leader: And dost crown him with glory and honor.

People: **O Lord, our Lord, how majestic is thy name in all the earth!**

Pastoral Prayer:

O God of new beginnings, we gather as a people who yearn for the vision you have given us in Jesus Christ. As we start on new days and we have our new, clean calendars in front of us, our hope is high. Yet we know that for our lives to be truly conformed to your intent for us, we must train our eyes on your kingdom and our ears to the word you have given us in scripture.

Grant us the wisdom to learn from our past, but let not our past hold us hostage. Give us the good courage to confess our sin before you and release these our sins to your mercy. Open our lives to the grace you offer us in Christ. Let us experience the new thing you do through Jesus. Help us give our best to the master every day of the twelve months that will comprise our journey of faith for 2004. In Jesus' name we pray. Amen. (David Mosser)

SERMON BRIEFS

ETERNITY IN THEIR MIND

ECCLESIASTES 3:1-13

This passage holds the danger of being an inkblot test for the preacher. Similar to familiar passages such as, "You will have life and have it abundantly," or "the truth will set you free," this passage puts the preacher in danger of projecting onto the text almost anything he or she wishes. The challenge is to preach the text rather than the preacher's issues. While this challenge is inherent in all preaching, we need to take particular care when preaching texts such as this one.

The commentators remind us that Ecclesiastes is the somewhat cynical work of a disillusioned thinker who finds little meaning in life. This is hardly the basis for Christian proclamation! Yet, this passage, set to popular folk music in the 1960s, remains a favorite. On the first Sunday of the year, how does the preacher work from this text to a message for the day?

The Jewish translation, commonly called *The Tanakh*, translates verse 11 as: "He brings everything to pass precisely at its time; He also puts eternity in their mind." On the first Sunday of the year this verse, and the book of Ecclesiastes as a whole, invites reflection on keeping our perspective. One of the easiest things to lose in life is a sense of perspective. We become consumed by our tasks, pressures, and schedules. Small things become large. We often take ourselves too seriously. Today's text invites us to renew our perspective.

Resolutions abound on January 4. Some in the congregation (and in the pulpit) have already abandoned their well-intentioned New Year's resolutions. Others are still struggling along attempting personal reform. Still others, somewhat in the spirit of Ecclesiastes, have long since given up the practice of New Year's resolutions.

In any case, the perspective on life to which the text invites us can be a way to put the new year in the context of eternity. The year to come is unpredictable. It will dish out what it will into our lives. The smorgasbord of life experiences enumerated in the text will befall our neighbors or us each year. If we approach life in a reactive way, then we are always dependent on the events of the moment to shape our feelings and attitudes. When life provides birth, planting, healing, building up, laughing, dancing, gathering, embracing, seeking, keeping, sewing, speaking, loving, and peace, then we believe life is great. When life's diet consists of dying, uprooting, slaying, tearing down, weeping, wailing, throwing stones, shunning embraces, losing, discarding, ripping, hating, silence, and war, then we think God has abandoned us. Such is the cost of a short-term perspective.

A person rooted in the gospel knows that life will swing wildly from blessing to curse, but that beneath the unpredictability of each day are the "everlasting arms." God puts eternity on our minds. A faith that God's love and care are eternal and dependable makes hope and security possible even when earthly life is uncertain.

The year to come is unpredictable except to say that there will be both good and bad, both joy and sorrow, both birth and death. Our year will be full of experiences at all places on the continuum. Our perspective is not in the events of the moment, but in the eternal promise of God's grace. The contrasts of life will befall us, but will not define us. We have eternity on our minds. (Carl Schenck)

ALL THINGS NEW

REVELATION 21:1-6*a*

"There is nothing new under the sun," does not describe life accurately. To believe this quotation leads to apathy or cynicism or both! New things form a familiar theme in the Bible. We hear a lot about a new covenant, a new commandment and, in our text, a new heaven and a new earth.

A new year offers to each of us a new beginning. Although accompanied by a bit of nostalgia about the ending of a year, there is joy and excitement about beginning again. In a sense we close one door and open another.

Our Bible opens and closes with the story of a garden. The garden before time ends in a garden beyond time. By human choice, sin came into that first garden and with it, suffering, sorrow, separation, and death. Whatever we lost in Adam, however, we gained in an infinitely grander scale in the second Adam, Jesus Christ. What we lost by sin, salvation restores. In the words of John Milton, the Bible tells the story of "Paradise Lost," and "Paradise Regained."

John saw "a new heaven and a new earth" (v. 1). There are two basic words in the Greek New Testament for *new*. One means new in time; the other means new in kind. The word used here means new in kind. In verse 5 God says, "I am making all things new." Thus, this new heaven and earth transcends the first one in every way.

There will be no more sea. The Hebrews viewed the sea as mysterious, even threatening. The sea separated John from his friends and from his churches. In the throne scene of Revelation, the sea separated humankind from God. In the new creation, nothing will separate the faithful from the presence of God.

The "holy city, the new Jerusalem" (v. 2a) is the city of God which Abraham and others of faith sought (Heb. 11:16). The tabernacle of the Exodus, as well as three successive Jewish temples in Jerusalem, symbolized God's presence. In his Gospel, John described God's presence with his people thus, "The Word was made flesh, and dwelt [literally "tabernacled"] among us" (John 1:14 KJV). But even that circumstance was temporary. In this new creation, God's presence and fellowship with the people will be eternal. Moreover, the heavenly state will be free of pain, sorrow, and death. As God's children we shall have resurrection bodies not subject to the limitations of our present mortal bodies. And, history as we have experienced it will be no more (v. 4b).

After God announced the renewal of all things, God instructed

John to write that these "words are true and faithful" (v. 5 KJV). This is because God is Alpha (the beginning) and Omega (the end of all things). The redeemed will enter into constant and continuous communion with our Lord forever and ever. This promised togetherness should inspire a closer togetherness with God now, even in difficult circumstances.

We use these biblical verses frequently in funeral services, especially graveside services. This is understandable. These dramatic words describing a new heaven and a new earth give people assurance, comfort, and peace. If for no other reason, we ought to study these words carefully and believe them completely.

This belief enables each one of us to make this new year one of new commitment. Let us renew our dedication in the name of the one who made us a "new creation," gave us a "new name," enabled us to sing a "new song," and promised us a new home (2 Cor. 5:17; Rev. 3:12; 14:3). (Jerry Gunnells)

A NEW KIND OF KINGDOM

MATTHEW 25:31-46

In any democratic society, it might be a hard question to answer, but when you think of royalty, what comes to mind? Several years ago, the British buried their beloved Queen Mother, with all the attendant pomp and pageantry we expect to see when we inter such an important person. Colorfully uniformed soldiers, horses bedecked in royal fare, a crown sitting atop the casket of the honored queen—all these marked this event. These, indeed, are the symbols of a kingdom, and the images that speak of rank, status, and power.

Yet the Gospels present a starkly different picture of what God's vision of royal life entails. Our Gospel passage today, in fact, troubles us by its countercultural perspective. It's so different from our worldview. Perhaps like the disciples, we are left scratching our heads and wondering, "Can God really expect things to be so different?" The setting is the Mount of Olives after Jesus has cleansed the temple and foretold its destruction.

The disciples, sounding every bit the awe-struck pupils, initiate this conversation by asking Jesus, "Tell us, when will this be, and what will be the sign of your coming and of the end of the age?" (Matt. 24:3). From this one question, Matthew presents Jesus as launching into a significant discourse that, while never answering the disciples' question directly, provides an opportunity to expound on the nature of this new kind of kingdom.

Included in this longer discourse is our passage. Jesus is here speaking of the parousia, the second coming of himself in power and glory to consummate his mission of redeeming all creation. Its royal nature is unmistakable, although Jesus frames his view of the second coming in a parable about sheep and goats. As we take in this passage, we see words like "glory," "throne," "king-dom," "king," and the royal title "Lord." Matthew pictures the righteous as sheep, uncommon animals of great worth, valued for their wool, and the Lord as their shepherd. The parable portrays the unrighteous as goats. Goats are common animals, good for meat and milk, but not much else.

What separates the sheep and goats in terms of an invitation into the kingdom? Clearly, both sheep and goats had no idea of what the qualifiers were by which their Lord judged them. However, also clear is that the Lord is just in holding both to the same stan-dard, a standard of selfless service to others with no thought of reward or glory. Jesus' penetrating words sink into our conscience like a hot needle into flesh: "for I was hungry and you gave me food, I was thirsty and you gave me something to drink, I was a stranger and you welcomed me, I was naked and you gave me clothing, I was sick and you took care of me, I was in prison and you visited me" (vv. 35-36). In this kingdom, the Lord bestows royal privilege on those who spend their lives in faith, caring for others in the world. Indeed, as Jesus portrays it, caring for others is the same as caring for Christ. The faithful will not hide in the har-bor of religion; they will push their craft out onto the sea of human suffering. As we begin this new year, then, how do we measure up to this high standard of the returning Christ? Are we worthy of a royal welcome into his glory, or an ignominious exile apart from him? A new kind of kingdom indeed. (Timothy Mallard)

JANUARY 11, 2004

Baptism of the Lord

Worship Theme: Jesus' baptism reminds each of us that as baptism became part of God's plan for a sinless Jesus, then it must come as a precious gift. As we remember Jesus' baptism, may we remember the divine blessing our baptism confers on us.

Readings: Isaiah 43:1-7; Acts 8:14-17; Luke 3:15-17, 21-22

Call to Worship (Psalm 29:1-4 RSV)

Leader: Ascribe to the LORD, O heavenly beings, ascribe to the LORD glory and strength.

People: **Ascribe to the LORD the glory of his name; worship the LORD in holy array.**

Leader: The voice of the LORD is upon the waters;

People: **The God of glory thunders, the LORD, upon many waters.**

Leader: The voice of the LORD is powerful,

People: **The voice of the LORD is full of majesty.**

Pastoral Prayer:

Gracious God as we remember together and celebrate our Lord's baptism, fill us with expectation as you did those who waited for Messiah. Jesus, who submitted to baptism, is the one to whom John referred when he said, "I baptize you with water; but he who is mightier than I is coming, the thong of whose sandals I am not worthy to untie; he will baptize you with the Holy Spirit and with fire" (Luke 3:16 RSV). We pray, O God, for you to send your Holy Spirit to us. May it fill us with a new passion for the ministry you give to us as a sacred trust. May the Holy Spirit unite us as it did those in Jesus' day who caught a vision of the kingdom. Let us soak up your spirit and spread the good news of Jesus far and wide. Grant us a fulfilling vision of what you created your church to be and to become. In Christ's name we pray. Amen. (David Mosser)

SERMON BRIEFS

GOD WITH US

ISAIAH 43:1-7

On September 11, 2001, as many watched the haunting image of people running in the clouds of dust in the wake of the collapse of the twin towers, we searched for some meaning about how such a tragedy could occur. Why would God allow such horror? As many gathered that night at churches around the world, we shared with one another our disbelief of the day's events. "Do not fear, for I am with you" (v. 5a). Through each other, we remembered that God is surely with us even amid the terror of the day and the days following. Moreover, we prayed for those who lost their lives and shared our belief that God was with them in the towers, at the Pentagon, in a field in Pennsylvania, and with their families. The prophet Isaiah proclaims to the people of Judah that God is with them. As the enemies of Judah gathered at the borders, Isaiah reminded the people that God had brought them to their land and was with them still. Sometimes, like on September 11, we search our hearts to remember Immanuel, God with us.

In the most difficult times of life, we wonder if God is with us. The Lord promises to protect us through the elements of life. The rivers shall not overwhelm us. Sometimes the pressure of life makes us feel as though we are drowning in a deep pool with no room to breathe. God promises to be our comforter, to give us peace, and to help us see the surface of the water above our heads. When we were children we used to challenge one another

41

to see who could swim under the water the longest. As we swam from one end of the pool to the other, we knew that eventually we could come to the surface for a breath of air. Every so often, life throws something at us that makes us wonder if we can get to the surface or not. This is symbolized by the advertisement that asks, "are you drowning in a sea of debt?" God promises to see us through the troubled waters of our lives.

Then there is the opposite extreme, "if you can't stand the heat, get out of the kitchen." Stress is a major cause of many health problems in the world today. The causes of stress are many. Despite the fact that technology has made it easier than ever to get our jobs done, we are working more hours than ever before. Jobs that keep us apart from our families create a whole new set of pressures. We worry as our children go out into a world that is not as safe as it was when we were their age. The pressures of our lives are real. The prophet Isaiah proclaims that God will be with us as the pressures increase in our lives. "The flame shall not consume you" (v. 2). As we seek time alone with God, a sense of peace may ease the pressures of life.

Isaiah reminds the people of Judah who makes these promises. "For I am the LORD your God, the Holy One of Israel, your Savior" (v. 3a). The prophet Isaiah challenges us today to remember that the LORD is our redeemer. God gives those who trust in the Lord a special peace to walk through the pressures of life and to overcome the storms that surround us. God is holy. God is our salvation. When we call on God in prayer to help us, the Lord promises to be there. (John Mathis)

HOLY SPIRIT BAPTISM?

ACTS 8:14-17

When baby Jesus was a few days old, his parents took him to the temple for circumcision and purification, in accordance with Jewish initiatory custom. It was the job of the priest to perform the circumcision. The early church chose baptism, rather than circumcision, as the necessary mark of membership in the Christian community. God marks Christians in our hearts, not on our bodies. I am grateful for this, because if preachers still had to perform circumcisions, I would be selling used cars instead!

In Acts 8, we come across a character who seems as slick as the stereotype of a greedy used car salesman. Simon, a magician and entrepreneur, was impressed with the miracles that accompanied the "laying on of hands." He tried to persuade Peter and John to sell him their power. But we know that we cannot buy, sell, or manipulate the Holy Spirit; the Holy Spirit is not a "thing" at all, but a personal indwelling of God's own Spirit in ours.

From God's perspective, we may appear just as foolish as Simon in our confusion regarding the topics of the Holy Spirit and Baptism. An odd statement in verse 16 adds to this confusion: "the Spirit had not come upon any of them; they had only been baptized in the name of the Lord Jesus." Christian baptism is an outward symbol of something happening inwardly and invisibly. We hope that baptism *includes* the receiving of the Holy Spirit into the believer. When John baptized Jesus, the Holy Spirit descended "like a dove." The baptismal ritual of most denominations includes an invocation of the Holy Spirit, for Jesus commanded us to baptize "in the name of the Father, and of the Son, and of the Holy Spirit."

So why had the Spirit failed to come upon the believers at Samaria? Was it as simple as a failure by Philip to recite the proper Trinitarian sentence? Surely the coming of the Holy Spirit is not restrained by the theological equivalent of a typographical error! To believe so is to make "Holy Spirit baptism" as formulaic and magical as Simon mistakenly believed it to be. Signs, miracles, and other joyous fruit accompanied Philip's preaching and baptisms, and we read no report in Acts of anything incorrect about his ministry. Perhaps those Philip baptized became believers largely at a cognitive level and, later, when Peter laid hands upon them, they opened up their hearts and emotions to a more powerful indwelling of the Spirit. If anything, these events tell us that the Christian life unfolds in layers and levels, not in a single, solitary package or fleeting moment.

To gain clarity on these questions we look beyond Acts. In Luke 11:13, Jesus promises that God will give the Holy Spirit to anyone who asks, without requiring a particular form or liturgy. In Titus 3:5-6, Paul ties baptism to the reception of the Holy

Spirit, writing: "[God] saved us, not because of any works of righteousness . . . but according to his mercy, through the water of rebirth and renewal by the Holy Spirit. This Spirit he poured out on us richly through Jesus Christ our Savior." Baptism is the sign of that outpouring of grace and Spirit, that overflowing fountain of love which God gives to us even as we are born and which envelops us more each day of our lives.

"Baptism of the Lord Sunday" comes, appropriately, in the afterglow of Christmas. At Christmas, we recall the Christ Child in a lowly stable and remember that God's gifts of baptism and salvation come not for the righteous, but for sinners, and not just for adults, but for children. Just as Peter and John came to a place which Jews viewed as unclean (Samaria) to offer the gifts of baptism and the Holy Spirit, so God comes to our world today and offers us those same gifts, without cost. Simon did not recognize a bargain when he saw it. Do we? (Lance Moore)

FILLED WITH EXPECTATION

LUKE 3:15-17, 21-22

We all have expectations of the church. We expect it to be there for our weddings, funerals, baptisms, confirmations, holy communions, and a whole host of things that give us faith and hope. We expect it to be there when we need it. We think the church has little or no limitations and rarely makes mistakes. We think it is there to serve us and those who seek its help.

We all have expectations of pastors. The following portrait speaks to such expectations. It is called "Perfect Pastor Found." It goes like this:

The perfect pastor has been found:
He preaches exactly twenty minutes and then sits down. He condemns sin, but never steps on anybody's toes. He works from 8 in the morning to 10 at night, doing everything from preaching sermons to sweeping. He makes $60 per week, gives $30 a week to the church, drives a late model car, buys lots of books, wears fine clothes, and has a nice family. He always stands ready to contribute to every other good cause, too, and to help panhandlers who drop by the church on their way to somewhere. He is 36

years old, and has been preaching 40 years. He is tall on the short side, heavyset in a thin sort of way, and handsome. He has eyes of blue or brown (to fit the occasion), and wears his hair parted in the middle, left side dark and straight, right side brown and wavy. He has a burning desire to work with the youth, and spends all his time with the senior citizens. He smiles all the time while keeping a straight face, because he has a keen sense of humor that finds him seriously dedicated. He makes fifteen calls a day on church members, spends all his time evangelizing nonmembers, and is always found in his study if he is needed. Unfortunately he burnt himself out and died at the age of 32. (Michael Hodgin, ed., *1001 Humorous Illustrations for Public Speaking* [Grand Rapids: Zondervan Publishing House, 1994], p. 253)

Whether or not we expect this of our church leaders, particularly pastors, it does touch on some of the unrealistic expectations we have from time to time.

We all have expectations of each other. Parents have expectations of their children and vice versa. Parents expect their children to make good grades, keep their rooms tidy, maintain responsibility for household chores, pick good friends, and go to church regularly. Children expect their parents to support them emotionally and financially, be there for them when they need things, and provide for their college education. Church members expect each other to support the church's ministry with their time, talents, and treasures. Pastors expect their churches to offer the best benefit packages and be on the forefront of ministry growth. Sometimes we are realistic; sometimes we are unrealistic.

What are our expectations of Christ? John the Baptizer noticed that the people had unrealistic expectations of the Christ, the anointed Messiah of God. Some expected John to be the Christ. Even John had his own expectations when he answered the people, "I baptize you with water; but one who is more powerful than I is coming; I am not worthy to untie the thong of his sandals. He will baptize you with the Holy Spirit and fire" (v. 16). John expected Christ to be a powerful person. Christ's power would be his spirit, God's Spirit, and have a transforming power—"His winnowing fork is in his hand, to clear his threshing floor and to gather the wheat into his granary; but the chaff he will burn with unquenchable fire" (v. 17). John does not interpret this power. He only states its qualities. We are left to interpret

45

this power as it influences our own transformation as a baptized people. This is a baptism from within a person and it has an ongoing quality that interprets us: our lives, our ministries, our present, and our future. It will never be quenched, and it is eternal. In Jesus we find all this packaged in one person.

"Baptism of the Lord Sunday" is a good time for you and me to consider our own baptisms. What do we expect from our baptisms? Do we expect baptism to influence our entire faith journey? Was baptism simply an act, a religious ritual having no ongoing influence? Today is a good day for us to consider this. Jesus did. After all is said and done, maybe the question needs to be turned upside down. It is not so much what we expect of Jesus Christ as it is, "What does Jesus Christ expect from us, the baptized?" (Michael Childress)

JANUARY 18, 2004

Second Sunday After the Epiphany

Worship Theme: Scripture testifies that the Lord delights in the Lord's people. Therefore, through Jesus' ministry and the Holy Spirit, God distributes gifts to believers. By these gifts we spread the gospel's good news.

Readings: Isaiah 62:1-5; 1 Corinthians 12:1-11; John 2:1-11

Call to Worship (Psalm 36:5-7, 9-10 RSV)

Leader: Thy steadfast love, O LORD, extends to the heavens, thy faithfulness to the clouds.

People: **Thy righteousness is like the mountains of God, thy judgments are like the great deep. . . .**

Leader: How precious is thy steadfast love, O God!

People: **For with thee is the fountain of life; in thy light do we see light.**

Leader: O continue thy steadfast love to those who know thee,

People: **And thy salvation to the upright of heart!**

Pastoral Prayer:
O God, giver of all spiritual gifts, remind us that we are your vessels. We are those who merely embrace your gracious words of life for all creation. Remind us, therefore, that we do not create the glory of life, but we are rather your stewards of the limitless possibilities of sharing the divine glory. Grant us your joy in the celebration of abundant life. As Jesus used a wedding to

reveal in part who he was and why he had come, let us employ our celebration of worship to share the good news. Let us share the joy of Christ to a world in need of the gospel. May we offer our thanksgiving for all the spiritual gifts of faith we manage in your kingdom, O God. Give us a purpose that extends far beyond what we can make of our lives. Let us pour ourselves out for others because this is your will for us. Make us a congregation worthy of bearing Christ's name. We pray this in the precious name of Jesus Christ. Amen. (David Mosser)

SERMON BRIEFS

I WILL NOT BE SILENT

ISAIAH 62:1-5

Imagine being lost in the mountains or adrift on the sea. Hope exists in the belief, however faint, that rescuers have not given up the search. Those who have endured the exile exist with this hope against hope. After returning to Jerusalem and setting themselves to the task of rebuilding, they look forward to a new day of peace and justice. Yet as the years mount, the longed-for restoration slips away and the plaintive cry of "how long, O LORD, how long" can be heard on the lips. Such is the context for this passage from Isaiah. It comes as an answer to the lament. It is the prophetic response to those who believe themselves abandoned by God. The prophet offers a cry of hope and the coming of God's triumph set against the bleak world's despair. The prophet cries out for the sake of God's people, for Zion, and for Jerusalem.

Coming as it does on the second Sunday of Epiphany, the text invites the preacher to adopt the prophet's role. The light comes to the Gentiles. The Word of God to a hurt and broken world is not a cry of despair, but an urgent proclamation that God has not forgotten them. Dramatically, verse 2 points to the public nature of God's eventual triumph. "The nations shall see your vindication, and all the kings your glory."

There is urgency and passion in this passage. "I will not keep silent." A sense of expectancy pulses through the verses. Despair not! God is at work in the world. The vindication and triumph of the Lord will shine out "like the dawn." The reader must carefully note that this triumph is a sovereign act of God's grace. God gives a new name, signifying a new relationship. The old names reflected the suffering of exile and the humiliation of defeat.

It is common for people to have nicknames for their spouses. We call our loved one "honey" or "darling" or some other similar term of affection. It reflects the intimacy of the relationship. So it is here in this passage. The marriage metaphor employed by the prophet reflects an intimacy with God in a new relationship. Despair is to be displaced by the closest of affections "for the LORD delights in you, and your land shall be married." Verse 5 is concrete in its expression: "As the bridegroom rejoices over the bride, so shall your God rejoice over you."

The thoughtful preacher may faithfully present this passage in a number of ways. The emphasis could be on placing our hope for the future in God's hands. The preacher might instead focus faithfully on Isaiah's urgent passion to proclaim the good news of God's coming to the downtrodden, brokenhearted, and abandoned. The marriage metaphor offers the possibility of exploring the covenantal relationship with God. Whichever avenue we take, faithfulness must focus on God as the one who acts for us. There is no room here for boasting in our own accomplishments or weighing the hearer down with a guilt-driven message of "try harder." The new name and new relationship is the gift of God. (Mike Lowry)

GIFTED PEOPLE

1 CORINTHIANS 12:1-11

Gifted is a marvelous word. I don't recall that it was commonly used in the towns in which I grew up. Oh, we knew that there were "gifted" people, but they all lived someplace else. We associated giftedness primarily with the arts. All of the gifted people were back East in special academies. Some of us were smarter than others, some made better grades, but "gifted"? That was a remote concept.

In recent decades the term "gifted and talented" has arisen in educational circles. There's no uniform philosophy about how to identify such students. Nor is there agreement on how to treat them. One strategy is to *broaden* their education, while another is to go *deeper* into basic subjects with them. Most agree that the gifted need special attention. Those who administer gifted and talented programs say the students get along fine. It's the parents of students who miss the cut who make waves. They often demand that their child be retested.

Giftedness was an important concept to Paul and the early church. Paul's understanding is quite different from that of modern educational theory. The heart of his message is in verses 6 and 7 of our text where he includes the words "everyone" and "each [person]." Paul says that the Spirit bestows gifts on *all*, on *everyone*, on *each person*. Nobody's left out! No student, no parent, no person needs to stand at the principal's door and demand to be retested! Paul says, "You're *all* included. *Everyone* is gifted. The Spirit is working in *every* life!"

Giftedness is exceedingly individual and personal. Could the Gettysburg Address have come out of a conference report? Could "My Old Kentucky Home" have been composed by a governor's committee? The first came forth when a man named Lincoln contemplated what it meant for people to make ultimate sacrifices. The second was born when a man named Foster delighted in a place and a people he loved. Giftedness and inspiration are intensely individual and personal. The Spirit works one-on-one, individually. *Individuals,* not committees, are instruments of creation.

In writing about giftedness to the Corinthians, Paul does so in a particular context, the context of life in the church. He writes that the Spirit gives appropriate ability to all believers for their particular service. In our text, Paul names nine gifts as examples. In other places, such as Romans 12, Paul gives other lists of the Spirit's gifts.

Gifts must be developed. That's *our* part. We should not waste energy comparing ourselves unfavorably with others. Our task is to develop *our* gifts for use in God's service. This requires work. When asked about his marvelous gift for oratory, George Bernard Shaw said, "I learned to speak as people learn to skate or cycle, by doggedly making a fool of myself until I got used to it." Paul says that *everyone* is gifted; the Spirit has left no one out. And it takes all of the gifts, fine tuned and working together, to accomplish God's work.

The most satisfying thing in the world is for you and me to take a gift and develop it and offer it up to God, to make this very personal response to God's call on our lives. We long for an experience like that. It's the most exciting thing that goes on in churches: people getting in touch with their giftedness. I pray that this will be a year for all of us to claim and develop our gifts and offer them up to God together. (Sandy Wylie)

THE INFALLIBLE SIGN OF CHRIST'S PRESENCE

JOHN 2:1-11

There is an old saying that you will never get a second chance to make a first impression. Perhaps this is the reason Jesus appears to be resistant to performing a miracle at the wedding feast in Cana. Jesus' mother insisted, and Jesus relented.

Why should a miracle story, which was embarrassing to our forebears who supported prohibition and the Women's Christian Temperance Union, be significant to us? Why should an account of Jesus rescuing a wedding steward and a bridegroom from an embarrassing situation be considered an important word from God?

Look first at who else in scripture transformed water. Moses turned the water of the Nile into blood, didn't he (Exod. 7:14-15)? Jesus turned water into wine. Blood is a symbol of death. Wine is a symbol of life and joy.

Another interesting contrast in scripture, which can cast light on this passage, is between John the Baptist and Jesus. John was an antisocial ascetic who refused wine. He was a Nazarite, and it was part of his vow (Num. 6:1-4; Luke 1:15). Jesus attended parties and was accused by his enemies of being "a glutton and a drunkard" (Matt. 11:19).

By allowing his first miracle to be turning water into wine,

Jesus sent a clear message that the Kingdom he had come to embody, proclaim, and inaugurate would be characterized by life and joy. Jesus said, "I came that they may have life . . . abundantly" (John 10:10). Jesus also said, "These things I have spoken to you, that my joy may be in you, and that your joy may be full" (John 15:11 RSV).

A French priest, put it this way: "Joy is the infallible sign of the presence of Christ." Whenever the Lord Jesus is present, he produces the fruit of joy in us (John 15:5; Gal. 5:22-23).

I am not suggesting that there is something sub-Christian about sadness or grief. There are some things in life that should make us sad. And God wants us to taste the pain of our losses. After all, Jesus was "a man of sorrows, and acquainted with grief" (Isa. 53:3 RSV). But even in sadness and grief, joy can bubble up from the bottom of our being if Christ is present. Joy has nothing to do with circumstances.

Tradition says that the six stone water pots that Jesus used to hold the wine he created had been used to wash the feet of the wedding guests. They were unclean vessels, yet Jesus had them filled with water and transformed the unclean water into wine.

Jesus does the same thing in us. Jesus' presence causes things that are tragic, painful, and difficult to be transformed into situations in which we experience his joy. As a pastor I have seen this happen hundreds of times.

Where does our joy come from? It comes from knowing that God is with us, that God is for us, and that God is smiling at us. Many people I know think God is angry with them. They, therefore, interpret everything bad that happens as God's punishment or God's injustice. God is not angry with you. Right now the Spirit is saying to you, "You are my child, and I am well pleased with you" (Mark 1:11; Rom. 8:14-17; Gal. 4:3-7). If you could hear this word and receive it, then you would know joy.

A second-century bishop once said, "The mark of Christian saints is that they are hilarious." John Wesley agreed with this when he wrote, " 'Sour godliness,' so called, is of the devil." Does gloom and doom, negativity and cynicism characterize your life? Then you need to receive Christ's joy.

Dante's *Divine Comedy* has an interesting twist near the end. After carrying his readers on a horrifying tour of hell, Dante finally approaches heaven, and the first thing that could be heard coming from the Holy City was laughter. He wrote, "It is like the laughter of the universe." Dante was right!

Several years ago I buried one of my favorite relatives. As we left the funeral, one of my aunt's friends made a comment to me, which I have never forgotten. She said, "From now on, God is going to have a lot more fun." I hope that when you and I die someone will be able to say this about us. The closer you walk with Christ, the more likely it is to happen. (Jim Jackson)

JANUARY 25, 2004

Third Sunday After the Epiphany

Worship Theme: Paul tutors believers to "strive for the greater gifts." The greater gifts, which we find in God's Word, unify the people of God. We stand under God's authority because Jesus, whom God filled with the power of the Holy Spirit, is the one who mediates God's will for us.

Readings: Nehemiah 8:1-3, 5-6, 8-10; 1 Corinthians 12:12-31*a*; Luke 4:14-21

Call to Worship (Psalm 19:7-9, 14 RSV)

Leader: The law of the LORD is perfect, reviving the soul;

People: **The testimony of the LORD is sure, making wise the simple;**

Leader: The precepts of the LORD are right, rejoicing the heart;

People: **The commandment of the LORD is pure, enlightening the eyes;**

Leader: The fear of the LORD is clean, enduring for ever; the ordinances of the LORD are true, and righteous altogether.

People: **Let the words of my mouth and the meditation of my heart be acceptable in thy sight, O LORD, my rock and my redeemer.**

Pastoral Prayer:
God of Divine Revelation, you show yourself to all believers in many and various ways. To some you reveal yourself through

scripture, while other believers encounter your magnificence most completely in the risen Christ. Regardless of our mode of knowing or coming to faith, draw us together as a church that recognizes that today is a day to hear and celebrate the good news. Make us a people intent on proclaiming with Jesus that this is indeed "the year of the Lord's favor." Forgive us where we have failed to permit your assurance of divine favor to permeate our lives. Forgive us for not wisely following Jesus. Furnish us the foresight to become part of your kingdom of which there is no end. Especially, let us fulfill your Holy Scriptures by our lives. Give us the vision and discernment to live out the mandates of scripture through our discipleship. Remind us that it is for such a time as this that you created us as you inspire us by your spirit. In Jesus' name we pray. Amen. (David Mosser)

SERMON BRIEFS

KEEP STANDING FOR THE GOSPEL!

NEHEMIAH 8:1-3, 5-6, 8-10

"Please stand for the reading of the gospel," we say on Sunday mornings when the scripture is read in worship. The symbol of our standing is a mark of respect and recognition that the words about to be offered are important. Listening to them should be done with care and attention, for these words have the ability to bring us into the presence of God.

Scripture tells us that when Ezra the priest opened the book of the law of Moses, all the people stood up. Through such action the people recognized the importance of the words they were about to hear. Standing was a gesture of respect and anticipation.

A few years ago a young minister was leaving a congregation to take an assignment at another church. His last sermon was titled, "Keep Standing for the Gospel." He related how it had been his privilege in worship to read the gospel Sunday after Sunday, always preceding the reading with the words, "Please stand for the reading of the gospel."

The young minister used that phrase to remind the church that the very core of its ministry is to stand for the gospel. He related times in his experience with that congregation when the church stood for the gospel. He reminded the church of the time it had welcomed an African American pastor to its staff to serve in a predominantly white congregation. Some people opposed such an appointment, saying that the time was not right. But the church "stood for the gospel" and insisted that its pulpit be open, and the congregation had been blessed by the ministry of the African American pastor.

The minister remembered the time the church had undertaken a very costly ministry of providing housing for poor persons in the community and how some said it was economic foolishness to do such a thing, but the church had "stood for the gospel." The sermon that day concluded with a ringing plea to the people: "Keep standing for the gospel!"

Isn't this the essence of the church? We stand for the gospel as we minister in communities where economic injustice or racial alienation compromises the quality of life for some of God's children. On the day of his final sermon, that young minister helped the church know that its action Sunday after Sunday was a powerful symbol of its ministry in the community week after week.

The people stood when Ezra read from the book of the law of Moses. And they were blessed. Ezra told them to go their way and "eat the fat and drink sweet wine . . . for the joy of the Lord is your strength" (v. 10). It is always the case when people of faith stand for the way of righteousness and truth. The joy of the Lord is discovered in our acts of faithfulness as people who "stand for the gospel." There is no higher calling. There is no more noble work. Let us stand for the gospel! (Chris Andrews)

DEVELOPING A SENSE OF WE

1 CORINTHIANS 12:12-31a

William Glasser, founder of "Reality Therapy," believes humans have four basic needs beyond survival needs. One of these is the need for love and belonging. All of us strive to fulfill

this need. When we don't succeed, we get sick and display symptoms. God made humans social creatures, to be touched and
stroked and loved—literally. Babies who are not touched and
cuddled won't thrive.

The most basic place for us to meet our need for love and
belonging is in a family. Langdon Gilkey writes, "Somehow each
self needs a 'place' in order to be a self, in order to feel on a deep
level that it really exists. Unless we can establish roots somewhere in a place where we are at home . . . we feel that we float,
that we are barely there at all" (*Shantung Compond: The Story of
Men and Women Under Pressure*. San Francisco: HarperSan-
Francisco, 1975).

Do you have a place that's home? That "place" may be within a
biological family or within some other family. It may be a group of
singles who get together at a restaurant regularly or a couple of widows who call each other every morning. Families come in all sizes
and shapes. We work hard to nurture them and keep them alive.

Today's text concerns a family that's special to all of us: the
church. What holds this family together isn't great preaching or
anything like that. It's the feeding and nurturing that each of us
gives to it. In the churches I've served there are always members
who don't attend worship even though they could. Yet some of
them have a point of contact—they send contributions. These
gifts are these people's point of contact with the church. Somehow it's important to them to stay in touch with their church, to
feed this community, to be a part of it.

I once worshiped at a synagogue. Synagogues have a sense of
community that one can *feel*. There's a rootedness and a sense of
confidence that really give life to a community. On this occasion
the rabbi was preparing to read a passage about the wilderness
wanderings of the Hebrews. In his introduction he said, "When
WE were in the wilderness . . ." Something sounded strange to
me. In his next sentence he used "we" again. After a couple of
seconds I solved the puzzle. Of course! By saying "we," the rabbi
was identifying the congregation in front of him with those early
Israelites: "*We* were in the wilderness."

I have never heard a Christian who was about to read from the
book of Acts refer to the early church as "we." I realize that there
are dimensions to Jews' We-ness that we Christians don't share

with each other. But here's a thought: What if we Christians started reading the book of Acts this way? What if our sense of community was such that we read our history and thought our thoughts in the first person plural? What if the church were truly We?

In today's scripture Paul explores a fitting, enduring image for the church: the body of Christ. He says three things about this body: (1) every part of it is important, (2) there's no reason for jealousy, and (3) every part makes a unique and vital contribution. This is the most wonderful kind of belonging I can imagine. In the church *everyone* is important, and every contribution is significant.

A little girl was sitting on the steps of a cathedral. A passerby who paused was surprised to hear her ask, "Do you like it?" "Yes, it's beautiful," the man answered. "I'm glad you like it," replied the girl, "because I helped build it. My father's a carpenter. Every day he worked on this church, I brought him his lunch." In this great body of Christ all of us are important, all of us count. All of us are anchored in Christ and in each other. There couldn't be a more wonderful fulfillment to our need to love and belong! (Sandy Wylie)

FILLED

LUKE 4:14-21

There was a commercial in the sixties promoting a hair tonic called Brill Cream. The black-and-white commercial leaves a lot to be desired by comparison to today's commercials. However, aside from that, the buzz line was very striking and memorable: "A little dab will do ya!" The point was that just a little bit of the hair cream would make your hair the envy of everyone.

Jesus has returned to his hometown. Jesus is back in Nazareth after a hiatus. It is the Sabbath and, as he did when he was a young boy living in Nazareth, he goes to worship. It was the same synagogue in which he and his parents had worshiped each and every week of his youth. However, on this return visit, something was different. There is a stir among the worshipers, an air of electricity in the congregation. Luke is sure of why the air is electric with anticipation and awe when we read: "Then Jesus, filled with the power of the Spirit, returned to Galilee" (v. 14).

A little dab will not do you when it comes to being the church in the twenty-first century. In fact, just a little of God, so to speak, is not what biblical faith is about. Jesus returned to the place of his youth, a place where his ministry could flourish and conclude. Thus he returned home to inaugurate his Galilean ministry and it would require giving his whole life to God. Luke and those who reported about Jesus quoting Isaiah 61:1-2 were convinced that Jesus was "filled with the power of the Spirit." Now here is the rub: Whenever we are to launch into some extraordinary work for God, some new venue of ministry in the church, we need more than a dab of God to bless our ministry. We, like Jesus, need to be filled with the Holy Spirit in order to face and embrace the extraordinary nature of the work ahead of us.

But there is something else about being "filled with the power of the Spirit." It means being filled with God's courage. Too often we lack the necessary divine courage to face the mountainous tasks of being God's grace and power in this world. In order to bring good news to the poor, proclaim release to those who are captive, offer sight to those blinded by life, let the oppressed go free, and proclaim all this as in God's favorable time, then we'd better be filled with God's Spirit. A dabbing of God's Spirit will give us the fortitude and courage. We need all of God to face the huge challenges that are inherently part of God's salvation journey.

A speaker at the 2000 Indiana-Kentucky Conference's Annual Education Day posed a question to all laity and clergy present: "When is it the best time to be the church?" Somewhat stunned and hoping he meant the question to be rhetorical, we sat waiting for his answer. He replied, "There is no better time to be the church than today." Sounds simple, does it not? Further reflection on his answer makes us wonder if we have accepted that fact. Could it be that we have too often seen the church as having lived past its more powerful days? If not careful, we may relegate the church's effectiveness to a time when it was more powerful and influential. There is no better time to be courageous and faithful than today. There is no better time to be filled with God's Spirit than today. Only when the church is filled with God's Holy Spirit is it truly the church of Jesus Christ. (Michael Childress)

59

REFLECTIONS

FEBRUARY

Reflection Verse: *"Between the vestibule and the altar*
let the priests, the ministers of the LORD, weep.
Let them say, 'Spare your people, O LORD,
and do not make your heritage a mockery,
a byword among the nations.
Why should it be said among the peoples,
"Where is their God?"' " (Joel 2:17)

A person of national preaching stature, both as a teacher and
as a fine preacher, said something that struck me as odd. Yet, the
longer I am in the ministry, the more I recognize the deep truth
of this preacher's words. This preacher said, "Of all the temptations that the ministry throws at us, the most seductive temptation of all is that in handling holy things daily, we lose our own
sense of awe with regard to the very things that make life sacred."
When we think about this prophetic truth, we may see a whole
lot of reality in it.

Most pastors in most parish settings rarely worship God. Certainly we are "in worship," but are we in an attitude of worship?
We attend, and indeed lead, a multitude of worship services for
any number of people. However, we all know that leading worship with all our anxiety and anticipation, we tend simply to go
through worship motions. We do this naturally to allow others a
sustaining and spiritual worship experience. Perhaps what we
have here is the ecclesiastical equivalent that mirrors the phrase:
"The cobbler's children had no shoes."

Every pastor I know felt the call of God in Jesus Christ when
he or she surrendered to the ministry. Yet, over time, our call can
become muddled, indistinct, or distant. Too often pastors by the
nature of their vocations disconnect from colleagues. Sometimes
the disconnection has to do with simple geography. Other times

our disconnection lies in a sense of competition among pastors in the same denomination or in our towns. Whatever the reasons, we do detach ourselves from others or at least allow our circumstances to isolate us. One way or another, we need help.

The psalmist asks, "from where will my help come?" The answer comes around like a litany: "My help comes from the LORD, who made heaven and earth" (Ps. 121:1-2). We know the truth of this psalm. Yet we pastors are too prone to forget it. A pastor's greatest sin is the sin of arrogant pride. This sin whispers into our ears that in the ministry we can go it alone, although we all too often extol the virtues of Christian community or urge community spirit upon our congregations. Nevertheless, we cut ourselves off from the community with frequent regularity. As Proverbs 16:18 reminds us, "Pride goes before destruction, and a haughty spirit before a fall." Pride keeps us from seeking help. Pride foils our addressing a spiritual barrenness that is simply part of the faith journey. We each have our reasons to hide from others, yet this is an excuse and not a reason for emptiness.

Are you handling holy things daily to the extent that you lose your own sense of awe with regard to the very things that make life sacred? If so, you are in good company. The church's great saints have stood where we stand. Luther, Wesley, Augustine, Bonhoeffer, and a host of others poured out their souls to God over the spiritual aridity within. We can relate.

Ash Wednesday in my experience generates little enthusiasm among the holy days we celebrate. Whether the imposition of ashes service occurs morning, noon, or night, few people attend. It is painful to confess that we are dust, and to dust we shall return. It is awkward to have a black smudge in the middle of our forehead all day long. It is unnerving to be counted among those who have fallen. In this admission, we find God's help.

For pastors who have lost their way, Ash Wednesday is a place to find the path again. For us the isolated, cut off from brothers and sisters in the ministry by competition or geography, Ash Wednesday helps us reconnect. For pastors who recognize that "Of all the temptations that the ministry throws at us, the most seductive temptation of all is that in handling holy things daily, we lose our own sense of awe with regard to the very things that make life sacred," Ash Wednesday invites us to reality.

Joel helps modern day Protestant priests address our own sin, whether it is the sin of pride or despair. In either incarnation of sin, it grips us. We find our way toward wholeness in confession and through the pardon that ultimately only God gives. Clearly our people look to us for comfort. But truly when Joel writes, "Between the vestibule and the altar let the priests, the ministers of the LORD, weep," he clearly knows our frame. Truth about God and us is paramount.

Dick Murray taught at Southern Methodist University's Perkins School of Theology for twenty-nine years and knew what it took to be a pastor. He also was honest to a fault. Once in class a young, budding theologian said, "Dr. Murray, something happened to me in my church last Sunday night, and I didn't know how to handle it."

Murray said, "So, describe your situation. Perhaps we can give guidance out of our collective wisdom."

The student replied, "Someone in my church asked me a question, and I did not know the answer. I wasn't sure what to do. What do you think I should have done?"

With acid in his voice Murray offered a counter question, "Did it occur to you to tell them you didn't know?"

From the student's look, Murray's suggestion never crossed his mind. Murray shrewdly detected that this student's attitude was also that of everyone in the class. We all suppose that we are the resident authorities in our churches on psychology, theology, biblical studies, and the Christian faith. This is dangerous for our souls.

Ash Wednesday reminds even preacher-types the truth about which Paul wrote: "all have sinned and fall short of the glory of God" (Rom. 3:23). Perhaps we might all get back on the ministry pathway to which God calls us by being human and not feigning infallibility. We are all sinners. Ash Wednesday offers us a good dose of human reality. Only by recognizing our sinfulness do we fully appreciate God's offer of grace in the sacred things that we pastors daily handle. Amen. (David Mosser)

FEBRUARY 1, 2004

Fourth Sunday After the Epiphany

Worship Theme: When the Lord calls on God's prophets to speak, the Lord also empowers their speech. Even today, the Lord will guide our testimony about the gospel's saving power demonstrated in love.

Readings: Jeremiah 1:4-10; 1 Corinthians 13:1-13; Luke 4:21-30

Call to Worship (Psalm 71:1-6 RSV)

Leader: In thee, O LORD, do I take refuge; let me never be put to shame!

People: **In thy righteousness deliver me and rescue me; incline thy ear to me, and save me!**

Leader: Be thou to me a rock of refuge, a strong fortress, to save me, for thou art my rock and my fortress.

People: **Rescue me, O my God, from the hand of the wicked, from the grasp of the unjust and cruel man.**

Leader: For thou, O Lord, art my hope, my trust, O LORD, from my youth.

People: **Upon thee I have leaned from my birth; thou art he who took me from my mother's womb. My praise is continually of thee.**

Pastoral Prayer:

Gracious God of Love and Mercy, we gather on this Sabbath day to hear again the life-giving words of the gospel. Help us so comprehend these words of love that our lives become loving. Help us so comprehend these words of mercy that our lives become merciful. Remind us that it is your divine love that gives our lives meaning and purpose. When we gaze upon our society and its manifold needs, we are apt to fall into despair. However, when we look to the teachings of Jesus and to the message of hope-filled living that our Christ inspired, we are again secure in our faith. Be with us as we witness to your love. Make us a people filled with the love that Jesus shared with others. Help us be bold as we proclaim the gospel with our words and with our lives. Make us disciples worthy of the name of Jesus Christ. We pray this and all things in the power of your Holy Spirit. Amen. (David Mosser)

SERMON BRIEFS

I HEARD A WORD—YOU CAN DO THIS

JEREMIAH 1:4-10

B. B. King was born in 1925 in Mississippi. Growing up black in the South during the Great Depression wasn't easy. Life was always hard and often unfair. As a young man he traveled to Memphis where he heard such great blues guitarists as Lonnie Johnson, Elmer Jefferson, and Charlie Christian. He said his soul understood the music, and then he heard a word spoken: "You can do this." For fifty years B. B. King has played the blues. He still records, performs, and tours the world. He doesn't compare himself to the legends he saw in Memphis, but he continues to play because he still hears that word that was spoken to him (Thomas Conner, "Long Live the King," *Tulsa World,* 1 February 2002).

I believe there is a word spoken for all of us that allows us to play out our lives in a meaningful way. Jeremiah was a young man when he heard the Word of the Lord. For Jeremiah it was the call to be a prophet. It wouldn't be an easy job. He would be asked to pluck up and break down, to call people into accountability, and to attack injustice. He would be asked to plant and build up, to encourage people, and to sow seeds of hope. It was an awesome and difficult responsibility, and Jeremiah's response was predictable: "I don't know how."

To feel called to meaningful work, yet to feel totally inadequate is a common experience. We want to engage in a task that makes a difference, but we hold back because we are afraid. Our fear comes because we only know our human abilities; we forget that it is God calling us to a great work. God promises us strength and guidance.

We are like Moses who hears the voice from the burning bush, like Gideon thrashing wheat in the cave when the angel comes, like Isaiah grieving in the temple when God appears. Like all of them, we respond in unison, "Who me? How? I can't!" Left to our own knowledge and resources we are right, we can't! But the message that God gives to Jeremiah is the same one he gave to Moses, Gideon, and Isaiah, the same one he gives to you and me, "do not be afraid, for I am with you."

God gives us a call and the guidance and strength to respond. On May 20, 1927, Charles Lindbergh took off by himself from New York to fly nonstop to Paris. No one had ever done it, and many felt the transatlantic flight was impossible. Lindbergh would encounter many problems. He ran into thick, blinding fog. His compass quit working. Ice formed on his wings, so he flew a few feet over the ocean to try to melt it off. Sleep was always a struggle. The flight would take thirty-three hours, and he had been up almost a whole day getting ready before he took off.

While alone over the vast ocean, Lindbergh said he felt a presence come, a presence that gave him strength to stay awake, guiding him through the fog. When he finally crossed the coast of Ireland, he was only three miles off course! After successfully landing in Paris, Lindbergh became a world hero, but for the rest of his life, when he talked about the historic solo flight from New York to Paris, he would describe it as, "The flight *we* made." (Robert Long)

THE GREATEST GIFT OF ALL

1 CORINTHIANS 13:1-13

Up to this point in his letter, Paul has been discussing spiritual gifts. Like every effective writer, he builds to a climax. He now takes up the greatest gift of all: love. Paul begins discussing love by comparing it to other important things. The list of important things is quite impressive. First is language or eloquence. History demonstrates the power of words. The problem is that orators often serve unworthy causes. For every Isaiah or St. Francis there's a Hitler or a Jim Jones. Evil and deception always do their best to come to us in soothing words. Language will fail! It's ironic for us that Paul asserts this in koine Greek, a language that's now dead.

Second is knowledge. In our information culture, knowledge is a key to power and wealth. But knowledge is also an indifferent tool. It was the intellectual elite who dragged innocents to the scaffold in Salem and who directed the Nazi war machine. Furthermore, knowledge quickly becomes obsolete in every field today. Knowledge will fail!

Third is faith. What we *believe* is supremely important. We're always finding ways in which our attitudes and beliefs affect our health and our destiny. But faith is often illusive and is easily perverted, especially when it involves belief in some party line. The atrocities of the Crusades and the Inquisition were done in the name of faith. Faith, too, will fail!

There's something far more important than all of these wonderful gifts, says Paul. If you don't have this thing, you'll never have enough. If you have only it, you'll have all that matters. This thing is love. Paul describes how love behaves. First, love isn't "envious or boastful" (v. 4). Jealousy is that subtlest of all demons, a green-eyed monster. It's the first thing we learn to disguise. Lord Byron wrote, "he was jealous, though he did not show it, / For jealousy dislikes the world to know it" (*Don Juan*, canto 1, st. 65).

Second, love isn't "arrogant or rude" (vv. 4-5). It's never selfish. Harry Stack Sullivan writes, "When the satisfaction, security, and development of another person become as significant to you as your own satisfaction, security, and development, love exists" (*Conceptions of Modern Psychiatry*). This is a good definition of *agape*, the Greek word for this kind of love.

Third, love doesn't "insist on its own way; it is not irritable or resentful" (v. 5). The New English Bible (NEB) reads, "Love keeps no score of wrongs" (v. 5). Unfortunately, we humans are creatures who do keep score! We save up our negative feelings just as some people save trading stamps. Many people save and trade stamps, but stamp saving is highly destructive to all parties. "No stamps for Christians!" Paul seems to say.

Finally, love "does not rejoice in wrongdoing, but rejoices in the truth" (v. 6). The Jerusalem Bible (JB) reads, "Love takes no pleasure in other people's sins. . . . It is always ready to excuse." We know the secret delight we get from someone else's sin. Others' wrongdoings make us seem a little less wicked by comparison. But love knows that we sometimes fail each other. And when that happens, there's only one remedy: to forgive. To offer and accept forgiveness is a special form of love. And, in the end, love is the greatest thing we can be a part of, for it's the only thing that will last. (Sandy Wylie)

FROM HEAD TO HEART!

LUKE 4:21-30

The Gospel writers had a problem: How do you tell the story about the sinless Son of God who somehow got himself killed? In other words, "How did a nice Jewish boy like you manage to get yourself in such a mess?"

Agreed, Jesus' fresh word from God would no doubt wreak havoc in the religious community, upsetting the status quo! Vested interest has no desire to alter its entrenched position. But, in Jesus' own town they tried to kill him! How could that have happened?

Our text describes such a scene. Jesus preaches before the hometown crowd and the audience overflows. The hometown-boy-made-good is back and the town is abuzz! He begins harmlessly enough by taking a text from Isaiah, and ears perk up awaiting his commentary. Jesus states that he is the fulfillment of this messianic text. Smiles of pride and nodding heads flitter throughout the house. But then Jesus "goes to meddling." Jesus reminds them of their own scriptures which tell about Elijah going to the widow at Zarephath when there were Jewish widows unattended. Jesus had the audacity to remind them that God healed the leper Naaman, a Gentile, while Jewish lepers still contended with the hated disease.

How quickly the tide turned! Now the hometown "good ol' boys" were ready to string up their native son. "Who does he think he is?" "Remember the circumstances under which he was born?" "That's Mary's boy!" What could have caused these folks to react with such intensity to violence?

Was Jesus too familiar to them? It is true that familiarity sometimes breeds contempt. Even the Bible says that Jesus' own brothers did not believe in him. But, in a sense, is not the opposite true as well? One of the greatest testimonies about the nature of the life of Jesus is that after the Resurrection, Jesus' brother James did believe in him and became the pastor of the Jerusalem church. Those who know us best and love us are a true indication of who we really are.

Maybe the people of Nazareth were not so much at war with Jesus, the person, as they were at war with the nature of his ministry. "You are the Jewish Messiah, and you are going to the Gentiles? We are God's chosen people. We have followed the law, endured the persecution, guarded the traditions. Now it is going to be offered to them?" To the Jewish faithful, Jesus had quickly destroyed the notion of privilege. (The notion that says, "Grace is good when it is extended to me, but I'm not so sure my neighbor deserves it.") It is still difficult for many to accept that God loves everyone.

Or, possibly the reaction was so radical because these people were at war with their own Bible. No one is so angry or evasive as those who are condemned by their own book. They knew! They had read Genesis 12, Exodus 19, and Amos 9:7. They knew they were to be a kingdom of missionaries through which the whole world was to be blessed. They knew that God had provided an "exodus" for the Philistines and the Arameans just as he had for the Israelites! They knew! They knew it in their heads! But they did not yet know it in their hearts. Fred Craddock says that the longest journey you ever take is from your head to your heart. We know that God plays no favorites. But, yet, the church still harbors racial, gender, social, and religious prejudice within its walls. We know—in our heads. Possibly one day we shall know in our hearts. Possibly one day we shall see people as Jesus saw them.

A four-year-old girl was at the pediatrician's office for a checkup. As the doctor looked into her ears, he asked, "Do you think I'll find Big Bird in here?" The little girl stayed silent.

Next the doctor took a tongue depressor and looked down her throat. He asked, "Do you think I'll find the Cookie Monster down there?" Again, the little girl was silent.

Then the doctor put a stethoscope to her chest. As he listened to her heart beat, he asked, "Do you think I'll hear Barney in here?"

"Oh, no," the little girl replied, "Barney's on my underpants; Jesus is in my heart!"

Oh, that Jesus would dwell within us all! (Gary Carver)

FEBRUARY 8, 2004

Fifth Sunday After the Epiphany

Worship Theme: Fear immobilizes the best of people. Yet in Jesus' assurance to "fear not" we take good courage to follow him wherever he leads us.

Readings: Isaiah 6:1-8 (9-13); 1 Corinthians 15:1-11; Luke 5:1-11

Call to Worship (Psalm 138:1-5, 8 RSV)

Leader: I give thee thanks, O LORD, with my whole heart; before the gods I sing thy praise; . . .

People: **For thou hast exalted above everything thy name and thy word.**

Leader: On the day I called, thou didst answer me, my strength of soul thou didst increase.

People: **All the kings of the earth shall praise thee, O LORD, for they have heard the words of thy mouth;**

Leader: And they shall sing of the ways of the LORD, for great is the glory of the LORD.

People: **The LORD will fulfil his purpose for me; thy steadfast love, O LORD, endures for ever. Do not forsake the work of thy hands.**

Pastoral Prayer:

God of Grace and God of Glory, we magnify your holy name. Frequently when we wade into the deep waters of life, we sometimes lose heart. When relationships break and conflict looms on the horizon, we feel unequal to the task of loving others as we love ourselves. Too often we want to flee and leave the conflicted situation. However, we know in our hearts that conflict between we creatures is never resolved until confronted. In the confrontation you have given a marvelous weapon—the weapon of love. Make us the loving people that Jesus intended when he called his disciples. Let us be numbered among those who see the radiance of your plan for our lives and the path that you have provided for life abundant. In Jesus we have a guide for the way. Like Isaiah, let us see you high and lifted up in all that we say and do. Forgive us where we have failed and open to us the blessed life that Christ offers us today. In Jesus' name we pray. Amen. (David Mosser)

SERMON BRIEFS

BEGINNING AGAIN

ISAIAH 6:1-8 (9-13)

King Uzziah's reign lasted more than fifty years. As a ruler, Uzziah's glory was second only to that of the fabled King Solomon. In the year that King Uzziah died it must have seemed like the end. The stable, strong leadership the nation so relied upon passed from the stage of history. No one looked forward to that new year.

As we move into the second Sunday in Epiphany, the setting of this great text is significant. We often enter the new year like those who experienced the death of Uzziah. Despite promise and possibility, there is a sense of life hanging at loose ends and structures teetering on the brink. The simple, seemingly throwaway, opening phrase sets the stage for God to act. It is descriptive of our time as well as of Isaiah's.

Isaiah focused his attention on the Lord in that year of struggle and tragedy. It is as if he is saying, "When my world shook, I saw the Lord!" In the opening days of this new year, God offers us the same challenge. Where is our focus? Do we gaze longingly on the casket of Uzziah, remembering the good old days of a bygone

71

era, or do we instead focus our attention on the Lord? Aristotle is said to have insisted that the direction of our gaze determined the outline of our thoughts. On a very practical level the prophet Isaiah instructs us that we begin again in a new year by refocusing our attention upon God. With the holidays behind us, we are tempted to get back to the routine of everyday living. The Lord speaks to us through the prophet that this just will not do.

The theophany occurs in the scene of a throne room. (The true king is not an earthly ruler but the Lord God!) The seraphim both guard access to the throne and sing God's praises. The encounter with God is so overwhelming that it shakes the temple. To transpose such insight for our day is to place ourselves in Isaiah's shoes. We, too, stand before the awesome presence of God. We, too, are called to account.

Focusing on God, Isaiah is flooded with an awareness of his own failures and frailties. Verse 5 is a confession. It is based on three indisputable facts. First, Isaiah is an individual of unclean lips. Second, he dwells among a people of unclean lips. Third, he has seen the Lord. The application to our time seems obvious.

It is of great significance that the confession leads to a cleansing ceremony. This theme alone is worth careful reflection by the preacher. Confession evokes the cleansing action of God's grace. Through confession Isaiah is able to experience forgiveness and become empowered for mission. Only after confession and cleansing does he hear the Lord speak.

The rhythm of the text moves decisively. Isaiah enters the presence of God, confesses, and God cleanses and empowers the prophet. The tendency is to skip immediately to verse 8, but to move there too quickly is a mistake. The grace of God lives in this text through the cleansing action of God.

Set against the plaintive cry, "somebody ought to do something!" is the final, most critical claim of Isaiah's call. "Then I heard the voice of the Lord saying, 'Whom shall I send, and who will go for us?' And I said, 'Here am I; send me!' " (v. 8). It is the heroic and yet humble response of obedience. The text drives the reader to this critical focal point: Isaiah offers himself before he clearly knows the shape and nature of the Lord's call. He does offer himself in humble and eventually sacrificial obedience. (Mike Lowry)

THE HEART OF THE GOSPEL

1 CORINTHIANS 15:1-11

Every preacher is asked the question, what do Christians believe? People want to know how Christianity differs from other religions. Even Christians are interested in explanations of the faith that give the "simple answer." This text is often quoted as an answer to those kinds of questions.

It does not appear that Paul was trying to give such an answer. He was attempting to address issues that the Corinthian congregation discussed. The Corinthians raised some of these issues in correspondence with Paul. Other issues came to Paul's attention from reports of those who had been in the Corinthian congregation. It is not clear from 1 Corinthians 15 whether Paul responds to an issue posed by the Corinthians or whether he has simply heard about a problem in the congregation. What is clear is that people had questions about the resurrection of Jesus.

Apparently, there were some who said, "there is no resurrection of the dead" (v. 12). In chapter 15 Paul gives his longest and best defense of the Christian belief about resurrection. The first part of that defense is a summary of the message that Paul himself preached in Corinth. At the heart of that "good news" was a clear affirmation about the resurrection of Jesus. Although Paul's defense of the Resurrection doesn't include all of the elements of the apostolic preaching in Acts, it does contain the core elements. It is belief in the truth of this proclaimed message about Christ's resurrection that brings salvation. Paul makes clear the necessity of holding firm to this central teaching. Without it he says, "you have come to believe in vain" (v. 2).

The argument, which Paul presents, has several parts. First, he claims that the Christian belief in Christ's resurrection is the primary Christian teaching. Second, he admits that his information about Christ's resurrection is second hand. This is not a denial of his encounter with Christ. It is an admission that Christ's revelation to him was a later revelation. He was passing on what had been "passed on" to him. Third, Christ's death, burial, and resurrection fulfilled the Hebrew Scripture. Although Paul doesn't quote any scripture here, he may have had passages like Isaiah 53 and Psalm 16 in mind. Fourth, the risen Christ appeared to a number of individuals and groups. All the apostles saw him. In fact, that became a criterion for apostleship. That's why James, the brother of Jesus, and Paul are entitled to be called apostles.

Paul concludes this passage with another reminder that "this is what we preach, and this is what you believed." Doubt descended on the Corinthian congregation. Had God really raised Jesus from the dead? The same kind of doubt is present in today's church. Paul's answer is simple and straightforward: Look at the record. Christians throughout the centuries have dealt with doubts about the Resurrection by noting the transformation that took place in the lives of those who claimed an encounter with the risen Lord. Those who had fled from persecution when Jesus was arrested were the very ones who became Christian martyrs in the years to come. What made the difference? It was their belief in the gospel message. The heart of that gospel is still confirmed by the changed hearts and lives of believers. (Philip Wise)

LEAVING BEFORE THE INVITATION

LUKE 5:1-11

John and Mary have been married over twenty years and have two teenagers. She put him through medical school. Last year they finally paid off those school bills. Last Sunday John announced, "God has called me to be a missionary to Bosnia. If Johnny and Susie get part-time jobs, Mary goes back to work, and my sister takes care of Mary's sick parents, I can go to seminary and we can fulfill God's calling!" Everybody happy?

We sometimes forget that Jesus called the disciples to a second career. They, too, had families, careers, bills, and aging parents. The phone rings, "Peter did not come to work again today. Is he running around the countryside with that itinerant preacher?" Think of Peter's wife! She married a successful fisherman. Now she is the preacher's wife with a mother who tends to be ill. Everybody happy?

No wonder people leave before the invitation. Too risky to stay. Why become vulnerable to an experience that could change the rest of your life? You could hear the life altering call of God. But there are positives as well.

74

The call of God can be an awesome experience. How awed Peter must have been with this miraculous catch of fish. It was a miracle in the ordinary experiences of life. God does that, you know. He reveals himself and his call to a shoeless shepherd through a burning bush. He calls a redheaded kid from tending sheep to be the shepherd-king of Israel. Gideon heard God's call on the working end of a hoe. Paul was gathering troublemakers. Could it be that God cares about us and is involved in the everyday happenings of our lives? The film *Oh, God!* tried to portray the message that God comes to us and wants us to be happy. In 1978 it received the award "Best fantasy film of the year"! Fantasy? That God cares?

For Peter this also was a humbling experience. It humbled Peter as he was astonished at the power of Jesus. Part of Peter's eventual greatness was his ability to admit his own powerlessness in the face of the awesome power of Jesus. But the same power that caused him to fall on his knees also lifted him up. We answer Jesus' call not in our strength, but in Jesus' strength.

The call of God is not only an awesome and humbling experience but also a joyful one as well. Obedience to Jesus' call starts us on the progressive road to Christlikeness. There is no more joyful journey in life than that of using our gifts to become more and more like Jesus. Doing what God calls us to do makes us happy. We may not always know what we are to do tomorrow, but he will show us what to do today and supply to us his power with which to do it. That is joy!

William Bausch tells the story of a nun that received some extra grant money. She worked as a chaplain in a women's prison in Chicago. She went to the women and said, "I have some money that I want to spend on you, and I'm going to give you an option. I can hire an attorney to come and talk with you on how you can shorten your sentences. Or I can hire a welder to come in and teach you to weld so that you can have a marketable skill when you leave the prison. Or I can hire a dancer and a painter to teach you how to dance and how to paint." Ninety-five percent chose the dancer and the painter because, as they said, "they always wanted to express themselves but never had the chance." The most positive, fulfilling, joyful experience you will ever know is walking in the middle of God's will for your life! Everybody happy? (Gary Carver)

FEBRUARY 15, 2004

Sixth Sunday After the Epiphany

Worship Theme: Paul asserts that God resurrected Christ from the dead. This means that God fulfills in Jesus the promises that Jesus makes in his Sermon on the Plain.

Readings: Jeremiah 17:5-10; 1 Corinthians 15:12-20; Luke 6:17-26

Call to Worship (Psalm 1 RSV)

Leader: Blessed is the man who walks not in the counsel of the wicked, nor stands in the way of sinners, nor sits in the seat of scoffers;

People: **But his delight is in the law of the LORD, and on his law he meditates day and night.**

Leader: He is like a tree planted by streams of water, that yields its fruit in its season, and its leaf does not wither. In all that he does, he prospers.

People: **The wicked are not so, but are like chaff which the wind drives away.**

Leader: Therefore the wicked will not stand in the judgment, nor sinners in the congregation of the righteous;

People: **For the LORD knows the way of the righteous, but the way of the wicked will perish.**

Pastoral Prayer:

We too, like those near the lake, come to worship to hear the words of Jesus and for Jesus' healing touch, O Lord. We all seek the blessing that life in you offers, but too often we follow the ways of our own hearts rather than your divine will for us. Give us the mind of Christ to discern the blessing you bestow daily on your people. Create in us a heart for others and the mercy that you have given us to share through Jesus' life and death. In addition, give us the will to accomplish our tasks of discipleship for which you called us. The road toward your kingdom often makes us weary, but you offer to us a new spirit. By this spirit may we offer the fruit of our lives as our living sacrifice. It is your people who carry your mandate and your love to the world. May you count us in their number. In the name of Jesus Christ, we pray. Amen. (David Mosser)

SERMON BRIEFS

THE WATER OF GOD

JEREMIAH 17:5-10

Water is a precious gift of God. Water refreshes, sustains, and nourishes. Our bodies are made up mostly of water. We can go many days without food and survive, but we can only last a short time without water. In this passage from the prophet Jeremiah, water is also a symbol of the refreshing, sustaining nature of God for our lives.

The text begins with a statement of warning and admonition, "Cursed are those who trust in mere mortals . . . whose hearts turn away from the LORD." This is not a portrait of God as a mean deity who places hexes and curses on the people whom God has lovingly created. It is a statement of outcome, of the consequences of our actions when we deny the reality of life with God. Life apart from God is not a viable reality but a cursed experience of despair and loneliness.

The message is originally intended for a time and people whose lives and livelihood revolved around rain, fertile soil, and successful crops. They understood the importance of moisture for nurturing and sustaining life. This makes the message even more powerful.

[Those who turn away from God] shall be like a shrub in the
  desert,
    and shall not see when relief comes.
They shall live in the parched places of the wilderness,
    in an uninhabited salt land. (v. 6)

Any good farmer knows that growing anything in salt flats is
utterly and completely hopeless. The futility and despair of such
a metaphor is overwhelming and complete.

The message is not lost for people of the present time either,
for the human need for the sustaining and refreshing power of
water has not changed. We may use technology to get water in
ways impossible in biblical times, but the need remains. We need
water, and the metaphor points to the greater truth, we desperately need God.

My father was born and raised near the West Texas town of
Graham in Young County. Cattle ranchers and farmers knew the
value of water then, and they still do today. Dad learned to swim
in a "cattle tank," an earthen pond that gathered rainwater and
sometimes ground water from a spring or well. He was baptized
in the same place where he swam. The same rain that fed that
pond also nourished the soil that provided grass for the cattle to
eat and green pastures in which the horses could graze.

The symbolism of our need for water and our need for God is
as constant and relevant today as it was in Jeremiah's time.

Blessed are those who trust in the LORD. . . .
They shall be like a tree planted by water,
    sending out its roots by the stream.
It shall not fear when heat comes. . . .
in the year of the drought it is not anxious,
    and it does not cease to bear fruit. (vv. 7-8)

It is by the fruit that we bear and the faith—or lack thereof—
that is written on the heart that God knows whether or not we
are a part of the kingdom. If we drink in the precious water of
God, that is, we live in God's Spirit, and are strengthened by
wrestling with God's Word, we grow healthy and strong as God's
people. No storms of life can rip away such deep roots. (Gary
Kindley)

ORDINARY RESURRECTION

1 CORINTHIANS 15:12-20

An oxymoron is a combination of contradictory words. "Ordinary Resurrection" would be an example. It is hard to imagine what an ordinary resurrection would be like. Any resurrection would be miraculous. First-century Corinthian Christians could believe in the resurrection of Jesus; it was an extraordinary occurrence. However, they did not believe in ordinary resurrections, that is, the resurrection of ordinary folks.

That was the problem Paul was trying to address in this passage. There were preachers in Corinth who proclaimed the resurrection of Christ while denying that resurrection from the dead was a possibility. We don't know the precise nature of their objection. We do know that Christians took their belief in resurrection from the Jewish teaching that those who died would be raised bodily from the dead in order to receive their rewards or punishment at the Last Judgment. Jesus affirmed his belief in this understanding of resurrection. Jesus' resurrection became the proof Christians needed for this theological belief. There were some Jews, such as the Sadducees, who did not believe in resurrection because they couldn't find it taught in the Hebrew Scriptures. This fact may explain the teaching that was happening in Corinth. It seems more likely that the Corinthians were taking their cue from the Greek belief in the immortality of the soul. The Christian belief in the resurrection of the body may have been incongruous with the commonly accepted beliefs of their culture.

Paul argues for a belief in resurrection. His argument is simple and logical. If there is no such thing as resurrection, then it makes no sense to preach about the resurrection of Jesus because Jesus could not have been resurrected. If Jesus was not resurrected, then Christian claims about Jesus are false. If he was not raised from the dead, then claims about his ability to forgive sins are untrue. For Paul the resurrection of Jesus was the linchpin of the Christian gospel. Without resurrection the whole Christian teaching comes uncoupled. The result is clear: Those who have died believing in Christ's resurrection and power to forgive sins have died in vain. If Christianity is only about how to live in this life and is irrelevant to the life to come, then Christians are a pathetic group of false witnesses and should be pitied and ignored. But, argues Paul, since Christ has been raised from the dead (he's given his evidence for that in 15:1-11), those who have put their trust in him will also be resurrected.

There are times when we accept most of what a group affirms, but deny some specific tenets of that group's beliefs. For instance, we might identify with a particular political party but disagree with the party on a particular plank in its platform. Paul says that this is not possible for Christians when it comes to resurrection. It is the indispensable ingredient in the Christian belief system. That's why belief in the resurrection of "ordinary" folks is so important. Resurrection is not an experience that is reserved for Christ alone. It is promised to every believer.

I have a hunch that the Corinthians were more sophisticated than the text might suggest. Perhaps they didn't deny believing in resurrection, but rather suggested through their preaching that they were open to other possibilities. Christians are often tempted to adjust their beliefs to the popular beliefs of their time. If the Corinthians had done that in the first century, they would have given up a core belief. What beliefs are we tempted to compromise in our setting? (Philip Wise)

WOE TO THE BLESSED?

LUKE 6:17-26

In an episode of *M*A*S*H*, Frank Burns and Hotlips Houlihan were foiled in their efforts to get Hawkeye in trouble. "Get revenge!" was the essence of Radar's advice. "Oh, no!" replied Hawkeye. "They are just two half persons barely together making a whole person."

Someone said of a powerful but insecure denominational leader, "It is a shame that such a big man can be so little." "Half people" cast small shadows. In our text Jesus is talking about half persons becoming whole persons. Those who *don't* get it *can* get it! They can get life!

After an entire night in prayer Jesus delivers what we commonly call the Sermon on the Plain. Some Jews believed that one was blessed—rich—because they were good and favored by God. Is Jesus saying God hates the rich? Talk about upsetting theological apple carts! The broader perspective of Jesus' teaching emphasizes that God loves everyone. Jesus is not saying that God hates someone merely because they are "blessed." Jesus seems to say that if their lives are centered around their possessions, already they have their reward. They are "paid in full." He also says that to whom much is given, much shall be required. The "blessed" have a responsibility to channel their resources and energies to others.

Jesus may be suggesting that success often is much harder to handle than failure. Leon Spinks upset Muhammad Ali, winning the heavyweight championship, and initiated a year of personal chaos for himself. Thirty people joined Spinks's entourage for the rematch. After his defeat, he sat alone in his dressing room.

Jesus could also be stressing that there should be more to our living than the collecting of toys. Rabbi Harold Kushner tells of a caterpillar, native to South Wales, that lays its eggs then turns into a moth with no mouth and no digestive system. It dies within a few hours (*When All You Ever Wanted Isn't Enough*. New York: Simon & Schuster, 2002). There has got to be more to life than to show up, further the species, and die!

Or is Jesus saying in verses 20-23 that God loves the poor? This is Luke, remember, not Matthew. Jesus, in Luke, speaks about the poverty-stricken, not the poor in Spirit. God certainly loves the poor. Maybe God loves the poor because they come to him in abject poverty with nothing to offer. They can't even attempt to buy off God. They are perhaps more aware of their need for God. So God becomes the center of their lives.

Now Jesus is not necessarily saying we ought to take a vow of poverty and join a monastery. In fact, the Talmud states that we will be brought into judgment for every good thing God put on this earth that we refused to enjoy. What did Jesus mean as he spoke to those in his Sermon on the Plain?

I think Jesus meant that we should put him, not our abundance or our need, at the center of our lives. Through our personal relationship to Jesus, we understand that we should enjoy the fullness of life when it is abundant. We should enjoy with exuberance and generosity. We also understand that when nothing seems to be going right, we remind ourselves that we should not be weary in well doing, for God rewards faithfulness in God's time and in God's way. Our relationship to Jesus works on the best and worst of days. (Gary Carver)

FEBRUARY 22, 2004

Transfiguration Sunday

Worship Theme: God reveals Jesus' glory to three privileged disciples: Peter, James, and John. In this revelation on the Mount of Transfiguration these disciples get a foretaste of the glory of the Lord.

Readings: Exodus 34:29-35; 2 Corinthians 3:12–4:2; Luke 9:28-36 (37-43)

Call to Worship (Psalm 99:1-5, 9 RSV)

> *Leader:*   The LORD reigns; let the peoples tremble!

> *People:*   **He sits enthroned upon the cherubim; let the earth quake!**

> *Leader:*   The LORD is great in Zion; he is exalted over all the peoples. . . .

> *People:*   **Mighty King, lover of justice, thou hast established equity; thou hast executed justice and righteousness in Jacob.**

> *Leader:*   Extol the LORD our God; worship at his footstool! Holy is he!

> *People:*   **Extol the LORD our God, and worship at his holy mountain; for the LORD our God is holy!**

Pastoral Prayer:
O Lord of Wonder, allow us to experience the marvel of Jesus' transfiguration as did Peter, James, and John. Cover us with the

cloud of your glory so that we too might be convinced of your power. May the witness of prophets like Moses and Elijah confirm for us the wonders of your love. This love provides for us that which we seek. We hunt the world over and yet will never find a life comparable to the one you offer us in your only begotten son, Jesus, our Christ. Guide our witness. Make us those who know how and when to share this wonderful good news with others. Help us to be sensitive to the needs that pervade our hurting world. Let us be those who not only speak of peace but also are, in fact, peaceful. Let us be those who not only speak of grace but also are, in fact, gracious. As those who serve the risen Christ, be with us through your spirit as we walk faith's pathway. In Jesus' name we pray. Amen. (David Mosser)

SERMON BRIEFS

FINDING OUR SHINE

EXODUS 34:29-35

In even the most humble person lies the lingering desire to shine. Our ambitions may be great or small, but in the circles in which we travel we would like to stand out as exceptional in some way. The most ordinary of us want to be extraordinary in some fashion.

Our text tells us that when Moses returned from Sinai with the tablets of the law, his face shone. There was brightness about him. In fact, the text says that Moses' light was so bright that he had to put a veil over his face because, without it, he was frightening to the people. But Moses was unaware of his frightening countenance. Only in the people's reaction to him did he become aware of the shine that was on him.

The brightness of Moses' face came not from his desire to polish his reputation or from his efforts to look good in the eyes of the community. Moses' shine was a gift of God, which came to him as he devoted himself to doing God's will and work. Moses was on the mountain receiving God's law. He was engrossed in the task to which God had called him. There is no reason to suppose that he was distracted by thinking about his own place in the community or by considering ways to enhance his image. Moses was giving himself to the will of God and his shine was a by-product of his commitment and focus. He was unaware of the brightness of his life as he lived it in God's light. In fact, his brightness was not his at all, but the reflected light of God.

Too often we try to be about the light rather than about the work. We would like to shine in our communities. In our better moments, we would like to make Christ shine through us. In any case, our attention and focus are on the by-product rather than the underlying cause. We call attention to Christ best when we do Christ's work in the world. In fact, we can cry out that Christ is the light of the world until we are hoarse and tired, but few will see the brightness.

Instead, God calls us to keep our focus on doing Christ's work. As we visit the sick or imprisoned, as we feed the hungry and clothe the naked, as we love both our neighbor and our enemy, as we forgive over and over again we immerse ourselves in the ministry of Christ and then, and only then, do we shine with his light. Our faces are brightest when we forgive rather than seek revenge, when we give ourselves wholly to serve others, and when we do not count the cost of discipleship.

John Ruskin lived in the time when English villages were lighted by gas lamps that had to be individually lit each evening. He was once talking with a friend as the lamplighter moved slowly on a distant hill. Ruskin said, "There is what I mean by being a real Christian. A Christian's course can be traced by the lights that are left burning."

Moses' face did not shine because he sought to make light. In fact, he was so absorbed in the great task of doing God's will that he did not even realize that he shone. Only when we are similarly engaged in doing God's will do we find our shine. (Carl Schenck)

REMOVING THE VEIL

2 CORINTHIANS 3:12–4:2

Has anyone ever told you an "inside joke"? Certainly, a comic story could potentially fill a room with laughter when each listener has the privileged knowledge that makes such a wise-crack funny. When we are excluded from the details of inside information, the joke does not make any sense. It might even make us feel excluded from the group in which we are participating. We end up wondering why we were left out, while everyone else has been transformed into a state of amusement.

In 2 Corinthians, Paul writes of Moses reading the Old Covenant to the Jews. The Jews wear veils over their heads out of caution and respect for God. Ironically, the veil comes to symbolize unenlightenment. Although the people hear Moses' words, they are unable to understand the meaning of God's law for a "veil lies over their minds" (v. 15). It is as if this veil has kept them in the dark, unable to either see God or fully appreciate the divine commandments. From Paul's perspective, these Jews are incapable of understanding the Old Covenant because they lack the details of inside information. Without the inside scoop of Jesus Christ, the words of God's law fall on deaf ears.

Perhaps there are times when we feel that a veil lies over our minds. We read scriptures and hear the Bible read in worship. These spoken words seem to disperse before ever reaching our ears. The substance of God's Word disappears. Our efforts to encounter God seem futile. We even wonder if God's Word has any power at all to transform our lives. In instances like this, we strive extra hard to experience God in the monotony of life, but when such encounters fail to happen, we become disappointed and discouraged. The veil can seem so great and burdensome that we lose our direction in life.

Paul provides the Corinthians with a hopeful message, which recognizes that such a veil is not permanent. He reminds them "when one turns to the Lord, the veil is removed" (v. 16). Jesus, as our Lord, reconciles us with God by removing the veil from our hearts and our minds. Our veils may be different. Some of us may have veils of apathy, ignorance, or intolerance to name a few. We are nonetheless assured that Christ takes on our sins so that we may be forgiven. It is through Christ that we gain life, and we are reminded that we worship the living God.

Through our encounters with this living God, we become transformed into God's own image. This transformation causes us to do things differently and to look at the world from another perspective. Paul tells the Corinthians that the new perspective they gain through Christ enables them to hear and understand the message in the Old Covenant. Like the Corinthians, we too can have our veils removed through Christ. We are not to assume this removal will be an immediate event. Paul cautions the church to acknowledge that transformation is neither easy nor smooth. The change we experience through Christ is a process moving "from one degree of glory to another" (v. 18). God's Spirit includes us in the divine plan for this world by granting us the power to transform our lives. It is this Spirit who gives us life and hope to overcome the veils that lie over our minds and prevent us from encountering God. (Mark White)

INSPIRATION AND APPLICATION

LUKE 9:28-36 (37-43)

It is surprising to see how much of the ministry of Jesus was invested in the education and preparation of the disciples. The transfiguration was a key factor in this process. Like so many other experiences, the transfiguration seemed to be more mystery than education to the three disciples who witnessed the event. The three disciples clearly did not understand what was happening, but the transfiguration takes its place along with so many other puzzling experiences, which would become clear later. Any profound education has in it notable pieces of puzzling information and experience, the importance of which evolves over a period of time.

The transfiguration took place as Jesus was about to set out for Jerusalem. So many things would be said and done on the way to and in Jerusalem that would be over the heads of the disciples. The greatest of all frustrating puzzles was yet to come—the cross. Soon Jesus would be snatched from their midst in what to them was a heartrending tragedy that would leave them in a profound state of shock. His words and deeds, which they had so vaguely understood, would continue to instruct them later.

This is what we know about what happened on that unnamed mountain. Peter, John, and James went with Jesus up the mountain to pray. The three selected disciples must have been tired. They dozed while Jesus prayed—a scene repeated later in the Garden of Gethsemane (22:46). They awoke to see Jesus in a transformed appearance. Jesus conversed with two individuals whom the disciples recognized to be Moses and Elijah, who also had a glorious splendor in their appearances. They were discussing Jesus' departure, which would take place in Jerusalem, their eminent destination.

When the disciples were fully awake, and the heavenly duo was about to leave, Peter felt called upon to say a few words—as he often did. He proposed enshrining the experience with three tabernacles, one each for Jesus, Moses, and Elijah. The biblical text parenthetically said that Peter did not know what he was saying.

While Peter was still offering his commentary, they were enveloped by a cloud. An unseen voice from within the cloud said: "This is my Son, my Chosen; listen to him" (v. 35). The apostolic trio was so mystified and terrified by what happened that they did not tell anyone until much later. Little wonder at their silence! How could they explain what they had just seen?

The next day they came down from the Mount of Transfiguration. Before they could even consider trying to understand what had happened they were suddenly in the middle of an uproar over a failed attempt of the remaining nine disciples to heal a child suffering seizures.

Taken by itself, what does Luke 9:28-45 have to say to us today? It is important for us to go to the mountaintop and be exposed to the glory and awe of heavenly things, even if we do not understand them. Even in our ignorance, something of the importance of such experiences penetrates our lives. Many glorious mysteries, which puzzle and frighten us at the time, later serve to give us strength and confidence as we eventually discern their meaning. It is not unusual to be exposed to some experience for which we are momentarily unprepared, but for which time will prepare us.

We are not unlike Peter who, while he did not really know what was going on, knew instinctively that something great was afoot. He wanted to freeze the moment. Let this moment last forever! But life does not work that way.

There is always suffering, anger, confusion, and hurt that awaits the attention and ministry of those who have been to the mountaintop. It is essential to go to the top of the mountain, but it is selfish to stay there. There must be a balanced interplay between the ecstatic inspiration and existential application.

I once heard a preacher at the dedication of a church which had been built by many laborers during difficult times say: "This is a place where workers dream and dreamers work." We must move constantly back and forth from the top of the mountain to the valley of human need, from transfiguration to application, from profound mystery to practical ministry. (Thomas Lane Butts)

FEBRUARY 29, 2004

First Sunday in Lent

Worship Theme: Not only does God liberate the Hebrew children from the oppression of Egypt but also grants us release from sin and death through Jesus Christ. As Jesus triumphs over temptation, he leads us toward the path of righteousness.

Readings: Deuteronomy 26:1-11; Romans 10:8*b*-13; Luke 4:1-13

Call to Worship (Psalm 91:1-2, 9-12, 15-16 RSV)

Leader: He who dwells in the shelter of the Most High, who abides in the shadow of the Almighty, will say to the LORD, "My refuge and my fortress; my God, in whom I trust."

People: **Because you have made the LORD your refuge, the Most High your habitation,**

Leader: No evil shall befall you, no scourge come near your tent.

People: **For he will give his angels charge of you to guard you in all your ways.**

Leader: On their hands they will bear you up, lest you dash your foot against a stone.

People: **When he calls to me, I will answer him; I will be with him in trouble, I will rescue him and honor him.**

All: **With long life I will satisfy him, and show him my salvation.**

Pastoral Prayer:

O Lord, as we enter Lent between the mountains of Transfigu-ration and Calvary, we ask for your protection as we make our spiritual journeys. We know that the path through life is often treacherous. We seem to encounter stumbling blocks at every turn. The decisions life asks us to make too often overwhelm us. We must choose the good over the evil. Frequently we find our-selves torn between these important decisions. Just as your Spirit of love and compassion accompanied Jesus on his journey, we would ask that you send your Spirit upon us. May we drink from the deep well of scripture and the tradition of our ancestors who found hope and strength in every time of need. As we meet impediments to the righteous life to which you call us, may we remember that your promise is to always be with us—even to the end of the age. For this promise we give you thanks and praise your holy name. We pray this and all things through the power of Jesus Christ. Amen. (David Mosser)

SERMON BRIEFS

PROMISES YET TO BE FULFILLED

DEUTERONOMY 26:1-11

How many times have you sat with your muscles tightened, your hands grasped together and your teeth clenched, only to breathe under your breath, "God, please, just tell me what to do! If you will just give me some kind of direction, I promise I will do whatever you want. I need direction." It is to be hoped that this desperate prayer is not a routine of our daily conversations with God, but in some way or another, we are constantly asking for God's direction in our lives. We want to know what, when, where, and how we can best live our lives to please God. An instruction booklet would be fantastic; an outline would do, or even a sign—could I at least have a sign, God? Give me some direction, and I will do whatever it is that you would have for me to do. Today's text is an answer to our prayer. As the author outlines a form of liturgy for praising God after the fruits of harvest have been collected, we find both clear and underlying actions, which bring pleasure and praise to God.

There is no doubt that those to whom this text is addressed need direction. They descended from a wandering Aramean and lived for many generations under the cruel hand of Egyptian oppressors. After many years of wondering if their God still remembered them, they were finally delivered to their current location, the land flowing with milk and honey. It is time for a new life, a fresh start, and an even more reverent way of worshiping the God who keeps promises.

The instructions for how to please God are clear. They are to give the firstfruits of the land back to God and recite before the altar of the Lord the path of their ancestors, which brought them to the fortune they now have. A celebration should fill the air in thanks for the bounty God has given among the people.

But would we be celebrating if we were in their shoes? We have all heard plenty of sermons with inclusions of specific, not so biblical, formulas about how our tithe should be calculated and given. This text clearly states that God requires a portion of the firstfruits. Imagine how difficult that must have been for the people of Israel. They were finally in a good place, no more Egyptian oppression, no more wandering in the desert, no more wondering if God would continue to care for them. For once, they were actually getting to feel like and being treated as God's chosen people.

What about a sense of entitlement? Haven't they earned all of their fruits? They have been through unbelievable sufferings for multiple generations. Just when we would expect the people of Israel to be bitter and angry when having to give up the firstfruits of their new land, we find that they celebrate. They have suffered, been oppressed, and lost family members, friends, and fearless leaders, yet through it all, they still know a good thing when they see it. God kept a promise to them. God promised they would come to the land of milk and honey. Giving up the firstfruits is the least they can to do please a God who keeps promises.

We are blessed to continue to serve a God who still keeps promises. The season of Lent reminds us of the most important promise God ever made. God sent Christ into the world so we may have another promise, that of eternal life.

This text makes clear what it takes from the chosen people to please God. They are to give back from that which God has first given to them. God made a promise of provision among all God's children. Indeed we are all provided for, because we serve a God who keeps promises. The instructions are here, give back from that which you have been given. Heed this command, for there are promises yet to be fulfilled. (Victoria Atkinson White)

THE RESPONSE OF FAITH

ROMANS 10:8*b*-13

On this first Sunday in Lent we turn to Romans. In the beginning chapters of Paul's great theological epistle he clearly outlined God's provision of redemption. In these verses of our lesson Paul moved to the premise that God's amazing and bountiful plan demanded a response on the part of recipients. Paul explained that to know alone was not enough. To know and fail to act was fatal. For God's redemptive movement to have meaning, people must respond to it by faith in Jesus Christ.

While theoretically one might be saved—achieve righteousness—by the law, practically speaking, this was impossible because the law demanded perfect obedience, an impossible task for imperfect humanity. Thus, our only hope was to accept in faith what God had done in Jesus Christ. In verses 5-8 Paul contrasted these concepts. We cannot save ourselves; therefore we are provided with a Savior by God's gracious act. The only demand is that we listen to the gospel and respond to it in the proper way.

The proper response is delineated clearly in verses 9-10 of our text. To miss the poetic construction of these verses is to miss half the message. In verse eight Paul quotes Deuteronomy 30:14, making a play on the phrase "in thy mouth, and in thy heart" (KJV). In a characteristic form of Hebrew poetry, parallelism, Paul repeats the same thought in different words and in reverse order. Thus we have the series: mouth-heart-heart-mouth. Matching this series is another: confessing-believing-believing-confessing. Paul was not writing about two different ideas but about one, the word of faith. In Paul's mind when one believed, one confessed. Paul never grants the possibility that one could believe and not confess.

Paul's own experience formed the background for his teaching. In the beginning Paul believed the gospel to be a lie and Jesus an imposter. Paul's dramatic encounter on the Damascus road changed all that. His conversation with the risen Lord convinced him that Jesus did indeed rise from the grave (Acts 9:5-6). Paul believed. And what was his response? It was confession with the mouth. "Lord," he said, "what wilt thou have me to do?" (Acts 9:6 KJV). Spiritual apprehension of the reality of the resurrection demanded immediate and unconditional surrender. The confession could not precede belief in the resurrection; belief could not be real without acknowledgment of his Lordship.

Although centuries away from the historical event, our problem too often is that Christianity has become a mere philosophical discussion. For many, mental assent to propositional truth is all that is needed. Belief has become reciting a creed or repeating a formula. The meaning of Christianity has been lost because it has been removed from the heart to the mind.

To confess means to acknowledge, to own, to declare a thing to be true. What is to be confessed? The Lord is Jesus! In contrast to the pagan assertion, "Caesar is Lord," Christians were to confess Jesus as Lord. Let us stress the fact that faith demands the absolute lordship of Christ in our lives. "Jesus is Lord" is one of the oldest expressions of the Christian faith. Paul insisted that only the Holy Spirit could enable one to say this (1 Cor. 12:3).

In verses 11-13 Paul made clear that this salvation was offered to all. Quotations from Isaiah (28:16) and Joel (2:32) emphasize that God saves all people by like means. The key word is "whosoever." "Believing on the Lord" and "calling on him" are synonymous as are "shall not be ashamed" and "be saved."

Just as bread is composed of several elements, with none of them individually being bread, so it is with faith. Believing in the truth of the gospel, surrendering to the Lordship of Christ, and living an obedient life must be fused into one essential reality to produce saving faith. (Jerry Gunnells)

TESTING THE BOUNDARIES

LUKE 4:1-13

We seem to be living in a day and time when people test all the boundaries of human existence. In the 1940s the sound barrier was broken, and human travel broke through the earth's atmosphere. Twenty years later, we landed a person on the moon. Not long after that scientists spoke of going beyond earth's moon and traveling to Mars and other terrestrial frontiers. Testing the boundaries of humankind's venturous spirit has always been part of the human journey. Time and space travel have challenged, and will continue to challenge, the boundaries of human ingenuity. Human beings have the penchant for discovering, testing, and pushing our potential in venturing beyond earth. Yes, we love going where no one has ever gone before.

We seem to also be living in a day and time when going inside of ourselves and testing the boundaries of the human spirit is apropos. It wouldn't be stretching the truth to suggest that books on spirituality are the fastest growing in popularity among readers. Spiritual gurus are springing up everywhere. Psychics have their own television shows. Nine-hundred numbers for getting a psychic reading about life are on the increase. These kinds of spiritual leaders lure people into spiritual travel that takes them where they've never been before. These impostors are nothing new on the landscape of human spiritual travel.

Jesus ran into their leader. Luke identifies this pretender as the devil. Whatever name we give this intruder of the human soul, there are some things that we need to keep in mind when we are tempted to test the boundaries of the human spirit.

The forces that oppose God in this world would have us believe that we can turn rocks into bread. Jesus does not test the boundary of human power to create something to eat from that which cannot be eaten. Jesus is "famished," as the scripture says. He's physically hungry to the point he is tempted to think he can do the unthinkable. When we're physically hungry, there are times when we might believe that stealing and taking from others justifies theft. For the drug dealer, turning drugs into money is the way to get rich and live off of other people's addictions. For the sexual predator, it is okay to prey on the vulnerability of others in order to justify the hunger of a distorted sexuality. The human appetite for testing spiritual boundaries cannot be satisfied with grandiose acts of super-human activities. Jesus faced his own temptation by simply saying, "One does not live by bread alone" (v. 4). We do not live by feeding our appetite for life with the food of selfishness or our hunger for displaying extraordinary power in serving ourselves.

Another aspect of testing our boundaries is the belief that we deserve to be rich, famous, successful, and have all the power and authority that go with such things. If careless, the church dupes itself into thinking that ministry is a venture in building huge repositories of wealth and influence. Ministry is more than a menu of things that cost money. If our vision of God's world is more connected to acquiring and consuming things, then we worship a god of consumerism. Ministry then becomes a venue for developing ministry based on who the biggest givers are. Jesus looks into the face of such a challenge and claims a higher call: "Worship the Lord your God and serve only him" (v. 8*b*).

Then the third test must be the charm. The devil takes Jesus up to Jerusalem and tempts him to jump off the highest point of the temple, all the while assuring Jesus that he will be protected by God's angels if he truly is who he says he is. The final boundary test arrives. Test the boundary of God's protection. We are forever being tempted to go where God never goes—harming self and others.

Jesus does not test the boundaries of God's love, grace, and mercy. Jesus lives within them because they have no limitations. (Michael Childress)

REFLECTIONS

MARCH

Reflection Verse: *"Hear this word that the Lord has spoken against you, O people of Israel, against the whole family that I brought up out of the land of Egypt:*
> *You only have I known*
> *of all the families of the earth;*
> *therefore I will punish you*
> *for all your iniquities." (Amos 3:1-2)*

This year the lion's share of Lenten Sundays fall within the calendar month of March. Naturally, for preachers, Lent is a time of year to wring every ounce of penitence out of our congregations. We have the lectionary on our side as we attempt to paint the human condition in the bleakest terms possible. In addition, our creaturely need for divine guidance becomes the answer to this dilemma of human sin. In former times I am certain that the texts offered by contemporary lectionaries were biblical passages over which fire and brimstone preachers licked their chops. With God on our side, we young and fearless prophets (indeed some not so young) couldn't wait to let the congregation have it. We all know fellow seminarians who played a variation on the colonial American theme of Jonathan Edwards's classic sermon, "Sinners in the Hands of an Angry God." Human sin well justified this incendiary preaching. Folks in the pew tolerated this style of preaching because their preachers had always done it this way.

Woe be to the modern preacher who preaches in churches who hanker for nothing but contemporary worship. In the new "baby-boomer" churches, "where never is heard a discouraging word," woe be to the pastor who follows Amos's route. Amos believed in the old-time religion. Amos believed in telling it like it is, never flinching from revealing to his people exactly what he, as a prophet of God, thought. Of course, Amos delivered the word straight, with nothing to water it down. He initiated many of his visions with the powerful words, "Thus says the LORD."

However, we live in a new day. Most preachers I know cannot get by on a steady menu of castigation. Many parsons cannot bring themselves to rail against their people this way. This is fortunate for these preachers, for even if they could in good conscience chastise their people again and again, few modern and sophisticated congregations would tolerate this kind of preaching in any event. We may justifiably ask, why not?

First, congregations today are unlike previous generations of congregations in several significant sociological ways. Plainly, this is a coarse generalization, but the exceptions to the rule make the rule all that more noticeable. Barely three or four generations ago, a resident pastor along with a local physician in any town was also that town's most educated person. These two people, at that time, invariably men, had the advantage of college and graduate school in theology or medicine. In many cases this situation is no longer true. Many individuals in any given congregation are college graduates. Not so rare are the impressive number of congregants who also possess Master's degrees. Some congregations even have a surprisingly large number of Ph.D. types within their church fellowship. This fact of education is not only intimidating to preachers, it is also a cause for homiletical humility. In an earlier day few church members challenged pastors regarding the specifics of a sermon or even scriptural interpretation. Today many pastors have mini-theological dialogues with parishioners as they pass by the pastor after worship. Thus, many pastors use the utmost caution in speaking out with verve. Who desires a good lampooning after worship for talking about things that clearly pastors have little knowledge to talk about in the first place?

Another fact of modern life makes bold and rancorous preaching dangerous. Many congregations do not grant the pastor carte blanche with respect to authority that a bygone day might have conferred. The lines of authority in any profession have been flattened. Some believers do regard pastors as "religious professionals." Simply put, most pastors no longer enjoy the hierarchical lines of authority that they once did. Today's listeners do not grant respect de facto; rather, individuals must earn respect, and pastors are no exception. When Amos spoke to his audience, he spoke what his audience perceived as a direct word from Yahweh. Today, many people in the pews, even if they love and respect their pastor, doubt if he or she has a direct pipeline from God's mouth to the preacher's ear. Add the fact of more assertive lay leadership to this issue of a different understanding of authority by moderns. No longer do people passively accept what the preacher says. We as modern people question everything. This makes the call to faithful and prophetic preaching a remote ideal that preachers can never quite recapture. Perhaps it is a good thing that the earlier phenomenon of passive congregations is a thing of the past. If this is so, however, it makes the challenging word that God commands preachers to proclaim a tricky business indeed.

Yet, a danger lurks in our reluctance to lay an Amos-like word on people. When Amos declared,

> Hear this word that the Lord has spoken against you, O people of Israel, against the whole family that I brought up out of the land of Egypt:
>> You only have I known
>> of all the families of the earth;
>> therefore I will punish you
>> for all your iniquities. (Amos 3:1-2)

At least people got the message. There is something in us, however, that creates a disinclination to preach like firebrands. One reason is that most of us genuinely love the people to whom we preach. It takes a special person to have the nerve and gumption to speak "the truth in love" (Eph. 4:15). This is doubly true for delivering a word of truth to those with whom we have a deep and abiding relationship. You tell me who wants to bring a hard-edged message to someone we love deeply? But, our reluctance to speak with boldness the word that the Lord has laid on us goes even deeper than our anxiety about wounding those whom we love.

Our anxiety reaches all the way down to our depths because we all know that we are preaching not only to the choir, so to speak, but also to ourselves. Paul understood this temptation for any who proclaim the word. He wrote to Corinth: "I do not run aimlessly, nor do I box as though beating the air; but I punish my body and enslave it, so that after proclaiming to others I myself should not be disqualified" (1 Cor. 9:26-27). Paul knew that the greatest of all ministerial temptations was the sin of hypocrisy. Thus our preacher's dilemma: Either we say nothing of consequence so that others cannot judge us by our own words, or we preach the gospel. If we preach the gospel, then we can only pray that we will not be "weighed on the scales and found wanting" (Dan. 5:27). It is a self-imposed indictment without the grace of God.

God's preaching charge to us is no easy task. We have been called by God and not for our own well-being. Rather, God calls us to speak an appropriate "word in season, [but] how good it is" (Prov. 15:23)! To dodge this prophetic responsibility is to be a person who does not preach with good courage. For preachers, this issue is one worth long deliberation. The health of those placed in our care depends on our own answer to the upward call of Jesus Christ for the proclamation of the whole gospel. After all, it is the truth and only the truth that will set us all free. Amen. (David Mosser)

MARCH 7, 2004

Second Sunday in Lent

Worship Theme: Paul invites us to imitate him, but in reality Paul asks us to imitate the Christ who lives in him (Gal. 2:20). Jesus' life and ministry make visible God's covenant with God's people.

Readings: Genesis 15:1-12, 17-18; Philippians 3:17–4:1; Luke 13:31-35

Call to Worship (Psalm 27:1-3, 11-14)

Leader: The LORD is my light and my salvation; whom shall I fear?

People: **The LORD is the stronghold of my life; of whom shall I be afraid?**

Leader: When evildoers assail me, uttering slanders against me, my adversaries and foes, they shall stumble and fall.

People: **Though a host encamp against me, my heart shall not fear; though war arise against me, yet I will be confident.**

Leader: Teach me thy way, O LORD; and lead me on a level path because of my enemies.

People: **Give me not up to the will of my adversaries; for false witnesses have risen against me, and they breathe out violence.**

Leader: I believe that I shall see the goodness of the LORD in the land of the living!

All: **Wait for the LORD; be strong, and let your heart take courage; yea, wait for the LORD!**

101

Pastoral Prayer:

Gracious God of Eternal Covenant, we approach your throne of grace as people who need guidance and counsel from you, the Almighty. You have created us in your own image and made us your people. You, O God, have named us at our baptism and made us your own through Jesus' life, death, and resurrection. As we follow Jesus on his journey to Jerusalem, and the divine fate that awaits him there, let us experience the life-giving amazing grace found in his atoning ministry undertaken for the benefit of all humankind. Give us courage to stand up for the right and be advocates for those who have neither voice nor power in our society. May we be the voice of truth and justice for the least of these. Indeed, Lord, give us the will to reach out and not simply speak on the behalf of the last, the lost, and the least of these, our brothers and sisters in Christ. Seal our prayer in the name of Jesus our Messiah. Amen. (David Mosser)

SERMON BRIEFS

BELIEVING IN THE DARK

GENESIS 15:1-12, 17-18

I suspect all of us have childhood memories of being tucked into bed by one of our parents and having the lights turned out. Few things strike terror in young children like a dark room filled with shadows on the walls cast by leafy trees. There's something about the dark that makes us long for companionship, assurance, some tiny beam of night-light.

Abram is an old man. In what now seems like a crazy, impetuous moment, he said yes to a voice that told him he would become a great nation. He follows the voice, not for a day or a month, but from that moment on and across hundreds of miles of strange territory. Abram believes the voice, all the while knowing there is one seemingly insurmountable problem. He and his wife Sarai are childless.

With nothing but a faint glimmer of hope, Abram sees the Lord in a vision. "Do not be afraid, Abram, I am your shield; your reward shall be very great" (v. 1). Fear is the operative word in Abram's life. He is afraid that time has run out for him, afraid he has followed a pipe dream, afraid that today may be his last day, afraid that the promised heir is like the fuzzy dreams he keeps having. But God keeps talking and Abram keeps listening. God again promises the old man that his descendents—from his and Sarai's union—will be like the stars in the sky.

The story continues: "As the sun was going down, a deep sleep fell upon Abram, and a deep and terrifying darkness descended upon him" (v. 12). The season of Lent is such a time. We have heard and reheard the promises of God: that light dispels darkness, that grace will prevail, that life will triumph over every form of death. But the lengthening darkness cast by the ever growing reality of the cross suggests otherwise. Maybe sin, death, fear, tragedy do win in the end.

Lent is a time in our lives when God calls us to believe in the dark. Time is running out like the shrinking sun setting in the western sky. With every passing day, the cross looms larger and hope seems smaller. As we follow Jesus to Jerusalem, we can't help but be sucked into the cynicism of his opponents and the selfishness of his followers. Everything within us wants to concede to what is dark, negative, deadly.

So what do we do? Not much. Maybe nothing. God calls Abram to sacrifice a small zoo of animals, to kill them and split most of them in two pieces, and then to sit down and do nothing else. Isn't that where we are? We have given God the best we can give, sacrificed time and treasure, even health and hope, believing that God's purposes for our lives will prevail. But such is not always the case.

Lent is a season in which we accept the fact that darkness is not optional in the journey of life. When the darkness descends on God's vision for life—that vision of newness, of hope, of reconciliation—we, like Abram, can only sit down and let the darkness descend upon us as well.

The good news is that we do not sit in the darkness alone. For Abram, God comes to him as a "fire pot and a flaming torch" passing between the sacrifices he has offered (v. 17). When Abram has literally offered God all he has to offer, he sits in the darkness and believes all over again that God will fulfill God's promise.

Wherever you may be on the Lenten journey, believing in the dark may be the best you can do for now. God will do the rest, all the way to Good Friday and beyond. (Timothy Owings)

THE RIGHT IMITATION

PHILIPPIANS 3:17–4:1

I remember that one of the most annoying habits of my little sister when we were children was her insistence to do everything I did. She wanted to dress like me, walk like me, laugh like me, and do virtually everything that I did. I vividly remember how frustrated I felt with her constant mimicking. And yet, there was hardly any way to discourage her. As a parent, I realize now what I could not have possibly understood as an eight-year-old with a four-year-old copycat. I realize that my sister was copying my actions and behaviors to learn. It is the way that most of us learn, whether we admit it or not. It is much easier to learn something new or complex by watching someone else than by trying to figure it out on your own. All of the written or oral instructions in the world cannot top the learning opportunity of watching someone else.

The apostle Paul understood the human tendency and need to mimic. He particularly understood that the easiest way for those early Christians to live the Christian life was to learn by example. For the early missionary churches, like the church at Philippi, it was important for them to have positive Christian role models or examples. This new life that Paul and other missionaries were proposing, after all, was quite different than their previous ways of life. Merely teaching, preaching, and writing were not enough. During his time with the Philippian church, Paul tried to be a solid example for the faith. He sought to teach not only through word but also through actions. The Philippians were apparently a committed group of believers, and in today's text, Paul encourages them once again to follow the examples that he and other Christians tried to set and not to be distracted or misled by the examples in the world.

The Lenten season should be a time to reexamine our commitment as Christians. Lent is a time to intentionally focus on the depth and authenticity of our own faith. It is a time to reevaluate to whom we belong and on what we should base our life choices. Although the Philippians did not observe Lent, they were probably constantly in a state of reevaluation. They were, after all, in a time and place where the new faith in Christ that they were experiencing was still unpopular. They needed to be reminded that they were not alone in their Christian journeys. They had examples to follow. There were people in their lives whom they could trust as examples. Likewise, they were to grow in their own faith so that they could become faith examples for others. This is not only an important truth for the first-century converts but also an important Lenten lesson for twenty-first-century Christians. Despite the many diversions from Christ, we are to seek those who can teach and exemplify the gospel. At the same time, we have a responsibility to live our lives in a way that exemplifies the message of Jesus Christ.

Perhaps the message for us this Lenten season is a simple one. Perhaps, it is time for us to reevaluate by whose example we live our lives, and what kind of example we ourselves are to others. In the same way that my little sister needed to copy my actions in order to learn, as Christians, we should seek to learn by the example set for us by Christian leaders of both the past and present. We should, as Paul instructed the Philippians in 3:17 (NIV), "take note of those who live according to the pattern" established by those individuals who have allowed the light of Jesus Christ to shine through them as an example to others. (Tracey Allred)

WILL YOU LISTEN TO THE FOX OR THE HEN?

LUKE 13:31-35

Who are you afraid of? As a child were you afraid of harsh punishment from a parent? Does a boss who seems to have it in for you unnerve you? Do ongoing terrorist attacks around the world keep you in a state of fear and anxiety?

Today's gospel text begins with Jesus receiving word that a Herod is again seeking his life (remember his father's unsuccessful attempt to kill Jesus when he was an infant). But we quickly learn that Jesus is not afraid. Instead of fleeing or going into hiding, Jesus calls Herod a fox and sends the Pharisees back with the message that he will continue publicly healing and casting out demons. Jesus makes it clear that he will not fall victim to Herod's agenda but will journey to Jerusalem on God's timetable.

Although Jesus knows he is being faithful to God's redeeming intentions, he also knows and tells us that the end of the journey will not be a pleasant one. But instead of fear, we see sadness as he laments over Jerusalem, the city that kills the prophets. Jesus goes with his eyes wide open, knowing that it is the people there, not Herod, who will bring about his demise.

This passage reminds us of Herod's beheading of John, and it also points us forward to the stoning of Stephen in the book of Acts. In Acts 7:52, Stephen asks, "Which of the prophets did your ancestors not persecute? They killed those who foretold the coming of the Righteous One, and now you have become his betrayers and murderers." For the prophets, the cost of following remains high, yet there is an absence of fear.

In this passage we see God's redeeming nature as Jesus prepares for his final journey into Jerusalem. However, we also see God's loving and nurturing side as Jesus describes his desire to shelter and protect Israel. Although Jerusalem has sealed its own fate by persecuting the prophets, we see God's love for Israel. Jesus describes his desire for them as a hen who seeks to gather her brood under her wings. Like a loving mother, God seeks to protect the children from the foxes that stalk them and is grieved when they reject that protection. Although God chooses not to coerce them, God's heart grieves, anticipating what will happen to them outside the realm of divine protection.

Fortunately, the death and destruction described in this passage are not the end of the story. After the Resurrection, the risen Lord appeared in Jerusalem, offering the fearful disciples pardon and a second chance to welcome the reign of God. Through them, God's offer extends first to the residents of Jerusalem and then to the entire world. The offer still stands for us today.

The question remains, what will we do? Will we, like the evil foxes, seek to implement our own agendas and seek to thwart

God's activity in the world? Or, in the face of uncertainty and persecution by the foxes that surround us, will we participate in God's redeeming work whatever the cost? May we, like Jesus, choose to stay the course without fear, knowing that all the while God seeks to nurture even those who persecute God and God's brood. (Tracy Hartman)

MARCH 14, 2004

Third Sunday in Lent

Worship Theme: Those who listen to the voice of the Lord shall live! The Word of God always provides a second chance for people to respond to the gospel and produce fruit.

Readings: Isaiah 55:1-9; 1 Corinthians 10:1-13; Luke 13:1-9

Call to Worship (Psalm 63:1-4, 7-8 RSV)

> *Leader:* O God, thou art my God, I seek thee, my soul thirsts for thee; my flesh faints for thee, as in a dry and weary land where no water is.
>
> *People:* **So I have looked upon thee in the sanctuary, beholding thy power and glory.**
>
> *Leader:* Because thy steadfast love is better than life, my lips will praise thee.
>
> *People:* **So I will bless thee as long as I live; I will lift up my hands and call on thy name.**
>
> *Leader:* For thou hast been my help, and in the shadow of thy wings I sing for joy.
>
> *People:* **My soul clings to thee; thy right hand upholds me.**

Pastoral Prayer:

O Gracious God of the Second Chance, we assemble to hear the good news of Jesus Christ. Through Jesus' teaching, O Lord, you teach us about your divine nature and then guide us in the paths of righteous living. As Jesus confronts the meaning of suffering for humankind, Jesus also gives us a way to move forward into an uncertain future. Help us live with the assurance that as we meet unmerited suffering in life, you, O God, also call us to exercise our freedom in grace. You call us to be your people and to live in a manner that shares the gospel with a needy and hurting world. Help us seek your presence and then share this word of salvation with others. Make us sensitive to the necessary basic human requirements of others and allow us to respond to such people as those who have the confidence of your divine word of redemption. Because you have always provided for your people in every time of need, give us your assurance to live under the shadow of your mercy and grace. We pray this and everything in Jesus' holy name. Amen. (David Mosser)

SERMON BRIEFS

THE GREAT INVITATION

ISAIAH 55:1-9

In a memorable scene from the classic movie *Lawrence of Arabia*, Lawrence and his Bedouin guide stagger out of the desert bringing critical news back to British headquarters. Caked with sand and with their skin cracking from parched dryness, they stagger into the ultraproper officers' bar and demand something to drink. While the shocked and outraged British officers stand around, the two of them guzzle down huge glasses of lemonade without a pause.

The passage from the prophet Isaiah hits with similar impact. "Everyone who thirsts, come to the waters" (v. 1). The passage opens in the imperative. If you are thirsty, come to the waters of God! If you are hungry, come and experience that which is free! The only prerequisite is spiritual hunger and thirst. The prophet parallels Jesus' later invitation to the wedding feast in Matthew 22.

This passage reminds us of the common human condition of spiritual hunger and thirst. It is reported that Mother Teresa once said of America, "I have never seen a land so hungry." Isaiah challenges preachers to speak directly to the ravaging spiritual hunger that stalks so much of modern living. The challenge is directly placed before the reader in verse 2. "Why do you spend your money for that which is not bread, / and your labor for that which does not satisfy?" Modern examples abound.

There is a note of judgment that pervades the text: "Let the wicked forsake their way." In a time of spiritual starvation, the Word of God rings forth with a challenge: come, seek, call upon; it is the language of repentance. It is not God who has abandoned us, but we who have abandoned God. We are to return to the Lord so that the offer of pardon and mercy may be enacted.

Yet within the clear challenge to change, the text does not scold or berate, it invites: "Incline your ear, and come to me; listen, so that you may live" (v. 3). The prophet Isaiah speaks to a people who have experienced a visitation of calamity. With the nation's ruin all around, Isaiah offers good news. God still offers covenant relationship. God's offer of love is still given. "I will make with you an everlasting covenant, / my steadfast, sure love for David" (v. 3b). God will "abundantly pardon."

Amid the chaos and hectic pace of modern life, God offers the gospel. Disaster or tragedy does not mean that God has abandoned us. The offer of covenant grace is still available. God desires, longs for a relationship. The divine offer is made without price. Our only requirement is hunger and thirst. The action needed on our part is the willingness to seek God. Implicit in the text is the unspoken thought that the choice is ours.

Out of this good news comes the vocation of witnessing. "I made him a witness to the peoples" (v. 4a). We are called to witness. The good news of God's grace is offered to the "nations that do not know you" (v. 5b). Those who have come in from the desert are to carry water back to those who hunger and thirst.

Our lesson logically proceeds thus: (1) the human condition of spiritual hunger, (2) the invitation to seek God, (3) the good news of covenant love, and (4) the call to witness. (Mike Lowry)

DANGERS OF SPIRITUAL COMPLACENCY

1 CORINTHIANS 10:1-13

The church at Corinth is in disarray. The members quarrel about spiritual gifts, wallow in jealousy and sexual immorality, sue each other in civil courts, and practice gluttony and drunkenness at the Lord's table. What a mess!

Paul offers instruction by drawing a lesson from the past. Paul points back to the time God brought the Hebrew people from slavery into freedom. During these wilderness wanderings the people did much evil, bringing disaster on themselves. A great principle of human conduct is that every behavior has consequences. When the Hebrews did evil, they created their own destruction. Evil deeds always destroy life.

Paul says, in so many words, "Take this lesson to heart. Don't suffer the painful consequences our ancestors did!" Paul recounts God's saving deeds for them: God parted the sea, guided them with a cloud of divine presence, and sustained them with food and water. God blessed them through the preexistent Christ. God has also blessed us Christians through the *earthly person* of Christ! We Christians have the waters of baptism. God feeds us at the Lord's table on food and drink that nourish us into eternal life.

So with such blessings, how can we as God's children ever turn away from God? Our standard answer for our malady is "sin." But something else may also be going on. Our problem may not be "desiring evil," as Paul puts it in verse 6, as much as it is a stifling indifference, an attitude of complacency.

Consider this: a Gallup poll found that 40 percent of Americans attend religious services fairly regularly, but fewer than 10 percent of us are deeply committed. The majority of us appear to just drift along, satisfied with the way things are. Many churches today are in no better shape than the Corinthian church. We're still quarreling, suing each other, chasing idols, and practicing sexual immorality.

Fortunately, Paul does more than admonish. He closes this text (v. 13) with real words of grace. First, "No testing has overtaken you that is not common to everyone." That is, testing or tempta-

111

tion is universal. Testing doesn't signify divine judgment or disapproval. It's just the way life is. Wise people know how to gauge the test results and use them to their advantage. Fools don't.

Second, "God is faithful." The psalmist says, "his steadfast love endures forever" (Pss. 100:5; 118:1-4). Unfortunately, we don't always take what God offers. Someone has said that God has wonderful things to give us, but our hands are too full.

Third, God "will not let you be tested beyond your strength." Through testing we mortals discover what is true and valuable and what is not. Gold and "fool's gold" (iron pyrite) look the same. We test them in fire. Fire doesn't damage gold, but iron pyrite sizzles and smells of sulfur. Little survives.

The most important things we learn about ourselves are the things we learn when we're put into the fire, when we're tested. In Dostoevsky's *The Brothers Karamazov* one of the brothers says, "There's a new man in me, a new person being born in me. But that new life would not have arisen in me if God had not sent the storm." Good things can happen to us in times of testing! We discover what's true and valuable and what's not. And we become stronger. Without that strength, where would we be?

Paul addresses *us*. Thankfully, we don't have to go through life cursing every bump in the road. We'll all have trouble. And we don't have to worry about God's faithfulness. If we diligently seek God's help, God will deliver us. God can even save us from our complacency! For this we can only say, "Praise be to God!" (Sandy Wylie)

FROM FEAR TO FAITH

LUKE 13:1-9

In the midst of the tragedies of life, faith teaches us to live today, focused on the things over which we have control.

Lent is the season when the church grows quiet. We uncover our unexamined assumptions. When we turn inward in the quiet of this season, we realize that we live our days with a persistent fear. We fear a phone call in the night, or a shocking headline in the morning paper. We realize we only have so much time. One author said, "time is the joker in the deck of life. It not only marches on, but it finally marches right over a guy."

Jesus is running out of time as he walks the road toward Jerusalem. But along the way, Jesus hears that his kin, the Galileans, had their blood mingled with their sacrifices by Pilate. And Jesus knew of eighteen innocent people whose only sin was that they were standing too close to the tower of Siloam when it fell. "Who sinned? Who is at fault?" At the deepest we fear this answer: If all people who fall victim to such accidents are innocent, then God is guilty.

But Jesus felt no need to vindicate the ways of God. His Father was so loving that even if he and his disciples had been standing under that tower it would have made no difference. But our faith is not as strong as Jesus'. How should we respond when the "roof caves in?" "What if the same happened to me, or those I love? What if we faced up to death?" Jesus wants to teach us that the real enemy is our failure to live an intentional life. It is a life that is inward and purposeful that fills today with meaning. Tomorrow is a dream; yesterday is a memory. Today is what we have.

Twice Jesus makes the point: "Unless you repent, you will all perish as they did." Jesus meant that we will perish in the midst of an unexamined life. By coupling these disasters with the stories of the last-chance fig tree, Jesus gives a new twist on repentance.

Usually when we think of repentance, we hear some ne'er-do-well say, "Once I was like this, now I am like this." But here we are coached, if we are a fig tree, to "be a fig tree." To repent means to be fully human and free. That fact perhaps means there are things we are not meant to understand. It is a lifetime project to understand ourselves. The source of serenity is simply this: To accept the things we cannot change, to change the things we can, and to know the difference.

The key to a satisfied life is taking responsibility over the things we can control and leaving the rest to God. In the face of the violence and caprice of life, Jesus was not concerned about past sin or righteousness, but only present response. For us and for the fig tree, there is still time to change and bear fruit.

Our prayer then becomes that of the contented mother in Psalm 131:

O LORD, my heart is not lifted up,
    my eyes are not raised too high;
I do not occupy myself with things
    too great and too marvelous for me.
But I have calmed and quieted my soul,
    like a weaned child with its mother;
    my soul is like the weaned child that is with me. (vv. 1-2)

Let us live with souls calm and quiet, living responsibly today.
(Don Holladay)

MARCH 21, 2004

Fourth Sunday in Lent

Worship Theme: In Jesus' life and the Christ event revealed in his death and resurrection, we no longer regard others from the human point of view. Rather, God has made us, the church, a community of reconciliation for all people.

Readings: Joshua 5:9-12; 2 Corinthians 5:16-21; Luke 15:1-3, 11*b*-32

Call to Worship (Psalm 32:1-6*a*, 11 RSV)

Leader: Blessed is he whose transgression is forgiven, whose sin is covered.

People: **Blessed is the man to whom the LORD imputes no iniquity, and in whose spirit there is no deceit.**

Leader: When I declared not my sin, my body wasted away through my groaning all day long.

People: **For day and night thy hand was heavy upon me; my strength was dried up as by the heat of summer.**

Leader: I acknowledged my sin to thee, and I did not hide my iniquity; I said, "I will confess my transgressions to the LORD"; then thou didst forgive the guilt of my sin.

People: **Therefore let every one who is godly offer prayer to thee.**

All: **Be glad in the LORD, and rejoice, O righteous, and shout for joy, all you upright in heart!**

Pastoral Prayer:

Gracious God of Manna and Eucharistic Bread, each time we eat, O God, you provide us tangible reminders of your blessed providence for us. When our forebears wandered in the wilderness, you provided for them. When Jesus' bodily presence departed from the disciples, you offered to them the gift and presence of the Holy Spirit as counselor, advocate, and helper. Whenever we break bread together we feel and know your great care for us. As we have the blessings of food and drink remind us that not all in our world live happily with full stomachs. Help us see the need of the hungry and homeless. Inspire us to acts of charity and mercy by your Spirit. Due to our care, love, and concern, may we be those who fill with food those who hunger. May we be your hands and feet in the world as we share your bounty with others. We pray for peace with justice in our world through the name of Jesus Christ. Amen. (David Mosser)

SERMON BRIEFS

SKIPPING GILGAL

JOSHUA 5:9-12

Admittedly, upon first reading this text I had to ask why. Why did the church liturgists choose these particular verses? Wouldn't it make more sense to drop verse 9? I mean, the gist of verse 9 as we have it is to explain the origin of the name *Gilgal*. If you dig just a little, *Gilgal* has to do with the verb "to roll" and the allusion to the circumcisions that have just occurred. Maybe the church liturgists were not concerned with the references here, but nevertheless we are faced with them. Perhaps we should gloss them over and go on to verse 10.

After all, without verse 9 we would not have to consider the sticky mess of understanding inferred by the text, "roll away the disgrace of Egypt," and the scenes of slavery and hard labor those words conjure up. And without the "rolling," we need not mention circumcision at all. Of course we would not be reminded of God's covenant with Israel or of God's deliverance in rolling away the Jordan River or of the stone that would one day be rolled away from a tomb. We can skip in the text to celebrating the Passover in Canaan without being bothered by what has come before. For that matter, why don't we skip ahead in our own church calendar and just celebrate Easter since it is almost here. Certainly this is not as bad as John Grisham's characters in *Skipping Christmas*! At least we have mostly prepared to celebrate the holiday.

Or have we? Can we truly celebrate Easter in a few weeks without thinking of what came before the stone rolled away? This text suggests we cannot. Just as the Hebrew people renewed their covenant with God as they entered Canaan, we too need to renew our own baptismal covenant with God as we prepare to enter Easter. But how? The Hebrews, as Joshua tells the story, renewed their covenant of circumcision, reaffirming their self-awareness of being children of God. They celebrated the tradition of Passover, remembering joy at God's deliverance as well as the serious responsibility such provision demanded. Then they partook of the food Canaan itself had to offer as manna ceased to appear, celebrating the new ways God was present in this new land.

We, too, are called to reaffirm our identity as God's children and remember seriously our salvation before we celebrate the Easter message of God's new presence in a new year. Such work is not to be taken lightly. As children of God we are to be known by our unity and love. In the midst of diversity, finding common ground and developing genuine concern requires intent and effort. Perhaps we need to let God "roll away the disgrace" of jealousy or self-isolation or contentment. We must face whatever it is keeping us from accepting our ability to respond to God's love. Allowing God to work thus in our lives requires courage. Joshua reminds us that Israel, too, had to have an amazing courage to believe somehow, someway that unleavened bread and manna could sustain a nation. Now our hope comes from Jesus who, in going before us, assures us that "I am with you always, to the end of the age" (Matt. 28:20), no matter what you envision that end to be.

This year, do not skip Gilgal on the way to the promised celebration. Reaffirm yourself as a child of God, taking strength in the salvation already offered to you, accepting the challenge of allowing God to transform you daily. (Karen Hudson)

A RE-CREATED PEOPLE

2 CORINTHIANS 5:16-21

Have you ever caught yourself saying, "I feel like a new person"? These words may come from our mouths at the moment we put on a new dress or suit. We might feel radiant, glamorous, beautiful, and handsome because of the new outfit draped on our bodies. We expect our friends to make encouraging remarks about our new clothes so that our self-esteem might be fed. It is no wonder that people enjoy shopping for a new outfit when it has this kind of ability to lift our spirits and brighten our horizons.

Perhaps the Corinthians were doubting their self-worth when Paul wrote his second letter to them. It is possible that they questioned the value of being a Christian. So Paul found it necessary to remind them "if anyone is in Christ, there is a new creation" (v. 17). What is this new creation? Is it not more than being an improved or reformed person? A working definition for Paul began by identifying this new creation as having a new view of the world. Christians should no longer regard people simply from a fleshly perspective. Human standards of evaluation are unable to measure the depths to God's creative work. Our standards for value disappear when they are held in light of the cross. Our race, gender, financial status, and even our criminal histories disappear before God when we stand as newly created beings in Christ.

It is striking that our own definitions for being a new creation are often individualistic. We talk about the ways God has transformed "my life" and "forgiven me of my sin." Certainly, God has accomplished these tasks. God is reconciled to us, but inherent in this idea is the notion that God has sought us out, rather than the other way around. We might be estranged from God, but God is present in our world. Our sense of estrangement can occur for different reasons such as a guilty conscience for the way we live our lives or selfish living that is harmful to others. As we identify and repent of our sins, both individual and communal, we gain a sense of being a new creation.

When we recognize that we are in Christ, our lives indicate that we are becoming re-created beings. As individuals and as a community, we are in a process of moving away from the old way of looking at the world with a human perspective to what Paul describes as a fresh perspective and a new way of seeing the world. To become a new creation is not a magical event. We are on a journey with Christ, a journey with peaks and valleys. Times of trouble and times of celebration mark this life. The newness Christ gives us is not just for the future; we can enjoy newness now. It is in the church that Christ creates genuine community, and it is within this community that we celebrate changed lives.

As we approach Spring and Easter, there is a sense of newness in the air. The natural world awakes from its sleep. Trees bloom and flowers blossom. Signs of life are all around us. At the same time, we prepare ourselves for the crucifixion of Jesus Christ, while being hopeful for his resurrection. The preparation for Easter enables us to remember that we too are becoming a new creation through Christ. As individuals and as community, God re-creates in us a new life through Jesus the Christ. (Mark White)

THE STORY OF A LOVING FATHER

LUKE 15:1-3, 11b-32

The gospel story from Luke is a familiar one. We have come to know it as the story of the prodigal son. While the story certainly is about a son who leaves home, to make this son the focus of the story seems to miss the point. The focus of the story is on the father. To those who are listening, Jesus seeks to describe a God whose love is for all people—even those who have sinned and live in brokenness. The key to understanding the power of this story is to get a sense and feel for God's grace. A constant theme in the gospel is that those who should be the dispensers of God's grace are often those who withhold it. We must remember that Jesus tells this story in response to the Pharisees and teachers of the law who complain that Jesus is spending his time and fellow-ship with the wrong kind of people. You sense the church's same preoccupation with this misunderstanding when you hear the three stories in Luke 15 referred to as the stories about the lost sheep, the lost coin, and the prodigal son. From the larger context of the gospel why do we continue to struggle with realizing that we discover the power of these stories in the sheep being found, the coin being found, and the son being forgiven? Jesus tells this story to a group who have evidently missed the point of his coming. Luke 15 illustrates the theme of life; a theme which is about finding the lost and loving the unlovable. This parable must be about the love of a father who will stop at nothing in his love for his son.

At the heart of this story is the grace of a loving father. It is the grace Frederick Buechner describes in *Wishful Thinking* when he says, "Grace is something you can never get but only be given. There's no way to earn it or deserve it or bring it about any more than you can deserve the taste of raspberries and cream or earn good looks or bring about your own birth." The complaining of the Pharisees and teachers of the law centered on the judgment that the people Jesus fellowshiped with didn't deserve Jesus' interest or his time. Like the son in the story who squandered the inheritance, the Pharisees need to get what is coming to them. Left up to the Pharisees and the teachers of the law the wayward son got what he deserved, living with the pigs like a beggar. It seems to me that this story was not a popular one with those for whom it was told. Like the oldest son in the story the response of the father is inappropriate in relationship to the obvious sin committed by the younger son. The more pressing question for such people is where is the justice in such a response?

This is not a story about justice but one about grace. It is always easier to pronounce the judgment in the lives of people. Zero tolerance, assessment tests, entrance exams, closed communion, job interviews, job evaluations, all become ways in which we experience the judgment inherent in so much of what our lives have become. And yet, Jesus proclaims through this story that the nature of God's love is grace. In this season of Lent the church certainly encourages persons to take an honest look at who they are in light of their Christian journey. Luke shares one such journey of a father and a son. However, let us as the church not forget that while repentance is necessary it is all the more important to offer that powerful word of grace. Jesus reminds us that when all is said and done, regardless of how it might look measured against the backdrop of a judgmental culture, people like this young individual really need that gentle word and gesture of redeeming, loving grace. The father knew this the day the son returned, and so can we! (Travis Franklin)

MARCH 28, 2004

Fifth Sunday in Lent

Worship Theme: As a penitential season, Lent reminds humankind how it has fallen short of the covenant God made with us. However, in Jesus Christ, God is doing a new thing. Through Jesus, God issues a heavenly calling to God's people.

Readings: Isaiah 43:16-21; Philippians 3:4*b*-14; John 12:1-8

Call to Worship (Psalm 126 RSV)

> *Leader:*   When the LORD restored the fortunes of Zion, we were like those who dream.

> *People:*   **Then our mouth was filled with laughter, and our tongue with shouts of joy; then they said among the nations, "The LORD has done great things for them."**

> *Leader:*   The LORD has done great things for us; we are glad.

> *People:*   **Restore our fortunes, O LORD, like the watercourses in the Negeb!**

> *Leader:*   May those who sow in tears reap with shouts of joy!

> *People:*   **He that goes forth weeping, bearing the seed for sowing, shall come home with shouts of joy, bringing his sheaves with him.**

Pastoral Prayer:

Creator God of Infinite Love, abide with us as we take our Lenten journey with Jesus toward Jerusalem and the mission that he accomplishes there. The hope that you hold out for us on the far side of the cross is the chief expectation that makes our journey of faith worthwhile—indeed, bearable. In your prophetic word to us, you promise that you are doing a new thing. In fact, in the life, ministry, and death of Jesus you conquer sin and death. As we strain to move forward and live in your promises, O God, give us the passion and daring to be your people. Remind us to consider the poor, for in ministering to them we fulfill the law of Christ. But while we fulfill our social responsibility to the poor let us not forget the joy of your call to faithful life. Daily remind us that faithfulness itself is our paramount recompense for righteous living. We pray this in the glorious hope of Jesus Christ, our Lord and Messiah. Amen. (David Mosser)

SERMON BRIEFS

NEW BEGINNINGS

ISAIAH 43:16-21

A wise man once said that the good old days were good because they were gone. It is very easy to reminisce about the days of old and complain about the future knocking at our door. The future brings about change in our lives, and that scares us. The future also holds the promise of something new, and that excites us. The Lord tells the people of Judah to forget the past and to prepare for a new thing. As we prepare for Easter let us put aside the things of the past and think about the new way of life that the Lord gives us. Let us rejoice in the eternal hope that God is "about to do a new thing" in our life.

Spring brings about the rebirth of nature and the expectation of a new beginning of life. Each year about this time, the dogwoods begin to blossom. Their petals shine forth for a few short weeks and then they quickly fall with the blowing wind. The birds begin to appear. Frogs, crickets, and all the other noisemakers begin their symphony anew. I remember as a child staying out late at night catching fireflies and saving them in a jar. The possibilities are endless when spring comes around. The Lord asks,

"Do you not perceive it?" (v. 19b). Do we not perceive the joy of new beginnings each year during the spring season?

Have you ever felt as though you were alone and everyone had abandoned you, including God? Have you ever felt as if you were in the desert without a drop of water? Isaiah proclaims that the Lord will alter the very essence of the world to bring about a new Spirit to the chosen people. The Lord promises a refreshing drink in the driest of times. Personal tragedy affects many people's lives so that they feel as though they are in a desert. The Lord promises a new Spirit to see us through the desert. The people of Israel wandered in the desert for many years. Just when they thought the Lord had abandoned them, God provided for them. Isaiah reminds the people of Judah that the Lord is with them in this time of struggle. During this Lenten season, let us remember that the Lord is with us as we struggle with the personal trials of our lives.

This passage begins with a proclamation of who the Lord is. The armies of the world fall down beneath the mighty power of the "Creator of Israel" (v. 15). The prophet proclaims that the Lord snuffs them out like a candle. The passage ends with a proclamation of how all of creation worships the Lord. It is good to offer praise to God as we pray. The God of salvation loves the world. While traveling in Spain, I was amazed at how easily the people offered their love to God. It seemed as if every prayer ended with, "We love you, Lord." The prophet Isaiah strongly suggests that God expects us to offer our praise by proclaiming, "so that they might declare my praise" (v. 21). As we develop our relationship with the Lord, we should strive to nurture our love for our Divine Creator. As we approach Easter, let us prepare for the coming of God's new thing by rekindling our relationship with the Lord. Perhaps we may perceive the joy of something new about to burst forth in our lives. (John Mathis)

GIFT OF GRACE

PHILIPPIANS 3:4b-14

On what do you rely as a basis for your relationship with Jesus Christ? As a Christian educator, I have had the experience to ponder that very question with people of all ages within the church. I have found a variety of responses. Some people rely on what they have been taught since they were small children, never considering questioning or not taking that teaching at face value. Some people rely on what they discover intellectually through reading and investigation, embracing Jesus through academic proof. Others rely on their experience of grace as a basis for their relationship, always grasping the mercy offered by Christ in a time of difficulty or loneliness. A good number of folks rely on the work that they have done for God as the basis of their relationship with Jesus. I must admit that it is this "worker group" that both provide the most theological struggle and with which I most identify. It is the concept of working for your relationship with Jesus that was problematic for the apostle Paul, and he addressed it over and over, including these verses in Philippians.

In Philippians 3, Paul encourages the church at Philippi against the temptation of putting their confidence and trust in their own abilities and works. This was a topic near and dear to the apostle's heart. After all, Paul spent his adult life as part of the Jewish culture that encouraged a close obedience to the law as part of the quest for righteousness. As a Pharisee, Paul sought this righteousness with vigor. As part of Paul's commitment, he worked to discourage the Christian movement, and was on a mission to do so when he encountered the grace of Jesus Christ on the road to Damascus. Paul's encounter with Christ, and all that happened afterward, convinced him of the importance of grace over work. Paul taught his mission churches likewise. In this particular passage, Paul retells the story of his life as a Pharisee and of all his work and legalism, which was probably familiar to the Philippians. In verses 7 and following, he ascertains, however, that all of that life of work and accomplishment is nothing compared to the knowledge of Jesus Christ and his death and resurrection. In his new life with Christ, the only righteousness that Paul seeks is the righteousness that comes from faith in God. Paul completes this section of scripture in the verses that are perhaps some of the most well known in Philippians. In verses 13 and 14, he admits that he has yet to fully grasp this righteousness through faith but that he is pressing on toward that very goal.

Perhaps, it is verses like these that folks who sit on the pew and participate in the programs without ever doing any work cling to as their motto, but this is not what Paul is talking about. As a matter of fact, Paul obviously believed that it was important for Christians to work and care for one another and for the furthering of the gospel. He spent, and probably lost, his life working for the cause of Jesus Christ. On the contrary, Paul discourages the idea that it is possible to earn righteousness through hard work. True righteousness is through faith and faith alone. No amount of work can make up for a missing or neglected relationship with Jesus Christ.

What an appropriate reminder for the Lenten season! Jesus Christ does not require a certain number of hours or tasks. Being a good Christian is not about how much or how little you do. It is not about how many years you taught Sunday school, the number of committees on which you serve, or any other labor at which you toil away for Jesus. What matters most is your personal relationship with Jesus Christ, which comes by faith and cannot be earned. This Lenten season do not resign your church positions or stop doing whatever work you do, but remember what is truly required by God: faith. The righteousness that you receive is part of the gift of grace. (Tracey Allred)

BREAD AND OIL

JOHN 12:1-8

One summer morning at a beach house with my family, I woke up to the smell of baking bread, drifting up from the kitchen. I quickly dressed and went downstairs. I met my sister-in-law there. She was just taking a loaf of freshly baked bread out of the oven. "Wow!" I said. "Is this for breakfast?" I asked hopefully. "No, not this loaf," my sister-in-law said. "This one is for the birds." "What?" I asked, not at all understanding. "This one is for the birds. The next one is for us," she said, pointing to a lump of dough. "You mean you are going to give a new loaf of bread to the birds?!" "Yes, that's right," she said. I couldn't believe it, thinking "What a waste of homemade bread on those noisy seagulls." My sister-in-law smiled and walked past me, heading down to the beach. I ran to the deck, convinced she was kidding. She wasn't. She got to the sand, and began tearing off hunks of the loaf and throwing them up in the air to the birds, who swooped and ate it happily.

I must say that I did get my fresh bread that morning from the second loaf. But for a long while, I couldn't get over that loaf thrown to the birds. Birds get the leftover, dried-up crusts and end-pieces of store-bought bread, not the first loaf out of the oven! I didn't get it.

Judas didn't get it, either. He smelled the lovely fragrance of that pistachio-nut oil wafting through the house, but it did not move him to gladness. No, Judas was disgusted to find that Mary had taken one of the most expensive bottles of perfume and poured the whole thing on Jesus' feet. What a waste! That bottle cost a whole year's worth of wages! And for what purpose? Better to have used the money for a good cause—like a contribution to the poor, or saving it for the Disciples' Emergency Fund.

No, Judas didn't get it. But Mary was on to something. Like my sister-in-law feeding the birds of the air, Mary grasped the importance of the moment. Mary recognized who was with them. She knew that the presence of Jesus was a bowing-down occasion, one that called for the best in the house. This was the one who had raised her brother, Lazarus, from the dead and led him out of the grave. Mary knew in her heart that he deserved all honor and glory. So she was moved to anoint him, to mark him as king. She claims the moment: She takes the jar of costly oil and pours every last drop on his feet, then bows down to wipe it with her own hair. Mary gets it!

Do we get it? Do we grasp who it is that is with us and then throw ourselves down in adoration and praise? Or are we still on the deck of the beach house, stuttering in bewilderment about the waste on a bunch of birds?

Jesus affirmed Mary's anointing. In fact, he interpreted her action beyond what even she had understood; that is, that it was the preparation of his body for burial. His anointing as king would lead him not to an earthly kingdom, but to suffering and death. Jesus got it, and went willingly from that place to face the cross.

The smell wafts through the house, waking us up to go down-stairs and meet the One who gives life to the dead and goes to the cross for our salvation. If we smell it, then why not name it and claim the bowing-down moment? This is the moment to abandon ourselves to Christ in love, in gratitude, in devotion.

Hallelujah! What a Savior! Break out the oil! Throw the first loaf to the birds! Amen. (Laura Jernigan)

REFLECTIONS

APRIL

Reflection Verse: *"The LORD is good,*
  a stronghold in a day of trouble;
he protects those who take refuge in him,
  even in a rushing flood.
He will make a full end of his adversaries,
  and will pursue his enemies into darkness." (Nahum 1:7-8)

Easter, as you readers all know by now, occurs on April 11 this
year. Easter is an occasion of hectic simplicity for most pastors.
On the one hand, people understand (for the most part) the cultural activities around Palm Sunday and Easter Day. We do not
have to invent or even promote too extensively the reasons for
which folks flock to worship. The cultural hoity-toity attend worship on Easter for reasons not too dissimilar to Mother's Day.
Churches fill with individuals who regularly neglect the Sabbath
or find it irrelevant to modern life. Generally, preaching to this
kind of crowd is in some ways like speaking to the Lion's Club or
the Garden Club in that many of the attendees are not exactly
tuned in to the historic liturgy of the Christian faith. The good
news about this is that preachers at least have a crowd that has
gathered of its own accord, whatever their ultimate motive may
actually be.

On the other hand, however, the sheer challenge of preaching
the Resurrection to the modern, scientific, skeptical mind is a
daunting assignment. If there exists a more difficult subject to
sell to the modern ear, I cannot imagine what it would be.
Preaching resurrection texts reminds me of trying to preach, or at
least theologically justify, the Minor Prophet whose name is
Nahum.

If we were to read the whole of the Minor Prophet Nahum, we
too might decide that. Nahum is out. This prophet does not even

grace the table of readings that churches draw on for worship, teaching, and preaching. To the best of my recollection I have never preached from this prophetic book. I have never heard any of my preaching colleagues mention a sermon series, or even a single sermon, from this book, which contains but three chapters. Honestly, Nahum may have the distinction of being the most consistently and collectively ignored biblical book in church history. Why is this the case?

For Nahum's lack of recognition, the text itself is "exhibit A." No doubt Nahum does have several memorable turns of phrase. For a few examples we can read these expressions of the faith: "The LORD is slow to anger but great in power" (1:3), "Look! On the mountains the feet of one / who brings good tidings, / who proclaims peace" (1:15), and "I am against you, says the LORD of hosts, and will lift up your skirts over your face" (3:5). Yet, on the whole, the message we read in Nahum does reek of God's violence and retribution against Assyria, and more specifically, Nineveh. With the possible exception of churches that specialize in "texts of terror" from the most bizarre and violent prophecies of scripture, like parts of Ezekiel or Revelation, most tame Christian congregations prefer the loving Jesus representing a God who forgives human sin at any cost. Perhaps this is how it should be.

Nonetheless, in Nahum we have a prophet who says,

> A jealous and avenging God is the LORD,
> the LORD is avenging and wrathful;
> the LORD takes vengeance on his adversaries
> and rages against his enemies. (1:2)

Indeed, for Nahum this characterization of God is only the beginning. Unfortunately for preachers we can either embrace texts like Nahum or ignore them like we ignore those parishioners who suggest we could improve worship attendance if the local high school cheerleaders took up the offering in their uniforms (I am not making this up). We may either snub Nahum and side step such difficult texts or face up to the distress of preaching texts that not only make the congregation uncomfortable but also make preachers squirm as well.

One of the greatest burdens for preachers is to preach the whole Bible. Clearly, many of Scripture's ancient issues do not concern moderns in the least. Conversely, many biblical themes are our concerns but make us queasy to address the questions in forthright ways. Not only do we publicly proclaim the whole Bible, but we, as faithful preachers, must also come to terms with these theological ideas and biblical texts. Only by coming to terms with these questions can we speak convincingly about them. When we do speak, however, we cannot sacrifice our own intellectual integrity.

What do we do with Nahum, and how does this prophet fit into our faith? The key is the prophet's understanding of what he is doing when he speaks. It would indeed be an objectionable book, theologically and otherwise, if Nahum said what he thought and felt about Assyria and Nineveh. However, Nahum as a typical prophet does not speak for himself. Rather, Nahum speaks for God. In the prophecy's title we read: "An oracle concerning Nineveh. The book of the vision of Nahum of Elkosh" (1:1). Like any good prophet, Nahum knows that his vision comes from God. Therefore, it is not Nahum's human voice we hear, but the voice of God.

One reason modern people find parts of the Bible problematic is that scripture speaks occasionally of Yahweh's violent judgments. It is true also that we live in a world that specializes in relativisms. To many in our modern world today, everything is relative. We second-guess every thought or action. No idea, principle, or action is above suspicion. Beacon Press published a notable and striking book titled *Proverbs of Ashes*. In this book the authors attempt to scrupulously write off the doctrine of the Atonement. They write that, among other things, "When the Christian tradition represents Jesus' death as foreordained by God, as necessary to the divine plan of salvation, and as obediently accepted by Jesus the son out of love for God the Father, God is made into a child abuser or a bystander to violence against his own child" (Rita Nakashima Brock and Rebecca Ann Parker, 2001, p. 157). There is some merit in what they write, but my point simply asks, if we begin to judge God from the human perspective, then who becomes a final arbiter of human behavior? When we impugn the judge, then who lingers to adjudicate dependable justice?

Eventually all people must make a faith decision. To whom do we offer our ultimate trust? Do we offer it to human thinking that debates itself to death? Or do we offer it to a God whom the Bible depicts as one who fights on behalf of God's chosen people? No one can answer this question for us—it is our question! What Nahum does for modern readers simply reminds us that God rules and overrules. God is God. Not only this, but God also fights on behalf of God's people. When God lays waste to Assyria, according to the prophet's vision, it is Nahum's way of proclaiming the sovereignty of God over the enemy. God is sovereign regardless of how mighty and powerful this enemy appears to the frail and fearful people of God.

At Easter preachers stand and proclaim, as best we can, the seemingly preposterous truth that God raised Jesus from the dead. Do we fully understand the God who is at work here? No! Rather we merely proclaim the historic faith through our historic Scripture. These sacred texts teach that God is stronger than evil and that life in God is stronger than death. Once we make that decision of faith, we have the rest of our lives to sort out the thorny, theological details. (David Mosser)

APRIL 4, 2004

Passion/Palm Sunday

Worship Theme: To sustain the weary with a word is the task of Jesus as Messiah. As Jesus reveals himself to the disciples, he also demonstrates the capacity for self-emptying.

Readings: Isaiah 50:4-9*a*; Philippians 2:5-11; Luke 22:14–23:56

Call to Worship (Psalm 31:9-16)

Leader:	Be gracious to me, O LORD, for I am in distress; my eye wastes away from grief, my soul and body also.
People:	**For my life is spent with sorrow, and my years with sighing; my strength fails because of my misery, and my bones waste away.**
Leader:	I am the scorn of all my adversaries, a horror to my neighbors, an object of dread to my acquaintances; those who see me in the street flee from me.
People:	**I have passed out of mind like one who is dead; I have become like a broken vessel.**
Leader:	For I hear the whispering of many—terror all around!—as they scheme together against me, as they plot to take my life.
People:	**But I trust in you, O LORD; I say, "You are my God."**
Leader:	My times are in your hand; deliver me from the hand of my enemies and persecutors.
All:	**Let your face shine upon your servant; save me in your steadfast love.**

Pastoral Prayer:

O God, our Divine Teacher, morning by morning you quicken our spirits to thirst for the truth you offer us in your prophets, teachers, and the Messiah, Jesus the Christ. We long to know more of you and your ways in your world, yet far too often knowledge of your kingdom creates fear in us. We desire to be servants of others and to empty ourselves on behalf of those for whom Jesus died. Even so, as we approach the moment of truth, the moment in which we encounter others who are different from ourselves, we hesitate. Help us have the mind of Christ. Give us the good courage and strength of will to once again proclaim boldly that we do indeed serve a risen savior with our words and actions. As you provide opportunities for service and witness within your holy realm, O God, allow us to serve others with justice and equity. Remind us to guard others' pride in ways that we would want others to protect our dignity. All this we pray in the blessed and righteous name of the savior, Jesus Christ. Amen. (David Mosser)

SERMON BRIEFS

SUFFERING SERVANT

ISAIAH 50:4-9*a*

How do we proclaim a good word to those who are weary and seeking deliverance? How often do we begin the day with God? The prophet Isaiah trusts in the Lord to provide for him the words to say. The prophet is open to the calling of God at the dawn of every morning. He begins his day listening and seeking the Lord for guidance. Often it is a struggle to sit in silence and listen. In seminary, we began our spirituality classes with ten minutes of silence. I struggled at first to become comfortable with this exercise. Little by little, I began to welcome this time spent with God in silence. Unfortunately, I sometimes struggle to continue this discipline in my life. It is good for us to seek time alone with God to listen to what the Lord is calling us to do. Silence is truly golden.

Once we are open to what the Lord has to say, are we willing to listen? Are we willing to make the changes necessary in our lives that God requires? The suffering servant follows the Lord's calling, not counting the cost. The servant follows the Lord and is not rebellious. Jesus Christ lived out the life of the suffering servant proclaimed by the prophet Isaiah. Jesus teaches us to turn the other cheek, to offer our cloak as well as our coat, to love our enemies, and to go the extra mile. As Jesus rode into Jerusalem and the crowds were cheering and shouting "Hosanna," Jesus knew that soon the guards would be beating him and spitting upon him. The prophet proclaims, "The Lord GOD helps me; therefore I have not been disgraced" (v. 7). Isaac Watts writes in his hymn, "O God, Our Help in Ages Past," "Our shelter from the stormy blast, / and our eternal home!" He continues, "Be thou our guide while life shall last, / and our eternal home" (*The United Methodist Hymnal* [Nashville: The United Methodist Publishing House, 1989], no. 117). God is with us during the difficult times of our lives. Storms will come and go but our eternal hope will never fail. The Lord will guide us all the days of our lives. In the Sermon on the Mount, Jesus teaches us to be kingdom people. These are not easy lessons to learn and require the heart of the suffering servant to accomplish.

The suffering servant is victorious in humility and is vindicated by trusting the Lord. As long as the servant trusts God and follows the Lord's teachings, no shame will come to the servant. The servant is not alone as he faces his enemies. "Let us stand up together" (v. 8*b*). Together with God, the servant faces all foes. The suffering servant seeks out his adversaries with the faith that God is with him. Jesus fulfills the role of the suffering servant. Jesus faces the temptation of the devil, standing together with God facing his adversary. Jesus continually stands up against the Pharisees and Sadducees boldly proclaiming the word that the Father has given. Jesus disregards the standards of the time and speaks to a Samaritan woman at a well. Jesus heals on the Sabbath. He appears before Pilate not fearing what is about to occur. Jesus carries his cross to Golgotha with a humble heart taking the sins of the world upon his shoulders and bearing all our pain. "It is the Lord GOD who helps me" (v. 9*a*). Jesus bears our grief and helps us through our suffering. Jesus serves as our example to trust in God and follow the Lord as we are called to minister in the world. (John Mathis)

THE CORRECT LENS

PHILIPPIANS 2:5-11

Many of us wear eyeglasses in order to see the things of our world clearly. Our glasses serve as a kind of filter through which the images we look at are focused and defined. In the letter to the Philippians it is clear that for the apostle Paul there is but one "filter" through which to understand the Christian life. That "filter" is Jesus Christ, in his career of self-humbling and suffering and death and resurrection.

In one of the most impressive passages in the Bible, Paul describes the career of Jesus in unforgettable language. The rhythmical form of these verses suggests that they may have been taken from a hymn of the early church which served as a brief confession of faith. The words of this text serve as a rehearsal and reminder of the way members of the church are to live. In the same way we use creeds in worship services today, these ancient words focused and formed the congregation's life as it worshiped.

The formula expressed in these brief verses is dramatic. In contrast to Adam, who sought to be equal with God (Gen. 3:5), we see one who refused to snatch at equality with God. Instead, Jesus poured himself out and took upon himself the form of a servant. Jesus humbled himself still more, becoming obedient unto death. "Therefore," Paul cries, "God has highly exalted him and bestowed on him the name which is above every name" (v. 9 RSV).

This is the Christ whose spirit all must share! This is the Lord to whose authority every knee must bow! To be identified with Christ in humility and obedience is the noblest dignity to which any person can aspire. Paul gave his life to following this one, who became obedient unto death, and taught that Jesus' example is the "filter" through which we define all true discipleship.

The passage begins with a call to have "the same mind" that was in Christ Jesus. It is a call for deliberate living. As we begin the journey of Holy Week, these words remind us that discipleship is always born out of intention. We are those who bend our will to the greater will of God. For those who walk faithfully through the drama of this week, the journey will be hard. There will be the strange drama of the table where we break bread and share a cup as an offering of body and blood on behalf of the world. There is the darkness of Good Friday's crucifixion and all the agony that goes with it. It is a difficult journey. Is it any wonder that congregations are less present on these dramatic days of worship than on Palm Sunday and Easter?

The "mind of Christ" seems strange in a world that embraces self-improvement as the way to happiness. Yet the testimony of the church is that this mind is the way to glory! It is the disciples' challenge to cultivate the mind of Christ until we begin to see the world through the "filter" of Christ's example and know that his way is the way to true life. The words of the prayer of St. Francis capture the essence of living "the mind of Christ":

> Lord, make me an instrument of your peace.
> . . . .
> O Divine Master, Grant that I may not so much seek
> to be consoled as to console,
> Not so much to be understood as to understand,
> Not so much to be loved as to love.

As we embark upon the journey of Holy Week, let us be deliberate in cultivating the mind of Christ through which all truth we can know! (Chris Andrews)

SAVE US?

LUKE 22:14–23:56

For those who do not believe there is brutality and horror in the Bible, take a look at Luke 22:14–23:56. The passage is so familiar we easily disregard the extreme violence taking place. This is a cold-blooded murder. However, those called upon to preach on this text frequently ignore the terrifying aspects of Holy Week completely. Passion/Palm Sunday may begin in sunlight but it ends in darkness. Jesus is hailed as the "King of Kings" and the "Lord of Lords" one minute and then cursed at and spit upon the next. We shy away from this part of the passage because we don't like to admit the truth about ourselves.

The problem is that we cannot thrust this horror upon others; for example, the Jews, the Romans, the Pharisees, and so forth. Rather, the text suggests that all human beings are capable of just this kind of evil, even you and me. In that sense the text calls us to look within ourselves and admit that we are not superior to those who stood in the crowd at the foot of the cross mocking Jesus. One of my favorite teachers used to say, "The Bible is a book about us."

This passage is so difficult that we usually focus on the glorious entry, pass quickly over the cross, and then rush to the Resurrection. But the truth of the matter is that there is no resurrection without the cross and there is no light without the darkness. This is as it should be. Who would want a religion that could not address our deepest problems and our greatest fears? Who would want a fair-weather religion that is good only for the sunny days and has nothing to say when the sky falls? God in Jesus takes us to the heart of the matter. We do not need minor change. We need salvation. God takes us into the darkest part of human nature and is not overwhelmed by it. God, however, does not shy away from the mob. God comes among us acknowledging the worst within us. God comes to us not with rebuke, or scorn, or disgust, but with love.

What is said here is that despite the truth about us God loves us and always will, and because of that love we have a faith powerful enough to defeat any evil, a faith powerful enough to save even us. (Wayne Day)

APRIL 11, 2004

Easter Day

Worship Theme: Early in the morning on the first day of the week, Mary Magdalene witnesses and experiences the good news that is too good *not* to be true. Through the witness of the early church, we today proclaim, "Christ the Lord is risen today, Alleluia!"

Readings: Acts 10:34-43; 1 Corinthians 15:19-26; Luke 24:1-12

Call to Worship (Psalm 118:1, 14, 17, 19, 24)

Leader: O give thanks to the LORD, for he is good;

People: **His steadfast love endures forever!**

Leader: The LORD is my strength and my might;

People: **He has become my salvation.**

Leader: I shall not die, but I shall live, and recount the deeds of the LORD.

People: **Open to me the gates of righteousness, that I may enter through them and give thanks to the LORD.**

All: **This is the day that the LORD has made; let us rejoice and be glad in it.**

Pastoral Prayer:
   O God in whom we move and live and have our being, let our words of praise and thanksgiving reach heavenward this holy day. Through the power of your resurrection of Jesus our Christ, you,

O God, have thrown open wide the portals of heaven. If we are wise enough, you allow us a glimpse of the heavenly places. Our savior, Jesus, has made a pathway for us to follow. Give us the wisdom to follow him. In his earthly ministry he invited his disciples to walk the path of discipleship. These many centuries later, Jesus' invitation still stands. May we reserve our place with you in eternity by the confession of our lives. May we do more than simply mouth pious phrase, but rather, offer to you our lives as a living sacrifice by which people may see the joy and blessedness of the gospel. Give us the fortitude to once again claim our faith heritage that you freely offer us in Christ. Help us once again renew our solemn covenant that you make with us in Jesus' resurrection. May today be a day of absolute joy for us and your church as we celebrate the greatest event—the history of salvation. In Jesus' name we pray. Amen. (David Mosser)

SERMON BRIEFS

ADOPTING GOD'S AGENDA

ACTS 10:34-43

I was twenty-nine years old and had just become pastor of the county-seat church. Soon after I arrived, an African American schoolteacher showed up in a morning worship service to check out the new preacher in town. After she had returned for a few more visits, the first item on the agenda at our monthly deacon's meeting included a question: "Preacher, what are we going to do if she wants to join the church?" At first, I was shocked that someone would ask such a question, but then I realized the person was serious. I didn't quite know how to respond. I was caught totally off guard, but somehow I managed to say, "What do you mean what are we going to do? We will do what we would do if anyone else wanted to join the church. If we choose to do otherwise, we might as well shut the doors of the church forever." The awkward silence that followed my response seemed like an eternity. I feared that this might become my last deacons' meeting. Fortunately, the deacon chair finally broke the silence when he said, "If that is what you say we are going to do, then that is what we are going to do."

In Acts 10 and 12, the first-century church was faced with a critical decision: to push its own agenda or adopt God's. In order for that to happen, God had to change the mind and heart of the church's leader, Simon Peter. Change had never come easy for Peter, but the Holy Spirit used him to free the church from the chains of legalism and lead the body of Christ to become an inclusive fellowship without barriers.

Peter's message in Acts 10:34-43 is one of the best examples of the earliest apostolic preaching. It contains the essential elements around which all early preaching was built: the connection to John the Baptist, the crucifixion, the Resurrection, the post-resurrection appearances, the judgment, the witness of the prophets, the call for decision, and the offer of forgiveness.

According to Luke, God used a Roman centurion named Cornelius and the vision of a sheet with four corners to convince Peter that God does not play favorites. God makes salvation available to anyone who believes and trusts in God. Up until that time, Peter and the early church believed that one had to become a Jew before he or she could experience the grace of God in Christ.

God's new agenda shaped the whole presentation of the gospel that Peter shared with Cornelius. Two very powerful points stand out in Peter's presentation. The first point is that Jesus Christ is Lord of all and stands above all. The second point is that the gospel is inclusive and offers hope to everyone who believes and trusts God. Later, the apostle Paul wrote to the church in Galatia saying, "There is no longer Jew or Greek, there is no longer slave or free, there is no longer male and female; for all of you are one in Christ Jesus" (Gal. 3:28).

Unfortunately, the leaders of the church in Jerusalem found that message difficult to accept. The leaders of the church had a closed agenda, and that agenda did not include the conversion of Gentiles. Fortunately, the agenda of the Judaizers did not represent attitudes within the entire church in Jerusalem. The apostles and other believers in the mother church gave Peter a hearing. The future of the Church as a worldwide movement to reach all people, regardless of race, hung in the balance.

In Acts 11, we discover that the early Church chose to push aside its own agenda and adopt God's agenda. Have you adopted the Lord's agenda for your life? (Bob Buchanan)

DESTROYING THE LAST ENEMY

1 CORINTHIANS 15:19-26

Do you remember your childhood enemies? Most people do. For many those childhood enemies still exist as enemies. We never confronted, much less defeated, our enemies in childhood. So, they remain—distant reminders of failure, shame, and defeat.

Today's enemies require no effort to remember. Their image is constantly before us. We live with them through the day, go to bed with them at night, and see them clearly with our early morning eyes. We spend time developing what we will say when we finally confront them. We enjoy picturing their defeat and our victory. But these are dreams not reality. What would happen if these dreams became reality?

Paul urges us to picture a victorious moment like that—a time when we defeat our greatest enemy. He declares that our greatest enemy is not another human being, but the specter of death. Christians do not live for this life alone. They live for the restoration of the kingdom of God. That's why death is our greatest enemy. If death is the end, if there is no life beyond the grave, then Christians are the most pitiable people in the world. We are the deluded dreamers who fantasize about defeating death through resurrection.

The argument that Paul puts forward in this passage is an argument based on solidarity. We are human beings and are inextricably linked to our ancestors. It was a human being, Adam, who brought death into the world. We die because we are a part of the human race, which has inherited mortality. In the same way, Paul argues, we participate in the resurrection of another man—Jesus. As Adam's sin brought death for human beings, so Christ's resurrection brings life for human beings.

God incorporates the way we realize this "life" into a set process. God has resurrected Jesus. Paul describes Jesus' resurrection as the "first fruits" of the process. The rest of the process involves the resurrection of other human beings according to God's plan. This happens at the end of history after Christ confronts and defeats the evil forces arrayed against him, which Paul describes as "every ruler and every authority and power" (v. 24). Death is the last of these enemies that Jesus destroys. That fact is consistent with Revelation 21:4, where John declares that in God's kingdom "death will be no more."

What is the significance of this claim for Christians? First, it satisfies our desire to know how human history will end. It ends with the restoration of our original status before Adam's sin. Death is no longer a factor. Second, it explains the hope that motivates every Christian. The Christian message is "good news" because death is not the end. Third, this claim about the defeat of death is a motivation for Christian living. We live with the Resurrection in our eyes and in our hearts. Finally, this claim makes it possible for Christians to face death with confidence and peace. We know what is on the other side of the grave. Unlike those childhood enemies who can still haunt us, we are no longer afraid of the final enemy. To the Easter greeting, "Christ is risen," we can respond with joy: "He is risen indeed!" (Philip Wise)

LOOKING FOR THE LIVING AMONG THE DEAD

LUKE 24:1-12

One of the things I have never quite understood is why some people enjoy going to cemeteries. As a small child, I recall several of my family members making their periodic pilgrimages to the cemetery to visit the graves of loved ones. It was a puzzle to me but at the same time intriguing. I recall on occasion begging to go and visiting the grave of my paternal grandfather with my dad. The visit usually included taking some fresh flowers and placing them at the foot of the headstone. He would bend down and pull weeds and tidy up the grave area. Dad would treat his father's grave with great care, as though it was his dad he tended, not the grave site. Sometimes there would be prayers accompanied by tears. Occasionally there would be reminiscing about times with Granddaddy that were both challenging and happy. This behavior would usually last twenty to thirty minutes and then we would return home. I never really found anything important about going other than it seemed both fun and mysterious.

Maybe that was what was happening with the women who were visiting Jesus' tomb on that first Easter Sunday. Nevertheless, I have to admit that their visit was certainly more exciting, more mysterious than my own visits to my grandfather's grave. We always left my grandfather's grave the way we found it, albeit a little neater and presentable. We never went expecting to find the living among the dead. Mary and the others didn't either. Yet after two millennia, we still find it difficult not to think of Jesus as simply dead and gone. This attitude has been the church's dilemma ever since that first Easter Sunday.

Think of it this way: How might we still be visiting Jesus' grave and be confronted with the same two strangers who met the women that day with the question, "Why do you look for the living among the dead?" (v. 5).

One of the things I recall about my grandfather's death was that whenever his life experiences surfaced in family conversations, they always referred to him in the past tense. As Christians who believed in a bodily resurrection and believed Jesus' teachings, we had not grasped the concept of thinking of Granddaddy as alive and well. Somehow, going to the grave made that truth a little more possible, maybe. I don't ever recall conversations about him in the context of his present life, although we couldn't share his life as we had before his death. I don't go to graves of loved ones now. At the core of this behavior, I find these visits of no importance. That's a practical reason. But there's another theological and biblical reason: My loved one is not there. I have no reason to look for the living among the dead.

Today, Easter Sunday, let us all do what the women did. The text says, "Then [the women] remembered" (v. 8). The women remembered what Jesus had told them about his life and death and resurrection. Let us recall such words as "I am with you always, to the end of the age" (Matt. 28:20). A living and vital spirit is within us, the living spirit of God. Other words like "Listen; the time will come . . . when you will be scattered, each going his own way. . . . In the world you will have trouble, but be brave: I have conquered the world" (John 16:32-33 JB). We need to recall in the midst of our struggles that having such challenges are a natural part of being human and an inherent part of faith's journey. And the words "those who are judged worthy of a place in the other world and in the resurrection from the dead . . . can no longer die, for they are the same as the angels, and being children of the resurrection they are sons of God . . . for to [God] all men are in fact alive" (Luke 20:35-36, 38 JB). These are words that we can count on every day.

Today, Resurrection Day, is a fresh reminder about life, not death. It is a reminder to all who have ears to hear that God is God of the living. If we hope to find our loved ones, our friends, our fellow church members who have gone on before us, then we have to look for them among the living. (Michael Childress)

APRIL 18, 2004

Second Sunday of Easter

Worship Theme: Those who witness the truth of God's power through the resurrection of Jesus now obey God rather than any human authority. As the firstborn of the dead, Jesus provides hope for an anguished world.

Readings: Acts 5:27-32; Revelation 1:4-8; John 20:19-31

Call to Worship (Psalm 150 RSV)

Leader: Praise the LORD!

People: **Praise God in his sanctuary; praise him in his mighty firmament!**

Leader: Praise him for his mighty deeds; praise him according to his exceeding greatness!

People: **Praise him with trumpet sound; praise him with lute and harp!**

Leader: Praise him with timbrel and dance; praise him with strings and pipe!

People: **Praise him with sounding cymbals; praise him with loud clashing cymbals!**

All: **Let everything that breathes praise the LORD! Praise the LORD!**

Pastoral Prayer:

Everlasting God, you show your mercy for us in raising Jesus from the tomb. We live as a people who need hope. Yet, in our world, we know that violence, sickness, and death obscure hope. We want to be bold in the gospel, but our courage fails us. However, in your steadfast love for your covenant people, you reveal a greater power loose in our world than we can envisage. In the life, death, and resurrection of Jesus, O God, you offer us a cosmic view of your power and might through love. We see this assurance of your love played out in thousands of kindnesses your people offer to others daily. Help us confess by this assurance of your loving-kindness that you are our Alpha and Omega—our beginning and our end. Help us so live within the hope of this assurance that we transform our lives by the witness of the early Church. Let our voices join the chorus of this great cloud of witnesses to make our confession of faith. Help us believe the good news and live with the joy that befits the resurrection. We pray in the holy name of Jesus. Amen. (David Mosser)

SERMON BRIEFS

THE POWER OF PURPOSE

ACTS 5:27-32

God had a clear plan and purpose both in Christ's humbling sacrifice upon the cross and in his exaltation via resurrection. Christ did not seek glory and adulation for himself (see Philippians 2). The crucifixion would, Jesus predicted, "draw all people to myself" (John 12:32), that they might find forgiveness and salvation.

After being dragged before the Sanhedrin, Peter shared this plan with the chief priests, that they might know why he continued to "teach in [Jesus'] name" despite the council's directive to cease. They had feared that the disciples only wished to stir up trouble and blame them for the death of Jesus. Peter may have succeeded in persuading one of the Pharisees, Gamaliel, who then rose to Peter's defense with the suggestion that perhaps this movement might be "of God." He wisely stated (in Acts 5:38) that "if this plan . . . is of human origin, it will fail."

How true! Human undertakings may succeed for a season, but

in the end, only God's plans and purposes will endure. Indeed, the whole of chapter 5 tells the story of the power of godly purpose and the failure of all-too-human false motives. (Earlier in the chapter, Ananias and Sapphira paid a heavy price for their evil motives.)

Holy power comes when we align our intentions and purposes with God's. As a mischievous child, my favorite way of getting out of trouble was to say, "I didn't do it on purpose." Sadly, too many adults continue through life with this feeble excuse, living aimlessly, only for themselves, without purpose or direction or integrity. What a tragedy to live your life without purpose.

Alfred Nobel became famous and successful as a chemist. He invented a handy product called dynamite. He envisioned that his explosive would be a boon to construction and mining— which it was. Although his discovery brought him wealth and fame, he was horrified to also see others use his invention extensively for warfare.

Years later, Nobel picked up the newspaper and was shocked to read his own obituary. It seems that a relative of his had died, and the press confused the deceased with the famous Alfred Nobel. The obituary mentioned the usual things and gave Nobel credit for the invention of dynamite, which, it said, was used in bombs. Nothing much good was printed about Alfred Nobel, and this forced him to realize that for all his work and wealth, he had done little worthwhile. Thus, Nobel took all his wealth and set up a trust fund and a perpetual committee, which ensured that great achievements throughout history would be encouraged and marked by the Nobel Prize.

There is more power and purpose in a godly plan than in dynamite!

What will your obituary say? How will you be remembered? What is your purpose in being here? In Acts 5:35, Gamaliel cautioned: "consider carefully what you propose to do." Let us pause and carefully consider God's purpose for our lives. (Lance Moore)

THE PROMISE

REVELATION 1:4-8

There is perhaps nothing more needed and seemingly more absent these days than hope. It is practically impossible to go through a day without coming in contact with someone in desperate need of a little hope. The person struggling with cancer, the wife who has lost a husband, the abused child—all these need hope. The victim who suffers because of senseless crime, the man who does not know from where his next meal will come, the addict who cannot overcome his habit—all these need hope. The list could go on and on. Part of being human means being vulnerable to the tragedies of life. It is the unfortunate but searing reality that a by-product of life can sometimes be a feeling of hopelessness. An offering of hope can be one of the greatest gifts you could possibly give to a hurting person. In the midst of a complex apocalyptic writing with all of its symbolism and mystery, a very real theme in Revelation is the hope that Jesus Christ offers in the midst of hopelessness.

John, the author of Revelation, and his audience must have needed hope. From his description, they were victims of persecution because of their Christianity. He consistently encourages them regarding their suffering and need for perseverance. In our passage, John greets his audience, the seven churches in Asia, with a reminder of their common bond, Jesus Christ, and a recapitulation of his attributes in a doxology. Jesus is the faithful witness, the firstborn from the dead, and the ruler of the earth. It is Jesus who loves us, frees us, and makes us part of his kingdom of priests. John then reminds them of a key element in Revelation, the parousia, or coming of Christ. He reminds them that it is Jesus who will come and everyone will see him, even those who crucified him. For the churches to whom John wrote, this must have been an incredible message of hope. Although things might seem hopeless, God has made a promise and when God fulfills that promise, it will affect and change all people. On the other side of their difficult situation, there was the constant promise of hope from God.

What a powerful promise! The wonder and power of God does

149

not stop at the resurrection of Jesus. There is still part of God's promise that God will fulfill. Although it is true that we do not live in the same kind of persecution that John and his contemporaries experienced, the same hope that offered comfort to John should comfort us as well. Whatever situation or hardship we endure, God promises to deliver us. The hope in that promise is a wonderful gift that we have as Christians. I am reminded of an elderly woman who recently passed away in our congregation. Her life and death were hard and painful. She had gone through more in her life than most, but because of her devotion as a Christian, she had hope in the promise of God and knew that on the other side of her pain, there was something to be hopeful about. Her funeral was one of the sweetest ceremonies in which I have participated. From her story, I learned a valuable lesson in hope. With Jesus Christ, there is something to be hopeful about. The story is not over. There is more to come, and it is going to be good! (Tracey Allred)

RAISED TO MEET OUR NEEDS

JOHN 20:19-31

If I had been Jesus, the postresurrection accounts in the New Testament would read quite differently. After the resurrection I would have gone to Caiaphas's house. When I got through spooking him, I would have gone to the palace of Pilate. Then I would have been off to the barracks of the soldiers who crucified me. I would have had a lot of fun on Easter morning!

Jesus took a different approach. He only appeared to people who were already followers, he appeared to them at the point of their need, and the purpose of each appearance was to strengthen their faith so that they would be able to reengage in ministry. Our gospel lesson contains the accounts of two of these resurrection appearances.

In the first account, Jesus did two very important things to strengthen the faith of his fearful disciples. First, he showed them his hands and side. He wanted to make sure they knew his appearance was not a case of mistaken identification. Second, he spoke words to them that addressed their deepest needs.

Jesus' words offered four precious gifts to his disciples. The first gift he offered was peace (see also John 14:27). They needed peace desperately, because they were terrified. Jesus wanted them to know that believers do not find peace in the absence of danger, but in the presence of God. Our world, which is dominated by fear, needs peace from the risen Christ.

Jesus' second gift was purpose. The disciples were lost. They did not know what to do. Now Jesus says to them, "As the Father has sent me, so I send you" (v. 21*b*). Their purpose—and ours—is to function as Christ's representatives in the world. The decision to be a Christian is our choice. But once we make that decision, it determines our primary vocation.

The third gift Jesus offered the disciples in the upper room was power. Jesus "breathed on them and said to them, 'Receive the Holy Spirit' " (v. 22). He had previously told them that when they received the Holy Spirit, God would deposit a river of living water in their hearts (John 7:37-39), and now they received the Spirit. God's Spirit is available to us today. Have you received the fullness of the Spirit?

The final gift Jesus gave that day was an opportunity for penance—forgiveness and the power to loose people from their sins (Matt. 16:19; 18:18). Jesus gave them and us the privilege of listening with a discerning ear and speaking truth to people— either "God has forgiven you for what you did" or "I don't think you have fully dealt with this yet." What an awesome privilege and responsibility.

Thomas, however, was not present during this resurrection encounter. His response to hearing what had taken place was typical of many of the people I know: "You will have to prove it to me before I will believe."

If I had been Jesus I would have resented Thomas's doubting spirit. I would have said to him, "No magic tricks for you, my friend."

Instead of reprimanding him, eight days later Jesus appeared to Thomas and took up his challenge: "You say you won't believe until you touch. Okay then, come and touch." But wait a minute, Jesus. You told Mary on Easter morning that she could not touch you. Now you are inviting Thomas to touch. Let's be consistent! No, this is a different person and a different set of needs. Mary needed to be weaned away from being dependent on the physical presence of Jesus. Thomas needed to touch in order to believe.

Here is the bottom line: If you are seeking to follow Jesus and you have doubts, tell Jesus what you need to have happen before you will believe. He will meet your terms. But Jesus added, "Blessed are those who have not seen and yet have come to believe" (v. 29). The resurrected Christ is alive. The resurrected Jesus comes to all who seek to follow him, as Jesus did long ago, at the point of our need, strengthening us for ministry in Christ's name. (Jim Jackson)

APRIL 25, 2004

Third Sunday of Easter

Worship Theme: The risen Lord not only feeds our souls but also calls upon disciples to "feed my sheep" (John 21:17). As the community of Jesus, we are about the business of fulfilling Jesus' mandate to care for our sisters and brothers.

Readings: Acts 9:1-6 (7-20); Revelation 5:11-14; John 21:1-19

Call to Worship (Psalm 30:1-4, 11-12)

Leader: I will extol you, O LORD, for you have drawn me up, and did not let my foes rejoice over me.

People: **O LORD my God, I cried to you for help, and you have healed me.**

Leader: O LORD, you brought up my soul from Sheol, restored me to life from among those gone down to the Pit.

People: **Sing praises to the LORD, O you his faithful ones, and give thanks to his holy name.**

Leader: You have turned my mourning into dancing; you have taken off my sackcloth and clothed me with joy,

People: **So that my soul may praise you and not be silent. O LORD my God, I will give thanks to you forever.**

Pastoral Prayer:

Divine Sovereign of all that is and was and will be, we praise your holy name for the majesty of the world. If we listen care-

153

fully, we can hear the voices of angels proclaim your greatness. They surround your throne of grace and witness to your power made perfect in love. As we move through our days, help us remember the voices of old. Those heroic voices that have witnessed to the world and to us that your desire is to be in covenant community with us, your people. As we reflect your divine love for your world, O God, give us the strength of character to care for your world. Let us be those who reach out to others with care and compassion. Let us be the ones who feed the hungry and clothe the naked. Let the little children come to us so that we may share Christ's hope. In so doing may we offer them a taste of expectation and anticipation for the joy that life in you offers. In this and in all things we pray in Christ's blessed name. Amen. (David Mosser)

SERMON BRIEFS

HOW TO ANSWER A WAKE-UP CALL

ACTS 9:1-6 (7-20)

Many of the Bible stories contain wake-up calls. One of my favorites is the story of the prodigal son. It has a very good ending, but it has a wake-up call in it. The wake-up call for the prodigal son came while he was living in the far country and going hungry. His empty stomach was his wake-up call. Of course, we see a wake-up call for Saul here in Acts 9. Saul is on his way from Jerusalem to Damascus, a 140-mile journey. It is his task to search out the Christians, to persecute them, to smother this new faith that is threatening Judaism and the Pharisee approach to life.

The Bible puts it this way, "As he neared Damascus on his journey, suddenly a light from heaven flashed around him. He fell to the ground and heard a voice say to him, 'Saul, Saul, why do you persecute me?' "

"Who are you, Lord?" Saul asked.

"I am Jesus, whom you are persecuting," he replied. "Now get up and go into the city, and you will be told what you must do" (vv. 3-6 NIV). Saul got up.

The lightning of God's power hit him; Saul was knocked to his feet. The voice spoke, and Saul responded. It was Saul's wake-up call.

We live in a sleepwalk world. We just calmly reach over every time there is a wake-up call and hit the snooze alarm. The sleep-walk condition is here in this story. To sleep through the wake-up call is the rule, not the exception. Saul was simply doing what he was accustomed to doing when the wake-up call came.

As Saul neared Damascus, the light suddenly flashed from heaven, and he experienced a great pain. The Bible doesn't say that. I say that because he fell to the ground. Saul heard a voice and had his wake-up call.

Why don't you identify the wake-up calls in your life? Saul is sleepwalking. Then he gets a wake-up call and falls to the ground. The next lesson we learn from Saul is the follow-up to the wake-up.

How do we follow up? We can sleep a little longer before deal-ing with the life issue that has awakened us. Saul did not have to say, "Lord, I'm in touch." Saul did not have to get in connection with the Christian community. Saul did not have to keep living until the church named him Paul, as a way of declaring him a Christian disciple. He could have returned to Jerusalem, but he went on to Damascus.

Saul does get up right away. That's why it's a good story. That's why we have the book of Acts and the rest of the letters of the apostle Paul. It's because Saul got up.

When you walk out of this holy place, when you get up out of your pew, I hope you will get up in your spirit, you will wake up, you will do something different, you will do something about your wake-up call.

Acknowledge the difficulty of responding to the call. Gail Sheehy wrote in *Passages*, "The work of adult life is not easy." But remember that you are not responding on your power and strength alone. Jesus was in the middle of Saul's wake-up call. He'll be in the middle of yours also. (Tim Walker)

WORTHY OF WORSHIP

REVELATION 5:11-14

There is no more pertinent subject facing the church today than worship. Churches are dealing with varying styles of worship: traditional, contemporary, and blended. As strange as it may seem, worship styles may be dividing as many churches as uniting them! The debate is not only theological but also practical. The central truth about worship, however, is not so much *how* we worship, but *whom* we worship. John made no mistake at that point. We worship the Lamb of God who takes away the sin of the world.

The writing of the book of Revelation came during John's political exile on the island of Patmos. Here he had his moments of despair and discouragement. Humanly speaking, the forces of evil seemed to have prevailed over the forces of righteousness. In a very real sense John had felt the same way at the cross. No one would doubt that many of the disciples had similar feelings. Yet in a state of supernatural inspiration, John saw things from God's perspective.

In this passage John moved from a discussion of the existing conditions within the churches of Asia to the future of the universal church. He saw the course of coming events in ways similar to Daniel and Ezekiel. Some parts of this section of Revelation seem beyond our human ability to understand. Other passages present spiritual teachings that are clear and pertinent to our present situation. The overriding message of the entire book of Revelation is that God will defeat all evil in the end. Our individual and collective task as Christians is to live in obedience to our Lord who comes as Conqueror and Judge.

Look at the way John came to this conclusion. He saw in God's hand a sealed book (a scroll) and heard a "strong angel" ask, "Who is worthy to open the book, and to loose the seals thereof?" (Rev. 5:1-2 KJV). John then wept because there was no one to open the book. One of the elders, however, told John to stop weeping because "the Lion of the tribe of Juda" would open the book (v. 5 KJV). At that point John saw "a Lamb as it had been slain, having seven horns [complete power] and seven eyes [complete spiritual vision] which are the seven Spirits of God" (v. 6 KJV). Just as they had worshiped God the Father, the living creatures and the twenty-four elders worshiped the Lamb (the Son) and sang his praises with a "new song" (vv. 8-9 KJV).

The theme of the song is the redemptive death of the Lamb of God for all people. "Every creature which is in heaven, and on the earth, and under the earth, and such as are in the sea" will join together as a universal throng to worship the Lamb (v. 13 KJV). If you have ever joined in the singing of Handel's *Messiah*, you have enjoyed at least a taste of what this universal praise of the Savior will be like.

In this passage angels are seen as a vital part of worship. They were created to help carry out God's work on earth. They bring messages from God (Luke 1:26-28), they protect God's people (Dan. 6:22), they bring encouragement (Gen. 16:7), they bring punishment (2 Sam. 24:16), they patrol the earth (Ezek. 1:9), and they fight the forces of evil (Rev. 20:1). Eventually, the main role of these good angels will be in worship, offering continuous praise to God.

Worship, properly understood, is the major focus of the church. Without worship, we diminish the true nature and power of the church. With it, we grow and develop. The outgrowth of all worship is service to God and God's creation. There is nothing either mundane or trite about worship. Place the Lamb in the center of your worship experience, sing the Lamb's praises, study the word, and listen to Christ's Spirit. Then go from that mystical encounter to express what you have experienced. That kind of worship will change you and your world. (Jerry Gunnells)

STANDING IN THE KITCHEN

JOHN 21:1-19

As a mother I am constantly caught in the tension of needing to do two things (at least!) at once. Among others, I find I need to be in the kitchen a fair amount, preparing, serving, and cleaning up food. At the same time I am always trying to distract my seemingly never-full son away from the kitchen. Achieving balance between my being in and convincing our son to be out of the same space is a lesson in progress.

Knowing my own journey, I can empathize with Jesus at the end of his earthly travels. Throughout the Gospel of John, while Jesus has been working, the disciples have been constantly a step behind. They haven't quite gotten what is going on. They have been experiencing the miracles but missing the message of true faith. Jesus has just told the disciples explicitly, "Blessed are those who have not seen and yet have come to believe" (20:29). Certainly now they are equipped to go and preach the gospel, knowing that even people who have not seen Jesus on this earth can and will believe. So, as our scene opens, I can feel the anticipation and almost hear a muttered prayer. "Please, I need to be with them one more time to try to get them to understand that they keep going when I am not physically with them. Let it work this time."

The fact that it has not worked so far is evident. They have gone back to fishing, returned to their old means of living as if they were laid off from being disciples due to Jesus' absence. They don't get it. They do not get what they have been equipped to do. Hence Jesus redirects them one more time. Fish on the other side of the boat, he says. Feed my sheep, he says to Peter. Presumably, this time they get it, especially Peter who goes on to be martyred for the sake of Christ.

In John's account, it took three affirmations by Peter to counter his three denials of Jesus during the crucifixion. If we are honest, we would have to admit that our own reinstatement would probably require many more affirmations. It is a sobering exercise to look back over a day or week or year, examining our words and actions to see if they denied or affirmed Jesus Christ. "Do you love me? Then feed my sheep. Do you love me? Then feed my sheep. Do you love me? Then feed my sheep."

Whatever sheep it is that God is asking us to feed, we must know and accept that encounters with Jesus change lives. We cannot return to our old means of living. Our entire lives become means for discipleship even if the issues at hand do not seem particularly religious. Just as the disciples had to learn that the gospel ministry continued beyond Jesus' earthly life, we must realize that the gospel ministry of our own lives continues past the walls of church and Christian communion. A relationship with Jesus not only turns our lives into a ministry but also enables us to live that ministry.

Standing in the kitchen, my son in his own way says, "Feed me." I offer him something healthy and send him on his way. Standing in my life are numerous people asking for food, some literally, others figuratively. Standing in my heart Jesus says, "Feed them," offers me his own love, and sends me on my way. (Karen Hudson)

REFLECTIONS

MAY

Reflection Verse: *"But you should not have gloated over your brother*
on the day of his misfortune;
you should not have rejoiced over the people of Judah
on the day of their ruin;
you should not have boasted
on the day of distress." (Obadiah 1:12)

I suppose that in "trivia circles" Obadiah is known best as the shortest of our Old Testament witnesses. In fact, this prophet speaks to a very large issue. One of Obadiah's most scathing prophecies is his fulmination against Edom's sin of pride. Edomites, by biblical reckoning, are a sort of sibling people to the Hebrews (see Gen. 25:30; 32:3; 36:1, 8-9). This little nation of Edom stands idly by and observes the Chaldeans (or Babylonians) ravage Judah. Verses 10 and 11 create the atmosphere for Obadiah's attack against Edom, for in these verses the prophet indicts Edom:

> For the slaughter and violence done to your brother Jacob,
>> shame shall cover you,
>> and you shall be cut off forever.
> On the day that you stood aside,
>> on the day that strangers carried off his wealth,
> and foreigners entered his gates
>> and cast lots for Jerusalem,
>> you too were like one of them. (Obad. 1:10-11)

Perhaps it is one thing to stand by in idleness and watch the misfortune of others, but to Obadiah's way of thinking, this is not behavior befitting a near relative. For this idleness Obadiah castigates the people of Edom with a vision from Yahweh. This prophecy is about the sin of pride. For their pride demonstrated in gloating, Obadiah implies that Edom will pay a price. Wouldn't it be wonderful if the sin of pride were a thing of the past? However, we all know that in most congregations pride is one of the most difficult transgressions we preachers address. In fact, we may even know a preacher or two who also is guilty of an overweening pride.

My guess is that most Christians—and this includes preachers—instinctively know how to handle the needs of the poor, the down-and-out folk who come our way. Many of these people need assistance because they have been victims of poor education, dreadful family life, or alcoholism or drug addiction. The church has taught us for years that these individuals need to confess their sin, repent, and believe in Jesus' name. Revivalists yell at people from behind pulpits in tent meetings reminding them that they are nothing but "sinners in the hands of an angry God." I know of a church where the preacher each week recounts in sordid detail his misdoings as a former "pagan heathen" (his term). He smoked pot, beat his wife, and generally was a miserable person—in thought, word, and deed. Then he found Jesus, and his life was changed. The problem is that not every person who needs Christ can bring to the altar the credentials of a miscreant. For people in the sin of despair, Jesus as an answer to life's problems is pretty convincing. However, what is a so-called normal and well-adjusted person to do? Does Jesus have a word for these?

When I was in seminary, I remember reading Reinhold Niebuhr, who wrote about the two basic forms of sin: pride and despair. Much later and with many books under my belt, I realized that in all honesty the theological assertion of sin in the form of pride and despair had been around long before Reinhold Niebuhr. I would rather suggest something like this: Niebuhr wrote that Luther wrote that Augustine wrote that Paul wrote that God said, "Sin comes in two varieties: the sin of pride or control and the sin of despair or of giving up." Either form is sinful and alienates us from God and from each other. Obadiah speaks a word to us preachers today about the temptation of sin—and by this I mean the sin of pride. (Reinhold Niebuhr, *The Nature and Destiny of Man*, 2 vols. (New York: Scribners Press, 1941 and 1943).

In a nutshell, Augustine wrote that the sin of despair asserts that our problems are so bad that not even God Almighty can help us out of the mess we have created for ourselves. The sin of pride, on the other hand, suggests that we, on our own, are self-sufficient and have no need for the grace and salvation that God offers us in Christ. Either way we sin. Augustine said that all sin comes from one of these two attitudes. In despair we profess that our sin is so great that God cannot help us; this is pride. The sin of pride in self-reliance is obvious. From the source of pride comes despair and from pride comes, well, pride.

It is a well-established fact that most preachers love the congregations they serve. Unloving preachers commonly don't last too long in one place. However, do we love our brothers and sisters in the ministry? These brothers and sisters are far too often the objects of our competition for respect, esteem, and better church positions. We in the ministry might do well to attend to the needs of fellow ministers for a healthier church. The body of Christ never looks too healthy when preachers bicker among themselves over minutiae that most laypeople find trivial—or worse—blatantly silly. Paul himself addressed this issue of pastoral competition. He writes, "as long as there is jealousy and quarreling among you, are you not of the flesh, and behaving according to human inclinations? For when one says, 'I belong to Paul,' and another, 'I belong to Apollos,' are you not merely human? What then is Apollos? What is Paul? . . . We are God's servants, working together; you are God's field, God's building" (1 Cor. 3:3-5, 9).

I want to urge each of us to seek out other pastors. They may be in your denomination or in your community. Seek them out and be a pastor to them. We, more than anyone, know what it is like to be lonely and cut off from others. Every pastor needs a pastor.

I suggest further that what repeatedly keeps us from connecting with other preachers is a sense of pride. It is our own pride that too frequently impedes our stretching out ourselves to others in common Christian compassion. We all need one another. Further, are we not working for the same Lord? Our model in dealing with other pastors sets a tone for our communities of faith. Our example also provides a blueprint for those who want to reach out to others. We all knew what Obadiah thought about those who stood idly by and watched their sisters and brothers in distress. May God help us release our vain pride and extend ourselves to other pastors who plant and water the good news alongside us. Amen. (David Mosser)

MAY 2, 2004

Fourth Sunday of Easter

Worship Theme: Jesus tells his followers that his sheep hear his voice. As our Good Shepherd, Jesus not only protects us but also leads us in right paths.

Readings: Acts 9:36-43; Revelation 7:9-17; John 10:22-30

Call to Worship (Psalm 23)

Leader: The LORD is my shepherd, I shall not want.

People: **He makes me lie down in green pastures; he leads me beside still waters; he restores my soul.**

Leader: He leads me in right paths for his name's sake.

People: **Even though I walk through the darkest valley, I fear no evil; for you are with me; your rod and your staff—they comfort me.**

Leader: You prepare a table before me in the presence of my enemies; you anoint my head with oil; my cup overflows.

People: **Surely goodness and mercy shall follow me all the days of my life, and I shall dwell in the house of the LORD my whole life long.**

Pastoral Prayer:
We pray to you, O God, in thanksgiving and gratitude for your sending us the Good Shepherd who watches over us. Like those of old, we too often feel like sheep that have been scattered, for

we have not regularly paid heed to the shepherd who gently leads us. Help us to awake, O God. Give us ears to hear his tender voice calling to us, a voice that leads us to abundant life. Give us the vision and discernment as people of your pasture to regard with deep faith and obedience the voice of our shepherd who calls to us with love and compassion. May we proclaim with the angels, elders, and the four living creatures who proclaim in worship,

> Blessing and glory and wisdom
> and thanksgiving and honor
> and power and might
> be to our God forever and ever! (Rev. 7:12)

Make us again your people, O God, a people who recognize the Word of the Lord. In the name of Jesus we pray. Amen. (David Mosser)

SERMON BRIEFS

WHAT WOULD JESUS SAY?

ACTS 9:36-43

The promise of the angel at the empty tomb—to the women and the disciples and even to Peter—was that the risen Christ would go "before [them] into Galilee" (Mark 16:7 KJV). Jesus is no longer bound by time and place, but will lead his disciples wherever they go, preparing their way, empowering their ministry. This morning, we can discern that Christ has gone before Peter even into Joppa.

She was called Tabitha in Aramaic, but in Greek, Dorcas. In either language she was a Gazelle, quick and graceful as she ran here and there doing God's work. How beautiful were the feet of this disciple, how beautiful the work of her hands, as she devoted herself to acts of charity among the believers and people of Joppa. The charity of her faith stayed at home.

The feet of Peter, too, have been swift and beautiful on the mountains north and west of Jerusalem, preaching good news "here and there among all" the sheep Christ had commanded that he tend (v. 32). The ministry of Peter's obedience carried him far from home.

Different as they are in many ways, Dorcas and Peter share faith in the one Lord and in the ministry at the summons of the one Lord. Together they will also experience the power of the risen Lord and unexpectedly so.

In Luke 9:1 (and parallels), Peter and the disciples had received Jesus' commission, had been given power and authority not only to preach but also "over all demons, and to cure diseases" (Luke 9:1). Near the end of that same chapter, however, they are unable to demonstrate that authority. They prove themselves powerless against the demon in the boy whose father had brought him to the base of the Mount of Transfiguration.

In Mark's account, by the time Jesus comes down the mountain the man has seen so much of the disciples' inabilities that he doubts Jesus' abilities (Mark 9:22). Jesus barks at the man and the disciples, and at the demon too as he heals the boy. Later, the disciples ask Jesus why they had failed. After all, Jesus commissioned them. The were empowered, but they had failed to pray.

Peter will not make that same mistake in Joppa.

When Peter got to Dorcas's house, her friends had washed her body and laid it out in an upper room. Peter put everyone outside, knelt beside the bed, and prayed. We might well wonder what went through his mind, what prayer he prayed from his heart. Something like this, maybe: "Jesus, I wish you were still here. You would know what to say and do. Like that time in Bethany. Like that other time, at Jairus's house. What would you do now, if you were here at Dorcas's house? What would you say? Jesus, what would you have me say?"

If Peter prayed such a prayer as that, perhaps the answer came at least in part as a memory. When Jesus had gone to the house of Jairus, his daughter was already dead. But Jesus said, "Talitha cumi" ("Little girl, get up.") Perhaps Peter heard the Spirit prompting almost exactly those same words from him: "Tabitha, get up." Arise, for Jesus is risen. And she did.

I wonder how Peter felt. All this time had elapsed since the original commission, and Peter had suffered several failures. But now he knew that he indeed had the authority—not of his own power and not without prayer—to be a channel of the risen Lord's once and continuing ministry in the world. Peter knows that Christ is not bound by time and place. Jesus goes before disciples into all the places of their prayer and service. (Thomas Steagald)

THE END OF THE STORY

REVELATION 7:9-17

In the old movie *Quo Vadis*, lions threatened Deborah Kerr as she was lashed to a stake in the Colosseum. Someone asked her, "Weren't you scared?" She replied, "No. I had read the script, and I knew that the hero would come and rescue me."

She was not afraid because she knew the end of the story. In this Scripture, John provides readers a glimpse of the end of the Christian story.

A multitude of people gathered before the throne and the lamb. You could not count their number. The assembly was cosmopolitan; all people were included. They wore white robes and held palm branches, symbols of victory. They cried out praise to God for being their salvation, the one who brought them through their travail. The angels and elders and four living creatures fell down and joined in the worship, adding their "amen."

Their praise was for the greatness of God. Listen to what they ascribed to God! Glory—God was a majestic God. Wisdom—God was the source of all knowledge. Thanksgiving—God provided for them. Honor—God was worthy of it. Power—God would accomplish the purposes of the kingdom. Strength—God provided power to get people through everything.

John was visualizing the end times. He knew the end would be terrifying, just as the persecution then was for them. But John felt that God would not be defeated and would deliver the faithful. Victory, triumph, life—that was what the worship celebration was about.

It is to be hoped that this picture of praise to God for salvation is repeated every Sunday as we gather for worship. Worship reminds us of God's ultimate victory for us and an end of the divine-human story.

This passage ends with four verses that celebrate what God would do for believers.

Verse 14 is the promise that the martyrs for Christ would find victory. Those who trusted Christ whatever the cost would find themselves purified from sin ("washed their robes") and cleansed by Christ's death and resurrection (the "blood of the lamb"). God would not desert them, but justify them. They would stand before the throne of God.

Verse 15 describes the truth that there would be no barriers between God and the people. They would enter into the very presence of God, and God's presence would shelter them. It would be like the "Shekinah" presence of God in the temple, but this time, there would be no veil to keep them from the Holy of Holies.

Verse 16 refers to the promise that God would satisfy all their needs—no hunger, no thirst, no hot sun to scorch them. Maybe they remembered the wilderness days, or days as slaves, when they went hungry and thirsty and fainted from the heat of the day. No more! God would meet their needs.

Verse 17 promises the lamb would be their shepherd, meeting their spiritual need for the water of life. Also, God would get involved, coming to wipe tears from their eyes. They would be comforted.

What a promise for us! If we trust God, God will care for us, provide for us, and lead us to victory. This passage means that when we face injustice, or suffering, or death, we can go on in faith and triumph. Why? We know the end of the story. Justice triumphs, good prevails, right overcomes wrong, and life defeats death. That is the end of the story. (Hugh Litchfield)

THE GIFT OF SEEING AND BELIEVING

JOHN 10:22-30

In Hans Cristian Andersen's tale, "The Emperor's New Clothes," the emperor is vain and obsessed with new clothes.

Two scheming tailors took advantage of this and pretended to make a special cloth that could only be seen by persons worthy of their calling. Of course, this meant the emperor himself could not see the cloth. Reluctant as he was to admit he wasn't worthy of his calling, he pretended to see the garments. When the clothes were finished, the emperor modeled them for all the people. He thought he would know those who were capable of their jobs and worthy of being his servants. But, surprisingly, all commented on the beauty of the garments and the delicacy of the fabric. Suddenly, a small child's voice was heard above all the others, "The emperor has no clothes. The emperor has no clothes." And you know the rest of the story.

In the story from John about Jesus, the leaders of the Jewish hierarchy don't cry out, "Jesus has no clothes," but they continue to question him, "Are you really the Messiah?" Jesus answers, as he has before, telling them to look at what he has done.

In the fairy tale, the tailors tricked the emperor, sending him out into the world in his underwear. They tricked him into believing he saw something that wasn't there. But in the story about Jesus and the Jewish leaders we see a much more common kind of trickery—the kind we often play on ourselves—the act of seeing something and not believing it is real.

How easy it is to see something right before our eyes and not believe it. How easy it is to have our judgment clouded by our prejudices or previous experiences, by the blinders we put on.

Someone is spontaneously healed and we thank the doctor, because we don't believe God does miracles today. We see a beautiful newborn baby, perfect in every way, but we believe it is somehow less worthy because the infant has an unwed mother. We see the vast diversity of species in the beauty of the flowers of the field, but we believe that God created everyone to think alike. We see, but we don't believe, because we have already made up our minds. We see, but we don't believe, because what we see threatens the very foundations of our world, our carefully thought out notions of what is right and good and proper.

The Jewish leaders wore the blinders of the their traditions, of the law and all its regulations. They had seen Jesus heal, teach, comfort, provide, and interpret. But, they also had a picture in their minds of the Messiah, and Jesus simply didn't fit their picture. So when Jesus told them to look at what he had done, they found it easy to dismiss Jesus' actions and focus on what they thought he had said.

I am reminded of a story of a couple in counseling. The husband began, "She said . . ." And the wife continued, "He said . . ." The session went back and forth between them until the counselor interrupted, "Let's change the subject. Tell me what your spouse does for you that you enjoy." The husband and wife began to list the things each did for the other. "She rubs my back." "He does the dishes." "She irons my good shirts." "He mows the lawn." "She sends me cute cards for my birthday." "He sends me flowers for Valentine's day." After several minutes, the counselor said, "Let's talk a bit about the problem that brought you to counseling." The husband began, "She said . . . ," and the wife continued, "He said . . . !" "Wait, stop," said the counselor. "Remember what you've done for each other." "I don't care what she's done, I told you she said . . ." The couple overlooked the gifts they gave to each other.

Jesus tells the Jewish leaders that those who believe receive a special gift, the gift of eternal life. The leaders, in their insistence on arguing their points, had missed the gift God wanted to give them through Jesus. May we be like the little child in the emperor's crowd. May we see what God does among us and share what we believe. (Sharee Johnson)

MAY 9, 2004

Fifth Sunday of Easter

Worship Theme: God's way of reconstituting the divinely created world is through the agency of love. The spirit of love not only allows the Jerusalem church to hear Peter's testimony but also is the guiding principle of our common life as believers.

Readings: Acts 11:1-18; Revelation 21:1-6; John 13:31-35

Call to Worship (Psalm 148:1-2, 7, 9-13, 14d)

> *Leader:*   Praise the LORD! Praise the LORD from the heavens; praise him in the heights!
>
> *People:*   **Praise him, all his angels; praise him, all his host!**
>
> *Leader:*   Praise the LORD from the earth . . .
>
> *People:*   **Mountains and all hills, fruit trees and all cedars! Wild animals and all cattle, creeping things and flying birds!**
>
> *Leader:*   Kings of the earth and all peoples, princes and all rulers of the earth! Young men and women alike, old and young together!
>
> *People:*   **Let them praise the name of the LORD, for his name alone is exalted; his glory is above earth and heaven.**
>
> *All:*   **Praise the LORD!**

Pastoral Prayer:

O God, as you promised your people through the word of the prophet, you are indeed offering your people a new thing. You have revealed your new heaven and new earth in the life, death, and resurrection of Jesus, our Messiah and Savior. Reveal to us that the former things have passed away. We now stand in a brand new world wrought by your loving-kindness disclosed in Jesus. Create within each of us, O Lord, the new spirit that allows us to live in love and charity with our brothers and sisters. Give us a loving spirit as we reach out to others in Jesus' name. Help us regard the estate of the last, the lost, and the least of these. May we bear the glad tiding of peace for all God's creatures as we witness to the power of your love. During this season of Easter, we pray that you, O God, resurrect our lives to the new vision of creation that only you and you alone can provide. We pray this in the spirit of the one who gives us life in abundance, Jesus Christ. Amen. (David Mosser)

SERMON BRIEFS

RUBBING SHOULDERS WITH THE WRONG PEOPLE

ACTS 11:1-18

Soon after Peter returned from his visit with Cornelius, a disturbing report reached Jerusalem that Peter ate with the uncircumcised. Peter's decision to eat with the uncircumcised was more disturbing than Philip's baptism of the Ethiopian eunuch, perhaps because the Ethiopian returned to his homeland. While verse 2 says that Peter went to Jerusalem, it is entirely possible that the apostles and brethren in Judea summoned Peter to explain his irresponsible and reckless conduct. It is clear that Peter fully understood that the Jerusalem authorities would ask him to explain why he chose to violate Jewish custom.

Peter took a courageous stand before the Jerusalem council. He argued that the uncircumcised received the Holy Spirit, and their salvation was God's work. Peter made it quite clear that at no point was this result of his own initiative. Peter, rather, only acted as God directed him. To deny the validity of Cornelius's conversion would result in opposing God and hindering the propagation of the gospel.

Peter wasn't the first person criticized for rubbing shoulders with the wrong people. The scribes and religious authorities criticized Jesus Christ for the same crime. Jesus loved us to make us lovers of people. Our essential agenda is to love him by loving others. No matter who they are or what they have done, we never exclude people from the possibility of God's grace. The mission and ministry of the church must never be based on an inclination toward "our kind of people."

In *The Kingdom of God Is a Party*, Anthony Campolo tells one of my favorite stories. On one of his trips from the East Coast to Hawaii, he tells of the time when he found himself awake long before dawn because of the time difference. Rather than try to force himself to go back to sleep, he got dressed and wandered up and down the streets of Honolulu looking for a place to eat breakfast.

He found a little place on a side street, walked in, and sat down on one of the stools at the counter. Everything he touched, including the menu, felt sticky with grease. When the guy behind the counter came over and asked, "What do you want?" Tony Campolo ordered a cup of coffee and a doughnut.

As he sat there munching on his doughnut and sipping his coffee at 3:30 in the morning, the door of the diner swung open. Much to his dismay and discomfort, in marched eight or nine provocative and loud prostitutes. It was a small diner so they sat on both sides of him. Their talk was loud and crude. Tony felt completely out of place and was just about to make a quick getaway when he overheard one of the women say, "Tomorrow's my birthday. I'm going to be thirty-nine."

One of her friends snapped back, "So what! What do you want me to do? Throw you a birthday party?" The woman replied, "Come on, why do you have to be so mean? I was just telling you it was my birthday. I don't want anything from you. Why should you give me a birthday party? I've never had a birthday party in my whole life."

As soon as he heard that, Tony made his decision. He waited until the women had left then he called over the guy behind the counter and asked, "Do they come in here every night?" "Yeah," he answered. Tony went on to say, "I overheard the one named Agnes say that tomorrow is her birthday. What do you think about us throwing her a birthday party for her, right here, tomorrow night?"

A smiled crossed over the man's chubby cheeks. He called out to his wife and told her about the plan.

At 2:30 the next morning, Tony Campolo was back at the diner. They decorated the diner from one end to the other with crepe paper and made a big sign out of cardboard that read "Happy Birthday, Agnes!" Evidently word had gotten out, and by 3:15 A.M. the place was packed.

Promptly at 3:30 A.M., the door of the diner swung open and in walked Agnes and her friend. Everybody was ready and screamed, "Happy Birthday!" Agnes was stunned and shaken. Her mouth fell open. Her legs seemed to buckle a bit. One of her friends grabbed her arm to steady her and led her to one of the stools at the counter as the crowd sang "Happy Birthday" to her. Her eyes moistened, then, when the birthday cake with thirty-nine lit candles was carried out, Agnes totally lost it and sobbed like a child.

When the party finally came to a close and Agnes walked out the door, there was a stunned silence in the diner. Not knowing what else to do, Tony Campolo broke the silence by saying, "What do you say we pray for Agnes?" He prayed that night for Agnes. He prayed for her salvation. He prayed that her life would be changed and that God would be good to her. When he finished, the guy leaned over the counter and said, "Hey! You never told me you were a preacher. What kind of church do you belong to?"

In one of those rare moments when just the right words came, Tony Campolo answered, "I belong to a church that throws birthday parties for prostitutes at 3:30 in the morning." The guy waited a moment and then he almost sneered as he replied, "No you don't. There's no church like that. If there was, I'd join it. I'd join a church like that!" (Bob Buchanan)

SEPARATED NO MORE!

REVELATION 21:1-6

At every graveside service, I read these verses. For me, they are strong words of comfort, giving a beautiful picture of the believer's future. John saw a "new heaven and a new earth"—not a replica of the old, nor a remake of the old. This was an entirely new creation of God. God would give the faithful a new place to dwell.

There will be no more sea. This is a key phrase. These ancients perceived the sea often as an enemy—mysterious, full of the unknown. They feared it; many would sail out into the sea, never to return. However, the most powerful idea the sea symbolized was that of separation. The sea cut them off from lands and nations and other people. John, from his island exile, would look out at a sea that separated him from his loved ones. So the vision: one day, no more sea. No more separation, especially from God. This passage highlights a new and deeper relationship with God.

John likens the believer's relationship with God to a "bride adorned for her husband" (v. 2). This is the most personal and intimate relationship we have, that of marriage. Marriage is based on total commitment to one another, which enables the "two to become one." That was the kind of relationship that God initially envisioned. God was totally committed to dwell among God's people.

God came to dwell with them. The idea was that God came to "tent" with them, to be where the people were all the time. All that they struggled against, God would take away. God would wipe away the tears from their eyes. No longer would believers suffer and mourn. Death would be no more. What good news this must have been! John's congregation faced so much persecution, which in turn, brought suffering and mourning and death. But God would remove it. To emphasize this, for only the second time in the book of Revelation, God personally speaks, "I am the Alpha and the Omega, the beginning and the end" (v. 6). God was the start of all things, the end of all things, the source of all things. God said that these words were "trustworthy and true." They could bet their lives on them (as most of them did). God was serious about this relationship.

What a word of hope! We, too, struggle still with too many tears, too much suffering, too much death. There are times when it feels that God is so far away, unaware of what we are going through. A father, whose daughter had died suddenly, said, "I can find God nowhere." He felt separated from God.

While it may sometimes seem like that, it isn't so. As this passage emphasizes, God comes to dwell with us, to stand by us, to comfort us, and ultimately, to bring us through the pain and suffering to joy and life. This is the divine promise.

We introduced my three-year-old granddaughter to the Atlantic Ocean last summer. As she stood there on the beach and looked at it and heard the roar of the crashing waves, we could tell by the look on her face that the ocean frightened her. Despite that, she went into the water. Why? The two people she trusted more than anyone—her parents—each took a hand and walked with her into the water. She trusted them and overcame her fear of the sea.

God comes and takes our hands and walks with us into the water. We can go on because we are separated no more! (Hugh Litchfield)

LITTLE CHILDREN

JOHN 13:31-35

On the occasions when I leave my children at home with a baby-sitter, I often must face their tears, objections, and questions: "Where are you going? Can I come? When will you be back? I don't want you to go!" I tell them where I am going, that I will come back soon, that the baby-sitter will take care of them, and that they will be fine. Since I have three children and the opportunities for fights and arguments is a live issue, I get in this word before I head out the door: "Be good! Play nicely with each other, ok?"

The Christian life is something like being a little child whose mother leaves for a little while. We live in that "little while" between the time of Jesus' death and resurrection and the time when Jesus will come again. We often feel uncertain about God's presence in our lives and what we are supposed to do in the meantime. Jesus knew this. Calling the disciples his "little children," Jesus prepares them for his leaving. He tells them two things: where and why he is going, and how they are to behave while he is gone.

Jesus tells his disciples that he departs in order to do his work. No, they can't go with him, for this work is uniquely his, motivated by love for God and his children. Jesus' work consists of suffering and dying on the cross, and in so doing he will glorify God, and God will glorify him. It does not sound like much in the way of glory to our ears. Yet this is Jesus' way, not of worldly glory, but of willing self-offering for the sake of the children he loves.

This brings Jesus to his second point: "I give you a new commandment, that you love one another. Just as I have loved you, you also should love one another. By this everyone will know that you are my disciples" (vv. 34-35). Jesus' love that brought him to the cross and the Father's love that glorifies the Son brings about a new way of life for the children who are left behind, one marked exclusively by love. I plead with my children, "While I'm gone, please be kind to each other!" And I mean starting now, because I'm leaving now! Just so, Jesus is telling us that he expects us to practice real love for each other now, the kind of love he poured out for us on the cross.

How hard a commandment is this? It comes easily sometimes, but more often loving one another is very hard: when we disagree, when we are angry, when we do not want to share, when we are jealous, when we have been hurt. Yet that's the word to us children who live in this time of "a little while." Love is our work while our parent is gone. Thank goodness God gives us the Holy Spirit as our "baby-sitter": to comfort us, to remind us, to help us, to forgive us. The Spirit is working now to rebirth us into children who practice Jesus' example of loving one another and who demonstrate to the world the love of God.

Jesus leaves us for a little while, but promises to return and take us with him. Until then, little children, love each other as Jesus has so loved us. (Laura Jernigan)

MAY 16, 2004

Sixth Sunday of Easter

Worship Theme: God not only calls believers to share the good news but also calms our fears. God does not give to God's people as the world gives. Rather God gives in God's own unique way—through love and compassion.

Readings: Acts 16:9-15; Revelation 21:10, 22–22:5; John 14:23-29

Call to Worship (Psalm 67)

Leader: May God be gracious to us and bless us and make his face to shine upon us, that your way may be known upon earth, your saving power among all nations.

People: **Let the peoples praise you, O God; let all the peoples praise you.**

Leader: Let the nations be glad and sing for joy, for you judge the peoples with equity and guide the nations upon earth.

People: **Let the peoples praise you, O God; let all the peoples praise you.**

Leader: The earth has yielded its increase; God, our God, has blessed us.

People: **May God continue to bless us; let all the ends of the earth revere him.**

Pastoral Prayer:
   O God of Peace, grant us in this hour a sense of the tranquility that is your will for all people. Paul wrote, "I have learned to be

content with whatever I have" (Phil. 4:11). Let this faithful attitude bubble up within us so that we too might learn godly contentment. Each day material things bombard our lives. They
promise to provide meaning and value. Yet, O God, your church
is the one place where we can find true consequence and significance for the life you give us to manage as stewards. Remind us
that it is not in possessions or knowledge that authentic life
comes to us. Rather it is within the web of significant loving and
caring relationships that we find our genuine calling and worth.
Make us people who instinctively reach out to others in Jesus'
name. Let us be the bearers of food, clothing, and presence that
help those who have little hope of finding their way in the world.
Make us people who not only share of our abundance but also
speak the good news of the gospel with those to whom we also
minister. Grant us the joy of discipleship in Jesus' holy name we
pray. Amen. (David Mosser)

SERMON BRIEFS

WHEN NO ALSO MEANS YES!

ACTS 16:9-15

There is an old Celtic benediction that contains the words,
"And may the wind always be at your back." As Paul and his missionary colleagues embark on their second missionary journey,
they set sail with a clear and decisive call from the Lord. Luke
writes that they made a "direct voyage" (v. 11 RSV). Paul used a
Greek nautical term for sailing in front of the wind, of having a
following sea press a vessel on through the sea. The wind, and
more than that, the Holy Spirit, pushed the early church on to
the next phase of God's strategy for growing the kingdom.

The apostle Paul's next step of strategy for introducing the
gospel to Europe and reaching the Gentile world included a
trip to the province of Bithynia. However, according to Acts
16:7, the Holy Spirit did not permit Paul and his companions to
go there.

Luke doesn't tell us why Paul didn't go to the area where he had hoped to go. Some suggest Paul became ill. Others suggest that Paul learned that the Judaizers waited to disrupt his preaching there. Others believe Paul might have had another Damascus road experience that convinced him simply to do otherwise. Centuries before Paul, the writer of Proverbs advised,

> Trust in the LORD with all your heart,
> and do not rely on your own insight.
> In all your ways acknowledge him,
> and he will make straight your paths. (Prov. 3:5-6)

MPC | HIC   04|07

Talking about trusting God is easier than actually trusting God. At a big camp meeting, a young man was asked to preach right before the Sunday morning service began. Hundreds of people were in attendance, but the main speaker had not shown up. So they asked the young minister to preach. Scared half to death, he went to the bishop's tent and asked, "What shall I do, Bishop? They've asked me to preach, but I don't have any sermon." The bishop replied, "Just trust the Lord, young man. Just trust the Lord."

After leaving the tent, the young man picked up the bishop's Bible and turned through its pages hoping to find an inspiring passage. Instead, he found a few typewritten sermon notes he really liked. So taking the bishop's Bible and the notes he walked into the service.

The young man amazed everyone and the people crowded around him after the service. Everyone was impressed except the bishop. He stormed up to the young man and thundered, "Young man, you preached my sermon that I was going to preach tonight. Now what I am going to do?" With a smile on his face, the young man said, "Just trust the Lord, Bishop, just trust the Lord."

For the apostle Paul, a no from the Lord about going to Asia meant that a new and greater yes was about to be revealed. Whenever God closes one door, God always opens another. Paul remained open and flexible to the leadership of the Holy Spirit. The Holy Spirit also went ahead of Paul and prepared the heart of a prominent businessperson named Lydia to receive Paul's preaching and teaching. She became the first convert in Macedonia. Paul baptized her, along with her entire family. (Bob Buchanan)

A GLIMPSE OF HEAVEN

REVELATION 21:10, 22–22:5

The most troublesome question on my ordination council was, What did I think heaven was like? I answered by saying that I really didn't know for sure, but it had to be magnificent because God was there. Some of the council wanted me to use phrases like "pearly gates" and "streets of gold" in a literal sense. I felt that such language was symbolic and far too restrictive to describe the ultimate nature of heaven. While not completely agreeing with my assessment, they let me pass the examination.

In this passage, John attempts to describe what heaven—this city of God—is like. It is an amazing description. At least six truths are given.

First, God's presence fills heaven. In his vision, John sees no temple. They didn't need one, for God is the temple. God's presence floods the place. As the temple symbolized the presence of God among the people, so God dwells with them. There is no sun or moon, for the glory of God is the light. Whatever else heaven is, it is the place where God dwells, and that makes it overwhelming.

Second, the redeemed share heaven. Those whose names are written in the lamb's book of life will be there. John mentions that the "nations" and "kings of the earth" will bring glory to God. Some interpreters feel that this is a reference to the Gentiles, that God's grace covers all. The gates of heaven will never be shut and anyone may enter. Who will be in heaven? This vision indicates that all who trust in what God has done in Christ will be there. God's name will be on their foreheads (22:4). The redeemed will share heaven.

Third, evil is gone. Where God dwells, evil cannot dwell. Nothing "unclean" will be there, nor anyone who practices evil. "Nothing accursed will be found" (22:3). There will be no "night" there. Night often symbolized evil. In the past, bad deeds often occurred under the cover of darkness, but no more. Throughout the book, John writes about the triumph of God over suffering and pain and death. They feared those then; we fear them now. But in heaven, they will be no more.

Fourth, God meets our needs. A river of water of life flowed from the throne of God through the middle of the city. Water was a precious commodity and if you didn't have it, you died. In God's city, water flows abundantly. On either side of the river are the trees of life, with twelve kinds of fruit, producing every month. God's provisions are plentiful. We won't have any unmet needs in heaven. We get the abundant, eternal life we want.

Fifth, we offer worship in heaven. Worship is a part of heaven. The servants surround the throne, offering their worship to God. They will see God's face. God's name will be on their foreheads. Is this not a reason to worship? God has made them children of the kingdom. Somewhere I read that a former slave preacher, John Jasper, said that when he got to heaven, he wanted to spend the first 10,000 years there just praising the Lord, because the Lord was the one who got him in. So should we all.

Sixth, we offer our service in heaven. "They will reign forever and ever" (v. 5). While the reign of the millennium was for one thousand years, the time in heaven will have no such limit. They will serve God forever. God will bless them forever. The bliss of heaven will be forever. The "we" consists of the communion of all saints.

After forty-five years of ministry, I still can't say exactly what heaven is like. However, as the language of this passage indicates, heaven will be magnificent, because God is there. (Hugh Litchfield)

AT HOME WITH US

JOHN 14:23-29

"My Shepherd Will Supply My Need" by Isaac Watts is a beautiful hymn based on the 23rd Psalm. The last stanza interprets verse 6 ("and I shall dwell in the house of the Lord forever") in this way: "No more a stranger, nor a guest, / But like a child at home." For a child in a healthy family, home is where you can be yourself, kick your shoes off, let a caring parent attend to you, play and relax, even express sadness and anger in a safe environment. We all need a valued place in a family and to know that we are truly loved. "Like a child at home"—what a wonderful image of communion with God.

The lesson from John's Gospel evokes such an image. Home and family are what Jesus promises: "I will not leave you orphaned; I am coming to you" (v. 18). And, "we will come to them and make our home with them" (v. 23). Jesus promises the disciples that he will not abandon nor leave them, but actually come and live with them. There will be closeness in this home, for Jesus also promises: "On that day you will know that I am in my Father, and you in me, and I in you" (v. 20). There will be great love in this family: "those who love me will be loved by my Father, and I will love them." Christ living at home with me, dwelling in me, loving me. What a wonderful image of communion with God.

On this sixth Sunday of Eastertide, on the verge of Pentecost, we need such an image to become real and working in our lives. The Easter stories of Jesus rising from the dead and appearing to the disciples derive their power only when we open our minds to the possibility that Christ now lives in our hearts. Easter continues when Jesus comes to the believer, creating true communion with the one God, and making a true home for us right here on earth in our everyday existence. Easter moves naturally into Pentecost, for Jesus also promises that God will send the Spirit, the Advocate to dwell with us as well, who will comfort and teach us and bring us peace. We are embraced and loved and spiritually equipped. The good news of this Sunday of Eastertide is that we have the company of a good Parent, a devoted Brother, and a strong Helper living within us to help, to encourage, to guide, to correct, to forgive, to love.

What would it be like to start each day with an image of Jesus coming to us and making his home with us? It could make a big difference in the way in which we think and act, in the way we feel about ourselves and respond to the people around us. If I could remember that Christ has not left me an orphan but adopts me into the family of God, then I would consider myself a worthy and beautiful child of God. If I could focus on how Christ knocks on the door to my home and asks to be involved intimately in my life, then I would be more aware of the path that Christ wants to walk with me in the world. If I would pause occasionally and consider that the Spirit of the Living God is living inside me, then I would open up conversations and discern what the Spirit is saying to me. My spiritual home would flourish and overflow with love for the other children of God.

Jesus promises: "We will come and make our home with you." Come into our hearts today, we pray. Amen. (Laura Jernigan)

MAY 23, 2004

Seventh Sunday of Easter

Worship Theme: Love is the theme that binds all believers to God in Jesus Christ. When we display love for others we act in concert with God's regard for God's created order. In fact, out of love alone did God send us our Messiah, Jesus Christ.

Readings: Acts 16:16-34; Revelation 22:12-14, 16-17, 20-21; John 17:20-26

Call to Worship (Psalm 97:1, 5-9, 12)

Leader: The LORD is king! Let the earth rejoice; let the many coastlands be glad!

People: **The mountains melt like wax before the LORD, before the Lord of all the earth.**

Leader: The heavens proclaim his righteousness; and all the peoples behold his glory.

People: **All worshipers of images are put to shame, those who make their boast in worthless idols; all gods bow down before him.**

Leader: Zion hears and is glad, and the towns of Judah rejoice, because of your judgments, O God.

People: **For you, O LORD, are most high over all the earth; you are exalted far above all gods.**

All: **Rejoice in the LORD, O you righteous, and give thanks to his holy name!**

Pastoral Prayer:

O God of Love and Fidelity, remind each of us that it is out of your heavenly love that you created us in your divine image. Since you, O God, are a God of love then you created us for love too. As we consider your handiwork, worshiping and praising your holy name, let us also consider our relationship to your created order. Give us a will and passion to extend your love and concern to the sisters and brothers with whom we dwell. Give us that fervent spirit to be your hands and feet in the world. Help us recognize the diverse opportunities you place in our path to speak a good word on behalf of our Lord and Savior, Jesus Christ. As Jesus practiced holy hospitality toward others, let Jesus be our model for our relations with others. May our acts of charity help heal the hurts that the world inflicts upon the discouraged. Let us be companions with those who have lost their way and guide them toward your paths of righteousness. We pray this in Jesus' name. Amen. (David Mosser)

SERMON BRIEFS

LIFE'S MOST IMPORTANT QUESTION

ACTS 16:16-34

Brian Harbour tells the story of visiting a lady who had made some contact with his church through a "Mother's Day Out" ministry. He had visited with her only a few minutes when her husband came home from work. As he walked into the room, she said, "Honey, this is the pastor from Woodland Hills Church. He came to talk to you about God." Then she left! After a few awkward moments, it was as if a dam broke and all of the desires, needs, and hurts of his soul came gushing out. For over an hour, he talked about his needs, emptiness, hunger, and fears. When he had talked himself out, Brian shared with him how Christ could meet his need. That afternoon, the man knelt in his living room and gave his life to Jesus Christ. Later, just as Brian was leaving the man's house, he said, "Preacher, I have been waiting five years for someone to help me get straightened out with God."

The scene in the Philippian jail was different than one might expect. Paul and Silas were cold, uncomfortable, and shackled with chains. You might expect them to be depressed, but instead they sang. Initially, the Philippian jailer was the one in charge. Yet, near the end of the story, we hear the jailer ask the prisoners what he should do. In verse 30, he asks life's most important question: "What must I do to be saved?"

It is a pressing question because no one escapes answering it. Soon or later we have to face it. It is a personal question that only we can answer. It is also a practical question. We don't wake one morning and discover that we are now Christians. We don't go to the church our entire life and automatically become a Christian. We don't become a Christian by being born into a Christian family.

We must do something, and that something is stated in Acts 16:31. "Believe on the Lord Jesus." Believing involves more than intellectual assent. It involves the mind and emotions and leads to a public profession of faith.

The conversion of the Philippian jailer demonstrates that the experience of salvation includes two steps. The first step involves recognizing our need for salvation. You and I need salvation because the Bible declares that we are all sinners (Rom. 3:23). You and I need salvation because sin alienates and separates us from God (Rom. 6:23). You and I need salvation because that is the only way that God can take care of sin. The second step involves realizing that Jesus Christ can meet our need for salvation. You and I can receive the gift of salvation through repentance and belief. To repent means more than just being sorry for our sins. It means to turn away from our sins. To believe means to turn to God and trust God to do what only God can do.

During World War II, Helmut Thielicke was a pastor in Stuttgart, Germany. Allied bombing virtually destroyed the city. One morning Thielicke stood in combat boots and military fatigues before a gaping hole. It was a cellar that had sustained a direct hit from a bomb during the previous night where approximately twenty people sought shelter. A woman approached Thielicke and asked, "Are you Pastor Thielicke?" When he replied, "Yes," she said, "My husband was down there last night. All they found of him was his cap. We heard you preach many

times. I want to thank you for getting him ready for eternity."
How will you answer life's most important question? (Bob
Buchanan)

EPILOGUE: THE SUM OF IT ALL

REVELATION 22:12-14, 16-17, 20-21

In these last few verses, John seemed to give a recap of the
message and hope of Revelation. In fact, Jesus offers a magnificent promise. Jesus says that he is coming soon, bringing a
reward, to repay others according to their work. Those who had
been faithful would be granted entrance into the eternal city of
God.

One of the beatitudes in Revelation saying, "Blessed are those
who wash their robes," refers to the martyrs who shed their blood
for the faith (v. 14). They will enter the gate of the city and enjoy
the tree of life, the fruits of eternal life. Note that they "washed"
their robes. They participated in the work. While Christ saved
them, they needed to trust salvation by faith. Christ promises the
eternal kingdom of God to the faithful.

Jesus gives not only a promise but also an affirmation. Jesus,
who came to give John this testimony at the beginning of the
book, returns at the end to underscore the trustworthiness of
the message. Jesus identifies himself as from the root and the
descendent of David (Rev. 3:7; 5:5). Jesus is the bright morning
star. To the church at Thyatira, he would give the morning star, a
symbol of the dawn of a new age and of immortality (2:28). Here
Jesus identifies himself as that morning star. He was the new age.
Jesus affirms that what John wrote was true.

Beyond promise and assurance, Jesus also issues an invitation.
The Spirit [probably Christ] and the bride [the churches] say,
"Come" (v. 17a). This was an invitation to the martyrs. Also, whoever hears should say, "Come." This is a call to witness to Christ.
What a person experiences of Christ must be passed along. Also,
anyone who wishes could come and take the water of life as a
gift.

It was not too late. Maybe someone who heard this message

might need to accept Christ. Jesus offers an invitation. That offer is still available now.

In addition to the above, Jesus furnishes hope. In the end, Jesus says, "I am coming soon." To that, John writes, "Amen." John looked for that coming at any moment. John wanted the persecution and the suffering to end. John lived with that hope.

With that same kind of hope, we can now look forward to Christ's coming. It might be today, or tomorrow, or in thousands of years. But then, it could be at any moment. Do we want it to happen? Can we say "Amen" to that?

In the end, John gives a blessing. He leaves the saints with "The grace of the Lord Jesus." What better blessing to give than to remind believers to trust God's grace. For no matter what they faced—or what we face—God's grace is sufficient. God would get them through, to the end, and beyond.

So, what is the sum of it all? For me, it is symbolized by a seminary student I knew. From early days, she lived with cystic fibrosis, but was determined not to let that keep her from living. And live she did! Finally, her lungs failed and she underwent a double lung transplant. She survived it, finished seminary, got married, and started preaching. After about three years, these new lungs failed. On the day she died, she encouraged her family to let her go, for she was ready. She also told them she wanted me to preach her funeral. She gave me a text and a thesis. The text was Lamentations 3:22-24. The thesis: "Great is thy faithfulness." She never doubted that. Her funeral was a true celebration of that faith.

This is the sum of it all. God is, and always will be, faithful to us. (Hugh Litchfield)

THE 80% RULE

JOHN 17:20-26

A skeptic once told me, "I like Jesus. It is Christians that I can't stand. I despise the way they take cheap shots at one another. Rather than helping one another, they actually hinder one another's work. They treat those who do not bear their sectarian brand name as enemies who are bound for hell."

I caught my skeptic friend by replying, "I agree with you. If that is Christianity, I'm not interested either. But that is not real Christianity!"

But, I know where he was coming from, don't you? I'm embarrassed at how Protestants and Catholics kill each other in Northern Ireland. I grieve over the disunity and hostility between Protestants, Catholics, and Orthodox Christians around the world. If you do not believe that the problem my skeptic friend talked about is real, visit the famous churches built over holy shrines in Israel. The competing denominational groups cannot even agree enough to keep the buildings in repair!

Jesus was not the least bit sectarian. John reported to Jesus that he had found people performing miracles using Jesus' name. These people were not part of their group and so John stopped their ministry. Jesus reprimanded John and said, "He who is not against us is on our side" (Mark 9:40 NEB). That should be our attitude toward others who claim the name of Jesus.

Jesus prayed for his church to be "one" so that the world would believe that Jesus is God's gift to the world. The truth is that the disunity of the church always confuses the world.

Can you imagine what a powerful witness it would make for Jesus if the two billion people in our world who claim to be his followers would look past their differences and disagreements and love each other and work together? Wow! Protestants, Catholics, and Orthodox churches agree on virtually 95 percent of the gospel's essentials. We disagree about marginal issues like form, style, organization, and doctrine—nonessential to salvation. So, why can't we just get along?

Many years ago a crop duster taught me an important principle. He said that any crop duster who consistently tried to spray more than 80 percent of the fields he contracted to dust, would sooner or later get his plane caught up in a power line and die. From him I adopted what I call "the 80% rule." If I can go along with 80% of what is being said or done, whether it is in my home, at church, or in my neighborhood, I'm okay. I can live and let live. It is only when I start to agree with less than 80% of what is being said or done that I begin to have problems. I commend to you the 80% rule.

Trust me, your agreement with your Protestant, Catholic, and

Orthodox fellow believers runs well over 80% when it comes to the essentials of Christianity! So look for ways to build bridges not walls. Let's not be guilty of name calling, characterizing, or belittling. Overlook your differences and cooperate with one another. When you ride by another church, pray for its people. When you read or hear about another denomination being in crisis, refuse to pile on. Remember, Jesus prays for our unity that the world would believe that God sent him.

In 1749, John Wesley and a Roman Catholic man had a theological disagreement. In a letter to the man, Mr. Wesley established four rules that he proposed might guide their relationship. Wesley wrote they should resolve not to hurt one another, to speak only good of one another, to harbor no unkind thoughts toward one another, and to help one another in every way that they could.

They agreed to disagree about theology, but they resolved to love one another. (Jim Jackson)

MAY 30, 2004

Day of Pentecost

Worship Theme: The Spirit of God, the Holy Spirit, comes upon those gathered as disciples of Jesus. The Holy Spirit animates the community of faith and gives it power to become the new people of God. The arrival of the Holy Spirit once again confirms God's promise to God's people.

Readings: Acts 2:1-21; Romans 8:14-17; John 14:8-17 (25-27)

Call to Worship (Psalm 104:24, 27-30, 33-34, 35*b*)

Leader: O LORD, how manifold are your works! In wisdom you have made them all; the earth is full of your creatures.

People: **These all look to you to give them their food in due season; when you give to them, they gather it up; when you open your hand, they are filled with good things.**

Leader: When you hide your face, they are dismayed; when you take away their breath, they die and return to their dust.

People: **When you send forth your spirit, they are created; and you renew the face of the ground.**

Leader: I will sing to the LORD as long as I live; I will sing praise to my God while I have being.

People: **May my meditation be pleasing to him, for I rejoice in the LORD.**

All: **Bless the LORD, O my soul. Praise the LORD!**

Pastoral Prayer:

Like those souls on that first day of Christian Pentecost, O Lord, we gather as an all-too-often frightened people awaiting a sign or a word from you. Help us face our uncertain future with the certainty of your promise fulfilled in Jesus Christ. Send to us the assurance of your covenant relationship with us through the agency of the Holy Spirit. Let the Spirit speak to our minds and hearts that great, divine pledge of old. As we live in the shadow of your love, O God, allow us to receive the compassion of Jesus in the deepest core of our character. Make us a people who practice the love of Christ as we minister to others in Jesus' holy name. Let the Spirit continue to breathe into our lives a vision of a better world—the world you created in your divine imagination and by your word. Forgive us where we have suffered failure of nerve. Give us instead a spirit of willingness to serve in newness of dynamic Christlike life. In Jesus' name we pray. Amen. (David Mosser)

SERMON BRIEFS

FRESH BREEZE IN THE HEART

ACTS 2:1-21

The late Cardinal Cushing told of an occasion when he was administering last rites to a man who had collapsed in a general store. Following his usual custom, he knelt beside the man and asked, "Do you believe in God the Father, God the Son, and God the Holy Spirit?" The Cardinal said the man roused a little bit, opened one eye, looked at him, and said, "Here I am dying, and you ask me a riddle."

We get ready by waiting. Jesus had said just a few days before, "stay here in the city until you have been clothed with power from on high" (Luke 24:49).

There's a lot of power in a good wait. A good wait increases anticipation, sharpens our expectation, and energizes us for the event that follows the waiting. Time has a way of preparing us, of getting us ready. Waiting is a spiritual activity. Jews say the Sabbath begins the sundown of the day before. Friday night was the waiting time for the Jews. The Holy Spirit's coming to us may be thwarted because of our unwillingness to spend time getting ready. Getting ready for most of us involves a season of experiences that, upon reflection, reveal a deep need for spiritual empowerment.

We get ready by acknowledging our spiritual emptiness. The disciples were empty that day. They were unsure of their relationship with Jesus. They were unsure of their own power. They were unsure of their mission. Do you know what a sinkhole is? The disciples had experienced a spiritual sinkhole that had grown larger and larger in their hearts since Christ's death. Even after Jesus appeared to them, they were lifeless and without a mission.

In the book of Acts, getting spiritual means getting in touch with the Spirit of God to the degree that there is a corresponding spiritual empowerment for you. After waiting, the disciples received power. The Spirit empowered them and made them adequate.

However, the Spirit moves as it will. Religious folk have trouble with this, unless it's planned spontaneity. Although the disciples had been waiting, they were in no way prepared for what happened. The event described in Pentecost is an unusually wild one; by the response, we can believe that no one expected it.

Would you like to get spiritual? Then open your life to the possibility of the spontaneous, the dramatic, the bold, the big, the surprising. One big surprise is that we can help the Spirit's spontaneity. This is the boring, bashful way to get spiritual. This is getting spiritual through establishing spiritual habits. The disciples established or continued the habits of meeting together for worship, for fellowship, for study, and for prayers. The disciples on the day of Pentecost came to the temple day after day waiting for the Spirit. They came back to the temple day after day to worship after the Spirit had come.

Some of us need both the spontaneous and the systematic and need to hold them in tension to get spiritual, to know God's empowerment for our lives.

For others, however, it's either/or. By the nature of your personality and your understanding of discipleship, some of you will experience a high spiritual moment of empowerment for living. Others, however, simply cannot comprehend anyone ever getting spiritual in a moment of drama. My point is not *which* method but *a* method of getting spiritual. It's not so much in a method as in the miracle of God's empowerment, adequacy, and strength.

After the Spirit came, Peter preached, and the people, being made sensitive to the things of God, were "cut to the heart," and they repented and were baptized and received into the church that very day (v. 37). Their question was, What shall I do? The response: Whatever it takes, I'll do it. (Tim Walker)

SOUL-SATISFYING PATERNITY

ROMANS 8:14-17

Both of my children sounded the syllables "Da Da" in the early months of their lives. Now, I am not sure if they understood what they were saying, but I would like to think they did since I was a proud and doting father. However, as they grew and came to understand the love I had for each of them, the endearing word of Daddy became real and meaningful. When they fell from their bikes and cut their chins or when they swam out a little too deep in the swimming pool, the cry for "Daddy" spoke of a relationship that meant to them an identity full of security and stability that they could count on. Other nights when I tucked them into bed, read stories like "The Pokey Little Puppy" to them, and prayed with them before lights out, the sound of "Daddy" became even sweeter.

Regrettably, many children will never experience a father-child relationship where they can call to a "Daddy" who will respond to them in love and sacrifice. As I ponder the state of such children, I envision a malnourished child who stands in the hallway of an orphanage, longing, yearning for something, but he knows not what. He cannot imagine what it would be like to be held in the arms of a strong, loving father and be caressed and cuddled before being put to bed at night between soft, warm sheets. How grateful this child would be if some childless couple were to adopt him, shower him with loving compassion, and remove him from a life of hopelessness and squalor.

The apostle Paul used this adoption metaphor in Romans 8:14-17 to explain the new relationship that believers share as children of God. He knew that a childless Roman man would go to great lengths to adopt a child to perpetuate his name and inherit his estate. Paul understood how the rights of an individual were transferred from one binding, legal entity to another to cause the adoption process in a family to be sure and complete. In the same manner that a fatherless baby with little hope of happiness, love, and a future suffers from an identity crisis, so does a lost person before experiencing a new life in the Spirit with Jesus Christ. The Holy Spirit gives the believer a new identity. The believer no longer suffers the plight of an orphan with no parents or sense of belonging.

The born-again believer has the hope that an adopted child has when the child enters his or her new physical home. The orphan is not referred to anymore as an "orphan," but as "my child." He or she is given a room with toys and clothes. He or she is named just like all the other members of the family. No difference is made. As a matter of fact, no one ever wants to think of the child anymore as adopted. The new identity is sure and strong. The new identity supersedes all other titles, relationships, and possessions. No wonder Paul says that the Christian will cry "Abba, Father!" because such a term of endearment is appropriate. Before an adoption, a child would be fearful, not daring to share any affection with adults that he knows. But after the parent establishes the adoption relationship, the child spontaneously cries "Daddy!" and knows now that this familiar person is the father who will take care of his or her needs. This man is now a real father! This individual is now a special person whom no one can replace. A caring, kind father has turned a homeless, helpless orphan into a satisfied, happy child.

In the same way, our heavenly Parent reaches out in saving grace and love to each one who will enter such a relationship. From such a relationship, the believer has a new identity as a child of God. As Paul says, "The Spirit that God has given you . . . makes you God's children, and by the Spirit's power, we cry out to God, 'Father! my Father!' God's Spirit joins himself to our spirits to declare that we are God's children. Since we are his children, we will possess the blessings he keeps for his people, and we will also possess with Christ what God has kept for him." (Rom. 8:15-17 TEV). (Billy Compton)

GOD THE SPIRIT

JOHN 14:8-17 (25-27)

"Philip said to him, 'Lord, show us the Father, and we will be satisfied.'"

There is a deep yearning in our heart of hearts to see God. We want to see God, know God, find fulfillment in God. Philip expresses this yearning to Jesus, and Jesus responds, "You got it! You who have seen me have seen the Father. What's more, the Father will send you the Holy Spirit in my name." This is the good news of Pentecost: God comes to be present among us in the Holy Spirit. We can see God; we can know and be satisfied, for the Spirit of God is with us.

John's Gospel does not describe a Pentecost with the rush of a mighty wind or tongues of fire. But John's Gospel does promise the coming of the Spirit. With the presence of the Spirit, we begin to see and know God in three persons: Father, Son, and Holy Spirit. These are intimately related to one another and in perfect unity with one another.

Who is the Holy Spirit? The Spirit is the continuing presence of Jesus in our lives, who makes God known. To use a musical analogy, the Holy Spirit "is the third movement of a single sonata, indispensable because it completes and fulfills all that has gone before" (Jan Milic Lochman, *The Faith We Confess*, p. 179). When I studied piano, I played Beethoven's sonatas. What was most fun and challenging about them was the recurrence and development of a certain theme and the way in which Beethoven would play with it: transposing it to different keys, splitting and mixing it up, even sneaking it in backwards. It would all come together in the third movement during the recapitulation, when Beethoven restated the theme in an even larger way and the sonata moved to resolution. God wanted so much to be shown and known to us that God did not end the sonata at the second movement, that is, in the human person of Jesus Christ, but went on to compose the third movement, that is, the Holy Spirit, so as to be intimately near us and currently available to us. The third movement is the Spirit of God, the Spirit of Jesus, the same theme in a new key.

For Philip and the rest of us who yearn to see and taste God's presence, the coming of the Spirit is a welcome, exciting third movement. Because we are given the Spirit, we come into the very presence of God. Not only that, but we have the Spirit among us, inside us! We bear in our lives the Spirit of God.

This has huge, direct consequences. If Father-Son-Spirit, are One-in-Three, Three-in-One, and if we are bearers of the Spirit, then we are one with God and therefore, one with the mission of the Three. "Very truly", Jesus tells us, "the one who believes in me will also do the works that I do . . . and will do greater works than these" (v. 12). Could this be true? Yes! The Spirit comes to take us up into doing what the Father commands and what Jesus came to do on earth. As the Spirit moves among us, our Pentecost becomes one of keeping Jesus' commandments and obeying and serving as Jesus did. We ourselves start playing this third movement of God's sonata, or, perhaps, it plays us! The Holy Spirit theme starts to have its way with us as the Spirit moves us to learn of Jesus' way, teaches us the truth, makes our wills one with God's will, and emboldens us to pray in Jesus' name. Our very lives are worked into the recapitulation of God's own theme and mission.

"Show us the Father, and we will be satisfied." We have the Spirit of God. The Spirit of God has us. Thanks be to God. (Laura Jernigan)

REFLECTIONS

JUNE

Reflection Verse: *"Woe is me! For I have become like one who,*
after the summer fruit has been gathered,
after the vintage has been gleaned,
finds no cluster to eat;
there is no first-ripe fig for which I hunger.
The faithful have disappeared from the land,
and there is no one left who is upright." (Micah 7:1-2b)

Some Protestant denominations hold their annual meetings in the summer. My church always meets the first week in June. After sitting through some twenty-five of these annual meetings, I feel as though I have the crucial routine down pat. I would never say that these events are unimportant. Nonetheless, in the vein of weddings, some of the luster wears off after the first half dozen or so. If you don't believe me, ask Elizabeth Taylor.

While sitting at a church conference table for three and a half days, listening to many drone on about budgets, trustee reports, and special ministry projects, the eye wanders and the ability to listen grows feeble. Gazing about the convention center and at the thousand or so participants, I recognize that these are my people. These folks stationed at the microphones speak of plans and strategies. They are my sisters and brothers in the ministry. Our church rises and falls on their response to their call to ministry and to the commitment they bring to the gospel. It would be hard to image going it alone to speak for God to a culture like ours. We need each other. A solitary voice speaking for God is a lonely voice. Yet, the prophet Micah seems to be a contemporary to the voice of which John the Baptizer spoke when he quoted Isaiah: "The voice of one crying out in the wilderness: / 'Prepare the way of the Lord, make his paths straight' " (Matt. 3:3). Micah plainly says,

> Woe is me! For I have become like one who,
> after the summer fruit has been gathered,
> after the vintage has been gleaned,
> finds no cluster to eat.

He states forthrightly that he feels as if he is alone.

Our faith is a community-shared faith. In the exodus every Hebrew fled Egypt, even all the livestock. Although Israel broke itself into tribes, the Hebrews understood themselves as one individual people. Even when the nation divided into the northern and southern kingdoms, the hope remained that the Messiah would unite the people again. Thus, Micah must have sensed a palpable feeling of aloneness among the unrighteous.

Too often, I suspect, many of today's ministers feel remote from others who have also taken up the ministry mantle. Given pastors' geographical spread and the different embodiments of churches that from the outside look quite similar, we know all too well that each congregation is definitely unique. For these isolated pastoral souls, however, there is much to encourage. You are not alone. Prior even to the prophetic ministries of Isaiah and Micah, another prophet voiced similar reservations. His name was Elijah.

To make his theological point to old King Ahab, Elijah prophesied that, "As the LORD the God of Israel lives, before whom I stand, there shall be neither dew nor rain these years, except by my word" (1 Kings 17:1). And Elijah's word came to pass. Later, after a showdown with the prophets of Baal, Elijah asked the assembled crowd, "How long will you go limping with two different opinions?" To the timid Yahweh followers among the spectators, Elijah even declared, "I, even I only, am left a prophet of the LORD; but Baal's prophets number four hundred fifty" (1 Kings 18:21-22). Eventually after a bit more hoopla, Elijah obliterates the prophets of Baal and then he must run for his life. Jezebel, Ahab's queen, was none too pleased that Elijah publicly humiliated her prophets. He also embarrassed the king and queen and effectively disestablished the entire existing religious institution. After running from the queen's threats, Elijah was about to give up. Yet, Yahweh encouraged him, after the prophet reminded the deity that "I have been very zealous for the LORD, the God of hosts; for the Israelites have forsaken your covenant, thrown down your altars, and killed your prophets with the sword. I alone am left, and they are seeking my life, to take it away" (1 Kings 19:14).

Even deep in Romans, Paul addresses the idea of a faithful remnant when he quotes Elijah, "Lord, they have killed your prophets, they have demolished your altars; I alone am left, and they are seeking my life" (Rom. 11:3). Of course Paul offers counsel to those who feel isolated and abandoned by others in the faith. He writes to the Romans that God answers Elijah's fervent pleas. Paul writes, "But what is the divine reply to him? 'I have kept for myself seven thousand who have not bowed the knee to Baal.' So too at the present time there is a remnant, chosen by grace" (Rom. 11:4-5). Paul's words instruct us when we feel at times like saying to God, "It is I and I alone who is faithful." Not only are we never alone because God is an ever present and abiding companion but also because God provides a remnant of faith-minded people to walk with us on the faith sojourn.

In the decisive moments in which God reveals God's will to people, conflict is certain to occur. Micah alludes to this "crisis time" when he writes,

> The son treats the father with contempt,
>   the daughter rises up against her mother,
> the daughter-in-law against her mother-in-law;
>   your enemies are members of your own household. (Mic. 7:6)

It is doubtless worth mentioning that Jesus as well alludes to this same phenomenon, perhaps even quoting Micah, as Jesus instructs his disciples before sending them out into the world.

The call to ministry that God lays upon God's people can be an exacting call. That call will beckon its recipients few times to a life of ease or comfort. Rather, the call, in many cases, summons us away from the world's alternatives—and this often involves going against conventional wisdom. Common sense or conventional wisdom often calls us to take the path of least resistance. However, in listening to and hearing the voice of God, the Lord calls us to be more than we could be left to our own devices. Therefore, we take comfort in the fact that God provides us a select group of like-minded sisters and brothers who share our faith and walk the path of discipleship with us. In this happy circumstance we gain the strength of character to be God's people. Despite his condemnation of the unfaithful, Micah's faith retains the hope key to prophesy. This hope and faith Micah demonstrates even to modern people when he suggests:

> But as for me, I will look to the LORD,
> I will wait for the God of my salvation;
> my God will hear me. (Mic. 7:7)

Amen. (David Mosser)

JUNE 6, 2004

Trinity Sunday

Worship Theme: Believers celebrate the three modes by which God reveals the Godhead. As Father, Son, and Holy Spirit, God discloses God's loving character to people. Humanity reflects on this revelation and, although in an incomplete way, recognizes divinity.

Readings: Proverbs 8:1-4, 22-31; Romans 5:1-5; John 16:12-15

Call to Worship (Psalm 8:1-5, 9)

> *Leader:* O Lord, our Sovereign, how majestic is your name in all the earth!
>
> ***People:*** **You have set your glory above the heavens.**
>
> *Leader:* Out of the mouths of babes and infants you have founded a bulwark because of your foes, to silence the enemy and the avenger.
>
> ***People:*** **When I look at your heavens, the work of your fingers, the moon and the stars that you have established; what are human beings that you are mindful of them, mortals that you care for them?**
>
> *Leader:* Yet you have made them a little lower than God, and crowned them with glory and honor.
>
> ***People:*** **O Lord, our Sovereign, how majestic is your name in all the earth!**

Pastoral Prayer:
We pray this Sabbath day to you, Our Triune God: Father, Son, and Holy Spirit. Give us holy breath to sing our praise to your

majestic glory. "In him we live and move and have our being" (Acts 17:28). Outside of your love we fall into despair and hopelessness. Within the margins of your love and mercy you give us life—the most precious of all gifts. Guide our stewardship of gifts and graces. Give our ministries truthful integrity and blameless authority. Inspire us to reach out to those who have few advocates in this world. As we feed the hungry, clothe the naked, and visit the infirmed and those in prison, bestow on us a holy sense of your mission. Let us accomplish your will through our commitment to your kingdom. You, O Lord, have revealed your truth in the form of the trinity. Let our Trinitarian doctrine, our feeble and creaturely effort to put your inexpressible nature into human speech, guide our life and action. Remind us that Jesus as a divine incarnation of love abides with us in all and through all. Make us worthy of the name "Christian" in the name of Christ. Amen. (David Mosser)

SERMON BRIEFS

EVERYTHING WE NEED

PROVERBS 8:1-4, 22-31

The older I get, the more multi-faceted my persona becomes. I must admit that sometimes those many facets leave me feeling a bit fragmented. I am a wife. A mother. A daughter. A sister. A minister. A neighbor. The list could go on and on. Sometimes it is hard to believe that although I am the same person that I have been since my earliest memories, the dimensions of who I am have changed. For me, each added dimension seems to complete me even more. Nearly every person could probably recognize the same things about themselves. As humans, we are complex, multi-faceted beings. Ironically, even with all of our complexity, we sometimes have difficulty grappling with the vast array of dimensions of God. Although we recognize that as human beings God creates us in God's image, we sometimes have difficulty grasping the idea that one God possesses so many different dimensions.

This is a concept believers have contemplated for centuries. Because of the plethora of deities found in most cultures, it has always been a challenging idea for Jewish believers, and later Christians, that their God can supply all of their needs without splitting into a number of identities. Throughout scripture, we can find incidences of humans doubting God's multi-faceted personality, and turning to other gods to meet their needs, only to betray their commitment to God. For the sages or teachers of wisdom responsible for writing and collecting the book of Proverbs, it was important to give attention to this aspect of God in their teaching. As in other proverbs, Proverbs 8 addresses the personification of wisdom. In this particular proverb, the writer depicts wisdom as a co-existing element of God present with God before and throughout creation. Proverbs 8:22 and following describe wisdom's origin, present from eternity. The writer even describes wisdom as the craftsman at God's side. This passage of scripture is important as it gives authority to wisdom which throughout Proverbs teaches readers a way to live righteously and not foolishly. This wisdom is not another god or deity for people to worship, although throughout time humans mistake wisdom as an independent divinity. On the contrary, this text describes wisdom as a part of God, an element of God. The author's audience needed instruction in how to live their lives successfully, productively, and righteously. Proverbs 8 reminds us that whatever we need the most comes from God. We cannot separate wisdom from God. Therefore, whatever our needs, God can meet them. The same God that gave us breath and hears our every prayer will meet our daily need.

Although we live in a totally different set of circumstances than the original recipients of the Proverbs, it is also important for us to remember that God can indeed meet all of our needs. It is tempting as twenty-first-century adults to rely so heavily on ourselves that we take God out of the equation, limiting what we think God can actually do. What an important reminder that God is so multidimensional that God can embrace and understand every part of who we are and what we need. Trinity Sunday is a good time to refocus on a God who is most complete as a complex combination of what we need the most. (Tracey Allred)

LIFE IN THE KINGDOM

ROMANS 5:1-5

Anyone who has received a valentine card has some taste of how special one can feel to receive a love message from an admirer. Actually, the definition of *valentine* is "a person chosen on Valentine's Day . . . a greeting card sent to one's Valentine . . . a day set aside as a day when valentines are traditionally exchanged." Valentine's Day cards represent special messages sent to those we care deeply about. In the same way, the Bible contains messages from God to those God loves, those born into the kingdom by faith in Jesus Christ. As the apostle Paul explains in Romans 5:5 (NIV), "God has poured out his love into our hearts."

No, God has not written to us in a Hallmark card nor sent us flowers but God has sent a personal word to all who by faith now live as a part of the kingdom. God's love message tells us specifically what faith in Christ provides. Paul identifies three special gifts believers receive as followers of Christ.

The first special gift we receive is the wealth of peace. Peace is very much a desired condition in our world. Even in this present time, the war on terrorism reminds us how evasive peace can be. History proves—and modern day life teaches us—that peace in the world is an elusive dream. Humankind knows no peace in the world. However, through Jesus Christ, a person can be at peace with God. A peace treaty has been signed and verified through Jesus Christ that sets us free from the state of hostility between God and human beings.

The second gift is the benefit of access. In the Old Testament the Jew was kept from God's presence by the veil in the temple and a wall at the temple warned that any Gentile going beyond that wall would be killed. But when Jesus died on the cross, the Bible teaches that the veil was torn and the wall broken down. Now, through Jesus Christ and by faith, any person has access into the very presence of God.

The third gift is a foundation of hope. When I visit sick people in the hospital, I become intensely aware of what hope means to them. At first, they hope nothing is amiss with their health. Then,

205

they hope their illness is not serious. They also hope something can be done to cure their illness. Yes, a sick person would tell us the old maxim is true: If it were not for hope, the heart would break.

In these verses from Romans Paul declares that a Christian can live with a confident expectation of sharing hope in God. The believer has a future built on this hope. Regardless of how bad a day may be, a better day is yet to come. (Billy Compton)

LEGACIES OF THE LIVING LORD

JOHN 16:12-15

Have you ever been remembered in someone's will? It happened to me once, at a critically important time in my family's life. A distant relative, whom I had only met once, left me $5,000. We needed the money! Yet I felt so undeserving. If I had mowed my Aunt Edna's grass every Saturday for years and she had never paid me, I would have felt differently. But I had done nothing to earn what she left me. Why did she leave me money in her estate? There is only one possible reason: She looked at her family tree and found my name in it.

In John 14–16, Jesus gives us his last will and testament. These three chapters contain the legacies Jesus left behind for all who would follow him. These are gifts of grace, unearned and undeserved. They have been given to you strictly because you are a member of his family, and, therefore, you are a joint heir (Rom. 8:16-17; Gal. 4:7).

John 16:14-15 are verses that explain how Jesus intends to deliver the things in his will to you. It speaks of the Holy Spirit and says, "he will take what is mine and declare it to you." In other words, the work of the Holy Spirit is to be the delivery person for Jesus. The Spirit takes the things in Jesus' estate and delivers them to his heirs.

Consider some of the items in Jesus' will and how the Holy Spirit delivers them to us. Jesus has promised you a supernatural dwelling place in heaven (John 14:1-6). The King James Version calls it "many mansions." Compare that to the body you are living in now, which Paul describes as a "tent," a temporary, fragile structure in which we all "groan." We long, Paul says, to be "clothed" with this new body and for "what is mortal [to] be swallowed up by life" (2 Cor. 5:1-4). But how can we be sure that God will fulfill this hope? Because God has deposited the Holy Spirit into our lives as a down payment, a guarantee that the promise is true (2 Cor. 4:5).

A second promise Jesus left you in his estate is supernatural power (John 14:12-14). Many theologians note that Pentecost reversed the Tower of Babel (Gen. 11:1-9) because people speaking different languages were able to understand each other (Acts 2:1-11). But why did God confuse the tongues of people at Babel? Genesis 11:6 states that God determined that if humans remained united they would be able to do anything they proposed to do. Jesus promises in his will that when the Spirit comes we will be able to come together and do "greater works" than even Jesus did in the flesh. Jesus suggests that what God will give us is limitless.

Jesus promises a third benefit: a supernatural helper (John 14:15-18). Jesus says that the One who will come to fulfill this promise will be able to stand beside each of us and live within each of us simultaneously. Praise God for the Spirit!

There are many other important legacies in Jesus' last will and testament. Jesus has given you the promise of supernatural peace (John 14:27-31), supernatural friendship (John 15:13-15), and supernatural witness (John 15:26; 16:11).

But consider with me one final legacy: the promise of supernatural guidance and instruction. Jesus told those remembered in his will that they would continue to hear from him. Jesus said that he had many things to tell them that they were not ready to hear. As they became ready, the Spirit would guide them and instruct them. The Spirit would take the words of Jesus and deliver them to us. The words of Jesus to us will include messages about "things to come."

Jesus said that the sheep hear the shepherd's voice (John 10:3, 4, 16). We are his sheep. Our task is to find time to be quiet, to be still, to remove the static from the line, and to listen to Jesus' voice. Chuck Swindoll calls these breakthroughs of the Spirit UIPs (as opposed to UFOs). They are "unidentified inner promptings." I experience this the way Isaiah did when he wrote, "your ears shall hear a word behind you, saying, 'This is the way; walk in it' " (Isa. 30:21).

Reach out to the Holy Spirit today. The Spirit is the one who takes the promises of Jesus and delivers them to you. Your name is in the will. (Jim Jackson)

JUNE 13, 2004

Second Sunday After Pentecost

Worship Theme: We worship a loving God who sent Jesus as a sign of love that proves itself to human beings. As followers of Jesus, God asks us to forgive others as God has first forgiven us.

Readings: 1 Kings 21:1-21*a*; Galatians 2:15-21; Luke 7:36–8:3

Call to Worship (Psalm 5:1-8)

Leader: Give ear to my words, O LORD; give heed to my sighing. Listen to the sound of my cry, my King and my God, for to you I pray.

People: **O LORD, in the morning you hear my voice; in the morning I plead my case to you, and watch.**

Leader: For you are not a God who delights in wickedness; evil will not sojourn with you.

People: **The boastful will not stand before your eyes; you hate all evildoers. You destroy those who speak lies; the LORD abhors the bloodthirsty and deceitful.**

Leader: But I, through the abundance of your steadfast love, will enter your house, I will bow down toward your holy temple in awe of you.

People: **Lead me, O LORD, in your righteousness because of my enemies; make your way straight before me.**

Pastoral Prayer:

God of Everlasting Forgiveness and Mercy, hear our prayer. You know, O God, that we live in a world where the word *revenge* is active. We see revenge played out on our family televisions and read about vengeance in novels and newspapers. We hear people say that "they don't get mad, they get even." This attitude of retribution too often becomes the desire of the human heart. Yet, Jesus taught that forgiveness is the seal of the Christian life. Help us confess our need to get even. Lord, we pray that you might send your Spirit upon us to be more ready to forgive than seems humanly possible. Give us the strength of character to bear the burden of our anger so that others might see the love of Christ by our reaction to the hurts that the world often imposes. We do not pray to suffer injustice, but rather to let the insignificant insults and slights pass by us. Make us big enough to absorb others' insensitivities and insecurities. Remind us that we have a savior who absorbed the world's evil so that we might have abundant life. We pray for this strength in the name of Jesus. Amen. (David Mosser)

SERMON BRIEFS

DOES EVERYTHING HAVE A PRICE?

1 KINGS 21:1-21*a*

Does everything have a price? Our story helps us to think about the value of things as it speaks of one's rich heritage and as it speaks of the lure of riches. We see the "rich heritage" as the scripture speaks of Naboth owning a vineyard in Jezreel. It was inherited land. Do you have land that has been in the family for years? There is usually more value to that property than just dollars and cents. In Naboth's culture, the heritage of the land forbid Naboth from parting with the vineyard, for land and its occupants were thought inseparable. In our western culture, we don't quite understand this practice, but we do understand protecting the family name. To sell the land would be to turn your back on your family and to turn your back on God, who provided the land for you.

Our story also shows us the lure of riches. It is what I call the rich mentality that many people absorb when they begin to have money, power, or authority. Ahab wanted Naboth's vineyard for a vegetable garden near his palace in Jezreel. Ahab perhaps thinks of it as a business deal. The text does not suggest he tries cheating Naboth. Ahab said, "I'll pay you whatever it is worth," and offers Naboth a better vineyard. But when Naboth refuses, Ahab becomes angry and sulks, and so his wife, Jezebel, plots for a way to get the vineyard.

Jezebel mocks her husband, "Act like a king! Do what kings do!" In her mind, kings could do whatever they had the power or money to do! She epitomizes the "rich mentality," which says, "We have the money, power, and authority. Everything has its price, and we have the right to get what we want if we have the means to get it!"

Jezebel concocts false testimony against Naboth. She looks for an easy way to get rid of Naboth, and a death penalty fits the bill. To get the death penalty, she technically needs two or three witnesses, prescribed by the Deuteronomic code. So, Jezebel gets some elders and the nobles to join her. She has Naboth accused of reviling the tribal leader, which was equivalent to cursing God. Jezebel does everything behind closed doors. Soon, Naboth dies unjustly.

When Jezebel gets word that Naboth is dead, she urges her husband to go and take what is "rightfully" his. Once Naboth was out of the way, it's easy to justify taking the land. Now, we are not sure if the property of slain criminals went to the crown or if it was an illegal confiscation. We do know that the "rich mentality" is thought to have won. It's like a flashing neon sign saying, "those who have can always find ways to get what they want." Everything has its price and if you've got the money and power to get it, then you will always win!

But, then the Word of the Lord came to Elijah the Tishbite. Isn't it just like God to raise a prophet when something unjust is happening? The Word of the Lord counters the lure of the "rich mentality." Just as Nathan proclaimed judgment before David after Bathsheeba, here, Elijah pronounces the verdict to Ahab. The text says that Elijah has become the king's "enemy."

Elijah says, "I have found you, because you have sold yourself

211

to do what is evil in the sight of the LORD" (v. 20 RSV). Jezebel forgot the scriptures, and we too can often fall into this same trap. We too can often forget Psalm 24:1 (RSV), "The earth is the LORD's and the fulness thereof." We are merely stewards and not owners. The earth, our possessions, and our money are transitory. The earth is not just some purchased commodity. Whereas they stoned Naboth for breaking the law, others discover the king and queen to be the real lawbreakers.

In a way, the "rich mentality" was right, everything does have a price. But the prophet Elijah helps us to see that the price doesn't always have dollars attached to it. Everything does have a price. That price may be our own souls. That price may affect our own lives or even the lives of our sons or daughters. For in this story, disaster won't come until later. We are again reminded that our whole family tree can be affected by the decisions we make today. The decisions a church makes today impact the life of its church family for years to come!

Does everything have a price? Does our economy place a dollar figure on everything in today's world? Does capitalism promote the idea that everything is a tradable commodity? We have to ask ourselves this question when we see the abuse of disadvantaged persons. We have to ask ourselves this question when we watch as some people seem to have no voice and no rights. We have to ask ourselves this question when the lottery is up to $325 million, but our ethics tell us we shouldn't play it because we are convinced to our core that the lottery promotes irresponsible use of money.

What do you think? Does everything have a price? What was the price for the elders and nobles who joined in the plot with Jezebel? What is the price today? What is your price? (Ryan Wilson)

MADE RIGHT BY CHRIST

GALATIANS 2:15-21

In this passage Paul speaks to the very heart of the gospel—both its promise and vulnerability. Paul uses language that was easily understood in his time, but which falls strangely on the ears of people today. Just what is this justification business? What does it have to do with my life or my soul? Does the law of which Paul speaks mean traffic law, criminal law, civil law, the Ten Commandments, or what?

The word *justification* does not point the twenty-first-century person to religious or spiritual concerns. To the extent that we use the word in modern English, *justification* refers to a process of making something true, right, or acceptable. For Paul, the overwhelming task of humanity was to find a way to feel accepted and in right relationship with God. While today's people may not be consciously aware of the need to be right with God, people are driven to find acceptance and worth. We work too hard. We eat too much. We may drink too much. We search for a spouse who will make us feel wanted and needed. We fight for affluence and a secure future. For the most part, these efforts appear secular, but beneath the surface they betray a deep longing for justification. These drives we feel express our spiritual hunger.

The great power of the gospel is its ability to address and satisfy this hunger. Paul's gospel disarms all of our secular or religious efforts to earn God's favor. Here lies the deep faith/works divide. In Paul's day, religious people tried to feed their hunger for acceptance and worth by performing religious duties. People sought justification through moral, liturgical, or charitable acts which they deemed might satisfy God's demand for goodness. Paul referred to these acts generically as "the law." For Paul, faith stood in stark contrast with the law because it promised that we were made right with God not through our efforts but through God's action in Christ. The acceptance and worth we never quite feel we have earned, God gives as a gift. The Christian relies not on his or her efforts or accomplishments, but on the embracing and accepting love and mercy of God. Morality, religion, charity, citizenship, and honor mean nothing. The cross means everything. To experience justification, Christians must let go of their own striving and receive God's gift.

This leads to the great vulnerability of the gospel that Paul addresses. If our morality, piety, charity, citizenship, and honor have no impact on God's love and acceptance, then why not "eat, drink, and be merry"? This question challenged Paul in his time and in our own modern hearts we also wonder about it.

Paul declares that faith in God's mercy not only justifies us but also claims and changes us. The gift of the gospel overwhelms in the flood of baptismal waters and makes everything different. When we are loved enough we are made better by that love. This is true of mature human loves, and it is true of the love of God. Right living becomes the natural and desired outcome of being made right with God through the cross of Christ. We have been given so much that we now respond in right living. Rather than creating reckless lives not needing goodness, the gospel creates holy lives by the power of its grace.

Here we have the heart of the gospel. It is a call to let go and receive that which God eternally offers. Those who are "justified by faith" are no longer driven to prove their worth, but are made worthy by God's mighty act in Jesus Christ. (Carl Schenck)

SCRIPT WRITERS!

LUKE 7:36–8:3

Have you ever seen one of those movies where it seemed that no one acted according to script? The good guy turned out to be the bad guy, the bad guy turned out to be the good guy and almost no one turned out to be what you thought they would be in the beginning. Confused? Me too! Particularly when I look at our text.

Jesus is at dinner with a Pharisee. Now, I thought that the Pharisees were the bad guys who were constantly trying to trap Jesus and later teamed up with the Romans to put him to death. Maybe Jesus ate with him and did not refuse table fellowship with Simon because then, Jesus too, would have been guilty of prejudice—the sin that later took his life. So, Jesus is definitely a good guy.

So, maybe Simon is a good guy, a friend to Jesus. If that is so, why then did Simon not extend to Jesus the common courtesies of hospitality: foot washing, anointing, and a kiss? Why then did a "bad" individual do for Jesus what Simon seemingly refused to do? Luke says that a woman with a bad reputation extends these characteristics of graciousness because she is good; she has loved much.

Following the script? Me neither! I do understand that we have two religious leaders who are suddenly in the presence of a sinful or bad woman. One leader, Simon, feels that to be righteous or good, one should shun such women, putting as much distance between oneself and the other as possible. The other religious leader, Jesus, feels that to be righteous or good, one should move toward such a woman with forgiveness and with one's blessing of peace or pronouncement of wholeness. One leader feels that to be good, one must stand back and stay clean. The other leader feels that to be good, one must move forward and risk defilement.

So it seems that according to Jesus' script, the "best of the best," the good Pharisee, we see in a bad light, and the bad woman Jesus pronounces good through grace. Then Jesus commends her for her faith and bids her go in peace.

Now I ask you, where is she going? She cannot go back to her family. They have long forsaken her, because of her evil ways. She cannot go back to her "profession," because she has exhibited faith, and Jesus forgives her and grants her peace. God too has touched her. So, where is she going?

You would hope that she could go and find acceptance in the church. You would hope that she could go and find acceptance in your church. Better yet, could I give her your address?

Maybe Jesus wants you to write an ending to the script. (Gary Carver)

JUNE 20, 2004

Third Sunday After Pentecost

Worship Theme: God speaks to God's people in many ways. God even speaks to us in the still, small voice within us. God does so much for us that we need to take holy time to be thankful for the gifts and graces that God bestows on God's people.

Readings: 1 Kings 19:1-15*a*; Galatians 3:23-29; Luke 8:26-39

Call to Worship (Psalm 42:1-3, 5, 8, 11*c*)

> *Leader:* As a deer longs for flowing streams, so my soul longs for you, O God.

> *People:* **My soul thirsts for God, for the living God. When shall I come and behold the face of God?**

> *Leader:* My tears have been my food day and night, while people say to me continually, "Where is your God?"

> *People:* **Why are you cast down, O my soul, and why are you disquieted within me? Hope in God; for I shall again praise him, my help and my God.**

> *Leader:* By day the LORD commands his steadfast love, and at night his song is with me, a prayer to the God of my life.

> *People:* **Hope in God; for I shall again praise him, my help and my God.**

Pastoral Prayer:

O Compassionate God of Elijah, the Prophets, and Jesus, we lift our voices in prayer and praise. We thank you, O Lord, for the endowment of tender mercies you dispense to us each day. You have sent your son for us and for this gracious gift we are grateful. Allow us to pour ourselves out for others as Christ emptied himself for us. Help us where our faith fails us. We know that it takes great courage to live with righteousness in a world where many take the path of least resistance. Too often it is easy to look the other way regarding the suffering and needs of others. Yet we have Jesus as our model. Jesus is "the pioneer and perfecter of our faith" (Heb. 12:2); therefore let us cling to him as we aspire to the upward call in Christ. Open us to the gospel's new truths that you reveal to us in our daily walk with Jesus. Grant us the wisdom to follow him, as did those first disciples. Above all, furnish us the assurance that faith is its own reward and grant us peace in it. We pray in the name of the one who brings us perfect peace. Amen. (David Mosser)

SERMON BRIEFS

WHAT ARE YOU DOING HERE?

1 KINGS 19:1-15a

That's a question that we have all been asked at one time or another. It is the kind of question that a principal, a police officer, or your mother might ask. There is an implied criticism: You don't belong here. That is certainly the implication of God's question to Elijah in this passage.

The previous chapter outlines the story of Elijah's great victory on Mount Carmel. By any standard this is one of the Bible's great stories. Elijah challenges and defeats the four hundred fifty prophets of Baal and then kills them. As a result God sends the promised rain to drought-plagued Israel. Elijah celebrates with a victory run. He runs ahead of King Ahab's chariot all the way to the royal residence in Jezreel.

There are four pictures of Elijah in this passage. The first is of

"Elijah the Runner." Elijah seems invincible, but when Ahab's queen, Jezebel, threatens to kill Elijah, he "ran for his life." He knew how to run to victory, but he also knew how to run away. Isn't it amazing how quickly our victories and our courage vanish? We have all felt like running away. Like Elijah, we dream of greener pastures. All too often, when we run away, the green pastures end up being broom trees in the desert. The truth is that you can't run away from your problems or from God. The good news is that God does not discard us when we run away. Perhaps, this is the point of Jesus' story of a runaway in Luke 15.

The second picture we see is "Elijah the Quitter." Do you identify with Elijah? Many folks can't handle victory. They don't do Mount Carmel very well, but they are on familiar turf under the broom tree. The good news is that when we quit, God doesn't. God comes to us or sends someone to care for us. When we accept God's provision, we have the strength to do what God asks us to do. Elijah has the strength for a forty-day journey to God's mountain, Mount Horeb. If you are discouraged today, listen for God's voice and accept his provision.

The third picture is of "Elijah the Whiner." Elijah travels to God's mountain to hear a word from God. When God asks, "What are you doing here?" Elijah begins to whine. A popular lapel button has the word whiner written on it with a red slash drawn through it. The message is: "No Whining." Every Christian has felt like Elijah. "I'm the only one holding the rope. Everyone else has quit." Elijah wanted God's pity, but God doesn't respond well to whiners. Rather, God tells Elijah to get out of his cave of self-pity and go outside. There Elijah is to look for God. That is always the solution to our whining: Get away from your despondency and look for and listen to God.

The fourth picture is of "Elijah the Seeker." When Elijah doesn't know what he needs, God provides. When Elijah doesn't know where he should go, God directs. And, when he doesn't know what God is like, God speaks. God gives Elijah direction: Go back the way you came. God assigns him a task: Anoint a new king. God gives him encouragement: God will prevail. And, God gives him a revelation: There are other faithful believers besides Elijah. Deuteronomy 4:29 promises, "seek the LORD your God, and you will find him." (Philip Wise)

ONE IN CHRIST

GALATIANS 3:23-29

Paul turns from his examination of the relationship between law and faith to proclaim one of the fruits of faith in the community of believers. In doing so, Paul offers the preacher opportunity to address issues of importance in the current lives of the church and community.

How radical was Paul's vision? When Paul sees oneness in Christ between Jews and Greeks, slaves and free, male and female, Paul teaches that God overcomes the most basic and even bitter human divisions in Christ.

Jew and Greek: Here we have the most fundamental religious and ethnic division of Paul's world (especially from Paul's point of view). For Paul, *Greek* represents all those people, nations, and groups that are outside of God's covenant with the Hebrew people. To the Jews, these are thoroughly pagan people and entirely hopeless in their estrangement from God. They do not know God's law; they worship idols; they are immoral; and they are cruel in their oppression of Jews. To the Greeks, Jews appear backward, superstitious, and stubborn. To them, the Jewish practice of circumcision amounts to mutilation of the sacred human body. They perceive Jewish dietary laws as superstitions and Jewish unwillingness to accept "modern" social progress as foolish. To the Jews, circumcision was the sign of the covenant; dietary laws were forms of obedience; and resistance to Roman social convention was resistance to evil. The lack of understanding, mistrust, and even hatred between Jew and Greek was intense.

Slave and free: What could separate persons more than the practice of slavery? In Paul's time there were few, if any, voices raised to oppose slavery in principle. The social, economic, and psychological distance between the slave and owner was vast and unbridgeable. Profound damage was done to the personal honor and psychological health of the slave because the slave was owned and treated like a object. Slavery made things of persons and made it impossible for the owner and the owned to relate as equals.

Male and female: Differences in social roles, training, expectations, legal status, and biology all made understanding and mutuality between the sexes difficult in Paul's time. The same is true today. Men and women remain mysteries to each other and too often the source of deep hurt and pain.

When Paul declared that God overcame these profound differences in Christ, he claimed that the Christian faith created a community of equals. They were equals in the sight of God. Paul's message struck at the very root of the fractures that ran through his time and his society. (Carl Schenck)

THE POWER OF JESUS TO CONQUER WHAT LIES BEYOND OUR POWER

LUKE 8:26-39

The miracle of casting out a legion of demons from a man so seriously mentally impaired that his family and his community had given up on him is a powerful drama. However, the power of the drama widens when seen in the light of the miracles that preceded and followed. We should always study scripture in the light of its setting. We should see the part in light of the whole.

On the voyage across the lake from Galilee to the district of the Gerasenes the disciples encountered a violent storm. It was so violent that it frightened even the disciples who, no doubt, had weathered many storms on that same lake. Jesus rebuked the raging storm, and the waters became calm. Jesus has power over the forces of nature!

As soon as they landed, Jesus encountered a man possessed by demons. He was so deranged that he had torn away his clothing and lived in the local cemetery. The demons (who are of the spirit world) recognized Jesus (who was also of the spirit world). The demons challenged Jesus. The possessed man was so violent that he broke the chains and fetters with which he had been bound. When Jesus asked the man his name, he said, "Legion." A legion was about six thousand soldiers. The man felt he had six thousand demons controlling his life. Jesus commanded the demons to come out of him. Jesus set the man free. When the people of the town came out to see what was happening, they saw the man—once so violent—sitting at Jesus' feet, "clothed and in his right mind" (v. 35). The people were frightened at such power. Jesus has power over demons and evil spirits.

As soon as Jesus came back across the lake a crowd was waiting for him. The daughter of Jairus, leader of the synagogue, had died. Accompanied by Peter, John, and James, Jesus went into the house where the dead child lay and raised her from the dead. Universal amazement spread among those who learned of the miracle. Jesus had power over death. But wait! There's more!

There was a woman in the crowd who had been ill for twelve years. She had spent all she had on doctors, and none of them could cure her. In a gesture motivated by desperation, she came up behind Jesus and touched the hem of his garment. She was immediately healed of her chronic disease. Jesus had power over physical illness. What manner of man is this? He has power over the forces of nature, the world of demons, physical illness, and even death.

The healing of the demoniac of the Gerasenes is the center-piece of this quartet of miracles. We could never begin to understand this miracle or the special meaning it had to the man whom Jesus healed or to those who were privy to it unless we understand the intensity with which the people in Jesus' day believed in the vast underworld of demons and evil spirits. Our modern understanding of mental illness (as incomplete as it may be) makes it difficult for us to put ourselves in the conceptual framework of people who believed so intensely in demons and evil spirits. They controlled everything! The cause of all phenomena not otherwise understood was attributed to demons and evil spirits. These demons controlled the weather, illness, natural disasters, and personal misfortunes.

The manifestation of Jesus' power over demons and evil spirits was central to convincing the people who he was. What has this to say to our age in which we know much more about causality than the people in Jesus' day? For all that we know, or think we know, there are vast areas about which we are still ignorant. Every new discovery seems to bring a flood of new mysteries.

We still have our demons and evil spirits. They manifest themselves in personal and social illnesses and behaviors that are as mysterious to us as the condition of the Gerasene demoniac was in his day. We have different tools now for getting at these illnesses. We hope they are better tools, but we live in a world of people engaged in never-ending battles with depression, addiction, anxiety, and illnesses as yet unconquered by medical science. We see people every day whose lives are so fragmented by unseen forces that they could say their name is "Legion."

The power of God through faith in Jesus Christ has miraculously cured and saved many people in every age whose conditions were not subject to conventional remedies. Jesus still walks across the troubled waters and calms the raging storms in our lives. He knows about our demons too. He knows them by name. He can help us turn them loose or get loose from their grasp. He knows our condition. We see miracles every day. Some we half understand. Some we do not. If you have ever walked in the valley of the shadow of death with someone you love or by yourself—even in the darkest hour—you were not alone.

The last verse of Francis Thompson's poem, "The Kingdom of God," illustrates this.

> Yea, in the night, my Soul, my daughter,
> Cry,—clinging Heaven by the hems;
> And lo, Christ walking on the water
> Not of Gennesareth, but Thames!

When I read this, I can see Jesus coming across the sea of Galilee to the demented demoniac of Gerasene. (Thomas Lane Butts)

JUNE 27, 2004

Fourth Sunday After Pentecost

Worship Theme: God calls God's people to freedom in the gospel. Within that freedom, however, we bear the yoke of Christ. God's kingdom offers us perfect freedom in the perfect obedience to the call of Christ.

Readings: 2 Kings 2:1-2, 6-14; Galatians 5:1, 13-25; Luke 9:51-62

Call to Worship (Psalm 77:1-2, 11-15)

Leader: I cry aloud to God, aloud to God, that he may hear me.

People: **In the day of my trouble I seek the Lord; in the night my hand is stretched out without wearying; my soul refuses to be comforted.**

Leader: I will call to mind the deeds of the LORD; I will remember your wonders of old.

People: **I will meditate on all your work, and muse on your mighty deeds.**

Leader: Your way, O God, is holy. What god is so great as our God?

People: **You are the God who works wonders; you have displayed your might among the peoples.**

All: **With your strong arm you redeemed your people, the descendants of Jacob and Joseph.**

Pastoral Prayer:

As we gather to worship you, O God who is both Alpha and Omega, impart to us the saving knowledge of Jesus Christ. Reveal within the limitations of our worship the gospel's supreme truth. You sent Jesus to us, O God, as your only begotten son. Through Christ's life, teaching, death, and resurrection we glimpse a vital element of your mysterious plan for our life. You confirm Jesus' abiding presence through the agency of the Holy Spirit who is as near to us as our own prayers and breath. We confess that often our world pulls us toward its own vision of abundant life. Yet we know deep in our hearts that more possessions and our willful dominance can never provide the things necessary for a full and faithful life. You, O God, give our life meaning and value in terms of sacrificial love. Those who follow your rule recognize that perfect love casts out fear. Make us courageous for the gospel's call to service beyond self. Seal our community's spirit with a love that passes all human understanding as we strive to be your people in Jesus' gracious name. Amen. (David Mosser)

SERMON BRIEFS

CHANGING OF THE GUARD

2 KINGS 2:1-2, 6-14

Do you remember the people you admired as a child? Maybe the famous faces from television shows and your favorite cartoon characters caught your attention. Perhaps even an older sibling or a mentor significantly touched your life. As a regular part of your existence, this person may have taught you to ride a bike or may have built you a tree house. You admired this individual as your role model. You tried to emulate his or her every action and every word. You dreamed of becoming just like her or him.

In Second Kings, Elisha has dreamed that he would one day be an equal to Elijah. Elijah exemplified the role of prophet, and so Elisha wanted to follow in his footsteps. He probably imagined that as Elijah's successor, he would serve God well by speaking the truth and calling people to righteousness and justice. As we read in the text, Elijah has come to the realization that his work is finished. God is calling him home. He knows that when the ordained time arrives, Elisha will assume his role as prophet.

Both Elijah and Elisha are aware of this changing of the guard. Each are prepared to follow God's instructions. They set out for Bethel from Gilgal, the place where young prophets trained, until Elijah cautions Elisha to stay behind. Demonstrating his loyalty, Elisha quickly responds, "As the LORD lives, and as you yourself live, I will not leave you." Elijah concedes, only to ask Elisha to stay behind again on two other occasions as they travel toward Jericho and Jordan. Each time Elisha remains as his loyal companion. Perhaps Elijah was reluctant to leave his role and this life on earth. In fact, Elijah's actions seem quite human. Who really wants to give up the certainty of a life here on earth for the unknown of eternity?

Elijah realizes that the inevitable change will soon occur, so some loose ends need to be tied up. He questions what he can do for Elisha. Elisha does not ask for money or cattle, but rather he wants to inherit a double share of Elijah's spirit. The request itself is not that unusual. Among Israelites, the eldest son would expect his father to give him a double share for his inheritance. However, the unusual nature of the request begs the question, how would Elisha receive this gift?

In a mystical fashion, "a chariot of fire and horse of fire" descend from heaven, swooping up Elijah as he ascended in a whirlwind. Whirlwinds are often associated with the coming of God and it is in this instance that Elisha confronts the power of God. Just as God brings the power of the divine into the human realm, Elisha brings back Elijah's power to his community. Elisha receives Elijah's mantle, which identified him as the proper successor. Still unsure if he had received his inheritance, Elisha on his return trip through the Jordan River tests his power by striking the water only to discover that the Jordan does indeed separate.

As Christians, God often calls us to act in a similar fashion as Elijah and Elisha. We must be willing to pass the mantle of ministry from one believer to the next. We must be willing to serve when it is our turn, for we each are given opportunities to participate in the life of the church. Elisha received the mantle from Elijah, and like his predecessor, he too separated the Jordan. As both prophets discovered the power to triumph over the obstacles in their paths, may we also find confidence in our faith and the courage to overcome any difficulty we encounter as we minister to those around us. Like Elisha, may we loyally serve each other and God. (Mark White)

CHOOSE FREEDOM

GALATIANS 5:1, 13-25

Freedom may be the most slippery word spoken among the human family in these still yawning moments of the twenty-first century. One of the ironies of freedom, however, is that one can grant freedom to another, but living fully into one's freedom is always a choice we make. Viktor Frankl, who lived through and survived Auschwitz, discovered that one could find freedom deep within even in the face of brutal oppression and senseless death.

Galatians is Paul's "manifesto of freedom." The Galatians were a confused community of believers. Paul established the church (or perhaps the churches) in what is now central western Turkey. The first Galatian Christians were non-Jewish believers (Gentiles) whose lives were once oppressed by onerous pagan ritual. Now in Christ, they knew a spiritual liberty that released them to live free in God's grace (Gal. 4:8).

But something happened after Paul's exit. Galatians 1:6-7, 3:1, and 4:9 refer to a group of people who polluted the minds of the Galatians with a "gospel plus" theology. These people suggested that God's grace in Christ was not enough. Some of the Galatian believers were seduced by this spiritual nonsense.

So Paul writes this terse, at times testy, letter to recall the Galatians to choose freedom over legalism. We too would be wise to choose freedom as God's gift to us. And yet, so many Christians (particularly in the United States) seem to crave the seemingly secure assurances of fundamentalism: "Give me a faith I can prove, 'truths' that will validate my prejudices, five things I can do to verify I am a Christian." Are we free if we only exchange one form of idolatry (materialism, selfishness, you name it) for another (biblicism, legalism, self-righteousness)?

Paul says no. To be free means that we are free *from* sin, death, legalism, and all forms of spiritual "oughtness" and then made free by God's grace for life in Jesus Christ. Specifically, we are free to live fully in Christ in at least four ways. First, we are free "to stand" in the reality of freedom. "Stand firm" means to plant one's feet on the soil of spiritual freedom and not to move or be moved by the forces of spiritual slavery. The most profound thing we do as Christians is simply, quietly, faithfully, lovingly stand. We make no speeches, organize no marches, and collect no petitions; we stand in the freedom God has so generously given us in Christ.

Second, Paul says that we are free "to love." Echoing our Lord, Paul gathers in his arms the essence of biblical faith: Love God by loving "your neighbor as yourself." Someone has rightly said that the only way any Christian can visibly, experientially love God is by loving others freely, fully, faithfully.

John Claypool reminds us there are only two kinds of love: need love and gift love. "Need love" is inherently selfish; it gives because it hopes the receiver will give back. On the other hand, "gift love" is love given not from one's emptiness needing to be filled, but rather from what Claypool calls one's "muchness." People who are free in Jesus Christ can authentically share "gift love."

Third, Paul then says we are free to "live by the Spirit." How tempting it is to read these verses, draw up a checklist of spiritual *do*s and *don't*s, and live off our list. Don't go there. Paul contrasts the life of the Spirit and the life of the flesh to call us to be "led by the Spirit." Legalism requires coercion and manipulation: Freedom is a choice that bubbles up from love.

Finally, we are free "to become" the person God created us to be. Galatians 5:22-25 lists "the fruit of the Spirit," which is singularly "love." Becoming a whole person in Christ is authentic, liberating freedom, God's "gift love" to every believer. (Timothy Owings)

DO YOU KNOW TO WHAT SPIRIT YOU BELONG?

LUKE 9:51-62

This passage of scripture is a powerful lesson on how to deal with historical hatred as it takes on a personal focus. There are people who hate for reasons that go back beyond their memory. Inherited hatred is difficult because it is usually disconnected from its origins.

The lesson for today has to do with an ugly and complicated quarrel between Jews and Samaritans, the history of which goes back over seven hundred years. While many elements fueled the fires of hatred between Jews and Samaritans, the original and most abiding element was racial. The Samaritans were Jews who intermingled and intermarried with their conquerors both in Samaria and Assyria. For the Jews in those early days, this was an unpardonable sin religiously and culturally.

The passage of time sharpened rather than diminished the hatred of Jews for Samaritans. The Gospel of John (4:9 RSV) notes that Jews "have no dealings with Samaritans." Luke 9:51-62 makes it clear that the Samaritans returned the ill feelings.

Samaria consisted of a strip of land that separated Galilee in the north and Judea in the south. Jews traveling from Galilee to Jerusalem in Judea seldom took the most direct route, which was through Samaria, and took about three days. They went east, crossed the Jordan River and traveled south, past Samaria, then turned west to Jerusalem. The trip took twice as long as the direct route, but in this way they avoided contact with the hated and unclean Samaritans.

In this passage Jesus leaves his homeland of Galilee and sets "his face to go to Jerusalem" (v. 51). This phrase denotes an unshakeable determination. Toward what have you "set your face" in life?

On this occasion Jesus chose not to follow the usual route of Jewish pilgrims on their way to Jerusalem, which would have avoided Samaria. Perhaps he wanted to teach his disciples a lesson. Jesus is not going to just lead the apostolic team through Samaria, he plans to spend the night there. He sent two messengers ahead to arrange hospitality for the night in a Samaritan village. Hospitality was refused because they were Jews on their way to Jerusalem.

When James and John, the sons of Thunder, heard the news of the rejection, they were obviously very upset. They asked Jesus if he would like for them to call down fire from heaven and destroy the inhospitable Samaritans. Jesus rebuked them for their violent proposal and they went on to another village. Some ancient authorities add an interesting comment from Jesus to James and John: "You do not know what spirit you are of, for the Son of Man has not come to destroy the lives of human beings but to save them."

The lesson is clear. Jesus will not allow traditional prejudices as an acceptable attitude by those into whose hands he will leave his kingdom. He simply says: "You have forgotten who you are and who I am. I did not come to destroy, but to save." And, they went on to another village. One cannot help wondering if the "other village" was also Samaritan.

In the very next chapter (Luke 10:29-37) Luke records how Jesus told a poignant parable which reinforced the lesson of tolerance he taught the disciples in chapter 9. Understanding the entrenched prejudice against Samaritans, we can see how shocking the parable of the good Samaritan must have been to the first hearers. Most Jews did not believe there was such a thing as a good Samaritan. When Jesus told a story in which a Samaritan was the hero and Jewish clergy were the villains, you may be sure he got their undivided attention even if he did not have their agreement. Jesus did not accept intolerance then, or now.

A Hebrew legend tells of a stranger coming to the door of Abraham's tent. Abraham invited him in for supper. When he broke bread, Abraham noticed that he did not offer a blessing for the meal and asked him why. The man said he gave no prayer because he did not believe in God. He worshiped the sun. Abraham kicked him out. Later that night the Lord came to Abraham and asked about the stranger. Abraham said: "Lord, he did not believe in you, so I threw him out." And God said to Abraham: "I have put up with that man and his ancestors for hundreds of years. Could you not tolerate him for an hour or two?" Do you know to what spirit you belong? (Thomas Lane Butts)

REFLECTIONS

JULY

Reflection Verse: *"The* LORD *God appointed a bush, and made it come up over Jonah, to give shade over his head, to save him from his discomfort; so Jonah was very happy about the bush."* *(Jonah 4:6)*

Jonah as a prophet is far different from any of the other Minor Prophets. Yahweh sends him to an alien people whom Jonah hates: the Assyrians of Nineveh. We all know the story. Jonah reluctantly preaches a five-word sermon (in Hebrew) and promptly an entire city repents. The narrative reads, "the people of Nineveh believed God; they proclaimed a fast, and everyone, great and small, put on sackcloth" (Jon. 3:5). All this occurred to the great dismay of Jonah. He prays directly to God, "O LORD! Is not this what I said while I was still in my own country? . . . I knew that you are a gracious God and merciful, slow to anger, and abounding in steadfast love, and ready to relent from punishing" (Jon. 4:2). And, of course, punishment is precisely what Jonah wanted to see.

We all can remember the deep agony surrounding the tragic events at Columbine High School in Littleton, Colorado, in 1999. This tragedy moved most Americans to think deeply about human injustice and God's sovereignty. As reported, police found a suicide note written by one of the teenage gunmen. The note blamed parents, teachers and "your children who have ridiculed me" for their bloody rampage that killed twelve students and one teacher and finally themselves. What can anyone say about tragic events like this?

For one thing, like Jonah, we all want justice! I have heard people say with unintended irony, "It's too bad these two disturbed young men committed suicide because they deserved the death penalty." It is the nature of human life that injustice always seems to rule the day. Perhaps the worst sphere of injustice is when humans inflict suffering on other innocent humans.

A deep hatred of how those in their school had treated these boys drove them to do what they did. It was irrational, no question about it, but given the elaborate preparations for the unthinkable, they believed that their course of action exacted justice. Reports suggest that schoolmates had humiliated and bullied them. No one bothered to deny this claim. Too bad no one had taught the architects of this crime how to forgive those who thoughtlessly pushed them over the edge. None of us, I hope, knows what it is to experience this intensity of fierce hate. Most of us want to think we are quick to forgive and quicker to forget. Forgiveness of perceived or actual injustices committed against us is the secret to cope with a world that dishes out injustice in healthy (or unhealthy) measure. It is this kind of hatred of the Assyrians that made Jonah a reluctant prophet.

George MacDonald once remarked, with great insight: "It may be infinitely worse not to forgive than to murder, because the latter may be an impulse of a moment of heat, whereas the former is a cold and deliberate choice of the heart." Have you ever been so angry or humiliated that you wanted revenge?

Several years ago I attended a retreat at a local church camp. In a room of thirty people, someone invited me to sit at a table that happened to include our bishop. I declined the seat because I had just driven two and a half hours. However, one of the individuals got up and offered me a chair. I still declined, but the person persisted. So I moved around the table and as I sat, this individual pulled out the chair from under me. I did not know this individual well, and I'm certain the person intended no harm. However, when I hit my head on the chair on my way to the floor, I wish I could say I had "the sweet love of Jesus burning in my heart." I admit something was burning, but it was not love. A room full of people nervously laughed, but I felt the sting of every snicker. I felt totally embarrassed. I cannot imagine what the two students from Columbine High School, Eric Harris and Dylan Klebold, must have felt after being humiliated day in and day out by a group of mean-spirited students. But at that camp I got a little taste of humiliation, and I did not like it; neither would you. Each one of us, from time to time, feels the power of "an anger that will not let us go." Jonah and his people had suffered under Assyrian domination for years. Now God asks him to preach a revival meeting in the nation's chief city?

As pastors we all face unjust situations in which it is inappropriate to fight back either physically or verbally, despite the temptation to exact justice. However, we do have an alternative. Jesus has given us a "love that will not let us go." We have a power to forgive the indignities we endure because Jesus gives us that power. We do not let go of anger because we are morally superior, but because God has given us a Savior who provides an alternative response to injustice. Rather than striking back, the Christian response is forgiveness. Jesus' command to forgive seems hopelessly idealistic until we realize that it is upon such an ideal that God constructs the realm of Heaven. We can never break the cycle of violence and retaliation until someone takes the first step toward reconciliation: forgiveness.

Forgiveness is not inborn to human beings. In fact, we can only accomplish forgiveness by the spiritual power God gives us in Christ. Our Apostles' Creed that states, "I believe in . . . the forgiveness of sins," reminds us of the price Jesus paid so that God might reconcile the world to himself. If we believe and practice Christ's forgiveness, then we too become children of God.

Jonah was happy when all went his way, especially when he possessed a nice bush for shade. However, when the worm destroys the bush and the hot wind blows, Jonah loses his will to live. Jonah's expectations for himself and his life were unrealistic. However, Jonah does get one thing right. God does care even for the enemy. As the Lord asks Jonah point blank, "Should I not be concerned about Nineveh, that great city, in which there are more than a hundred and twenty thousand persons who do not know their right hand from their left, and also many animals?" (Jon. 4:11).

In our work as pastors the model that Jonah plausibly offers us, however negative, may possibly be a good reminder about forgiving those difficult people we encounter. Is it not worth noting that these demanding and recalcitrant people are ones for whom Christ also died? (David Mosser)

JULY 4, 2004

Fifth Sunday After Pentecost

Worship Theme: Jesus tells his disciples that the kingdom of God has come near just as Paul writes that we shall reap as we have sown. God places a choice for or against the kingdom within the heart of all people.

Readings: 2 Kings 5:1-14; Galatians 6:(1-6) 7-16; Luke 10:1-11, 16-20

Call to Worship (Psalm 30:4-12 RSV)

Leader:	Sing praises to the LORD, O you his saints, and give thanks to his holy name.
People:	**For his anger is but for a moment, and his favor is for a lifetime. Weeping may tarry for the night, but joy comes with the morning.**
Leader:	As for me, I said in my prosperity, "I shall never be moved."
People:	**By thy favor, O LORD, thou hadst established me as a strong mountain; thou didst hide thy face, I was dismayed.**
Leader:	To thee, O LORD, I cried; and to the LORD I made supplication: "What profit is there in my death, if I go down to the Pit? Will the dust praise thee? Will it tell of thy faithfulness?
People:	**"Hear, O LORD, and be gracious to me! O LORD, be thou my helper!"**

Leader: Thou hast turned for me my mourning into danc-
             ing; thou hast loosed my sackcloth and girded me
             with gladness,

People: **That my soul may praise thee and not be
             silent.**

All: **O LORD my God, I will give thanks to thee
             forever.**

Pastoral Prayer:
O Lord our God, let us magnify your holy name. Let us sing
with joy our decision for your kingdom. Let us rejoice that we
have made a decision of faith with our lips and fulfilled it by our
lives. As we go on our daily way, give us the good judgment to follow your divine directive and live lives that proclaim Jesus
Christ's gospel with our thoughts, words, and deeds. Help us recognize other people's struggle with life's great questions. Remind
us that these persons often see the gospel in the seemingly small
and insignificant ways we relate to them. Give us the confidence
to reach out in a manner that lifts Christ up in all that we do.
Help us remember that Jesus is often our silent partner in the
relationships we foster. In our work and in our play, grant us that
inner peace that radiates Christ's spirit deep within us. Let Jesus
be our all in all as we engage people for whom each day is a
struggle for consequence. Let us offer Christ to them as the
authentic means to a fruitful life. In Jesus' name we pray. Amen.
(David Mosser)

SERMON BRIEFS

FILLING OUR VOIDS

2 KINGS 5:1-14

Do you ever pay attention to the commercials that interrupt
your favorite television show? It seems that more often than not
we tune out commercials. Either we get up from our seats for a

snack or a bathroom break, or we channel surf looking for a better option. When we actually do pay attention to the advertisements that invade our homes, we hear a simple yet clear message. We are told that we are not complete. We need to fill a void in our lives. If we simply buy the product or service offered, we can become whole and fulfilled people.

As we read 2 Kings, we encounter Naaman, an individual searching for wholeness in his life. To some surprise we observe that even the most honored people can feel there is a void in their lives. Such is the case for Naaman. He has received great military honors as the commander of the army of Aram. Naaman comes highly decorated for his accomplishments and his status as a mighty warrior. However, he struggles with his shortcomings. He struggles with his leprosy and likely, he wonders why such a terrible disease plagues him.

Despite his leprosy, the Bible casts Naaman in a positive light. He acknowledges that his success in life is due to the God of Israel. But how could a non-Israelite have such a faith in God? Does Naaman have any hope of conquering his disease? The servant of Naaman's wife, a captured Israelite girl, gives him hope. She speaks of a cure for leprosy if he will only travel to Israel and visit "with the prophet who is in Samaria" (v. 3). Naaman's own master, the king of Aram, sends him to the king of Israel with a large present to offer as payment for his healing. Unfortunately the king is not the right person for the job. He becomes frustrated and, perhaps, afraid with the request to heal Naaman.

Fortunately for Naaman, someone sends Naaman to Elisha. Knowing that he is visiting a prophet, Naaman likely expects Elisha to provide him with immediate attention. He is struck by the prophet's impersonal response. Elisha tells Naaman to bathe seven times in the Jordan. This action will cure his leprosy. Naaman may have understood Elisha only in terms of evoking a ritual cleansing, which he could have received at his home. The simplicity of this solution irritates Naaman. He is annoyed that Elisha did not come out to heal him in a spectacular way. Rather, Elisha instructed him to bathe in the dingy Jordan River. Naaman's servants had better sense than to reject the prophet's recommendation. They persuaded Naaman to heed Elisha's advice, and to his amazement, bathing in the Jordan cured his disease.

Only the God of Israel could have healed Naaman, making him whole again.

Naaman's arrogant attitude toward Elisha needed reform as much as his leprosy. Physical, emotional, and spiritual wounds can leave us with a void and a feeling of emptiness. These short-comings make us wish for wholeness, just as Naaman dreamed of being a complete person. How do you fill the voids in your life? Where does true healing come from? Are we to discover God and to find our healing in the dingy places of life? May we be willing to hear God's healing voice wherever God utters it. God may speak through an unnamed person, or God may call us to immerse ourselves into the filthy places of life. A response to God's voice relies on the hope of healing and the assurance of peace. Just as Naaman experienced wholeness in his life, we too can have our voids filled by trusting in God. (Mark White)

DOING WHAT IS RIGHT

GALATIANS 6:(1-6) 7-16

Paul lived his life in the shadow of the cross. To the Corinthi-ans, Paul writes, "For the message about the cross is foolishness to those who are perishing, but to us who are being saved it is the power of God" (1 Cor. 1:18). To the Galatians, Paul so identified with our Lord's death that he wrote, "I have been crucified with Christ; and it is no longer I who live, but it is Christ who lives in me" (Gal. 2:19-20).

For all the wrong done to him in word and deed by the Gala-tian Christians, Paul has the last word. It is a good word; no, an excellent word. Our text brings the cross of Christ into the con-versation in such profound ways that Paul simply cannot end this tough letter without calling the Galatians to what is right.

Sometimes it is difficult, indeed, seemingly impossible, for those of us who follow Jesus Christ to do the right thing. We are tempted to do the expedient thing, that is, whatever will solve what we believe is the problem, regardless of the cost in human resources or strained relationships. We are all guilty of what someone described as "placing the urgent above the necessary;"

to live in a "knee jerk" fashion, reacting in fear and confusion to what happens to us and around us rather than acting in compassion. We so much want to be right that we often fail to be loving.

So Paul calls the Galatian believers to do what is right in four profoundly personal ways. First, do what is right in the work of restoration. All of us have lived through moments in a Christian community when someone's behavior or attitude was far less than Christian. For all the good a church may do in its community, if a congregation fails to do the work of restoration and healing among its own members who morally or spiritually stumble and fall, then the church has failed.

Second, do what is right in terms of sowing and reaping. Evangelism is a good and healthy word that every church would be wise to incorporate into its vocabulary. If your community is like the one in which I live, crime, family stress and violence, economic upheaval, and racial distrust punctuate the morning newspaper. When we are tempted to withdraw into the imagined safety of the church, we must not "grow weary in doing what is right" (v. 9). To share the good news of Jesus Christ with "the least, the lost, the confused," is to sow the gospel where God has placed us, believing that in God's time, harvest will come.

Third, we are to do what is right in terms of reconciliation. Paul and the Galatian Christians were not on the best of terms. They were hostile to Paul. He was upset with their rejection of the gospel of grace. The relationship, at best, was strained. At the conclusion of this most difficult letter, Paul returns to the cross, holding up God's radical work of dying love as our example to follow. In a word, reconciliation always requires a crucifixion. Something inside of me must die—an attitude, a memory, a prejudice, a hurt, a "get even" strategy—so that God can reconcile a valued relationship that is now broken.

At the end of the day, "grace" has the last word. As Paul closes this sometimes caustic letter, Paul prays "the grace of our Lord Jesus Christ be with your spirit, brothers and sisters" (v. 18). Can you hear the profoundly magnanimous love that lays gently on the parchment as Paul watches the ink dry? Paul calls his Galatian "brothers and sisters" to do what is right. Whatever we do, may grace be the right and last thing. (Timothy Owings)

KINGDOM CLOSENESS

LUKE 10:1-11, 16-20

Imagine the beginning of a work day. This day the "to do" items are straightforward enough, but deadlines press and the buck stops with you. Knowing this, you get up, get dressed, and brush your teeth. You grab your bag and head out the door. You zip to work uneventfully, give a perfunctory wave to coworkers, find your desk and get to work. Work goes matter-of-factly. You take care of tasks at hand, stay levelheaded when glitches arise, and at the end of the day you go home. It has been a good day, rushed and busy, but you have worked well; you have been successful.

If not for two verses and an ending moral in the biblical text, this scene could be a modern rendering of our Scripture passage. Like our scenario, Jesus' instructions relate a sense of both urgency and responsibility in a matter-of-fact way. To the appointed seventy he speaks along these lines: The responsibility is yours. Act now. Don't dawdle in getting ready; don't stop along the way. Give only a basic greeting, then get to business. Forget about being a social butterfly or a social prude. Just cure the sick and tell them God's kingdom has come near. Don't fret over rejection; keep going. The seventy go out and are successful.

If our scene and the biblical one can play out in tandem, what makes the difference? What takes the ordinariness of our story and turns it into something holy? Certainly Jesus gives an important focus at the end of the biblical story. Jesus compels ancient and modern listeners alike to rejoice not in their own success but rather in what God has already done. The Gospels tell this message over and over; true joy is found in God's redemptive work, not in human accomplishment.

Moreover, verses 9 and 11 further intimate an emphasis needed to transform ordinary days into extraordinary experiences of grace. The key comes from knowing that God's kingdom has come near. The kingdom of God, Jesus Christ, God's presence incarnate has come near. Unless we live as though we can confine this ancient event to ancient times, we must admit that through the Spirit and our fellow humanity, made in God's image, we also encounter kingdom closeness.

We need to receive that message daily in our lives. Knowing that we will experience the presence of God in the everyday rhythm of living gives needed comfort to some. To others it alters the light in which they view the world around them. Such were the effects on Brother Lawrence of the Resurrection, a seventeenth-century monk who found that practicing the presence of God is not an activity relegated to church or devotions, but is inextricable from carrying out daily chores.

We deliver the message of kingdom closeness as well. Note that the ministry actions of the seventy are to cure the sick and then declare the nearness of the kingdom. The two go hand in hand; one action implies the other. The way in which the seventy treat the townspeople shows that God's kingdom has come near. Likewise, the nearness of the kingdom empowers those sent to care for people in a way beyond basic human concern. How we treat people is inseparable from what we communicate to them about God's kingdom.

Imagine our scene again. In the midst of this rushed but rhythmic day any number of ordinary occurrences bring us the message that heavenly grace is near. Let us listen. In the midst of this same day any number of ordinary encounters deliver a message. Let them speak of kingdom closeness. (Karen Hudson)

JULY 11, 2004

Sixth Sunday After Pentecost

Worship Theme: God measures God's people by God's plumb line. When believer's show mercy to the neighbor, then God measures them as the faithful people of God.

Readings: Amos 7:7-17; Colossians 1:1-14; Luke 10:25-37

Call to Worship (Psalm 82)

Leader: God has taken his place in the divine council; in the midst of the gods he holds judgment: "How long will you judge unjustly and show partiality to the wicked?

People: **"Give justice to the weak and the orphan; maintain the right of the lowly and the destitute.**

Leader: "Rescue the weak and the needy; deliver them from the hand of the wicked."

People: **They have neither knowledge nor understanding, they walk around in darkness; all the foundations of the earth are shaken.**

Leader: I say, "You are gods, children of the Most High, all of you; nevertheless, you shall die like mortals, and fall like any prince."

People: **Rise up, O God, judge the earth; for all the nations belong to you!**

Pastoral Prayer:

Great God of Righteousness, in the assembly we gather to hear your claim upon our lives as revealed in our Bible. Help us not only to hear your work but also to act justly toward others in the light of scripture's truth. To you, O God, we owe our very lives. Yet, you have placed each of us in the community of your creation to arbitrate mercy and justice as it is in our quarter. Help us look to others as our neighbors and give to them the love, mercy, and justice that we have already received from your gracious hand. Make us a people who have a holy zeal for the well being of other people. Give us the vision and discernment to reach out a helping hand in the love of Jesus. Let us be those of whom you will say at the end of our ministry, " 'Well done, good and trustworthy slave; you have been trustworthy in a few things, I will put you in charge of many things; enter into the joy of your master' " (Matt. 25:23). Give us good courage; in Jesus' name we pray. Amen. (David Mosser)

SERMON BRIEFS

TRUTH OR TREASON

AMOS 7:7-17

In our tradition, the heart of a Sunday's worship experience carries this liturgical heading: "Proclamation and Response." At the heart of this text we also find a representative example of "proclamation and response."

The lesson for today is the third of five visions of judgment that the prophet relates. This proclamation of God's impending judgment—or rather of God's not preventing judgment—leads Amos into a confrontation with Amaziah, priest of Bethel and member of Jereboam's court.

Importantly, and seemingly unlike many past and current would-be prophets, Amos does not rejoice as he announces God's punishment. In fact, so terrible are the first two of Amos's visions (locusts and fire, which may represent either natural or military calamities) that Amos pleads with God to spare Israel. God relents, answering Amos's prayers in each case.

With the third vision, however (that of the plumb line), Amos ceases praying. It is as if he surrenders to the truth God has

241

known all along: that Israel's real problems are not external but internal. The gravest dangers arise from within. In this vision, God reveals to Amos that Israel's foundations are "out of whack." In addition, Jeroboam's opulent kingdom is a house of cards, and the "high places" are towers about to fall.

Against the plumb line's truth (the Law? a Davidic King? the Messiah?), Amos sees clearly how shoddy is the northern kingdom's construction, how it violates building code, how crooked Israel really is. That Amaziah and Jeroboam cannot see it for themselves only proves that they are so crooked that the crooked looks straight.

The house Israel built on the sand of idolatry and injustice will fall of it's own dead weight. The slightest breeze of God's justice will topple it entirely. Amos proclaims that the judgment is surely coming. The young will die in the vain hope of defending the land; desperate and starving ladies will become prostitutes; foreign authorities will parcel out old home places, and the enemy will exile the few survivors.

Amos proclaims the truth, but the Palace responds that his message is treason. Amaziah, puppet priest of the idolatrous Jeroboam, easily attains authority to censure the prophet. He tells Jeroboam, "Amos has conspired against you . . . ; the land is not able to bear all his words" (v. 10). But Amos's only coconspirator is God, and if the land is not able to bear his words, it is because the land no longer has sufficient rootage. The beautiful topsoil has no hope against the flood of judgment, for the land has long since been cleared of righteousness and faithfulness.

Amaziah proclaims that if Amos can't say something nice about the king and his country, he should go somewhere else. Amos responds by saying that he must obey God more than either the king or any of the king's agents. Amos informs Amaziah that he did not seek the job, nor did he create the message. Rather, God summoned him from one familiar place to another, from one kind work to another. Amos not only proclaims the need to repent and please God, he also models repentance for Amaziah and Jeroboam, and indeed, for all of Israel. Perhaps the prophet is himself the plumb line and the standard by which Israel, along with its king and its priests, can change so that "the crooked can be made straight." (Thomas Steagald)

PREACHING TO THE SAINTS

COLOSSIANS 1:1-14

In seminary, one of my professors complained, "There are far too many 'shouldy' sermons and 'musty' preachers!" He challenged us to create sermons that called people to action in positive and life-giving ways. Surely, Paul (and perhaps his coauthor, Timothy) gives such an example in this letter to the Colossians. In Colossians, we see an example of some of the most inspirational letter writing offered in our New Testament. This is particularly noteworthy when we realize that within this positive, uplifting letter, Paul challenges the Colossae Christians to reject false teaching and purify their walk with Christ. Paul's method convinces the listeners that they are such amazing children of God that they will want to live as fully in the light of Christ as possible!

Today, we begin by giving thanks to God for the opportunity to preach to our wonderful congregations, rich in faith and good works and abounding in love and hope. I can honestly state that I have been blessed in every place I have preached to see examples of inspirational, godly leadership and fruitful, mature Christianity. The woman who spent countless hours caring for aging parents, adolescent daughters, and a busy husband still found time to teach me how to be a good Christian educator. She served as Sunday school superintendent, Bible school coordinator, and children's music director for "just one more year" as I got my feet wet in ministry, and much of what I know about being a pastor to children I learned from her in that year. The church council chairperson who helped his church survive turmoil and transition inspired me to give many more of my hours to that part-time, interim pastorate. His maturity as a Christian minister volunteering his time taught me to give more freely of my ministry. The woman who continued to pay her tithe to the church while she survived a painful bankruptcy proceeding following a medical crisis continues to inspire and inform my giving decisions above and beyond the tithe.

For these precious saints of God, we give thanks! For this reason, people of congregations past continue to be in our prayers over the years. As I remember their faithful living, I pray for the growth and wisdom that we all need as children of God. Even the most faithful person can be led astray. Paul inspires us to be strong, courageous, and consistent in following the teachings of God in Jesus Christ. For in doing so, we are living in God's light. How easily we might buy into the world's wisdom that would have us argue over whether the tithe comes before or after taxes, when God's wisdom challenges us to give the first ten percent back to God! How easily we slip into the false knowledge that obedience to God's commands earns our way into heaven, when Christ promises a place for us through the simple gift of grace! How easily we fall prey to superficial Christianity that claims Jesus was just a nice guy or was perfect because he wasn't human, when scriptures teach that Christ was fully human and fully divine, however confusing and complex that concept may be! In a world where many people offer answers, Paul reminds us that Christ's answer is the true guiding light. In a time when many of us would give up on ourselves as not good enough to expect more of our Christian maturity, Paul challenges us to grow always in the knowledge and love of God, bearing fruit in every good work. (Mary Scifres)

WHOSE NEIGHBOR ARE YOU?

LUKE 10:25-37

Maybe you have had an experience like Jesus had with this text's lawyer. It's not that we have a Messiah complex; it's just something of a regular occurrence in human communication. I experience it in receiving lines at weddings or waiting for my turn at the covered dish dinner. Someone will ask a question beginning, "Don't you think that . . . ?" It is obvious from the question that they are not really seeking information. Sometimes it feels like a test to see if I agree with them. At other times it seems they just want the opportunity to share some pent-up conviction they are dying to tell someone. Usually it is not a happy experience for either of us if I disagree.

The lawyer is using a familiar process that tells us a great deal about how he deals with people. First, he asks rhetorical questions. Instead of listening to Jesus, the lawyer is thinking about how to correct Jesus. The lawyer wants to fix Jesus' thinking.

The problem is that Jesus associates with the wrong kind of people at the wrong time. How can you help someone find eternal life if they are unwilling to change the way they live? A person first begins to obey the laws, and then, as they straighten out their life, they can be brought back into the company of good people. Then they can be well on the way to earning eternal life. This is the message that the lawyer attempts to communicate to Jesus. It is not that the lawyer worries about eternal life. He is trying to find out if he can trust this rabbi. The lawyer is confident as he responds to Jesus' inquiry about how someone achieves eternal life. He knows what we must do: love God with heart, soul, mind, and strength and your neighbor as yourself. Jesus replies, "Do this, and you will live." Notice that he did not say eternal life. God is available for us to love today. God's life of grace is present now.

Hoping to get back on track, the lawyer once again steers the conversation. Here again we learn something about the lawyer. He does not ask questions about how we love God, rather he asks about the neighbor. Is this an indication that he has not made a connection with his loving God and its implications for his relationships? Jesus is not teaching about the kingdom of God as discussion or as doctrine. Living in God's grace is about relationships. So Jesus tells a story. The story tells us the truth about who we are. If we truly love God we become a neighbor to those in need. One follows the other as naturally as one breath follows another.

C. S. Lewis wrote that there are two important days in our lives. The day we are born and the day we discover why. Life takes on an eternal significance when we realize the two commandments create kinship with God's children. To love God and each other as we love ourselves provides a divine reason for our birth.

Loving in this way creates a life for which doors into the future continue to open for us. (Bob Holloway)

JULY 18, 2004

Seventh Sunday After Pentecost

Worship Theme: An element in the task of God's people is to listen to God's revelation in scripture, especially in Jesus' words. When disciples need spiritual refreshing we seek this refreshment in the Word of the Lord.

Readings: Amos 8:1-12; Colossians 1:15-28; Luke 10:38-42

Call to Worship (Psalm 52:1-3, 6-9)

> *Leader:* Why do you boast, O mighty one, of mischief done against the godly? All day long you are plotting destruction. Your tongue is like a sharp razor, you worker of treachery. You love evil more than good, and lying more than speaking the truth.
>
> *People:* **The righteous will see, and fear, and will laugh at the evildoer, saying,**
>
> *Leader:* "See the one who would not take refuge in God, but trusted in abundant riches, and sought refuge in wealth!"
>
> *People:* **But I am like a green olive tree in the house of God.**
>
> *Leader:* I trust in the steadfast love of God forever and ever. I will thank you forever, because of what you have done.
>
> *People:* **In the presence of the faithful I will proclaim your name, for it is good.**

Pastoral Prayer:

To you, O God, we pray for Sabbath rest and Sabbath remembrance. On the Sabbath we remake our lives in you and your holiness. We rest from our weekly toil and take time to renew our relationship with family and friends. On the Sabbath we also restore our vows to you, O Lord of the Universe. In our daily lives it is too easy to forget that you indeed are the center of our life and world. Our jobs and many sundry activities hinder our focused relationship to you. Yet around you, O God, our authentic life and its purpose revolves. On the Sabbath we recount the many blessings that you confer on us. On the Sabbath we also recollect your historic relations with your people. Help us, as we read the accounts of your activities in human history, to remember that you have always been the God for your people. Take us out of bondage as you saved Israel and make us again your steadfast people. In Jesus' holy and righteous name we pray. Amen. (David Mosser)

SERMON BRIEFS

MIRROR AND FAIR WARNING

AMOS 8:1-12

The season after Pentecost is sometimes called "ordinary time." The term does not mean "unexciting," but still, there is nothing extraordinary, like a birth or a death or a resurrection going on right now. We need to pay attention, however, and especially because the lesson is from the prophets.

Barbara Brown Taylor, musing on the power of the Bible in her life, writes, "I cannot think of any other text that has such authority over me, interpreting me faster than I can interpret it. It speaks to me not with the stuffy voice of some mummified sage but with the fresh, lively tones of someone who knows what happened to me an hour ago" (*The Preaching Life*, Cambridge: Cowley Publications, 1993, p. 52).

It can be unsettling (as well as comforting) that the Bible knows us so well as to reveal our folly and sin in stories and sermons that are both ancient and as current as, well, an hour ago. Or an hour from now: "When will church be over so that we can get back to the game, the house, the store, the shop, the office, back to what really matters?" (Amos 8:5*b*, my paraphrase).

Part of the extraordinary power of Amos's lesson, however, resides in the fact that it is aimed precisely at the "ways and means" of ordinary life—in Israel then, and here now. It is both mirror and fair warning, a warning Israel did not heed.

I am thinking of a wedding reception. The tables are fairly laden with all sorts of delights for the eye and tongue. Especially beautiful is the platter piled high with strawberries half the size of my fist and so shiny and red that they must be wax. But they aren't. Would that they were. I have bitten into wax fruit before, and that would be preferable to this. I pick up the biggest, reddest strawberry. Can you see this coming? It is putrid. I can only imagine the look on my face as I try neither to chew nor taste till I find a trash can.

How does Amos look as he tastes this fourth vision of judgment on the house of Israel? The fruit looks good, but it's rotten. Jeroboam's reign appears peaceful, but war looms. The country appears prosperous, but Israel is deep in greed and disparity and injustice. It is precisely because of the lack of justice and compassion that judgment, the end, is coming.

Earlier, Amos's vision revealed the corruption of king and altar. Here Amos reveals the corruption of society at large. He has already targeted the cruelty and avarice of the wealthy, who buy "the poor for silver and the needy for a pair of sandals" (v. 6). Here Amos aims again at those who "trample on the needy" and bring the poor to ruin.

Of particular interest is 8:6, reminiscent of slavery. Once they were slaves, these Israelites, in Egypt. There they saw that the judgment of God comes as surely as the inundation of the Nile. God freed them from their oppressors at the Red Sea. Now the Israelites have become oppressors—and even more heinously, of their own people! Amos proclaims they will get their Deuteronomic desserts in the desert. And should they inquire as to what happened or why, there will be no further word from God, no manna in the next wilderness. Only this word from Amos, and extraordinarily, for them and for us, in this ordinary time. (Thomas Steagald)

FINDING HOPE IN THE POWER OF GOD

COLOSSIANS 1:15-28

As I read this ancient hymn, I feel a connection with those ancient Christians. Together, we sing of the awesome God who is before creation and rules over creation, we praise Christ who is God's own image and fullness brought to earth, and we worship this same Christ who brings us into reconciliation to God so that we might be pure before God's holiness.

And yet, Paul didn't reference this hymn simply to sing praise to God. Paul did so to remind us of what it means to proclaim faith in Christ Jesus. The culture exposed the Colossians to many versions of religion and many types of gods. Although few of us today think of Zeus as the almighty God, we might find ourselves worshiping our country during times of national crisis. "God bless America. Make us strong, safe, and prosperous." Although many of us laugh at astrology charts, we might not laugh when we admit the times we blamed our bad behavior on our astrological sign. "Oh, I'm just kind of moody because I'm a Cancer." We might complain about religious books that claim to show how to manipulate God's created world, until we recall the times we prayed for our will to be done instead of God's. "Please, dear Lord, I really want my child to go to college. Can't you just talk to her?" Our situations today are still precariously balanced between our belief in Christ and our life in a world that assumes humans are in control.

In a church that too often sounds like an institution of rules and regulations, we overlook the similarity between our modern church that sets itself up as the gatekeeper to God and the ancient church that was just learning that grace is the only gatekeeper to God. We drift off for a Sunday morning nap when the preacher starts teaching about Christ dying for our sins. "Sure, I know the Easter message," we think. But on Monday morning, we're haunted by our angry words to the family during a harried breakfast. On Wednesday, we're complaining about those "hypocrite" church leaders who behave badly. By Friday, we're feeling guilt-ridden by our profit-driven week in the workplace and our selfish spending, and we can't wait to get to church again on Sunday so we can "feel better" about ourselves. Most of us live lives that fall short of the glory of God, but we look to other people to behave better than we do. We are precariously balanced between our belief in God's grace and our life in a world that assumes humans are responsible for what happens both now and after death.

Paul's words interrupt that precarious balance, singing of Christ's authority over "all thing in heaven and on earth . . . whether thrones or dominions or rulers or powers" (v. 16). Christ's promises shift that uncomfortable balance, offering "to reconcile to [God] all things, whether on earth or in heaven, by making peace through the blood of his cross" (v. 20). God brings us, who feel unconnected to God, near through the gracious gift of Christ. God establishes us, overwhelmed by the world's control, securely in divine power. This promise is ours as we "continue—steadfast in the faith" (v. 23). The balance is precarious, and our connection is broken if we lose the hope that is promised through Christ. So, we preach and teach, worship and study, pray and commune, all with the prayer "that we may present everyone mature in Christ" (v. 28). With this prayer, we find the hope to connect with God and worship Christ. (Mary Scifres)

THE MARY/MARTHA DILEMMA

LUKE 10:38-42

Edwin Friedman was a rabbi who devoted his life to helping people understand the sources of anxiety and the problems anxiety can cause us. There are two kinds of anxiety: chronic and situational.

We can be temporarily anxious over a test, a job interview, an event for which we are preparing. Once we take the test, complete the interview, or finish the event, we forget about these moments and move on. Chronic anxiety is like a low-grade fever that stays with us. It has to do with our fears about our life, our competence, and the value of our lives to others. It can be so pervasive that it disables and distorts our perception of who we really are and what we are capable of doing.

One classic symptom of anxiety is the need to diagnose others. This is what Martha does as we encounter her with Jesus and Mary. Martha begins to notice that Mary is not doing her fair share. Martha complains to Jesus. See how hard I am working? Doesn't anybody care about what is happening to me? The problem, according to Martha, is that Mary is not fulfilling the requirements demanded by the situation. Martha's complaint is one that nearly anyone in her day would make. It was not proper for a woman to sit at the feet of a rabbi. It was scandalous. It was not Mary's place. If Jesus were a proper rabbi he would know it was a waste of time to teach a woman.

This happens a lot in our day. It is easy to diagnose the problems. We know what people should and should not do. Listen to the talk shows. Everybody knows exactly what politicians, football coaches, athletes, community leaders, and other public figures should and should not do. If schools had better teachers we would not have all of these problems in our society. If our members were more dedicated we would be a better church. When we are anxious, problems are always the result of what someone else is doing or not doing. We know exactly what they ought to do. We are anxious, and it is just easier to focus on someone else.

We can learn from Jesus' response. Jesus says, "Martha, Mary knows what it is time for her to be doing now" (my paraphrase).

It is reminiscent of an incident we find in John's Gospel. At the very end of John, Peter receives a commission from Jesus to feed the sheep. Peter, perhaps feeling a little overwhelmed by the opportunity Jesus gives him, asks about another disciple. "What about him?" Jesus asks a pointed question. "What is that to you?"

Jesus is not trying to elevate action over reflection, doing over being, or working over learning. He is trying to teach us that there is a time for everything. Jesus asks us if we know what time it is for us? Where should we be focusing our time, our energy, and our interest? Jesus helps us to discover that the more critical we are of what others are doing the more likely it is that we are without a clue about what we should be doing. The more certain we are about how others should be changing the more uncertain we may be about our capacity to change. The more critical we are of the performance of others the more likely it is that we are afraid of taking risks and not succeeding.

Within Jesus' words to Martha is a question that we can all answer. What time is it for me? What is God calling me to be or do today? (Bob Holloway)

JULY 25, 2004

Eighth Sunday After Pentecost

Worship Theme: One of the great symbols of our faith is that in baptism we are buried with Jesus. Likewise, if we are buried with Jesus, then we are raised with him too. The Christian faith is all about new life in Christ.

Readings: Hosea 1:2-10; Colossians 2:6-15 (16-19); Luke 11:1-13

Call to Worship (Psalm 85:1-2, 6-11)

> *Leader:* LORD, you were favorable to your land; you restored the fortunes of Jacob.
>
> *People:* **You forgave the iniquity of your people; you pardoned all their sin.**
>
> *Leader:* Will you not revive us again, so that your people may rejoice in you?
>
> *People:* **Show us your steadfast love, O LORD, and grant us your salvation.**
>
> *Leader:* Let me hear what God the LORD will speak, for he will speak peace to his people, to his faithful, to those who turn to him in their hearts.
>
> *People:* **Surely his salvation is at hand for those who fear him, that his glory may dwell in our land.**
>
> *All:* **Steadfast love and faithfulness will meet; righteousness and peace will kiss each other. Faithfulness will spring up from the ground, and righteousness will look down from the sky.**

Pastoral Prayer:

Compassionate God of Truth and Light, we come together as your people again to hear the old, old story. It is a sacred story that reveals to us who we are and more especially, whose we are. Allow us to see ourselves as your people in the light of scripture. Let us read into the biblical characters the same motives and desires that we ourselves possess. Endow us the capacity to translate ancient words into contemporary faithfulness. Remind us that although the words in our Bible may be antiquated to some moderns, it is the truth contained therein that makes our days worth living. As we pray to you, O Lord of Life, help us also move closer to our sisters and brothers in the faith. Remind us that Christ died even for those who profess your holy name with doctrines foreign to our understanding and experience. Unite our hearts and minds in a universal quest for godly truth that will set us free from the bondage of differences that divide the body of Christ. In the name of Jesus we pray. Amen. (David Mosser)

SERMON BRIEFS

A LOVE THAT WILL NOT LET US GO

HOSEA 1:2-10

I like to collect comic strips. One has a minister coming out of the church one Sunday morning after worship. His wife is waiting for him. She has her tongue stuck out at him. He responds, "I guess I don't have to ask you what you thought of my sermon today?"

I must admit this has happened to me more than once, not so much because the sermon was so bad but because I used an illustration in it from our marriage relationship without first asking permission. I am learning on this aspect.

The truth be told, however, most of us preachers and teachers often draw upon that which is nearest to us to help us relate to and talk about God. Even Jesus used the image of "Father" in speaking of God. I really did not fully appreciate John 3:16, which speaks of God giving up the only begotten Son because of God's love for us, until I had a son of my own.

The prophets were the same way. They drew upon their own everyday lives to help them share God's message. Hosea is a perfect example. In his own troubled marriage with a woman named Gomer, he found a profound lesson about the faithfulness and love of God.

Hosea married Gomer. Whether she was already a prostitute in Baalism or went to be one after they married is not clear. It would seem from this passage that she was already one and that God commanded Hosea to take her for his wife. In other words, he married her already knowing what kind of woman she was—a woman who at best would not be faithful to him and at worst was deeply involved in the worship of other gods in the most intimate of ways. While she had a number of children, the implication is that it's not certain that any of them are the children of Hosea!

The point is that God's relationship with the people parallels that of the relationship of Hosea with Gomer. In his own marriage and family, Hosea sees what happens for the whole nation. Just as Gomer proved unfaithful to Hosea, the people proved unfaithful to God. They were having children and rearing those children, not as the children of God, but as the children of Baal! In the names of Hosea's children—Jezreel, Lo-ruhamah, Lo-ammi, we see God's impending judgment on the people. The people had broken the first two commandments. Those commandments talk of God being a "jealous God," a God who tolerates no rivals or second place. Hosea saw judgment ahead for his unfaithful people.

But this is hardly the end of the story. In chapter 2 Hosea sends the children to plead with their mother to cease her unfaithfulness, to return to them. Hosea does something incredible (see chapter 3). Apparently Gomer has left him, or he cast her out (as God was threatening to do with Israel). But Hosea buys her back, brings her back, forgives her, restores her. Hosea's love is a forgiving, long-suffering love, but God's love is even more so. God wishes to restore the covenant with the people just as Hosea wanted to restore his marriage covenant. Despite all that the people had done, despite all of the pain they had caused God, God sent the prophets like Hosea to beg them to see the error of their ways and return to God. God was ready and willing to forgive them and receive them back, just as Hosea was with Gomer.

Can we imagine such love? Such forgiveness? Think about how very deeply someone you love can hurt you. Who has not been hurt deeply by a loved one, and who hasn't caused some pain? But imagine being unfaithful, repeatedly, but still being wooed and loved back. Such is the love of God for us! (Bass Mitchell)

GROWING IN GOD'S GARDEN

COLOSSIANS 2:6-15 (16-19)

It's that time of year again, when squash takes over the garden. I will soon run out of ideas for all of the zucchinis in my kitchen. There are only so many loaves of bread my family will eat! Even so, I am amazed every summer by the strength and fertility of squash. If only we Christians could be such amazing results in God's garden!

That is the challenge offered in this reading from Colossians. God calls us, those of us who have been planted in God's garden as Christians, to live in Christ. We Christians live in the garden of life, planted by God, rooted in Christ. How often do we remember that our roots are in Christ? When we talk of roots, do we talk of family trees and ancestors, hometowns and teachers, or do we remember that our taproot is Christ?

Christ is not only our root but also our fertilizer and our garden stake. We are built up in Christ. As we come to know Christ more fully, living in God's light and trusting in the Spirit's guidance, we grow stronger and healthier. We are nourished and guided by Christ, held together by this strong root, connected through God's love at every twist and turn. As we grow in Christ, we become strong, established members of God's garden. No longer fragile flowers, we grow into tall firs or strong oak trees.

This sounds beautiful, but gardeners know that it's far from simple to grow strong, healthy plants. Soils are not always conducive to growth. Some plants don't react well to fertilizer. Flowers are picked, leaving roots behind to whither and die. Weeds and insects threaten the health of plants.

Likewise, growing in Christ is no easy task. We accept Christ, but find it hard to grow if we live among people who don't support our faith. We don't like the challenging lessons that Christ offers as we mature, even those that would make us stronger and healthier members of Christ's body. In some churches, we don't hear God's word as it is offered, but we are afraid to look elsewhere for nourishment. We hear Christ's call, blooming with enthusiasm, only to have someone else negate what we have heard and discourage us from growing in new directions. We offer our ministry without regard for our own nurture, and find others nibbling away at our healthy Christian lives, leaving us tired and weak after a season of faithful discipleship.

Growth is seldom easy. But we can grow in Christ by dying to all that would destroy that faith. When we give up the relationships that hinder our faith, we are free to build relationships that are life-giving and nurturing to our Christian growth. When we abandon the fears that prevent us from learning new lessons and growing in new directions, we become fearless followers of Christ. When we ignore negative attitudes that prevent us from following God's call, those attitudes die on the vine, and we are free to grow stronger as God's children. When we let die the attitude of giving so tirelessly that it kills us, we find new energy for lives of fulfilling ministry.

All of this growth happens because Christ is our root, our nourishment, and our purpose. When we let not only our sins die but also our self-centered worldview that thinks we have to make the growth happen, then we can be raised to new life in Christ. Then we can become the fruitful garden of God, the body that is Christ's church. (Mary Scifres)

NEVER TOO LATE TO LEARN

LUKE 11:1-13

Praying is not easy for us sometimes. We can feel guilty for not having the time. We may feel inadequate because we feel we do not know the right words to pray. We can become discouraged because of the distractions we experience when we try to pray. We may be confused because we are not quite sure how our prayers have any influence with God. Prayer raises all kinds of issues about God. Does God already know what we need? If God does know, why pray? Can we change the course of events by asking God's help? If that is true, why do really important requests not get answered?

We learn something very important from this passage in Luke about these issues simply because they are not addressed. Apparently the disciples know how important prayer is to Jesus, and they ask him to teach them. By handling prayer in this way, we are not invited to pray because of results we might get. We are not invited to pray because we understand how it fits into a neat theological understanding of how God works. In setting this scene in this way we are invited to pray because it was an integral part of Jesus' life and relationship with God. We can trust that we will learn what we need as we walk along the path of prayer.

The Lord's Prayer gives us a way of praying when we do not know what to say. It is a prayer that can focus our minds and hearts in time of stress. It opens our consciousness to the presence of Christ.

The Lord's Prayer also can reveal a pattern for us to use in our daily prayers. It can provide a structure that moves us beyond a time spent strictly on what we can think of to request. This is important because prayer creates a space where our deepest needs, fears, and challenges can emerge. If we stop there and do not allow ourselves the chance to listen we short-circuit the possibilities of a healing and empowering process.

The Lord's Prayer calls us to begin our prayers with adoration. We are called to declare what we know about who God is for us. We are moved to remember that our life is a gift and that the will that moves life forward is not our will but the will of God. As we live within that will God invites us to pray for our daily bread. God invites us to ask for that which we need to be God's person.

The scene shifts from our life with God and moves to our life with others. Jesus quickly moves us to the place where our relationship with God impacts our life in the world. Our prayers need to be moments when issues of forgiveness, confession, and repentance allow God to help us to resist and move past the times of trial.

Our prayer is set in the context of trust in the faithfulness and love of God. Jesus' promise of the Holy Spirit is the promise that becomes a launching pad for advancing our lives as witnesses and disciples. (Bob Holloway)

REFLECTIONS

AUGUST

Reflection Verse: *"The great day of the LORD is near,*
   near and hastening fast;
the sound of the day of the LORD is bitter,
   the warrior cries aloud there." (Zephaniah 1:14)

Joan Rivers used to begin part of her comic monologue with the question: "Can we talk?" As we read our reflection verse, I can only imagine my well-meaning pastoral colleagues asking something like Joan's question knowing that I was going to address a text such as this. This is because we can probably divide the Protestant world into two distinct groups. One group specializes in a steady diet of apocalyptic texts, while the other group avoids these sorts of texts with a steady ardor. Many readers of books like *The Abingdon Preaching Annual* are apt to lean toward the second option. Occasionally, however, difficult texts edify us.

From time to time we all hear some solicitous individual say that the content of one's belief doesn't matter as long as he or she is sincere. Too bad this is patently untrue. Almost three years ago terrorists flew airliners into the World Trade Center towers and the Pentagon. That day remains etched into our collective consciousness and changed the way that most Americans view life. Perhaps it even puts to rest the platitude, "It does not matter what one believes as long as they are sincere in that belief." What we think and believe does matter, and for this reason, theology is important. Theology, that is, how we think and talk about God, is of the utmost significance. For Christians, there is no human way to take too lightly what we believe about God. In fact, from the soil of our belief and understanding of God grows the harvest of our engagement with life and other people. We act on our beliefs, whatever they may be.

Perhaps none of us enjoys dangling congregations over the "fires of torment" for the desired outcome of simply "getting their attention." Levelheaded people understand that life throws enough heartache and tragedy our way to keep most of us in a constant state of attention. Therefore, it is ironic that when the prophets want to seize people's attention, they resort to reminding believers about God's wrath and power. The irony inheres in that people's violence to one another on earth provokes divine wrath in heaven. Does it not seem similar to the instance in which a parent threatens to spank children who hit one another?

Why is it that even God's prophets, like Zephaniah for example, resort to such "rough talk" to motivate people back toward the faith? Could it be that with every persuasive tactic being ineffective, with all the prophetic guilt laying, wheedling, cajoling, coaxing, and begging, the prophets sensed that they were running short on time? I suspect there may be something to this supposition. After all, Zephaniah prophesies, "The great day of the LORD is near, / near and hastening fast." Perhaps Zephaniah knew no other way to wake his people from their faithless slumber. THE DAY OF THE LORD IS NEAR—wake up! When governments become corrupt while a nation's religious institutions sit in silence, then those trusted to protect the poor instead allow violence against those who cannot exercise self-protection. Like Amos, Zephaniah decries the violence done to the weak because violence heaps more hardship on an already oppressed poor. Maybe Zephaniah can think of no other way to bring his people back to their theological senses than to pronounce judgment against the nation.

Governments and the religious establishment are too often in collusion when violence against the poor occurs. Whether Nazi Germany or a local community, when the church does not speak for justice, people suffer. Jesus himself was a victim of violence and deception that even today no one can fully explain. Who killed Jesus? Was it the religious authorities? The Jews? The tradition of the elders? The Romans? A band of zealots led by one of Jesus' own disciples, Judas? Or was it something else? Perhaps fire-breathing prophecy was all that Zephaniah felt he had in his arsenal.

One of my church members several decades ago asked me to

attend her brother's funeral. She needed support because, as she said, "This church does not believe as I believe." We arrived at a little country church and met the pastor, a self-professed "firebrand preacher." Formerly a plumber, he felt God's call as a tent maker late in life. After a few correspondence courses, he developed an uncompromising apocalyptic perspective, alternating his sermon texts (almost exclusively) from Joel, Ezekiel, Mark 13, Daniel, and, naturally, Revelation. The angrier he got while preaching the closer to God's Holy Word he thought he stood. Needless to say, I did not anticipate a pleasant afternoon. The two-and-a-half-hour funeral proved me correct.

The plumber/preacher yelled, screamed, shouted, cried, and generally took everyone to task that hot, summer afternoon, with the deceased laid out in front of the pulpit. We could feel Hell's flames licking up around us. The preacher shrieked that it was too late for Joe, who could only make it to heaven if God made an unusual exception in his case. However, the preacher reminded us loudly that it was not too late for us. We all needed to repent, live "by the book," and get right with God—now!

Afterward I was thoroughly rung out. I never wanted to get caught in that situation again. I have never responded to blatant guilt laying, wheedling, cajoling, coaxing, or begging. I hated every moment of that miserable afternoon while he assailed my every theological principle.

My older church member's comments after the service surprised me as we drove home. She said, "I guess you now know why I wanted you to go with me." I replied that I certainly did.

Then she remarked, "I disliked everything that preacher said, and more than that, I really despised the way he said it. But you know, I can't honestly say that he said anything that wasn't true. He was right about my brother and, I guess, there were many people there this afternoon who needed a good dose of God's own truth."

I was not bold enough to share with her how I am drawn to a God who loves his creation to the extent that God graciously sent Jesus to save us. But now as I think back on that day, perhaps that preacher had lived long enough to see that people without God are indeed a hopeless people. Maybe he, like Zephaniah so long ago, realized that some people don't "get it" unless you hammer them with the Word of God. My faith tells me that there must be another way. But, some of the folks I care about may get to the point that the fire of God may be the only thing that will get their attention.

Fortunately, in the very next chapter of Zephaniah, the prophet cracks the door of hope ajar, if only a bit, when he visualizes a faithful response to the day of the Lord. Zephaniah counsels,

> Seek the LORD, all you humble of the land,
>   who do his commands;
> seek righteousness, seek humility;
>   perhaps you may be hidden
>   on the day of the LORD's wrath. (Zeph. 2:3)

I know that I definitely hope so. Amen. (David Mosser)

AUGUST 1, 2004

Ninth Sunday After Pentecost

Worship Theme: God loves us so much that we are called as God's daughters and sons. As the children of God, Jesus appeals for us to treat one another with the respect and honor by which we expect others to treat us. Greed has no place in God's family.

Readings: Hosea 11:1-11; Colossians 3:1-11; Luke 12:13-21

Call to Worship (Psalm 107:1-9, 43)

Leader: O give thanks to the LORD, for he is good; for his steadfast love endures forever.

People: **Let the redeemed of the LORD say so, whom he has redeemed from trouble and gathered in from the lands, from the east and from the west, from the north and from the south.**

Leader: Some wandered in desert wastes, finding no way to a city to dwell in; hungry and thirsty, their soul fainted within them.

People: **Then they cried to the LORD in their trouble, and he delivered them from their distress; he led them by a straight way, till they reached a city to dwell in.**

Leader: Let them thank the LORD for his steadfast love, for his wonderful works to the sons of men! For he satisfies him who is thirsty, and the hungry he fills with good things.

People: **Whoever is wise, let him give heed to these things; let men consider the steadfast love of the LORD.**

Pastoral Prayer:

O Heavenly Parent of us all, guide us in the paths of righteousness for the sake and in the name of Jesus. We are a wayward people, O God, following too often the dictates and desires of our own hearts. Let us acknowledge our lives before you. Help remold and refashion our lives so they conform more perfectly to your Son, Jesus Christ, who came to give us life in abundance. Jesus taught us what it means to be fully present to others. Assist us to not only listen to the stories of other people but also, in fact, hear them. Let us move from our zones of comfort and assume the risks that characterized those who spread the good news from Jerusalem, to Judea and Samaria, and indeed to the ends of the earth. Provide for us the vision that makes the created order of Eden the perfect garden that beckons us toward our unknown futures. Nonetheless, as we move into this unknown region, assure us that you are with us. We pray this in the sanctified name of Jesus Christ, our Messiah and Lord. Amen. (David Mosser)

SERMON BRIEFS

LIKE A LOVING PARENT

HOSEA 11:1-11

The prophet Hosea compares the relationship between God and Israel to that of a husband (God) and wife (the people). In today's reading, we see that Hosea changes from one family analogy to another—to God being like a loving parent and Israel a wayward child.

The reference in the first verse is to the slavery of the people in Egypt. There they were no people at all. They were chattel. But God called them, which means to summon and name them. God gave them birth as a people and then adopted them as God's own child. Why? Simply because God loved them, not because they were powerful, great, or had wonderful achievements.

Verse 2 provides an image any parent can understand: that of calling after a child, and the more you call, the faster the child runs from you. I saw that one day in a grocery store parking lot. A mother had her arms full and the child started to run. But the more she called after her daughter, the farther the girl ran. Likewise, Israel, although God repeatedly called, had run in the opposite direction, to false gods.

However, it was not Baal who had given them birth, who had picked them up and healed them when they fell, who had lovingly provided their food and all their needs. What ungrateful offspring! They would give to false gods the thanks and credit and even the love that really only belonged to their true Parent—to God! The image here is a tender one of a God who loves them even more than a parent, but whose love they take for granted and even scorn. Surely there are few things more hurtful or disappointing to parents than this.

One cannot read this passage without also thinking about the story of the prodigal son or better, the "loving father." In it the son shows no gratitude at all for all that his father has done for him. But his father just kept right on loving him.

Despite God's long-suffering, Israel kept running away right into danger again. Just as they had been in captivity in Egypt so long ago, now they would return to captivity, perpetrated by the Assyrians. There was nothing God would or could do about it. God loved them. God, like a parent, lets them have freedom to choose for themselves.

In Israel's trouble, they will call upon Baal, but Baal will not be able to lift them up. Baal does not care for them. No one cares for them like their Parent does. But it takes a lot of suffering before they realize this. However, verse 7, problematic to interpret from the Hebrew, might mean that they would call upon God but too late. God would not then lift them up. God would not keep them from the results of their rebellion.

But, as we often see in Hosea, there is quickly a change of tone and emotion. God is truly torn between God's love for them and God needing to let them reap the results of their decisions. They deserved what was going to happen to them. Even the law states that parents can bring disobedient children before the authority and that these children could be stoned to death (see Deut.

21:18-21). God, however, could not contemplate such a thing! Why? Because God loved them. God could not give them up.

I have two children. I cannot imagine them ever doing anything that would stop me from loving them. I do not like all the things they do or approve of all the choices they make. But I will always love them. I could not stop loving them even if I tried. If that is true for us, how much more so must God love us! (Bass Mitchell)

WEARING THE NEW CLOTH OF CHRIST

COLOSSIANS 3:1-11

How many of you are secret keepers of clothing with holes in them? Jeans that are far too faded and tattered to wear in public? What about that favorite pair of pants that really doesn't fit now that you've gained a few extra pounds? Or the miniskirt that doesn't really fit with your role as a mature professional and wonderful mother? Most of us have a few clothes in our closet that don't really fit anymore. Most of us have some behaviors or attitudes that don't really fit our Christian life either. When I'm clothed in tattered jeans, it's difficult to imagine myself in a fine French restaurant. Quite frankly, I don't do my most creative thinking when I wear a miniskirt. And if I'm sitting uncomfortably in a pair of pants that fit better 10 pounds ago, I'm not all that enthusiastic about jumping on a bicycle for a ride that would improve my health. In the same way, when we focus our minds on the things of this earth that are tattered and torn, we can miss the beauty of God's realm all around us. When we try to hold on to the parts of our lives that no longer fit, we have trouble moving forward into new opportunities and better behaviors. When we hang on to ideas and patterns that we could long ago have outgrown, we hold ourselves back from becoming the mature people that the next stage of life can bring.

But as Christians, we are given a new opportunity and a new challenge. Even death could not harness our God, for God's love and power raised Christ from the dead. Surely, we need not be held back by the things of this world that would keep us from knowing and loving Christ more fully! "Set your minds on things that are above," for in doing so you will find that you are above much of the muck that would keep your feet and your lives stuck in places you don't want to be. "Seek the things that are above," and you will find that God's love surrounds you. Clothe "yourselves with the new self," your new life in Christ, and you will find the old chains rusting and falling away, giving you the freedom to become the very person that God sees in you when God calls you the body of Christ. We are that body, right here and right now. No distinctions between which of us wears holey clothes and which of us wears a miniskirt, no difference between which of us was born and raised Christian and which of us is just beginning to explore the Christian walk. Here, we are one. Here, we are all God's children. Here, God makes us in the image of God. Here, God calls us to reject the old life that would pull us down into sin and sorrow. God calls us to arise in order to live the new life that is ours in Christ Jesus. (Mary Scifres)

DEAD WRONG!

LUKE 12:13-21

It was his car. He had made all the payments. He was grateful that he had finally paid it off and was in the second year of feeling the freedom from a monthly payment. Since he had moved to a new state he was beginning the process of registering the car for license plates. He could not find the title. He called the state office to explain his dilemma. He was politely told to get a copy of it from the courthouse of his former hometown. In the process he made an interesting discovery: He had to prove he was the owner.

Something about that discovery made the owner angry. He had made the payments for the 60-month period. He had kept it running, tending it carefully so that it would last. It was his car! But if some sort of glitch in a computer system kept him from getting a copy of the title, he could not prove he was the owner, and he could not drive it. There once was a man who thought that his carefully tended fields that had been in his family for years were his. The bountiful harvest that the fields provided was his. He was dead wrong.

There is absolutely nothing that belongs to us. There is nothing that we will be able to keep or control forever. No matter how much we have invested in being a self-made person, we have no warranty for our work.

Jesus advises us against the kind of view that places riches and possessions in a place of prominence in our lives. Jesus strongly cautions us against using these as an indicator of the value of our lives. His story is a blunt reminder of where this idolatry leads us.

Why does he take this approach? Is Jesus trying to build a case for monasticism and asceticism as the only appropriate lifestyle? It is more likely that Jesus wants us to know the truth. The truth, after all, is what makes us free.

The truth is that God created all things and all of the potentiality of all things. Absolutely nothing that we possess or create was our idea first. Mark Twain once noted that the world does not owe us a living; it owes us nothing; it was here first. If we are rich toward God, as Jesus desires us to be, we are free to be amazed at the bountiful grace and love, which is the gift of life. We are then free to enjoy what God's creation offers, and not be enslaved by the gifts of this world. We are free to hold, to let go, to create, and to change.

The truth is that God created all things and the potentiality of all things for all of God's children. The wealthy landowner acted as if he were the center of the universe. He had no compassion, no sense of what others in the world experienced. If we are rich toward God, as Jesus longs for us to be, we can be free to experience the joy of sharing. We can know the joy of being a servant of God in blessing others. We experience the joy of empowering and healing others as their lives advance.

Once again we find how much Jesus loves us. He loves us enough to tell us the truth about how God, in love, has created the world. He loves us to know that we have more joy in being a person created in the image of that love. (Bob Holloway)

AUGUST 8, 2004

Tenth Sunday After Pentecost

Worship Theme: What the Lord desires of God's people is justice, mercy, and fairness in our relationships to the oppressed, the orphan, and the widow. If believers honor and esteem these persons, then the realm of God has come near.

Readings: Isaiah 1:1, 10-20; Hebrews 11:1-3, 8-16; Luke 12:32-40

Call to Worship (Psalm 50:1-4, 8, 23)

> *Leader:* The mighty one, God the LORD, speaks and summons the earth from the rising of the sun to its setting.
>
> ***People:*** **Out of Zion, the perfection of beauty, God shines forth.**
>
> *Leader:* Our God comes and does not keep silence, before him is a devouring fire, and a mighty tempest all around him.
>
> ***People:*** **He calls to the heavens above and to the earth, that he may judge his people.**
>
> *Leader:* Not for your sacrifices do I rebuke you; your burnt offerings are continually before me.
>
> ***People:*** **Those who bring thanksgiving as their sacrifice honor me; to those who go the right way I will show the salvation of God.**

Pastoral Prayer:

Help us God, to refrain from simply going through the motions of worship. Remind us that you set this Sabbath day apart so that we might see revealed to us the path of righteousness that you have laid out before us. When we walk with you, Lord, help us join hands and hearts with those who have not yet seen a holy vision of what life might indeed become. Let us witness to others by not only the words of faith that we profess but also by the very nature of our character discovered in the deeds we do on behalf of your creatures. Create in our lives a space for the last, the lost, and the least, just as Jesus did when he walked among mortals. Give your people, O God, an eagerness for compassion as we minister in the name of Jesus. You light our path with a holy light. May we share this life with a world lost in darkness. Seal our prayer with the Spirit of the one who unifies all in heaven and on earth. We pray in Jesus' consecrated name. Amen. (David Mosser)

SERMON BRIEFS

ANGRY, BUT WILLING TO DEAL

ISAIAH 1:1, 10-20

My friends, there is no gentle way to put this. This is an uncomfortable text to hear. And it is equally uncomfortable to preach. I should have taken this Sunday off. Truth be told, I almost did, for this text, lifted from the pages of history, beats us up badly. And nobody likes a beating. I could soften the blow by telling you that Isaiah will eventually apply salve to every wound he opens. But that will not help us today. No, it will not help us much at all.

One of the more famous word merchants of the Christian faith, William Sloane Coffin, regularly uttered painful truths from prestigious pulpits, including those of Yale University and Riverside Church in New York. Warning would-be preachers about prophetic utterance, Coffin was fond of saying: "Always remember, if you have something to say that is as harsh as it is true, say it softly." Alas, in his postretirement years on the "visiting fireman" circuit, Coffin seldom heeded his own advice. Quite to the contrary, he described his work as "blowing in, blowing off, and blowing out," leaving his host or hostess to sweep up the pieces.

Still, it would have been easier to invite Isaiah as a visiting preacher and maintain, for myself, a respectable distance. That way we could take the "hit" together, huddling under the umbrella "misery loves company." Or, I could simply pretend that none of the things that bothered Isaiah once, bother anybody now. Or bother God now. After all, it's been a while since we set fire to any bulls in the chancel. Moreover, were you to bring a bushel of barley and tell the ushers that you wanted it "rendered unto the Lord," not one of them would have the faintest idea of what to do. I can't recall the last "New Moon" festival I preached, here or in any of my previous assignments.

No, it would be easy to exempt ourselves from Isaiah's critique, simply by dressing him and his sermon in twenty-seven-hundred-year-old language and liturgy. Then we could chortle with superiority over how stupid "they" were once, how ticked "God" was once, how dramatic "Isaiah" was once, and how precarious "church" and "nation" were once. True, the picture of God wearing earmuffs so as to avoid hearing our prayers might pull us up short. And the image of blood draining from our prayerfully uplifted palms is nothing less than gross. But surely our worship isn't that bad. Haphazard, occasionally. Halfhearted, consistently. But utterly detestable? Not really.

Surely God doesn't feel that way. Wouldn't say so if God did. After all, God is patient and long-suffering. But in Isaiah's sermon, God sounds fed up, unable to stand the sight of us; isn't that what it says? Decidedly un-Godlike, wouldn't you say? Who selected this text, anyway?

Unless, of course, there's more to it. Something we're missing. Something that needs correcting. Actually, it's rather transparent, swinging from the end of Isaiah's diatribe with the subtlety of a two-by-four. I am talking about the admonition to clean up our act, cease to do evil, learn to do good, seek justice, correct oppression, defend orphans, plead for widows. It's the old "leave your gift on the way to the altar, be reconciled to your brother or sister, then come back and offer your gift" admonition (Matt. 5:24, my paraphrase). We have preached this message before and will preach it again.

But not today. What concerns me today is the vitriol that drips from the voice of God when Isaiah scolds us—all of us. It is tempting to say that Isaiah heard God wrong. But honesty compels the admission that it's not Isaiah's hearing but our doing that's wrong, which means that God may be feeling it still. The anger, I mean.

Maybe I've lived a charmed life. We preachers do, you know— more than we think. But nobody has ever laid me out like this. And in church, no less. Some people, hearing this, would lash back. Others wouldn't come back. But that's not my biggest fear. My biggest fear is that God might not come back, that this text is God's exit speech, a justification for divine abandonment. Save for this: "Come now, let us argue it out, says the LORD" (v. 18a).

Can you believe it? After all that, God is still willing to deal. (William Ritter)

HOW IS YOUR FOUNDATION?

HEBREWS 11:1-3, 8-16

Our daughter and son-in-law bought a new house between an onion field and an orange grove in a suburb of Phoenix. Their first house, they had it built and were so excited. We went to visit them, and Tamara, with great excitement, took us to see "the house." It was a hole in the ground, not a house! The workmen had just finished digging the hole for the foundation and besides a few measuring sticks with little neon orange tags attached and a stack of beams, there was nothing that remotely resembled a "house."

We appreciated the visit and a few days later, over the Internet came pictures. This time the "house" was a concrete slab with pipes sticking out of it. It looked a little small but we "oohed and aahed" and mustered up lots of enthusiasm for the "house." Their home is now completely finished and looks beautiful. I realize my daughter was smarter about house building than I: The foundation is the most important part. Without a good, solid foundation, the walls will not withstand storms or the ravages of time.

Abraham, by faith, lived in a tent as a stranger in a foreign land. Tents are definitely not permanent dwellings and do not have a foundation at all. Abraham and his descendants chose to wait for the "city that has foundations, whose architect and builder is God" (v. 10).

Foundations are basic, the starting place, in both the physical and spiritual realms. If there is a crack in the foundation, disaster is sure to follow. One of our previous houses had a crack. Any time it rained, we were flooded. We tried "painting" the foundation with tar, digging a ditch around it, piling more dirt around it, even laying plastic around the foundation. One little crack was very expensive; it ruined carpet, furniture, paneling and did not help on the resale of the property. And one little crack, if not fixed immediately, grows into a big crack. Real property is one thing but what about our spiritual foundations? On what do we base our faith, our beliefs, our hope, our actions?

Our spiritual foundations include the acceptance of Jesus, submission to God, love, faith, peace, prayer, forgiveness, and belief in the power of the Holy Spirit. Without a solid understanding and practice of these basic principles, we will have no power, no growth, no understanding of what lies ahead.

Abraham, Sarah, Isaac, and Jacob were content, even in periods of uncertainty and strife because they built their foundation on trust, faith, obedience, and love. They did not look back at what had been, nor did they desire to return. Their reliance and trust in God enabled them to see with their heart's eye the place God had promised them.

How much easier it is for us! We have written instructions and documented assurances of what is to come. We have the Son of God and the Holy Spirit to be our guide and companion on the way. Yet, do we live as though our foundations are built by the master builder? Or do we have some cracks in our foundation and tend to trust our employers, or our friends, or the checkbook balance for fullness of life? Do we give the physical foundations of our homes, businesses, and churches more attention than our spiritual foundations? May we take this opportunity to remember that our roots are in Christ and only by the diligent, intentional construction and maintenance of our foundations can we be powerful and live life to the fullness God intended. (Raquel Mull)

273

PREPARING WITHOUT FEAR

LUKE 12:32-40

The greatest antidote to spiritual fear is the spiritual readiness of a practiced generosity.

"Be dressed for action and have your lamps lit; be like those who are waiting for their master to return from the wedding banquet" (v. 36). Someone once said, "if you live every day as if it is your last, someday you will be right." But if we have the unfinished business of broken relationships and alienations of self and others, then it can be an overwhelming thought. If we think we must fix everything we have broken, there is surely not enough time.

But as Jesus' people, we do not have to handle it all. Jesus reminds us, "it is your Father's good pleasure to give you the kingdom" (v. 32). If we keep our instincts focused on the gifts which come with spiritual preparation, then we can trust God to fill our spiritual purses.

If we do not trust, we need to fear the judgment of unfulfillment in this life and separation in the world to come. No one likes to talk about judgment. The professor says "I would have the greatest job in the world, if I didn't have to grade papers." Her students agree! But it is a logical requirement that God must differentiate between holiness and evil. The age will not be completed until God purges evil and transforms it. In Luke, judgment focuses on generosity or its lack. We remember the rich man in chapter 16, "who was dressed in purple and fine linen and who feasted sumptuously every day" (v. 19). In the afterlife, the sight of Lazarus with Abraham tormented the rich man. Some years ago, Robert McNamara retired as head of the World Bank. In his closing address, he spoke of the difficulty of caring for the world's poor. He said Americans spend more on houseplants than they do on international development. Then he cried.

If McNamara cannot solve the world's problems, we probably will not either. But if God fills our "spiritual purses," then we can help transform lives. It often seems to be a black and white choice: If we store up earthly treasures our souls shrink smaller. But if we shed the things of this world, our soul grows large. Are we large enough to encompass a needing and hurting world?

We move from anxiety to acceptance by following the habits of a cruciform life. Recently, I was obsessing over a strained relationship. I thought, "If this person would just take my advice, things would be a lot better." But this person had no interest in "doing it my way." One night, while tossing and turning over this relationship, while this person was no doubt sleeping peacefully, it came to me to "try love." What if I tried to give my very best to pray for, share with, and listen to this person? What if I saw my role as to offer what help I could to see that person grow? I was at peace. That peace lasted for almost two days! One of those days could have been my last.

The key is not to fret over the needs of the world. Jesus is not asking us to read the morning paper and then click our tongues and shake our heads. Jesus counsels us to "love the one you're with." That way, when the master returns he will find a table spread with generosity, and the master will feel at home. (Don Holladay)

AUGUST 15, 2004

Eleventh Sunday After Pentecost

Worship Theme: By faith believers conform their lives to the will of God as revealed in Jesus Christ. By faith God calls us contemporary people to read and interpret the signs of the kingdom of God all around us. By faith God calls us to be faithful.

Readings: Isaiah 5:1-7; Hebrews 11:29–12:2; Luke 12:49-56

Call to Worship (Psalm 80:1-2, 14-19)

Leader: Give ear, O Shepherd of Israel, you who lead Joseph like a flock! . . . Stir up your might, and come to save us!

People: **Turn again, O God of hosts; look down from heaven, and see; have regard for this vine, the stock that your right hand planted.**

Leader: They have burned it with fire, they have cut it down; may they perish at the rebuke of your countenance.

People: **But let your hand be upon the one at your right hand, the one whom you made strong for yourself.**

Leader: Then we will never turn back from you; give us life, and we will call on your name.

People: **Restore us, O LORD God of hosts; let your face shine, that we may be saved.**

Pastoral Prayer:
O God, Father of our Lord Jesus Christ who is the pioneer and perfecter of our faith, draw us near to you in faith. Remind each

of us who gather to hear your holy word that you have called us by faith for faith. Often we forget that your divine faithfulness in us is the cornerstone of your plan for the kingdom. You have put your trust and fidelity in us so that we can proclaim your loving-kindness to all people. Sometimes our memories fail us. Living comfortably in your benevolence toward us, sometimes we forget that Jesus himself said, "Come, follow me." This willingness to follow the risen Lord is the hallmark of our faith. Give us hearts for ministry in the name of Jesus. Furnish us the aptitude and strength of character to truly follow the path upon which you have placed us. Let us with clear determination emulate the disciples of old who abandoned comfort and recognition to speak the truth in love. Our world needs what you offer through us. Make us disciples worthy of the name of Jesus and in his name we pray. Amen. (David Mosser)

SERMON BRIEFS

THE WILD VINEYARD

ISAIAH 5:1-7

There are many farmers in the rural church community where I live. These farmers take a great deal of care tending to their crops each year. They wake up early in the morning and work until the sun goes down in the evening. Each spring is full of great possibilities and the promise of a bountiful harvest. A farmer once related growing corn to the many different stages of life. You plant the seed and nurture it like a child. As the corn grows, the farmer takes care of the stocks applying the proper amounts of fertilizer to each. Eventually the plants mature and bear fruit as a child who grows to parent their own offspring. The time it takes for the tassels to form on the corn represents middle age to the farmer. Finally, the farmer harvests the corn as it withers away in the fall. Although the farmer provides all this care to the crops, farmers must wait on the one component that they cannot control, the rain. Water gauges are as common in my community as telephones. Similar to a child growing up, the corn needs the proper amount of guidance, but eventually the rain determines what will become of the harvest. One lives by faith that the rains will come and come at the proper time. The farmer will harvest whatever grows during the season whether it reaches its full potential or not. But as the winter approaches, the farmer will plow over his field and wait again for spring to continue the relationship with the land.

Isaiah 5: 1-7, the song of the Lord's vineyard, tells the story of a people who have not lived up to their creator's expectations. The details of Isaiah's words paint a vivid picture of the farmer in the field creating his vineyard with great care and accuracy. The farmer knew that only the best wine would come from his vineyard. To the farmer's disappointment, the grapes that grew were not fit for wine.

The Lord brought the people of Israel out of bondage in Egypt and to a land flowing with milk and honey. The Lord provided judges and kings to guide the people of Israel as they grew as a nation. They provided for the poor and cared for one another. As the nation of Israel grew, the people began to forget about their creator and to assimilate with the people in the land. They adopted their religions and religious practices. They no longer cared for the poor. They became wild and demonstrated a willful disobedience to God.

The Assyrians soon overran the nation of Israel. Judah lasted one hundred fifty years under its own sovereignty until the Babylonians destroyed Jerusalem in 586 B.C.E. Isaiah proclaims the nation of Judah as the Lord's vineyard and declares the Lord's intent for his nation. The prophet Amos proclaimed to the people of Israel, "they sell the righteous for silver, and the needy for a pair of sandals" (Amos 2:6). The Lord requires justice and the people of Judah provided bloodshed and injustice. We are to provide for the poor and hungry of this world. There are still starving children throughout the world, but there is more than enough food. The vineyard overflows with grapes. Let us strive to provide for those in need and adhere to God's call for social justice.

The farmer had given up on the vineyard. Therefore, he removed the hedge that surrounded it for protection. Anyone who wanted to have the wild grapes was welcome to them. The farmer knew that if he withdrew his protection that soon the vineyard would be little more than a field of thorns and briers. He took away the precious water that the grapes needed to grow; the fertile hill soon became a wasteland. (John Mathis)

HOZHO

HEBREWS 11:29–12:2

I am Navajo, born for the Bitter Water clan. My people have endured much through relocation programs, government imposed boundaries, and education that has zero tolerance for our culture and heritage. Yet, it is precisely because of our shared experiences, painful and joyful, that we maintain our identity as a people, as Dineh.

Not only do we share a culture and a heritage, we share an understanding with others who have suffered in similar circumstances, even if we do not share the same language. Because of our history, Native Americans may have a slightly different view of this letter written to those early Hebrew Christians, tempted to return to Judaism. The author is encouraging them, reminding them of what others have gone through to maintain their heritage and identity as Christians and the prize is worth the price.

"Lay aside every weight." Navajos have a guiding concept in their worldview, called "hozho." Hozho means harmony. Harmony with God, oneself, neighbors, and with creation. Hozho is the state of laying aside every weight. If there is weight in our lives, then we are dealing with symptoms of wrong choices, regrets, disappointments, fear, or lost hope. Regardless of one's ethnicity or background, we all can experience loss of peace.

Harmony is difficult to maintain, it takes practice and constant attention. Perhaps one of the most illusive tenets is harmony with oneself. We have allowed Madison Avenue and Hollywood to dictate what appears attractive and acceptable, instead of God. We try to please others for fear of rejection. We think our lives would be more pleasing if only we had more money, if we had a larger house, if we had a different job, if our spouse would do something we ask, or if we had not left our homeland. At times like

279

these, we need to remind ourselves of our spiritual ancestors and claim their history as our own.

Harmony with neighbor is just as important. Scripture tells us that our offerings are not acceptable if we have a quarrel with another person. Living with others is not easy, even if you love them. But loving a person does not ensure that you will always like them, like what they do, or like what they say. Ask any child if their parents never do anything that embarrasses them. Perhaps because they talk about it, husbands usually have one or two behaviors that their wives would prefer they never repeat. Others of us find that we have been given the unique and learning experience of working with a person whose every word and gesture drives us up the wall! Yet, even these are minor when we see what others have gone through.

Loss of peace can rob us of the joy and power God offers to us. Fear can immobilize us. Regrets can shackle us to the past. Disappointment can shroud the plans God has for us. Lost hope focuses our attention on our own weak efforts, not on what God can do. How much time do we lose, or how many opportunities do we miss by constantly looking backward, at where we have been? Christians are not immune to these emotions or reactions, but as the author tells us, we are to move beyond them.

For the Navajo, to restore hozho means reconciliation by repentance, forgiveness, restitution, or repayment. For us, this often means humbling ourselves, being the peacemaker, even when it isn't our fault. Once we regain hozho, then the person is free to move ahead, unencumbered by past sins. Instead of glancing backward, one's sight is clear to look ahead.

Claiming one's past and accepting it is an important part of our growth, as individuals and as Christians. Learning from our heritage as well as our mistakes clears our vision to see where we are going. Let us not be distracted from "looking to Jesus [as] the pioneer and perfecter of our faith" (Heb. 12:2). (Raquel Mull)

WATER, FIRE, AND WIND

LUKE 12:49-56

Somewhere in our walk with Christ, we will say, "There are things they didn't tell me about when I signed on with this outfit." Jesus will reshape our priorities and help us discern what is important. The important decisions are not those which help us know the weather but rather those which help us know the climate within.

Luke invites us to walk with Jesus to trial and glory in Jerusalem. Jesus' time is short. Actions are enlarged and have closer consequences. Jesus and his disciples must have known the cost of the road they had chosen.

No one needed to tell Jesus about the divisions in a family. His family had strained relations. His natural allies, the Pharisees, grew hostile. Such was the history of the early church. It is hard for us to imagine baptism bringing such division. Now the greatest controversy on baptism Sunday may be where to go for brunch. But in those early days, decision for Christ sometimes meant family division.

Discipleship is no different today. To read Dorothy Day's *The Long Loneliness* is to meet a young woman alive with passion. She befriends authors, marches for economic justice, and falls in love. But Forster, her common-law husband, opposed her growing faith, and objected to having their baby baptized. Dorothy turned away from the love of her husband, and all personal comfort and joy, in order to serve Christ in the church. Because of that bittersweet decision, she gave her all to Christ and to workers in our cities.

Some decisions are more important than others. They divide like fire; they divide like water. Our spiritual climate can be as turbulent as any weather. We love to talk about the weather. Some folks cannot start their day without the Weather Channel. Meanwhile, some say, icecaps are melting and our globe is warming. Some weather is more important than others. We spend too much time with the urgent, and not enough time with the important. Consequently, we make many decisions, but few of them matter much. We are busy. We are organized. We are impressive.

281

In the fall and winter of 1861, we as a nation divided between the north and south. President Lincoln entrusted the Union Army to the hands of a young soldier named George B. McClellan. McClellan was a cautious man. He wanted to get more intelligence about the strength of the army in Virginia. He needed more recruits, more guns, more time.

There was, out west, a low-ranking officer named Ulysses S. Grant. People reputed him as a clown and a drunk. When war came, the War Department gave him an emergency commission as a general, cast out in western Kentucky. Then Grant captured Columbus, Kentucky; Fort Henry; and Fort Donelson. Then Nashville fell. And what was McClellan doing back in Washington? In the fall of 1861, McClellan presided over the largest parade in military history.

We Christians are, one pastor said, happily weaving daisy chains, humming hymns, while many fall into an abyss of suffering and separation. Now is the time to act! In so doing, we may bring division with family and friends. The Gospel of Thomas says, "Whoever is near me is near the fire; whoever is far from me is far from the domain" (v. 82). Be encouraged by the examples of those who have gone before, and first of all by Jesus, the author and perfector of our faith. He will be with us, through the water of baptism and the fire of separation, as we make the decisions that shape our lives and our world. (Don Holladay)

AUGUST 22, 2004

Twelfth Sunday After Pentecost

Worship Theme: Jeremiah says that God knew him before he was born. Thus, Sabbath celebration rekindles a believer's remembrance of God's special relationship to creation. However, Jesus teaches that human need periodically overrides Sabbath's ritual observance.

Readings: Jeremiah 1:4-10; Hebrews 12:18-29; Luke 13:10-17

Call to Worship (Psalm 71:1-6)

> *Leader:*   In you, O LORD, I take refuge; let me never be put to shame.
>
> *People:*   **In your righteousness deliver me and rescue me; incline your ear to me and save me.**
>
> *Leader:*   Be to me a rock of refuge, a strong fortress, to save me, for you are my rock and my fortress.
>
> *People:*   **Rescue me, O my God, from the hand of the wicked, from the grasp of the unjust and cruel.**
>
> *Leader:*   For you, O Lord, are my hope, my trust, O LORD, from my youth.
>
> *People:*   **Upon you I have leaned from my birth; it was you who took me from my mother's womb.**
>
> *All:*   **My praise is continually of you.**

Pastoral Prayer:

O God, as the Author of All Life, you knew us before we knew ourselves. Thereby, O God, you understand not so much what we want, but rather what we need. We are a people who live in a society mired in what we want, what we desire, and what strikes our inadequate fancies. Yet, in Jesus Christ, you reveal to us, O Divine Light, not what we think will make us fleetingly happy, but rather those deeper things that bring true blessing and happiness to us over time. Provide us that inner visualization to see the wisdom in your overall plan for our lives. Give us the resilience to discipline ourselves not only for our sakes but also for the sake of your sacred realm. Provide for us an image of the blessedness we can bring to life when we act in accordance to your holy will. Bind us together with the single vision of our congregation's yearning for mission. Create in us the will to increase the good news wherever and whenever we encounter those who need the gospel. Make us a people who grow into the divine image that you created us to be. In Christ's name we pray. Amen. (David Mosser)

SERMON BRIEFS

DISCOUNTS ARE FOR GROCERY STORES

JEREMIAH 1:4-10

You stand in the presence of the Lord God. The voice of God speaks, affirming you as a precious child of the Divine. You have meaning and purpose. You have a mission. There is a sense of eternity and destiny in God's words. The omniscient Lord God has anticipated this moment even before you were conceived. You are a part of God's plan for bringing abundant life to a world searching for something more. What is your response to God's incredible gift? "I can't because . . ."

Jeremiah's call and commissioning is an important lesson to us all about the power of God to overcome our pathetic excuses. The list of excuses may be long, but not really unique. For Jeremiah it was "Truly I do not know how to speak, for I am only a boy" (v. 6). Do you hear our own excuses in Jeremiah's lament?

I am too young or too old. I am too little or too big. I am too dumb or smart, too thin or fat, too weak or strong, too cheap or generous. Notice that God knows Jeremiah's fear even before Jeremiah speaks it, and God says, "Do not be afraid of them, for I am with you to deliver you" (v. 8). God does not discount our value, and neither should we. We discount the gift of life, power, and potential God gives us when we live in fear, weakness, and hesitation.

With the aging of the baby boomer generation, sales of vitamins, hair color (for women *and* men), and antiaging products are soaring. The diligence with which this generation works to avoid, or at least postpone, the inevitable is almost comical. Science and technology can only do so much. The reality of our mortality is inescapable. So why resist and be afraid when we can focus our energy on that which does endure? We can live for a greater good—sharing God's love—and with a power that the "Grim Reaper" cannot stop.

Jeremiah had a call of God. God's call came with a promise of a presence, and it still does today. We may not be remembered as a great prophet like Jeremiah. Our call may not be to ordained ministry or foreign missions. We may never write a book, launch a ship, build a skyscraper, or be CEO of a Fortune 500 company. No matter, for whatever God's call on our life may be, taking up the yoke of God means accepting whose we are and why we are here. (Gary Kindley)

THE BETTER WAY

HEBREWS 12:18-29

I am full-blooded Navajo and look Navajo. People, when they first meet me, often try to guess "what" I am by asking where I come from. I believe I know what they want to know, but I am never sure how I am to answer. Of course, there are those who offer me multiple choice: "Are you Hawaiian or Mexican or what?"

Upon learning I am Native American, most people share their family tree and how they are related to American Indians. I usually respond, "How has that connection influenced your life?" For me, my heritage has taught me that in many respects, our worldview is similar to that of first-century Jews. For many Native Americans, their introduction to Jesus came only a few centuries ago, so to embrace a "new" religion is monumental. We, Native Americans and first-century Jewish Christians, both had established religions, based on centuries of practice and experience. To forfeit one's traditional religion is sacrilege, tantamount to turning one's back on much of one's upbringing and heritage.

The author of Hebrews is writing to encourage those first-century Hebrew Christians, the ones who had just recently left their traditional religion. These Hebrews were tempted to return to Judaism, something primary to their Jewish heritage, understandable, and acceptable to their culture. Christianity was new, based on God working through a human being claiming to be the Messiah.

Many Native Americans share a concept of God with the Jews of the Old Testament. God is not to be approached, priests are anointed for that purpose. Only on certain days, under certain conditions can one enter holy ground. To bring one's petitions to God, one uses the means provided by tradition.

In traditional Navajo culture, "hozho" is a ruling concept and a way of life. Hozho is harmony, a peace with all people, all creation, and oneself. If hozho is lost, one must determine where the harmony was lost, which relationship is out of balance. Upon discovering the break, one can follow some personal efforts to restore the harmony. Key for the person is to become whole, move on and grow is reconciliation. In some circumstances, an apology or restitution is not enough, too many spheres have been affected and a medicine man is called in. It is through his efforts and practices that healing and harmony is restored. It is not a quick fix for problems and cannot be done except by one trained in the art of sandpainting and chants.

Before we make any snap judgments about Native Americans using a medicine man to absolve us of any wrong doing, do we not sometimes rely on others to do the work for us? Perhaps we think sending a check in the mail excludes us from helping in a soup kitchen once in a while or actually rubbing shoulders with one who is in prison or hungry.

The author of Hebrews reminds early Christians that since

their conversion, things have changed. They are no longer tied to the law. The old mind-set must be revised. We need not fear, because we have Jesus, the mediator of a new covenant. We no longer need to bring in a priest to speak on our behalf—we have Jesus.

Another viewpoint that Native Americans share with the Jews is how people address God. To think of God, or the Godhead, as a pal or chum is disrespectful. Rather, the reverence and awe, which the author stresses, is important to maintain. Perhaps this is because our Native American roots to traditional religion are shorter than Christians to Judaism.

The book of Hebrews could have been written for first-genera-tion Native American Christians tempted to return to their native religion. Whatever our background or heritage, as we seek to spread the gospel message to all people, let us remember that not all people read, hear, and interpret God's message in exactly the same way. It is only when the message is given with genuine love that it can bridge the differences between cultures, classes, and worldviews. (Raquel Mull)

A DIFFERENT KIND OF HEALING

LUKE 13:10-17

The folksinger John Prine introduces us to a woman stooped down by the circumstances of her life: Unwed and pregnant, society pushed her further out on the margins, where the lost and forgotten dwell. Over and over in the Gospels, Jesus reached out and showed us that his work, and the work of the body of Christ, is on society's edge. Our mission is to carry on the work of Christ, among the stooped women and forgotten men of our culture. Christ teaches us to be obedient, always focusing on the needs of others, realizing that we too need Christ's healing touch.

Jesus teaches us to be obedient. Jesus revered the Sabbath and he practiced his religion faithfully. Six times in Luke Jesus is described as teaching on the Sabbath. But part of what it meant to honor God's day was to make sure that those on the periphery were included in his healing and teaching ministry.

The religious leaders would treat their animals better than they would this woman. They would water their ox or donkey on the Sabbath, but when the son of man offered healing to a stooped woman, they protested. In the community where I live, an attempt to develop much-needed affordable housing was blocked by those who were concerned for the prairie dogs that lived on the ground. Compassion for persons must dominate sentimental attachment to lesser things.

Christ makes it clear that religious leaders more concerned with ceremony than service will be put to shame. About midway through this passage, the focus changes from the ailing woman to the religious leaders, very likely Pharisees. These hypocrites lack one thing that Jesus had in abundance: compassion. They are so caught up in the ritual and ceremony of their religious life that they forget to care for those they exclude by their practices. Christian leaders realize that what we call orthodoxy is really a kind of "majority report." Those who stood on the periphery of the church, with different concerns, are often excluded from the conversation. We are learning that wherever the periphery is, there we are called to be. We are learning from the way women interpret scripture that they often read a different book than men. And we are learning from the poor who interpret scripture "from the ground up."

Every one of us, at one time or another, is the stooped woman or man who comes desperate and in need into Jesus' presence. If you get a group of spiritual leaders together and ask them what brought them to the field, they might say they entered for their own healing. We, like the stooped woman in Luke 13, are sons and daughters of Abraham, deserving healing and freedom.

Throughout our nation's history, women have always had a place of leadership in the church. Christian women led the way in the fight against slavery, for the temperance movement, and for women's suffrage. In business, politics, and academics, women were pushed to the outer office. But in the church, they have taken and will continue to take leadership.

Our mission is to carry on the work of Christ, among the stooped women and forgotten men of our culture. In that work on the margins of our world, Jesus will meet us and offer us healing. (Don Holladay)

AUGUST 29, 2004

Thirteenth Sunday After Pentecost

Worship Theme: The table of the Lord is where the human race observes the unrestricted nature of Jesus' new kingdom. Where all persons are welcome and all people eat together, here is an ideal portrayal of God's kingdom.

Readings: Jeremiah 2:4-13; Hebrews 13:1-8, 15-16; Luke 14:1, 7-14

Call to Worship (Psalm 81:1, 10-13, 16)

> *Leader:* Sing aloud to God our strength; shout for joy to the God of Jacob.

> *People:* **I am the LORD your God, who brought you up out of the land of Egypt. Open your mouth wide and I will fill it.**

> *Leader:* "But my people did not listen to my voice; Israel would not submit to me.

> *People:* **"So I gave them over to their stubborn hearts, to follow their own counsels.**

> *Leader:* "O that my people would listen to me, that Israel would walk in my ways!

> *People:* **"I would feed you with the finest of the wheat, and with honey from the rock I would satisfy you."**

> *All:* **Sing aloud to God our strength; shout for joy to the God of Jacob.**

Pastoral Prayer:

Lord God, you who prepares for us a banquet beyond our limited human comprehension, we offer to you our sacrifice of thanksgiving. You have blessed us with inclusion in your holy family, O God. Our sisters and brothers number those with whom Jesus taught, healed, and ate. Because these sisters and brothers are Jesus' kindred, they are our kindred as well. Bring to our minds that it is Jesus' love that unites all believers. Jesus displays his love for us throughout his ministry, but most forcefully on the cross. There on the cross he offered for us a perfect sacrifice and gave us an undeniable example of his unconditional and marvelous love. It is by this unqualified love that we receive your divine merit. Jesus' love frees us from our sins, but also frees us for bountiful life in his holy name. As we journey the path of discipleship and share the common loaf and cup with one another and the world, give us that same loving spirit that existed among those first blessed disciples who broke bread with Jesus during his days on earth. Inspire in us a life that we live "in remembrance" of him. In the name of Jesus we pray. Amen. (David Mosser)

SERMON BRIEFS

WHAT IS YOUR LEGACY?

JEREMIAH 2:4-13

Accusations fly in this passage, and it raises some troubling questions. The idea of God accusing future generations for the sin of a present generation appears to perplex us. Also, with the water metaphor, what cisterns are we digging to replace God as the fountain of living water? (See also Jeremiah 17 and the sermon brief, "The Water of God" for Feb. 15, 2004.) This powerful passage from Jeremiah points to a greater truth in life: When we ignore God we tend to seek a substitute to fill the void that exists in our soul.

People fill the void with many things: Alcohol, drugs, sex, relationships, gambling, money, success, and power all may have their allure and may become a mistress that seduces us away from faithfulness. Still, we are the ones who choose, and we can choose to fight the seductive nature of anything that leads us astray and away from God and those for whom we care. When we consider what we are doing by our actions, it is well that we consider what legacy we leave to the future. What will future generations be like if they follow our example? Will our children have faith, and will future generations come to know the holiness of God and the strength that comes from wrestling with the biblical text?

The people of Israel were led to a land of abundance. "I brought you into a plentiful land / to eat its fruits and its good things" (v. 7*ab*). Soon, the people forget the worship of the Lord God. Even those who are charged with leading the people in worship, the priests of God, did not say, "Where is the LORD?" (v. 8*a*). Through Jeremiah, God pleads the obvious question: "Has a nation changed its gods, even though they are no gods?" (v. 11*a*).

This leads us to another vital question: If we fail to model faithfulness to God, how can we expect our children to have faith? This much is clear, God is not cursing our children's children, we are. For the community of faith to live out our calling we must remember our heritage, learn from our history, and live in loving fidelity to God each day. Our birthright as baptized Christians is not an end in itself but an opportunity to live out our lives in faithful relationship with God and God's creation. What we do today is important. What we leave behind is all we have and all we are, for we cannot take with us from this planet anything we have built, created, or accomplished.

Dr. Gaston Foote was a great preacher, author, and pastor of First United Methodist Church in Fort Worth, Texas. He officiated at the funeral of a wealthy woman who possessed a considerable estate. After the service as Dr. Foote was greeting those departing the church, a woman known for sticking her nose into the affairs of others approached him. "Dr. Foote, you can tell me, how much did she really leave behind?" Without hesitation the wise pastor replied, "Why, my dear, she left it all!" So do we.

The philosopher and author William James said, "The greatest use of life is to spend it for something that will outlast it." What will be your legacy? Will a faith that endures be a witness and example for your children and for generations to come? (Gary Kindley)

CHRISTIAN HOSPITALITY

HEBREWS 13:1-8, 15-16

The man sounded desperate. He and his family were parked at a gas station. They were on their way to a new town where he had just gotten a job.

You could tell by looking at him, his wife, and their three children, that they had known some hard times. This was another one. They were out of gas and money. It was getting dark and cold. They didn't know what to do.

The man asked the owner of the store for some gas. He promised he would pay for it as soon as he could.

The store owner was a Christian. He responded, "No. I'm not going to do that." The man looked dejected, until the owner continued, "But I tell you what I will do. Pull your car up, and fill it up. Don't worry about paying me for it. Let me go in and call my wife. We want you to eat supper with us tonight and we've got plenty of room for you to spend the night." And they did! That's Christian hospitality! That's at the heart of this text. It describes the church as a community of hosts and hostesses.

"Let mutual love continue," the writer says in verse 1. Hospitality, love, and goodness to others should begin right where you are: with each other. Look out for one another's needs. Open your hearts, your homes, your wallets to your brothers and sisters in Christ right in your own Christian community.

Most churches do this very well. We try to keep up with what's going on with one another in terms of our needs: spiritual, physical, even financial. Countless amounts of money are spent each week, calls and visits made, cards sent to help one another in Christian communities throughout the world.

"Show hospitality to strangers" (v. 2). Seldom does the Bible share about how we should love one another within the Christian family without quickly stressing that our love is not just to be limited to this. Christian love is inclusive, not exclusive. How could it be otherwise? The love of God given on the cross was inclusive, that is, not just for one nation but for the whole world! This, too, is a chief characteristic of Christians—our love for all persons, especially those in need.

The writer here gives two examples of people in need whom we should love. First, show Christian hospitality to strangers. We find this same admonition throughout the New Testament (see Rom. 12:13; 1 Tim. 3:2; Titus 1:8; 1 Pet. 4:9). The hospitality that is written about is that of opening up your home to weary travelers. It includes providing them with food, a place to sleep, and even money and extra food when they leave.

This hospitality was a welcomed and needed ministry in those days. Inns were not plentiful, and those which did exist were often unclean and immoral places. Can you begin to imagine what it must have been like to travel in those days and not know where you would stay or how you would eat? Or, how much it meant to have persons who would welcome you into their homes and treat you like one of the family?

The second group of needy persons is prisoners, as described in verse 3. Christian love is expressed in ministry to prisoners. Perhaps the writer has primarily Christian prisoners in mind here. Being a Christian in those days meant risking prison and eventually execution. Christianity was an illegal religion.

Can you imagine what prisons must have been like in those days? Dark, foul smelling, and rat-infested tombs! Prisons today are luxury motels compared to those the writer has in mind. Most of us cannot even begin to understand what our fellow Christians must have experienced in those prisons. It must have been terrible. Imprisonment in those days was regularly a prelude to execution. If any person needed ministry, it was the prisoner.

Real love, you see, is like that. It does not consider whether a person is deserving. Christian hospitality is offered even to the unworthy, the unacceptable, the sinner, even the prisoner. (Bass Mitchell)

GOING BEYOND "MISS MANNERS"

LUKE 14:1, 7-14

After the September 11, 2001, terrorist attacks on the United States, it seemed that Americans became more courteous and polite. We went out of our way to assist and encourage each other. Unfortunately, our newfound manners did not last long.

The results of a survey taken in January 2002, indicated that eighty percent of the adults surveyed believed that lack of respect and courtesy in American society is a serious problem. ("Aggravating Circumstances: A Status Report on Rudeness in America." Survey taken by Public Agenda, a nonpartisan, nonprofit research organization. Results published in *The Orlando Sentinel*, April 2002.)

Upon first reading of today's text, it appears that Jesus is giving us a lesson in manners. In first-century culture, mealtimes were about much more than food and fellowship. They carried religious, social, and economic meanings as well. As a guest, one was seated according to his or her status or honor in the community. Hosts were occasionally known to invite a guest in order to gain power over him or to put the guest in his debt. Jesus, who was not known to be a model guest himself, addressed the behavior of both the guests and the hosts.

In addressing the guests, Jesus quotes Proverbs 25:6-7, reminding those gathered that honor cannot be presumed or seized by guests. Rather, Jesus said, practice humility by choosing the last seat, and allow the host to honor you if he or she chooses. These words bring to mind Jesus' teaching in Luke 13:30, "some are last who will be first, and some are first who will be last."

Next, Jesus addresses hosts and radically changes the guest list. Don't invite the usual folks: your family, friends, and rich neighbors who can return the favor and repay your hospitality. Instead, invite those who can never repay you, those who are normally excluded: the poor, the crippled, the lame, and the blind. Then, Jesus said, you will be repaid or honored by God.

So there we have it. Jesus used the setting of a meal to teach us a very practical lesson on how to exercise humility in important social situations. We have had our weekly lesson on manners. But wait, as usual, there is much more at work here. As Fred Craddock states, if the incarnation teaches us anything, it is that the frequent and familiar are not to be overlooked in defining life in the presence of God (*Luke*, Interpretation Commentary Series [Louisville: John Knox Press, 1991], p. 176).

What then is Jesus' message here? First, he reminds guests that we must not practice humility as strategy for gaining recognition. Picture a roomful of guests fighting over the "lowest seat," while trying to listen for the host calling them to a seat of higher honor (Craddock, *Luke*). Rather, Jesus says, true humility means knowing that our worth comes from our acceptance by God, not from the recognition of those around us. Since God accepts all who earnestly seek God, this mind-set levels the playing field. We are all humbly honored to be guests at God's table.

The message is similar to the hosts. Jesus modeled mealtimes that were inclusive of all, no matter what their station or status. God models this for us as well. For when we come to the Lord's table, are we not all poor or disabled in some way? Yet we are welcome as family at the table. So what does this mean for us as hosts? It means more than volunteering occasionally at the local soup kitchen or donating groceries to the local food pantry. It means opening our homes and our tables to those who can never repay us; not because they are a project in need of a rescue, but because God's radical reordering of our world calls for it. It is time we move beyond Miss Manners to a life of radical love and inclusiveness. (Tracy Hartman)

REFLECTIONS

SEPTEMBER

Reflection Verse: *"So I said, 'I will not be your shepherd. What is to die, let it die; what is to be destroyed, let it be destroyed; and let those that are left devour the flesh of one another!' " (Zechariah 11:9)*

Recently I received a beautiful embossed letter from my bishop. It was a letter of thanks to my congregation for all we have done for a special "second-mile giving" program for our denomination's judicatory. I looked carefully at the left-hand corner of both the bishop's envelope and the sheet of stationery. In each corner was a diminutive "shepherd's crook." This crook symbolizes the office of the bishop. I have even seen bishops wearing small lapel pins, tie tacks, or other small pieces of jewelry that depict this same shepherd's crook. In fact, from way back, the shepherd's crook has been a guiding image for church leaders. Why is this? No doubt because the crook is the tool of choice of ancient as well as today's discerning shepherds.

From Old Testament times, the image of shepherd has been a metaphor for those who exercised leadership of the community of faith. Often we think the image is one that came to us from Jesus, but the shepherd image far predates even our Lord. For example, when Joseph brought his two sons to his father Israel (Jacob) for a blessing, we read these words of the blessing:

> The God before whom my ancestors Abraham and Isaac walked,
> the God who has been my shepherd all my life to this day,
> the angel who has redeemed me from all harm, bless the boys;
> and in them let my name be perpetuated, and the name of my
>   ancestors Abraham and Isaac;
> and let them grow into a multitude on the earth. (Gen. 48:15-16)

When the tribes of Israel much later anoint David as king in Hebron, they say to him, "Look, we are your bone and flesh. For some time, while Saul was king over us, it was you who led out Israel and brought it in. The LORD said to you: It is you who shall be shepherd of my people Israel, you who shall be ruler over Israel" (2 Sam. 5:1-2). In the book of Chronicles we read that the prophet Micaiah prophesied, "I saw all Israel scattered on the mountains, like sheep without a shepherd; and the LORD said, 'These have no master; let each one go home in peace' " (2 Chron. 18:16).

The Hebrew Scripture writers fill their narratives about God and God's people with pastoral metaphors, and these include that of shepherd. The image of the shepherd is surely one of the most widely known to lovers of the Bible. One of our most treasured psalms begins with these comforting words, "The LORD is my shepherd; I shall not want. He maketh me to lie down in green pastures" (Ps. 23:1-2 KJV).

Naturally, most of us are more familiar with the shepherd images that come to us from the New Testament. For example, we read about Jesus' compassion for the people when Matthew writes: "When he saw the crowds, he had compassion for them, because they were harassed and helpless, like sheep without a shepherd" (Matt. 9:36).

And who can fail to be moved by Jesus' introduction to a brief parable, "What do you think? If a shepherd has a hundred sheep, and one of them has gone astray, does he not leave the ninety-nine on the mountains and go in search of the one that went astray (Matt. 18:12)?

For these textual reasons our lesson from Zechariah is all the more disturbing. Zechariah's image is almost scandalous. As a prophet he seems at wit's end and ready to surrender both his prophetic mantle and resign his prophetic calling. Evidently things in the nation have been so conflicted that the prophet borders between depression and fury. To refresh your memory, read only these few verses of Zechariah's prophecy:

So I said, "I will not be your shepherd. What is to die, let it die; what is to be destroyed, let it be destroyed; and let those that are left devour the flesh of one another!" . . . Then the LORD said to me: Take once more the implements of a worthless shepherd. For

I am now raising up in the land a shepherd who does not care for the perishing, or seek the wandering, or heal the maimed, or nourish the healthy, but devours the flesh of the fat ones, tearing off even their hoofs.

Oh, my worthless shepherd,
who deserts the flock!
May the sword strike his arm
and his right eye!
Let his arm be completely withered,
his right eye utterly blinded. (Zech. 11:9, 15-17)

Thus, someone has to be the shepherd of the flock. However, this is not a happy task since the flock has been doomed to death and destruction. As one commentator put it, "The picture painted of Israel's situation under the shepherd's leadership is one of horrible distress; Israel's own leaders pay no heed. There is constant strife between neighbors, and kings rampage the land" (William P. Brown, *Obadiah through Malachi*, Westminster Bible Companion [Louisville: Westminster John Knox Press, 1996], p. 174).

Fortunately, for believers today there is a new shepherd in town. His name we call Jesus. He is the one who says to his people, "I am the good shepherd. The good shepherd lays down his life for the sheep. The hired hand, who is not the shepherd and does not own the sheep, sees the wolf coming and leaves the sheep and runs away—and the wolf snatches them and scatters them" (John 10:11-12). Jesus is the one who says, "I am the good shepherd. I know my own and my own know me" (John 10:14). This is the Jesus who does not let one flock of sheep control his destiny either. Rather, this Jesus controls the destiny of the sheep and the sheepfolds. Jesus says, "I have other sheep that do not belong to this fold. I must bring them also, and they will listen to my voice. So there will be one flock, one shepherd" (John 10:16).

Which shepherd do we want to listen to as we walk the walk of faith? Do we want to listen to the discouraged despondent shepherd that we read about in Zechariah, or do we want to follow the shepherd that we call "the good" shepherd? Of course the choice is ours alone. But let me draw our meditation to a close with a modest example of Native American wisdom.

A grandfather was talking to his grandson regarding how he

felt about a tragedy. He said, "I feel as if I have two wolves fighting in my heart. One wolf is the vengeful, angry, violent one. The other wolf is the loving, compassionate one."

The grandson asked him, "Which wolf will win the fight in your heart?"

The grandfather answered, "The one I feed." (David Mosser)

SEPTEMBER 5, 2004

Fourteenth Sunday After Pentecost

Worship Theme: As Creator, God fashions and shapes God's people. In the course of God's self-disclosing love in Jesus, God makes available forgiveness and reconciliation by means of the community of faith we call the church of Jesus Christ. We count the cost of discipleship in Christ's name.

Readings: Jeremiah 18:1-11; Philemon 1-21; Luke 14:25-33

Call to Worship (Psalm 139:1-6, 16b-18)

> *Leader:* O LORD, you have searched me and known me.
>
> **People:** **You know when I sit down and when I rise up; you discern my thoughts from far away.**
>
> *Leader:* You search out my path and my lying down, and are acquainted with all my ways.
>
> **People:** **Even before a word is on my tongue, O LORD, you know it completely.**
>
> *Leader:* You hem me in, behind and before, and lay your hand upon me.
>
> **People:** **Such knowledge is too wonderful for me; it is so high that I cannot attain it.**
>
> *Leader:* In your book were written all the days that were formed for me, when none of them as yet existed.
>
> **People:** **How weighty to me are your thoughts, O God! How vast is the sum of them!**

All: **I try to count them—they are more than the
sand; I come to the end—I am still with you.**

Pastoral Prayer:

From your Compassionate Hand, O Lord, comes all the substance of our years. To you, O God, we offer our sacrifice of
praise—indeed without your guiding hand we are nothing. You
form us as a potter forms clay. You reached down at creation and
took the dust of earth and fashioned us in your image. From the
dust we came and to the dust we shall return. Between our
beginnings and our ends you constitute us as the stewards of all
the households we manage. You furnish us minds for thinking,
hearts for compassion, and human wills to do your bidding.
Guide us to the corridors of righteousness and once again, we
pray, make us your holy and sanctified people. Where we have
broken relationship in Christ's body, the church, mend them in
your holy places. Make us mindful of those in our midst who are
damaged by life and alienated from others. Bind us to one
another and seal us with your divine love, O Lord. Let us be your
holy people who proclaim with boldness your heavenly will for
the life of your creation. Let us be agents of your reconciliation.
In the power of Jesus' name we pray. Amen. (David Mosser)

SERMON BRIEFS

TIME FOR A CHANGE

JEREMIAH 18:1-11

The potter and the clay is one of the most familiar passages
and images from the prophet Jeremiah. Most everyone has
encountered clay at some point in their life. I remember in grade
school working with the wonderful stuff and feeling the squish of
the cool, moist earth under the pressure of my fingers. Jeremiah
declares that the people of God (Israel specifically in this passage) are to God like clay in the hands of the potter. God can
remold, reshape, and bring about change in God's creation. We
are wise not to ignore such power and possibility.

Texts that speak of God's changing mind have often bothered or puzzled students of the Scriptures. Something of the constancy of God seems altered or weakened by such passages. In verse 8 the text, speaking for the Lord God, says "if that nation, concerning which I have spoken, turns from its evil, I will *change my mind* about the disaster that I intended to bring on it" (my emphasis). Again in verse 10 the idea of the changing mind of God is repeated, "but if it does evil in my sight, not listening to my voice, then I will *change my mind* about the good that I had intended to do to it" (my emphasis). This concept of the changing mind of God is not something that we need to fear.

God has an amazing way of bringing about change when change seems impossible. At times when life seems the most immutable, God steps in and transforms the disastrous into a creative opportunity for growth and goodness. It is God's nature to transform despair into hope. We are partners in such transformation, just as God has made us partners in creation. Our call is to be faithful, obedient, and loving. When we pray and ask for God's help, we are not denied the vital presence and power that we need. God's timing may give us reason to doubt, but patience and perseverance can yield new perspective and amazing results.

After forty-four years of blindness from a dynamite explosion, my father received his sight through a cornea transplant. There were several factors that came together to make the surgery successful after such a long period, but the most vital was a donor family willing to offer their deceased loved one's corneas for transplantation. I am often asked to speak to groups to encourage organ and tissue donation and was at such an event in Austin, Texas, when something rather remarkable occurred.

We were lighting candles at the conclusion of the outdoor garden breakfast, symbolizing all the parties involved in organ donation. When a woman representing donor families came forward, she discovered that her candle would not light due to the windy conditions of the day. A man representing the Lion's Club, who sponsored the eye bank, made the same discovery. The executive representing the eye bank also failed to get her candle lit. Finally, I came forward representing recipient families. With all four of us gathered around, we could sufficiently block the breeze and succeeded in lighting all four candles. Working together, we changed the conditions to achieve success.

When we work with God, we set into motion conditions that can transform the seemingly changeless and desperate struggles of life into meaningful and significant opportunities of grace. God calls us to change our ways; work with God and in harmony with one another, and we will see the transforming power and nature of God to redeem, create, and sustain us daily. (Gary Kindley)

A DIFFERENT NARRATIVE

PHILEMON 1-21

"Christians are shaped by a different narrative," said theologian and biblical scholar Walter Brueggemann at a conference of church leaders. He was reminding us that the church lives by the narrative of the gospel, not the narrative of the culture. The narrative of the culture is about competition and power grabbing. The narrative of the gospel is about servant love. Perhaps there is no more practical example of what the contrast between these two narratives is like than the short letter of Philemon. In this letter Paul is making an appeal on behalf of a runaway slave whose name is Onesimus. The letter is addressed to Onesimus's owner, Philemon.

The letter is a model of Christian courtesy. By reason of his own authority in the church Paul might well make demands upon Philemon. However, Paul prefers to make an intimate personal appeal. His request is simply that Onesimus shall be reinstated and given a welcome such as would have been accorded to the apostle himself. If there is a debt to be paid, Paul pledges himself to be responsible for it. The letter closes on a note of complete confidence in Philemon and his willingness to respond to Paul's appeal that Onesimus be received as a "beloved brother."

In this short letter we see the result of being shaped by the narrative of the gospel of Jesus Christ. The culture in which the letter was written accepted the institution of human slavery without question. Now Paul sets forth a pattern of life which is a constant rebuke to and judgment of all forms of slavery. A master

303

who acknowledges "one Lord, one faith" and "one God and Father of all" (Eph. 4:5, 6) will regard his slave, not as a slave, but as a member of his own family.

A previously dishonest slave who has found new life in Christ, "who knew no sin" (2 Cor. 5:21) and "came not to be served but to serve" (Mark 10:45), will be ready to meet his obligations to his master regardless of the costs.

Having been shaped by the narrative of the gospel—of the example of the redemptive love shown on the cross, of the grace of inclusion evident in the fellowship of the early church—members of the community of faith are invited to practice a different ethic as we relate to one another in the day-to-day business of our lives. Paul's letter to Philemon is both an example and a guide for us as we live the ethic of love in a world of competition and status seeking. These brief twenty-five verses offer a template for lives shaped by the narrative of the way of love. (Chris Andrews)

IT'S ALL OR NOTHING

LUKE 14:25-33

Recently our daughter came home from school and asked if I would bake a cake for a dinner theater her drama class was sponsoring. I readily agreed. I didn't realize, until she came home later in the week with bags of ingredients, that we had signed up to make all the cakes for two hundred people. That wasn't quite what I thought I was signing up for!

You may have had similar experiences. Did you agree to sit on a committee that someone told you would take a minimal investment, only to find it all consuming? Did you sign up for the video or CD club without reading the fine print that contained the details of how much it would cost to fulfill your obligation? In today's passage, Jesus is seeking to avoid any such misunderstandings. Jesus wants to be sure that folks know just what the cost of following him will be.

As the story opens, the scene has shifted from the intimate mealtimes at the beginning of the chapter. Jesus is back on the road to Jerusalem, and large crowds are traveling with him.

Wisely, Jesus is not overly enamored by the size of the crowd. He rightly suspects that they are along for the ride, that they are even more unsuspecting than the disciples about what lies ahead. Cutting right to the chase, Jesus turns and makes it clear just what is expected of those who truly wish to follow.

Without historical context, Jesus' first words seem harsh and totally out of character. How can the Jesus who has preached radical love and inclusion suddenly call for his followers to hate father and mother, wife and children, brothers and sisters? To understand his intent, we must set aside the emotions of anger and hostility that we associate with the word *hate*. Here, *hate* is a Semitic expression of exaggeration used to mean "turn away from" or "separate from." Jesus is saying that not only is the call to discipleship the highest calling, it also reorders and redefines every other relationship we are a part of. "Count the cost," Jesus says.

Next, Jesus warns the crowd that they must carry their cross and follow him. In our society, our "cross to bear" is often seen as a problem or circumstance that we have no control over, something that we had no choice in assuming. Jesus' intent here is different. We are called to make a willing and intentional choice to take up our crosses and follow.

Jesus illustrates his point with two parables. In the first, a farmer is considering building an observation tower in his field. In the second, a king is discerning whether he has adequate resources to wage war on his enemy. The point is clear. All people, rural and urban, rich and poor have the same choice to make. The time of decision has come. Do we have what it takes to see the project through to the end? Jesus calls us to consider our answers carefully and not to respond without careful consideration. For us, much more is at stake than embarrassment in front of the neighbors or defeat at the hands of an enemy.

Although we must all make the same decision about whether or not we are willing to pay the price to follow, it may cost us different things. For some it may cost us the reordering of relationships, for others the price may be giving up possessions. For still others, the investment may be in the form of time or energy. Whatever the price, it will be costly. The end of the journey to Jerusalem cost God and Jesus everything. How can we expect less? (Tracy Hartman)

SEPTEMBER 12, 2004

Fifteenth Sunday After Pentecost

Worship Theme: Our God displays concern for each and every individual of creation. Jesus' parable brings this implausible and unlikely truth home to contemporary people who only think in terms of efficiency. Jesus Christ came into the world to save all—the last, the lost, and the least.

Readings: Jeremiah 4:11-12, 22-28; 1 Timothy 1:12-17; Luke 15:1-10

Call to Worship (Psalm 14:1, 3-7)

Leader: Fools say in their hearts, "There is no God."

People: **They are corrupt, they do abominable deeds; there is no one who does good.**

Leader: They have all gone astray, they are all alike perverse; there is no one who does good, no, not one.

People: **Have they no knowledge, all the evildoers who eat up my people as they eat bread, and do not call upon the LORD?**

Leader: There they shall be in great terror, for God is with the company of the righteous. You would confound the plans of the poor, but the LORD is their refuge.

People: **O that deliverance for Israel would come from Zion! When the LORD restores the fortunes of his people, Jacob will rejoice; Israel will be glad.**

Pastoral Prayer:

When we hold our lives up to the mirror of your uprightness, O God, we find ourselves lacking the fundamental humanity for which you created us. In the beginning, when you created the heavens and the earth, O Lord, you set us in the garden to cultivate it and keep it. Yet we have failed to be good stewards of the earth. We confess our failures and transgressions to you today, O God. May we sincerely repent. May we also search for your gracious forgiveness for which you alone provide. Remind us of our task. Help us see that we are either kingdom people or we are not. If we choose this day to serve you, O God, make us thirst after the compassion and mercy that Jesus lavished on those he encountered. Give us a purpose and direction for life that is pleasing in your sight. We pray this confession and appeal in the holy name of Jesus, our Messiah. Amen. (David Mosser)

SERMON BRIEFS

IT'S EASTER, ALL YEAR LONG

JEREMIAH 4:11-12, 22-28

Out of death comes resurrection. That's the promise of Easter. Death is the direct consequence of sin, God's judgment built into the universe from its very creation. But there is another law built into the universe—that in life, new life, resurrection follows death. Everything dies—people, ideas, relationships, feelings, cultures, nations. But everything lives anew, re-created by the power of God our Creator, who is constantly working for good in every experience of living, because God is Love.

Jeremiah was God's prophet of love and resurrection in times long before the birth and death of Jesus the Christ. Jeremiah was also God's prophet of judgment, pronouncing God's wrath on the people of Judah as judgment for their sins.

Jeremiah brings the Word of God. God has given several chances to the people.

> "For my people are foolish; . . .
> they are stupid children,
>   they have no understanding.
> They are skilled in doing evil,
>   but do not know how to do good."

God outlines their sins. Primarily, they do not know God (v. 22).

God announces that judgment is at hand. Their foolish ways have caused a sort of "uncreation" of the universe. The earth "was waste and void, and . . . the heavens . . . had no light" (v. 23). This is a vision of time before creation. God announces that judgment is at hand. Their sinfulness has caused a reversal of the historical gift of the covenant to Moses. "The fruitful land was a desert, and all its cities were laid in ruins" (v. 26). This is a vision of time before God led the people of Israel into the promised land. Human beings have the power to destroy both God's creation and the gifts of God given through the covenant. God proclaims that the earth itself shall mourn and the heavens shall wear black. Human beings have the power to cause creation to weep.

In the midst of pronouncing such judgment, God speaks words of grace, "yet I will not make a full end" (v. 27). Although destruction appears total, God still has the power. God continues giving opportunities for newness.

The return of the people of Israel from their captivity in Babylon some generations after the destruction of Jerusalem prefigures the resurrection of Jesus Christ by God's almighty power. God allows judgment to happen as a consequence of our missing the mark, but God continues to bring life from the deaths we experience.

The children of Israel experienced the death of their families and friends, the temple, their culture and communities, their ideas about religion, even the death of their understanding of who God was as the limited God of their small nation. But out of this tremendous loss, God worked to restore Israel as a light to the nations, re-created in God's image, rather than in images of their own making. And God invited the people to work alongside in this cocreating process. What a powerful statement to us in our time! The words of Jeremiah grab us by the throat, shaking us into awareness. We live in a time that seems, according to the newspapers and television, to be "skilled in doing evil." We live in a time when there seems to be little light coming from heaven as wars continue the long line of violent struggle. We live in a time when "the birds of the air [have] fled" and the earth mourns from our wanton destruction of earth's precious created resources (v. 25b). We live in a time when the consequences of our sinful actions and the sinful actions of previous generations have come together in a tidal wave of pain and suffering for many around us.

Although humans have the power to destroy, we have yet a stronger power. We have the power of God's re-creative Spirit. Life is always stronger than death. Love is always stronger than evil. That, too, is God's law built into creation from its very beginning.

In our time, we are God's people. Let us choose, with God's help, to be those who live life fully, and love deeply, acting as partners with God to bring about resurrection in our world. (Sharee Johnson)

GRACE AMID OUR IGNORANCE AND UNBELIEF

1 TIMOTHY 1:12-17

In light of September 11, 2001, this passage has become clearer in many ways, but more difficult in others. Because of September 11, many of us have had an even harder time coming to grips with the one who many view as the first and greatest missionary. What are we to think of this man named Paul?

For there was Saul, a religious terrorist, killing many Christians in the first century. No doubt, just as many of those who crashed their planes into the twin towers at the World Trade Center and the Pentagon, Saul thought he was following God. He thought he was as committed as anyone had ever been to God, and so out of his commitment, Saul breathed threats and murder against disciples of the Lord. His zeal for God could not be matched, but many of us wonder how someone so zealous for God could be so misguided that killing becomes his or her mission.

Saul was misguided until something happened. He encountered the risen Christ. He encountered the Prince of Peace. He encountered the One who helps us to look into the very heart of God and see how love plays itself out on earth. Saul's encounter clarified how a committed follower of God lives: not so much out of the law, but out of grace and the fulfillment of the law. This personal encounter with Jesus Christ changed Saul forever. He became Paul. The one who had brought death to so many followers was now enabling Gentiles, of all people, to find their way to life abundant in Christ Jesus.

Later, Paul speaks to Timothy about his journey. He basically says, "Although I was the worst sinner ever possible, God's grace and love in Christ Jesus came to save me." We might wonder why Saul wasn't destroyed by his righteous anger. Why does it seem like there is so much evil in the world? Why is it that much of the evil is rooted in religious people? How can many of us who think we are following God be lured into doing evil? Why is there so much unbelief?

But then we are reminded of Jesus' own words, "I came not to call the righteous, but sinners" (Matt. 9:13 RSV). If we already think we know it all and are closed to God's work in our lives, then Saul is already in our lives. For those of us who sit in our own worlds and think we are following God, who try to impose our religious beliefs and fervor onto others, Saul is a warning and a reminder for us! Yet it is Paul who helps us to see that we, who are also sinners, are only saved by the grace of God. Paul shows us that God can redirect any and every heart!

The exciting news is that for those of us who seek God, even when we are misguided and vengeful toward others, the Risen Savior will come to us. Out of that encounter, we will be new people. We will find grace amid our ignorance and unbelief. (Ryan Wilson)

WILL YOU JOIN THE PARTY?

LUKE 15:1-10

As this passage opens, Jesus is in trouble again. The beginning of chapter 14 found Jesus eating in the home of a leader of the

Pharisees, but now he is eating with tax collectors and sinners. How dare Jesus keep company with such folks? Doesn't he know that we are known by the company we keep? Doesn't he remember his mother's warnings not to run with the wrong crowd? Doesn't he know that separating the righteous from the evil helps preserve the righteous? Apparently not, for once again we see Jesus breaking down social barriers and welcoming outcasts to the intimacy of his table. And once again we hear the scribes and Pharisees grumbling about Jesus. In response, Jesus teaches the scribes and Pharisees through parables.

At first, these parables seem very straightforward. A shepherd loses a sheep and a woman loses a coin. When they find their missing items, both call their friends and invite them to come celebrate the return of that which was lost. The point is, there is joy in heaven when one who has been lost is found. But wait, something is strange here. Doesn't it seem absurd for the man to risk leaving ninety-nine sheep alone in the wilderness to go and search for one? The woman searching for the coin makes more sense; it was worth a full day's wage. But then they call their friends to celebrate. It seems to me that the parties may have cost more than the value of what was found. It just doesn't make sense.

And then, there is the issue of the folks Jesus used to illustrate his point. R. Alan Culpepper suggests that by the first century, shepherds had gained a bad reputation "as shiftless, thieving, trespassing hirelings. Shepherding was listed among the despised trades by rabbis" (*The New Interpreter's Bible*, vol. 9 [Nashville: Abingdon Press, 1995], p. 296). Now, Jesus has the nerve to liken God to a shepherd and to a woman. Do you see the Pharisees' outrage growing? First he welcomes tax collectors and sinners wholeheartedly, and then he likens God to those in society who are unworthy of such association.

Even after this, Jesus is not quite finished with the scribes and Pharisees, for the final twist is yet to come. Not only does God rejoice over finding the one—the one that would seem to have little value compared to the ninety-nine who are already righteous—Jesus said there will be more rejoicing over the one who is found than over the ninety-nine who are already there. How outrageous! How could Jesus say that God would rejoice more over one tax collector or sinner than over ninety-nine righteous Pharisees and scribes? It was the ultimate slap in the face.

Yet this is the message of today's story. God still calls out to those who are lost, and God still rejoices when one accepts God's invitation to come to the table. If we have recently been that one, we can relate to the tax collectors and sinners who found great joy at being included in the table fellowship. Unfortunately, most of us in the church are more like the scribes and the Pharisees. We would rather keep ourselves separate from the world in order to protect our righteousness than go with the shepherd and the woman in search of what has been lost. Too often, our sense of righteousness keeps us from extending mercy to the lost and celebrating with God when they are found. So, let us break down the walls that separate us, and let us become people of outrageous, expensive, reckless joy. I don't want to miss the party, do you? (Tracy Hartman)

SEPTEMBER 19, 2004

Sixteenth Sunday After Pentecost

Worship Theme: Modern people worship a wide variety of objects that take God's place as the center of our devotion. Yet, scripture reminds us persistently that shrewdness about the things of God always lead us back to God as creation's life-giving principle.

Readings: Jeremiah 8:18–9:1; 1 Timothy 2:1-7; Luke 16:1-13

Call to Worship (Psalm 79:1-5, 8-9)

Leader: O God, the nations have come into your inheritance; they have defiled your holy temple; they have laid Jerusalem in ruins.

People: **They have given the bodies of your servants to the birds of the air for food, the flesh of your faithful to the wild animals of the earth.**

Leader: They have poured out their blood like water all around Jerusalem, and there was no one to bury them.

People: **We have become a taunt to our neighbors, mocked and derided by those around us.**

Leader: How long, O LORD? Will you be angry forever? Will your jealous wrath burn like fire?

People: **Do not remember against us the iniquities of our ancestors; let your compassion come speedily to meet us, for we are brought very low.**

All: **Help us, O God of our salvation, for the glory of your name; deliver us, and forgive our sins, for your name's sake.**

Pastoral Prayer:

O Lord, too often it seems as if existence throws us into the midst of life. Frequently we feel as if we have no moorings or bearings by which to navigate the torrents we face. Life too often comes at us in ways that appear as whirlpools of dark waters. We are afraid. Yet in you, O Lord, there is great mercy. In you, O Lord, is a compassion that runs deeper than our need and wider than our imaginations. We can hardly fathom the grandness of your grace that surrounds our every day. Furnish the assurance of your love again as you, O Lord, beckon us toward the kingdom of God. In the gospel we hear Jesus' good news. It offers to each of us those wonderful words of life. Help us embrace this good news that seems too good to be true. Make us people who declare the gospel with glad hearts as your forgiven people in Christ's name. Amen. (David Mosser)

SERMON BRIEFS

BREAKING THE HEART OF GOD

JEREMIAH 8:18–9:1

"There is a balm in Gilead to make the wounded whole; / there is a balm in Gilead to heal the sin-sick soul." What beautiful, comforting words. ("There Is a Balm in Gilead," *The United Methodist Hymnal* [Nashville: The United Methodist Publishing House, 1989], no. 375).

Not so, cries the prophet!

> My joy is gone, grief is upon me,
>   my heart is sick. . . .
> For the hurt of my poor people I am hurt,
>   I mourn, and dismay has taken hold of me. . . .
>   and my eyes [are] a fountain of tears,
> so that I might weep day and night. (vv. 8:18, 21; 9:1*bc*)

Jeremiah is a man in deep pain: pain for the people who have died in the war between Judah and Babylon; pain for those who live, still begging to be rescued by the very God they have turned from, and pain for the heart of God, which is breaking over the people of Israel.

"Is there no balm in Gilead?" the prophet asks. And his painful weeping gives us the answer: no. Like a doctor, with trembling voice and teary eyes, who tells a family that their loved one is dying, God grieves and mourns the unnecessary pain of God's children. The Great Physician is weeping and wailing over children who are wasting away with an incurable, terminal illness.

Jeremiah is often called the prophet of wrath. His message repeatedly outlines the destruction of Israel. But, Jeremiah is a gentle and sensitive man, able to feel others' feelings, able to feel God's feelings. His wrath is God's wrath. His pain is God's pain. His anguish is God's anguish. His grief is God's grief. His love and compassion for his people are God's love and compassion for the people of Israel.

Jeremiah pronounces judgment upon his own people, not judgment that comes wielding a ball bat to strike those who get out of line, but judgment that is woven into the fabric of creation. Sin brings judgment. Repentance brings forgiveness and renewal. The people of Judah have sinned, turning to the worship of idols and ignoring God's call to justice and concern for all. Jeremiah has told them of their sins at great personal cost to himself, and time after time, they ignore him.

> They acted shamefully, they committed abomination;
> yet they were not at all ashamed,
> they did not know how to blush. (Jer. 8:12)

"They did not know how to blush." What an appropriate line for the times we live in. Like the people of Israel, we have turned to idols, worshiping money, sexuality, drugs, success, possessions, military strength—all other gods. Like the people of Judah, we find ourselves as a nation and as the church facing difficulty and destruction. Just three years ago on September 11, 2001, we were brought face to face with our own vulnerability as a nation in the tragedy of the very first foreign attack on American soil since the War of 1812. The church continues to decline in membership, finding itself on the fringes of society and facing front page scandals over sexual impropriety, financial difficulties, and theological infighting. And as we fight with each other, prisons are filled at a record high, children go to bed hungry, and people die because they don't have the means to pay for health care.

The balm of Gilead is the healing oil of forgiveness offered to us as it was offered to the people of Israel, but we continue to deny that our healing begins with confession and repentance for our own sins. God's love is a "tough love" allowing us the freedom to experience the consequences of our actions but promising to bring something new out of every destructive thing that happens in our lives.

A disciple is one whose heart is broken over the things that break God's heart. Jeremiah's heart was broken, but he always understood that God's love is a healing balm, bringing forth newness where there was death; resurrecting hope where there was despair; and rebuilding that which has been torn down. May we, like Jeremiah, have our hearts broken by what breaks the heart of God. Then we can sing with our voices and our lives, "There is a balm in Gilead, to make the wounded whole; / there is a balm in Gilead to heal the sin-sick soul." (Sharee Johnson)

WHAT IS YOUR PURPOSE?

1 TIMOTHY 2:1-7

Paul says that he is a herald, an apostle, and a teacher of the true faith. He is confident that he has understood God's purpose for his life and calling. Paul must have had a feeling that he was fulfilling his life's purpose! But I imagine that many of us don't feel like we know our purpose. It's not that clear to us, and we often struggle with knowing if we are in the right place or not. We ask ourselves, "Am I where God wants me?"

No doubt, Paul could relate to this question. He had thought he was following God's path for his life. He was so zealously following this path that he was willing to kill for God. But, it wasn't until the Damascus Road experience and the three years following that experience that Paul's direction became clearer.

It was out of Paul's experiences that he tells Timothy to pray. Pray for everyone. Paul was saying to pray even in the midst of persecution for your persecutors. I think Paul begins this section

by urging for prayer and worship because it sums up Paul's advice
for how to find our purpose in life. Paul says that God wants
everyone to come to knowledge of the truth. In other words, God
is always willing for humans to come join in a relationship. That is
why God raised Jesus! At the proper time, God gave God's Son to
be the mediator between God and humankind. If we are able to
pray for our persecutors, then our purpose and priorities will be
in the right order. It takes the focus off of us and puts it back on
God.

Who knows who was praying for Paul back when he was called
Saul and persecuting the early Christians? Maybe Stephen at his
stoning had prayed specifically for Saul. Whatever the case, it was
out of Saul/Paul's experiences that God was able to use him for a
specific and difficult mission.

God has given Paul the task of proclaiming the good news. He
has been given special importance and is appointed from the
highest authority to summon all who will hear (in Paul's case,
specifically the Gentiles) to heed the proclamation of Jesus
Christ; for Paul is convinced that it was only when he encountered Christ that his purpose began to take shape. Maybe that is
good advice for us. Maybe our purpose will become clearer when
we encounter the risen Christ. In the meantime, it is through
prayer and worship that Paul suggests that God invites us
through Jesus Christ to consider our purpose. What will we say to
God's invitation? (Ryan Wilson)

WHAT ARE YOU DOING WITH
WHAT YOU HAVE?

LUKE 16:1-13

Jesus tells a parable in this passage concerning the place of
stewardship in the life of a person of faith. The story reminds us
of the necessity of being faithful with all that we are given in life
including even the smallest of possessions. The theme of "those
who are faithful over little will be offered the opportunity to be
faithful over more" runs throughout the parable. The parable also
shares that it is the shrewdness of the steward that impresses the

owner and saves him from his judgment. This story is somewhat disturbing to many Christians who read it because of such emphasis. However, it seems that Jesus is boldly proclaiming that the kingdom of God, which he seeks to initiate and establish, is not one for the timid and shy. As one reads this story, one is reminded of other such uneasy statements Jesus makes regarding the kingdom, such as Matthew 10:16 where Jesus instructs the disciples to "be wise as serpents and innocent as doves." Obviously part of the picture Luke is trying to paint regarding the kingdom is one that demands that its participants be shrewd and clever.

One of the realities that the church must face in a culture gone mad with possessions and materialism is the concept of stewardship. It is not often a pleasant truth of which the church is willing to speak, but one that dominates the kingdom discussions of Jesus in the Gospels. It is important in our own kingdom preparations to realize that we will be held accountable for all that we are and all that we own. The nature of ownership is one of managing what one owns. The struggle for all people everywhere is discovering the balance that must exist between the owner and what is owned. Too many times we find ourselves in relationship to what we own by being owned by our possessions. Part of what this parable attempts to teach is that we must be responsible for all that has been entrusted to us. Although the story is told in such a way that it seems as though the manager cheats the owner, the reality is that he exercises wisdom in relationship to the request of the owner to give a report of how he had managed the money. The manager did not try to hide the work he was doing in settling the account. In light of how he responded to the owner's instructions the owner sees what he is trying to do and praises him for his cleverness. Had the manager tried to fool the owner about the accounts, the response probably would have been much different. Yet, what the manager did was done in full light of the owner's view. Such shrewdness in response to his original judgment helped the owner to see him in a new light.

Herbert F. Brokering tells the parable in his book, *"I" Opener: 80 Parables*, that "once there was a man who was given a beautiful empty bag as a gift. All he had to do was to fill it with anything he liked. He thought he didn't have time to do this, so he gave back the bag." The emphasis throughout Jesus' teaching on stewardship is that one had best be doing something with what one has been given. The story in Luke is one more example of such thinking. The image of the kingdom Jesus shares is one that demands from us accountability with all that has been entrusted to us. To miss that, to fail to respond to that truth, is to put at jeopardy our place in the kingdom of God. (Travis Franklin)

SEPTEMBER 26, 2004

Seventeenth Sunday After Pentecost

Worship Theme: In the face of a discouraging circumstance Jeremiah buys a field to reveal his hope in the Word of the Lord. Hope for human beings often comes through the generosity and compassion of other people.

Readings: Jeremiah 32:1-3*a*, 6-15; 1 Timothy 6:6-19; Luke 16:19-31

Call to Worship (Psalm 91:1-6, 14-16)

Leader: You who live in the shelter of the Most High, who abide in the shadow of the Almighty, will say to the LORD, "My refuge and my fortress; my God, in whom I trust."

People: **For he will deliver you from the snare of the fowler and from the deadly pestilence; he will cover you with his pinions, and under his wings you will find refuge; his faithfulness is a shield and buckler.**

Leader: You will not fear the terror of the night, or the arrow that flies by day, or the pestilence that stalks in darkness, or the destruction that wastes at noonday.

People: **Those who love me, I will deliver; I will protect those who know my name.**

Leader: When they call to me, I will answer them; I will be with them in trouble, I will rescue them and honor them.

People: **With long life I will satisfy them, and show them my salvation.**

All: **Amen.**

Pastoral Prayer:

O God of the Old and New Israel, remind us that Pentecost is not simply a day, but a holy season. During these autumn days, send again your refreshing Spirit upon us. May the Spirit guide us and comfort us. It is in your abiding presence that we sense the Holy Spirit that you gave us as an assurance of hope. Grant us the daring to stand up for the right when it is so much easier to take the path of least resistance. Far too often we have been silent when we should have spoken up for the rights of those not present in our daily conversations. Let us speak about others as if they were present. As Scripture tells us,

> Those who desire life
>   and desire to see good days,
> let them keep their tongues from evil
>   and their lips from speaking deceit.
>   (1 Pet. 3:10)

Make us faithful to the tasks that you set before us in the teachings of Jesus we pray. Amen. (David Mosser)

SERMON BRIEFS

FIELD OF DREAMS

JEREMIAH 32:1-3a, 6-15

Hollywood has so many wonderful stories about the improbable, or even the impossible, taking place. One of my favorites is the movie *Field of Dreams*. In this film, a farmer hears a voice saying, "If you build it, they will come." He is frightened and unsure of what this voice is telling him, but soon he undertakes a quest to discover what he is being called to build. On his journey, he meets many people and experiences many things. Slowly, through a series of amazing events, the farmer begins to understand this cryptic message. He is to plow under his cornfield and build a baseball field. His family and neighbors think he is crazy. Yet through his dogged pursuit of the message's meaning, he comes to realize that this is indeed a way of making his dreams come true. The farmer completes his "field of dreams" and finds his peace. He builds the field, and the final scene shows cars by the hundreds coming to this special place.

Jeremiah's land purchase at Anathoth could be understood as his own "field of dreams." The law of redemption meant that Jeremiah had the opportunity to purchase Hanamel's field, but logical people would have to inquire, "Why would he?" The Babylonian army was besieging the city, and Jeremiah himself was in jail! Yet Jeremiah heeded the divine word to purchase the land, in spite of outward appearances. Things looked dark, but God instructs Jeremiah, "Take these deeds, both this sealed deed of purchase and this open deed, and put them in an earthenware jar, in order that they may last for a long time. . . . Houses and fields and vineyards shall again be bought in this land" (vv. 14-15). God says that even this darkest hour will pass. God invites Jeremiah to show great faith by believing that the people of Israel will once again flourish.

In the *New Interpreter's Bible*, Patrick D. Miller writes about the courage and risk inherent in Jeremiah's stance of faith. Miller writes, "The text is about betting on the future. . . . The promise offered here is no generalized hope for better times. It is a call for putting one's money down now" (6:821-22). Jeremiah had no external reasons to trust that things were going to work out for him. This was not a purchase that showed great promise. All Jeremiah had was God's assurance and a commitment to act in faith. Jeremiah realized that faith is indeed "the assurance of things hoped for, the conviction of things not seen" (Heb. 11:1). Despite what the world might say, despite of what appeared to be rational or logical, Jeremiah took a risk and trusted in the power of God to work for good.

Jeremiah's "field of dreams" reminds us that the people of God are called to be in the risk-taking business. We are sometimes called to do outrageous things, trusting in faith that God will be there to help us in our times of need. We are to show great faith, having the assurance of God's promise that our hope is not empty. The question is, how many of us will exhibit our trust in God in concrete and real ways? Will we trust God with our financial resources, with our families, and with our churches? Will we risk the taunts of our neighbors by being obedient rather than rational? Will we take the risk of being faithful instead of successful? May we each find our own "field of dreams," and be faithful to God's promised future, which we cannot see. (Wendy Joyner)

LIFE THAT IS TRULY LIFE

1 TIMOTHY 6:6-19

The desire to be rich is always in our face. The desire to have more gives us the impression that the grass is greener on the other side of the fence. And, advertising tells us that worldly accumulations equal a better life! But do worldly accumulations really equal a better life? Most of us feel that having some worldly accumulations helps us to enjoy life more fully. It's nice to have air conditioning, running water, a car to drive, and some money to spend. But where does it end?

Is it that our human nature just desires more than the necessities of life? Or is it that the devil falsely puts worldly desires into our minds? Paul suggests that those who have money as their goal in life become easy prey for Satan, who is ruler of worldly things. I don't really think Paul believes that all worldly things are inherently evil. Rather, I think Paul was aware that Satan can use worldly things for evil purposes. The devil is able to use worldly things to scramble our priorities and take our focus off of God. Who can forget the story of King Midas, who thought that it was wonderful that everything he touched turned to gold. That is, until he touched his daughter, whom he loved more than money, but it was too late as she was entombed in gold.

When we become overwhelmed by our possessions, we lose our focus. When I was growing up, I loved to collect baseball cards. I lived, breathed, ate, and drank baseball cards. I became so consumed that I spent all my time and money on them. When I started having to deal with other people, I began to lose sight of right from wrong. Making a "fair" trade became skewed, and the thought of stealing a fifty-cent pack of cards didn't seem that bad.

Riches and worldly possessions can do that to us. The devil uses them to disguise what truly matters in life. How much fuller our lives would be if we filled them up with relationships rather than earthly possessions. How much richer our lives would be if we spent more time helping others than helping ourselves.

We can't buy God! We can't buy love! We can't buy life! Baseball cards were great, but they weren't truly life. When we can learn how to be rich in works of love, then we will begin to find life that is truly life. When we begin to make investments in people, then we will see true dividends. Our storehouses will be opened, our care and sympathy for others will increase, and we will share our resources openhandedly. We might enjoy earthly possessions, but they won't control our lives. Instead, we will begin to store up treasures in heaven, and we will have found life that is truly life. (Ryan Wilson)

MORE THAN POSSESSIONS

LUKE 16:19-31

Luke seeks in this passage to continue his concern around the place of stewardship in the life of a follower of Christ. The key to understanding this passage is discovered in verse 31 as Abraham responds to the rich man by saying, "If they do not listen to Moses and the prophets, neither will they be convinced even if someone rises from the dead." The response frames all that precedes it in the parable. The inference here is that evidently the rich man has come to the realization that the reason for his suffering is linked to his lack of interpretation of the law and the prophets or his misinterpretation of them. One can sense his realization of his failure as he begs Abraham to use different means to warn his family and friends who are still living so that they will not make the same mistake he has. The theme of this story is that there are consequences to what we do with what God gives us, especially as it relates to following the guidance God has offered through scripture.

This is not a popular story to preach in the church of a culture like ours. Prosperity theology runs amok in the church today as we attempt to not only justify our wealth but also to go so far as to say that it is a sign of how God has blessed us. Jesus told this parable as a response to such thinking in the lives of the Pharisees. Using the Deuteronomic law as a foundation of their attitudes surrounding their wealth, they sought to tie that wealth to their faith as a sign of God blessing them for being righteous in the eyes of God.

Jesus seeks to turn such thinking on its ear. Jesus seeks to reinterpret for his hearers the law and the prophets as he places the responsibility for such wealth and what one does with it squarely on their shoulders. Once again we find this theme of stewardship and its prominent place in the kingdom. The rich man suffers in the afterlife because of his inattention to being responsible with his great wealth during his earthly life, especially as it related to the poor. Jesus seeks to proclaim that in the kingdom of God people must respond to all that God has given them in a way that is fair, responsible, and with much love and compassion.

Jesus also seeks in this passage to relate to those listening that we are all held accountable by God for our own life, for all that we are, and for all that we own. Both Lazarus and the rich man are held responsible for who they were and what they did or did not do with what they had. The rich man's pleading for someone to warn his brothers goes unheeded as Jesus plainly states that God has given everyone the same guides to listen to in life. Our lives will be judged according to our response to those guides and their instructions. Such teaching will not be popular in a culture obsessed with instant gratification, the pursuit of wealth, and the "right" to fifteen minutes of fame. And yet, the church must seek to boldly proclaim this countercultural message, which demands accountability in relation to one's possessions. Such accountability also includes our interpretation of the Scripture that God has entrusted to us and how that interpretation plays out in our lives.

In 1962, four young musicians auditioned for Decca Records. The record executives dismissed them saying, "We don't like their sound. Groups of guitars are on the way out." The Beatles left without a contract. We had best be careful as to what we base our decisions on in life. Jesus' parable reminds us of the implications and consequences of such decision-making. After all, life, according to this parable, is about much more than possessions. (Travis Franklin)

REFLECTIONS

OCTOBER

Reflection Verse: *"If one carries consecrated meat in the fold of one's garment, and with the fold touches bread, or stew, or wine, or oil, or any kind of food, does it become holy?" (Haggai 2:12)*

For reasons that are hidden, I suppose only in my own heart, I have been thinking about my maternal grandfather who would have been one hundred three years old last fourth of July. Perhaps what made me think about him was the celebration of a one hundredth birthday this week of a dear saint in our local church. We had a grand time seeing photos of her as a young girl and listening to her speak of the "good old days."

My grandfather was the master of the quick proverb. He had been an admirer of Benjamin Franklin and had read most of Franklin's writings by the time he left high school. Granddad's proverbs had the effect of a quick, decisive boxing-type jab that settled whatever matter we were debating at any given moment. When my mother told me to get my homework done before supper, for example, Granddad would say, "A stitch in time saves nine." I had no clue what he meant, but he *sounded* so convincing that I did as my mother told me. When I wanted to buy a baseball or a pack of gum, what was then the equivalent of a modern fifty-dollar video game, Granddad would speak of squandering money by suggesting, "A penny saved is a penny earned."

Later on, when I was in high school and it was time to go out with some of my questionable buddies, my mother would caution me to take care about the people I spent time with, to stay out of trouble, and to uphold our family's good name. Granddad would pipe up, "Birds of a feather flock together." I would say back over my shoulder as I rushed out the door, "No, Gramps, we are not going bird hunting." But each time he said something along these

326

lines, we children did have a moment to ourselves to pause and ponder.

Our meditation text is the prophet's perspective on the holiness of the people of Judah immediately after the rebuilding of the temple. Haggai, as a resident prophet, asks the priests a question from the Lord. Haggai asks, "If one carries consecrated meat in the fold of one's garment, and with the fold touches bread, or stew, or wine, or oil, or any kind of food, does it become holy?" That is, does other food's contact with consecrated food make it consecrated too? "The priests answered, 'No' " (v. 12).

Then Haggai turns the question around by asking, " 'If one who is unclean by contact with a dead body touches any of these, does it become unclean?' " The priests answered, "Yes, it becomes unclean" (v. 13). Haggai's little parable, or series of questions at least, suggests that something cannot make other things clean by contact. On the other hand, contact with unclean things makes even those things that are clean unclean. Haggai then uses this as an example of Judah, the nation. The people think that they have become holy by rebuilding the temple, but in fact the temple remains unclean because unclean hands have constructed it. To use a tried-and-true proverb here, "One rotten apple spoils the barrel." However, a good apple cannot save a barrel of rotten apples. Thus, on both sides of the transaction, Haggai suggests something rather negative.

Most of us today don't think about church issues in terms of clean and unclean. However, to get a sense of the seriousness with which the Hebrews took these cultic issues, we might think in terms of some dreaded virus, such as Ebola or HIV. It was with this degree of seriousness that the people took the issues surrounding clean and unclean in their practice of their cultic religion.

After this reprimand, however, Haggai then continues relentlessly by asserting that "I struck you and all the products of your toil with blight and mildew and hail; yet you did not return to me, says the LORD" (v. 17). Haggai so much as admits that part of the people's problems were an edict of God's trying to get them to return to the Lord.

Perhaps Haggai suggests through his prophecy that the people got what they deserved. But there is more. There is a word of pledge at the prophecy's conclusion. Haggai prophesies, "Consider from this day on, from the twenty-fourth day of the ninth month. Since the day that the foundation of the LORD's temple was laid, consider: Is there any seed left in the barn? Do the vine, the fig tree, the pomegranate, and the olive tree still yield nothing? From this day on I will bless you" (vv. 18-19).

Readers, do you notice what those from Judah do to merit God's Word through the prophet who says, "From this day on I will bless you"? They do nothing. Suddenly, in the midst of dire prophecy of doom and gloom, the prophet announces that God will bless them. They do nothing. Haggai no more than suggests their acceptance of God's free token. This statement of gracious blessing is like a proverb that had the effect of a quick, decisive boxing-type jab that settled the matter of God's loving-kindness for God's people in a moment. We only acknowledge the Lord's gracious word to receive it.

Jesus once told a parable resembling this theological affirmation of grace to those who seemed to rely on their own righteousness, or good looks, or wits, or charm to win God's favor. Jesus sets up a scene in which a Pharisee prays, "God, I thank you that I am not like other people: thieves, rogues, adulterers, or even like this tax collector. I fast twice a week; I give a tenth of all my income." Subsequently, a tax collector also prayed. Note the utter humility of this prayer: "God, be merciful to me, a sinner!" Jesus informs those who listen to this teaching that it was the humble sinner who "went down to his home justified rather than the other; for all who exalt themselves will be humbled, but all who humble themselves will be exalted" (Luke 18:10-14).

Those who want God's blessing simply need to know that they stand in need of the grace that God alone offers. To assume God's good grace is to forfeit it. This is why we refer to the gospel as good news, for without God's grace we are all "done for." The good news is that God accepts us and receives us just as we are, without one plea.

In another of Luke's masterful parables of grace, the prodigal son, the son's only work is that he "comes to himself" and returns home (Luke 15:17). All the prodigal does is realize that his deep need of mercy and unlimited grace is his for the asking. Like the prodigal, all God asks of us is that we come to ourselves, name our deficiency, and know that we need divine help. I suppose the decision is ours.

The church that gets the blessing of God realizes it is in deep need of the grace that God alone provides. For Haggai the people of Judah will receive their blessing from God, but not because of anything they have done. Rather, they receive God's gift of grace and salvation because they know their deep need of mercy. This is true for any community of faith that calls itself a church. We don't "do stuff" to gain God's favor. We "do stuff" as our pitiful attempt to live in a thankful way of life that responds to God's gift of love to us. After all, as my Granddad always said, "Birds of a feather flock together." Our flock, our tribe, our church is at its best when it realizes that the one thing that unites us all is our need of the grace and mercy of God. (David Mosser)

OCTOBER 3, 2004

Eighteenth Sunday After Pentecost

Worship Theme: We serve God as a privilege not as a responsibility. Being servants of Jesus is the reward of faith. As we share faith through our words and actions, faith multiplies.

Readings: Lamentations 1:1-6; 2 Timothy 1:1-14; Luke 17:5-10

Call to Worship (Psalm 137:1-6)

Leader: By the rivers of Babylon—there we sat down and there we wept when we remembered Zion.

People: **On the willows there we hung up our harps.**

Leader: For there our captors asked us for songs, and our tormentors asked for mirth, saying, "Sing us one of the songs of Zion!"

People: **How could we sing the LORD's song in a foreign land?**

Leader: If I forget you, O Jerusalem, let my right hand wither!

People: **Let my tongue cling to the roof of my mouth, if I do not remember you, if I do not set Jerusalem above my highest joy.**

Pastoral Prayer:

O Lord, we pray today the request that Jesus' apostles asked of him: "Increase our faith!" (Luke 17:5). In our toil and turmoil of daily life, we often feel the temptation to despair. We too often want to throw up our hands and surrender because life for many of us is burdensome. Yet you, O Lord, give us a witness to the life of Jesus in the Gospels. This witness allows us to confront the demons that bedevil us. Perhaps our demons are unlike those that beset the first believers; but we possess our own modern demons, or rather, they possess us. For some, alcohol or drugs have assumed control of our lives. For others, the temptation comes in the form of our presumptuous desire for others to notice us and consider us important. For still others, our temptation assumes the guise of gossip, slander, or worse. Remind us who the source of all life is. Help us as we journey in faith to take time to be holy and meditate on your Word. Remind us that the Holy Spirit is as near to us as our breath and our prayers. For this and all things we give you our praise of thanksgiving. Guide us as believers who proclaim peace with justice. In Jesus' name we pray. Amen. (David Mosser)

SERMON BRIEFS

A CALL TO WORSHIP

LAMENTATIONS 1:1-6

She was lonely. She had no one to comfort her, no place to rest. No one came. She could find no clearing anywhere. Her world was turned upside down with no measurable hope of righting itself again.

What has it been for you that has made you feel like your world turned upside down, never to revert back again? The death of someone dear, a loss of health, an inner personal crisis, too many changes too close together? While driving to the funeral of a friend's eighteen-year-old grandson, glimpses of the family's complete upheaval came flooding into my thoughts. What sustained them; more pointedly, what in their faith enabled them to continue to move?

The "she" above, of course, is Jerusalem as portrayed in Lamentations 1:1-6. The picture of national disaster in these verses leaves little doubt as to the complete upheaval experienced by Israel. The city that was a princess became a vassal;

lovers and friends were now treacherous enemies; suffering and hard servitude, not festivals, befell the people; enemies became masters while defenders fled. The verses and chapters that follow do little to alleviate this picture of despair. If we, at the beginning of Lamentations, were to ask what sustained Israel in the face of exile, the book would be eerily silent.

So why did God deem these words worthy of being called holy, preserved as part of canonical scripture? Why remember such a time when hope was shattered and God seemed to abandon God's people?

After the exile old visions of God's creative and ordered plan for Israel failed the reality check. Hope for future relationship with God could come only as new visions emerged, ones shaped by the experience of suffering. But when there is no comfort, no rest, no help anywhere, how can the seeds of new vision find life? Through worship. After creating the world, God rested and allowed for worship. When the floods subsided Noah built an altar and worshiped. As they moved into the promised land, Israel stopped to worship. And now, when new ways of being were once again needed, Israel (and we) must worship.

Through worship, we honor and allow God to repair and sustain God's vision in us and the world around us. In worship we sing praises instead of harping over "to do" lists. We recognize sin and receive assurance of forgiveness. We shift our focus from our own agenda to that of God. In the flow of ordinary life we need such renewal and focus. How much more so do we need worship when upheaval comes!

Perhaps God deemed these laments worthy to be called holy because God knows and loves God's people far more than we can imagine. Perhaps God knew upheaval would come again and that we would need the hope that past experiences of salvation can offer. Perhaps God knew that we need reminders in the midst of good times, when demons of self-sufficiency creep in unawares.

We must lay the foundation now if we expect to stand on it later; rhythms of worship that beat with our everyday life are stronger than those felt only suddenly in times of need. I suspect that one part of faith which sustains my friends now is nothing that anyone has suddenly said or thought, but the cadence of worship embedded in their lives. Perhaps the silence at the beginning of Lamentations is there in part so that Israel (and we) can hear the beat of centuries of worship that continues to sound. May we be called to worship. (Karen Hudson)

NO FEAR

2 TIMOTHY 1:1-14

Have you seen the words "No Fear" emblazoned in bold letters on the rear windows of cars or pickup trucks? Perhaps you've wondered what they mean, or perhaps you know that the words advertise a popular brand of clothing designed for use in sporting events like bicycle racing and surfing. The words have become a part of popular culture. They've been adapted and even parodied, for instance, "Ain't Skeered!"

What place does fear have in your life? Are you afraid of something now? Fear keeps us from doing many things, and rightly so in some cases. Our sense of fear is a part of our warning system that keeps us from getting into harm's way unnecessarily. Fear can bring us to recognize our vulnerability in a given situation and lead us to take precautionary measures. Fear, however, can also keep us from responding courageously and boldly. Rather than being a signal to warn us of danger, fear can become our commander, our boss. Paul advised Timothy, "God did not give us a spirit of cowardice" (v. 7). The word translated as "cowardice" implies fear. This verse reminds us that sometimes we must disregard our fears and recognize that it is right and good for us to be right in the middle of harm's way in order to be faithful to our Lord.

Read through the Gospels and you will see one of the most frequent commands of Jesus: "Do not be afraid" (see Matt. 14:27; 17:7; 28:10; see also Mark 5:36; Luke 8:50; 12:4). Easy to say but hard to do? Yes, but notice what God gives us instead of fear: "a spirit of power and of love and of self-discipline" (v. 7).

Not a bad trade. God gives us power, love, and self-discipline instead of the fear that means "cowardice" (NRSV) and "timidity" (NIV). *Power* means, basically, "the ability to do a task." With the power God gives, we can face and deal with what we must. Further, love "casts out fear" (1 John 4:18). To know that we are loved even as we face difficult circumstances reassures us. *Self-discipline* can also be translated "self-control" or "sound judgment." The word implies the capacity for holding oneself together while things all around are threatening to come apart.

Paul reminded Timothy that such a spirit was God's gift. A self-help program won't bring such a spirit into our lives. Nevertheless, the passage around 2 Timothy 1:8 points us to some ways by which we can open ourselves to receiving and using that gift. Paul called on Timothy to "rekindle the gift of God that is within you" (v. 6). Imagine how foolish it would be to endure a cold winter day in an unheated house when all one had to do to get warm was turn on the furnace. We evidently have something to do with whether we receive, open, and use God's gift. We should "just do it."

To help Timothy rekindle the gift, Paul recalled the family background of faith from which Timothy had come. The implication is that Timothy could shore up his own faith and courage by recalling the saints who had gone before him in his family—his grandmother and his mother—plus remembering that the hand of the great apostle Paul was on his life. When you face fearful circumstances and challenges to your commitment, recall those who have influenced you in the faith. Their faithfulness in overcoming challenges can remind you that it can be done.

When we receive God's gift of "no fear," we too can confess with the psalmist "The LORD is my light and my salvation; whom shall I fear? The LORD is the stronghold of my life; of whom shall I be afraid" (Ps. 27:1). (Ross West)

JUST DO THE JOB

LUKE 17:5-10

In the face of the ambitious admonitions of Jesus, the disciples ask Jesus to increase their faith. Certainly we can understand this request. How can we really forgive others the way that Jesus has commanded us? Surely, we must be given something that supercharges our abilities. However, Jesus' remarks suggest that what is truly needed is for the disciples to simply do their job as they have been told. The Greek word for "commanded" is *diatasso* and it means to arrange, appoint, or ordain. How many pastors staring at a blank computer screen crave some supercharging inspiration that will inspire them to overcome the challenge of weekly sermon preparation? Yet we are reminded by this text that we are simply commanded to do our jobs: to tell the good news of what God has done in Jesus Christ. No elusive website can provide a substitute for the one thing needed: your thoughts and feelings. As an ordained representative of the faith, this is why you have been set apart. The disciples want to stockpile more faith so that they can begin to address the task of faith. Jesus commands them to address the task of faith first and then experience their growth in the faith. This is the equivalent of acting their way into a new way of feeling.

While ministry can seem like a thankless task at times (and most churches are lax in the area of volunteer appreciation), it is sobering to be reminded that we ultimately do not perform ministry because of what Søren Kierkegaard called "the reward disease." Rather, we are simply doing what we have been called and created to do. If one takes seriously the notion of call to ministry, the ordained person really has no choice but to serve. One could even argue that as God-seeking creatures, all baptized Christians have been designed and appointed to serve. Consequently, we must not hesitate at regular intervals awaiting a big pat on the back. After all, we are simply doing what we have been designed to do. The use of the word *slave* is problematic because we know that people were never intended to be enslaved to others. This is a violation of God's intent. However, the point is made: When we do that which we ought to have done, our behavior is its own reward. Refusing to follow the commandments of Christ embodies its own punishments as well. As we encounter the challenges that always confront service, God will give us faith. At the same time, this text stands as one of many warnings to would-be "super Christians" intent on earning their way to salvation. Most churches rely heavily on highly capable Christians who have a knack for compiling long lists of tasks and plowing through them at an effortless pace. For such capable souls it is sometimes hard to grasp that salvation is truly a gift. While God expects much from those blessed with this capability, they are really just doing what God has created them to do.

Conversely, others say that they will serve just as soon as they have a little bit more understanding and faith. Often such statements become excuses for procrastinating. God wants us to serve—no more and no less. In following our call, we are not heroic nor do we deserve a commendation. By commanding us to service, Jesus has appointed us to help approximate the kingdom of God. We must avoid paralysis through overanalysis. (John Fiedler)

OCTOBER 10, 2004

Nineteenth Sunday After Pentecost

Worship Theme: God on occasion places believers in circumstances that appear unfavorable to the gospel. Yet, the Lord in divine witness causes the flowering and growth of faith in surprising places and in extraordinary ways.

Readings: Jeremiah 29:1, 4-7; 2 Timothy 2:8-15; Luke 17:11-19

Call to Worship (Psalm 66:1, 6-12)

Leader: Make a joyful noise to God, all the earth;

People: **He turned the sea into dry land; they passed through the river on foot.**

Leader: There we rejoiced in him, who rules by his might forever, whose eyes keep watch on the nations— let the rebellious not exalt themselves.

People: **Bless our God, O peoples, let the sound of his praise be heard, who has kept us among the living, and has not let our feet slip.**

Leader: For you, O God, have tested us; you have tried us as silver is tried.

People: **You brought us into the net; you laid burdens on our backs; you let people ride over our heads;**

All: **We went through fire and through water; yet you have brought us out to a spacious place.**

Pastoral Prayer:

Faithful God of Covenant and Promise, we thank you for the opportunities you give us to proclaim your mighty acts on behalf of your people. You call all persons to come within your fold. You also direct us to spread the good news in appropriate and understandable ways. For this gospel task of proclamation, we give you thanks. Often we find the task demanding. Yet your promise to us, O God, is to always be present with us through the agency of the Holy Spirit. Let us turn to the Spirit in our time of need. Help us acknowledge that only by relying on your goodness and mercy can we participate in the abundant life you offer us in Christ Jesus. As Paul counseled Timothy, let us not wrangle over words. Rather let us outdo one another in showing to others honor, mercy, and forgiveness. Let us have the mind that was in Christ Jesus as we journey the path of faith that Jesus showed us. Give us the fortitude to once again claim the name Christian. In Christ's name we pray. Amen. (David Mosser)

SERMON BRIEFS

LIVING IN TIMES OF EXILE

JEREMIAH 29:1, 4-7

I find myself in no-man's-land. I am not at home. The land about me is stark and barren. Life is joyless and colorless. No matter where I turn, there is no shelter to be found. I have no familiar landmarks, no support from those that I love. All of the things that once brought me comfort and security have been stripped away. My soul is laid bare. I feel utterly and completely alone. The future seems without promise, and everything within me cries, "I do not want to be in this place!" All I want is to be at home, surrounded by those who love me, filled with contentment and blessings of God.

The scene I have just described could be about many people in many situations. It describes my feelings following the death of my parents. It describes a young man who has lost his job and worries about his family's security. It describes an older woman who has lost her independence while facing a terminal illness. It describes parents who are experiencing an "empty nest" for the first time in twenty years. It describes a student trying to adjust to life at a new school. It describes the people of Israel as they are carried into exile in the land of Babylon. All these people find themselves in places they do not want to be, and all they want is for things to get back to normal. They are grief stricken and despairing, and in the midst of this, Jeremiah speaks God's surprising words to them. "But seek the welfare of the city where I have sent you into exile, and pray to the LORD on its behalf, for in its welfare you will find your welfare" (v. 7). Surprising advice to those who find themselves in exile and just want to go home.

Jeremiah reminds us that God's way is not always the way we would choose. We often think of peace as being the absence of conflict. We think of peace coming from getting the things we want. Yet, in *The New Interpreter's Bible*, Patrick D. Miller writes that for those in exile, "Such peace is not to be found in resistance and rebellion . . . but in submission. It is not to be found in returning to home, land, and family but in settling into exile and building homes and farms and families there" (6:792). Sometimes God's word to us is that we must stay in this period of exile. The challenge lies in trying to settle in wherever we find ourselves in the moment, seeking God's presence and the blessings that might be found there. God promises to be present to us in these periods of exile. Even in a strange and foreign land, as we seek our welfare, we will find it.

Living in exile is not for the faint of heart. It takes a tremendous amount of energy, fortitude, and faith. It requires for us to continually seek God's Word to us in prayer. We must do our part: building, planting, and investing ourselves, even when we don't feel like it. Much like Jacob (Genesis 32), sometimes we must wrestle in order to come away with a blessing, and on occasion we are left limping. Jeremiah encourages the exiles to settle in and to befriend the very circumstances that are their adversary. As we face an uncertain future, may we know that God's promises are certain. May we continue to have faith in the God of the exiles. (Wendy Joyner)

REMEMBER JESUS CHRIST

2 TIMOTHY 2:8-15

"Remember Jesus Christ." When we hear these words, we may wonder how anyone could forget. Signs and symbols and words about Jesus Christ are all around us: churches, hospitals, television programs, crosses worn as jewelry or lapel pins, bumper stickers, billboards, and t-shirts.

But it was not so in Paul's day. When Paul wrote to Timothy the words, "Remember Jesus Christ," Timothy would have seen few signs and symbols of Jesus Christ as he looked around the city of Ephesus. No church buildings existed that bore the name of Christ. In fact, the only evidence of Jesus Christ that Timothy would likely have seen was in the lives of the small group of Christ's followers to whom he ministered.

So Paul said, "Remember Jesus Christ." Those words were important for Timothy to hear, for only in remembering Jesus Christ could the Christian movement go on and go forward. Despite the prevalence of the Christian symbols in our culture, we would do well also to take Paul's words to heart, lest we forget what the signs and symbols and words are all about. Indeed, we should ask ourselves whether Jesus would approve of all of the things on which his name and the signs and symbols about him are placed these days. "Remember Jesus Christ" is an imperative for us too.

What does it mean to "remember Jesus Christ"? Remembering is an activity of the mind, of course. What do we really look like when we are remembering Jesus Christ? Are we merely sitting in a quiet place with a thoughtful expression on our faces? Paul would have us go much further than that. Consider several actions in this passage of Scripture that indicate what remembering Jesus Christ means.

First, remembering Jesus Christ means emphasizing and sharing the good news about Jesus. The gospel we are to believe and share is not a self-help program, although it offers us help for our deepest needs. It is not a philosophy, although its ideas bring coherence to our lives. It is not an invitation to a meeting, although we find great strength as we learn, serve, and worship together. The gospel we are to believe and share is centered on Jesus Christ and what God has done in him, even resurrecting Jesus from the dead.

Second, remembering Jesus Christ means being faithful to him in our lives, even to the point of enduring suffering and difficulty for him. Remembering Jesus Christ—truly remembering him— can involve us in actions on his behalf that take us far beyond our comfort zone. That is the way remembering Jesus Christ had turned out for Paul (see 2 Cor. 11:23-28). That is the way truly remembering Jesus Christ may turn out for us.

Third, remembering Jesus Christ means focusing on what is truly important in life: presenting ourselves "to God as one approved by him" (v. 15). In Timothy's setting, as often in ours, people found themselves embroiled in controversies and arguments about religion, "wrangling over words." Paul was not saying that words and ideas are unimportant. Paul himself had confronted the Judaizers about their proclaiming "a different gospel" (Gal. 1:6), which perverted the gospel of Christ. Too, Paul urged Timothy to be about the work of "rightly explaining the word of truth." Clear thinking and clear statements about significant matters are important. We must admit, however, that many controversies among Christians these days are about things far less important than the gospel of Jesus Christ. To remember Jesus Christ is to remember to focus on what is truly important— on Jesus Christ himself—so that we, too, may be approved by God. (Ross West)

A BLESSING FOR ALL

LUKE 17:11-19

Luke once again turns his attention to the nature of Jesus' ministry to bless the marginalized and the lost. The story of the ten lepers is a story about human beings' tendency to not quite get all there is to get from what God offers. Ten lepers begged for Jesus to heal them. Jesus instructed them to go to the priests and show themselves, which was in keeping with Jewish ritual law. On the way all ten are healed even before they show themselves to the priests. Nine go their own ways rejoicing in their healing and one, the Samaritan, returns to Jesus to thank him. This story is much more than just a good story about giving thanks. Jesus once again tells a story that is loaded with meaning concerning God's kingdom and those who do and don't respond to its offerings.

The first observation to be made about this story is that the ten lepers are bold enough to ask Jesus to show them his mercy. It is an important gospel motif that asking for what is needed is not only accepted by the Christ but also expected. How can one know what is needed if one does not ask? Asking demonstrates one's ownership and responsibility in seeking that which is needed. So many times as Christians we mistakenly believe that humility prohibits us from asking for what is needed in life. Many times in our lives we believe that humility becomes our reason for not asking when in reality it is pride that keeps us silent. In Alcoholics Anonymous, the starting point for recovery becomes the realization by the alcoholic that he or she has a problem and that an individual must seek out the help so desperately needed. Ten lepers got healed that day because they dared to ask!

In response to their asking, Jesus grants their request for healing with the instruction to show themselves to the priests in keeping with Jewish law. The lepers were on their way when unexpectedly their healing took place. The healing happened as they responded to what Jesus told them to do. I wonder if they would have been healed if they had decided they should not follow Jesus' instructions. Part of God's blessing comes when we follow God's lead in terms of doing what God requires of us.

The healing that comes as they make their way to the priests gives us a look at the abundant nature of God's kingdom on earth. Such is the bounty of a God who loves God's children. Before they even did what was required God blessed them and brought the healing power into their lives by lifting the skin disease from them. Jesus said in John 10:10, "I came that they might have life and have it abundantly." This story reminds us once again of that abundance of the life Jesus seeks to bring to us all.

Once they were healed, nine of the lepers went their own way. But one, after he saw he was healed, went back to Jesus, praising God in a loud voice. After Jesus asks about the other nine, Jesus gives the Samaritan his blessing. Once again Jesus grants much more than healing to the one who returned. He shared with him salvation. For the Samaritan who returned it was a double blessing and a sign of the abundant life Jesus seeks to bring. In a world consumed with the attitude of "what have you done for me lately?" this story reminds us of the bounty of a world blessed by a loving God. Living in response to such blessing demands of us more than just taking what we need or want without so much as a thank you. We give God thanks that God's blessing isn't dependent on our response or lack thereof. But we begin to realize that part of the appropriate response to God's blessing and grace is an awareness of the magnitude of and gratitude for this gift, which leads to God's gracious affirmation and acceptance. The gospel Jesus proclaims isn't reserved just for those who think they have earned it or have some birthright to it. It is a gospel of abundance to all people everywhere, even Samaritans. How can there be any other response but joy and thanksgiving once one realizes such truth? (Travis Franklin)

OCTOBER 17, 2004

Twentieth Sunday After Pentecost

Worship Theme: Part of our assurance of God's covenant with us is that we know that we can pray to God continuously, and God will hear our prayer. We shall know the Lord because the knowledge of God will be within us.

Readings: Jeremiah 31:27-34; 2 Timothy 3:14–4:5; Luke 18:1-8

Call to Worship (Psalm 119:97-104)

> *Leader:* Oh, how I love your law! It is my meditation all day long.

> ***People:*** **Your commandment makes me wiser than my enemies, for it is always with me.**

> *Leader:* I have more understanding than all my teachers, for your decrees are my meditation.

> ***People:*** **I understand more than the aged, for I keep your precepts.**

> *Leader:* I hold back my feet from every evil way, in order to keep your word.

> ***People:*** **I do not turn away from your ordinances, for you have taught me.**

> *Leader:* How sweet are your words to my taste, sweeter than honey to my mouth!

> ***People:*** **Through your precepts I get understanding; therefore I hate every false way.**

Pastoral Prayer:

We worship you, O God, for both the joy of nature and the gift of our own salvation history that you have written on the soul of life. We gather to remember your great deeds of old and to recall the covenant that you made with your people. To Abraham you furnished a land of promise and descendants that are beyond count. To Moses you provided the Torah of teaching and laws and ordinances by which your people could live in holy community and thrive. By these holy laws we dwell secure as a people who have your divine social order as a mandate. Give us the discipline to follow the law's dictate, while never substituting the letter of the law for its spirit. Grant us the wisdom to deal with equity as we deliver judgments concerning your holy will through the law. Give us a passion for prayer that originates in our hearts, but a prayer that reveals itself through the compassion of our actions. Make us a people formed by a covenant, we pray, between sisters and brothers in Christ. Amen. (David Mosser)

SERMON BRIEFS

WITH GOD'S HELP

JEREMIAH 31:27-34

A friend of mine is a deacon in the Episcopal church, and we sometimes share stories about differences in our liturgical traditions. Many times, we have talked about the power of a more formal liturgy becoming ingrained in our minds and hearts. One day, my friend shared a story with me about taking an oath for a secular position of public service. During the ceremony, when they asked if she would serve to the best of her ability, she responded, "I will, with God's help." She had used some of the language from the Episcopal liturgy instead of their suggested response! She was somewhat embarrassed about offering this response in a public forum, yet as we reflected on this situation, we realized the truth it contained. "I will with God's help."

Since the beginning of history, the people of God have struggled to be faithful and obedient in their relationship to God. One of the

345

most important areas of struggle in this relationship has surrounded the notion of covenant between God and humanity in a reciprocal relationship with both benefit and mutual responsibility. Throughout the generations, the people of God have entered into covenant with God time and again, only to fail to meet their responsibilities as outlined in the covenant. God has forgiven, and then another covenant has been established. We see these cycles of covenant, disobedience, judgment, and restoration acted out over and over again.

Here in the book of Jeremiah, God had again called the nation of Israel into relationship, only to have God's heart broken after a period of unfaithfulness. The never-ending cycle seemed destined to repeat itself yet again. R. E. Clements writes about this cycle of obedience and disobedience as he asks, "If Israel's sins in the past brought such fearful judgment upon the nation so that it came close to total annihilation, what assurance can there be that after a future restoration has taken place the same fate will not befall Israel again?" (*Jeremiah,* Interpretation Bible Commentary [Louisville: Westminster John Knox Press, 1989], p. 190).

Yet Jeremiah promises in this passage that God is about to do a new thing. God says to the house of Israel, "I will put my law within them, and I will write it on their hearts; and I will be their God, and they shall be my people" (v. 33). Through God's grace, the previous obstacles to the covenant relationship will be removed. God will work within the hearts and lives of the people of Israel to help them in their quest for faithful relationship. Clements notes that "The old covenant of the law is dead; instead there will be an inner power and motivation towards obedience on the part of Israel written on the very hearts of the People of God, not on tablets of stone" (p. 190).

Perhaps it is time for us to again hear God's promises to the people of Israel. We need to be reminded that God not only calls us into a relationship but also gives us the strength and power to be obedient and faithful within that relationship. How many times in our own lives do we forget about the grace that God provides for us within covenant relationship? It is so easy to lapse into a "works righteousness," relying on our own strength to live up to our end of the bargain with God. We forget the gracious gift of God, God's Spirit working within us, changing our hearts. The good news, and the challenge, is to realize that we are able to be faithful only "with God's help." (Wendy Joyner)

SCRATCHY RELIGION

2 TIMOTHY 3:14–4:5

Cell phones seem to be everywhere, including some places they should not be found. Please, would you check now to be sure that your cell phone is turned off?

One of the problems users of cell phones encounter from time to time is poor reception. We lose the signal entirely, or we find ourselves straining to understand. Perhaps all we can hear is what sounds like scratching. This scratchiness can prevent us from hearing what we need to hear.

Paul warned Timothy about folks who had "scratchy religion." Actually, he said they had "itching ears." Their reception of "sound doctrine" was scratchy, unclear. In fact, they didn't want to hear "sound doctrine," healthy teaching of the gospel. What they were "itching" to hear was not the genuine teaching of the gospel but ideas that merely confirmed the beliefs and prejudices they already had.

How good it is that we have no such folks in the twenty-first century and that we ourselves never have to deal with such problems! Would that it were so! As we seek to be faithful in living and proclaiming the gospel, temptations to do otherwise come to us regularly.

In fact, we Christians are engaged in a great struggle about what the gospel is and how we are going to share it. How will we present the age-old message of the gospel so that folks today will pay attention? To what extent, for example, will we use certain marketing and communication techniques to connect our church and the gospel with people? We must not insist on using nineteenth- and twentieth-century methods and fail to seek new ways to minister. God is always calling us to seek creative ways, new ways, to get the gospel to people. Every generation of Christians at their best has sought new ways to minister. We must do that, too. At the same time, we must also be careful not to alter or even discard the gospel as we change the methods.

The gospel—what God has done in Jesus Christ for us—is what is unique about the church's message. We must not let ourselves get away from it. We can learn much about our world from the various disciplines of learning, and we should. They need not be a threat to our faith. Indeed, we Christians should be the leaders in encouraging intellectual pursuits. At the same time that we tap these resources, let us listen to and proclaim the truth of the gospel. That's what Paul urged Timothy to do in 4:2. That's what we are to do. When we do this, the gospel becomes the foundation for our lives, a foundation that cannot be shaken.

Paul had just finished reminding Timothy of the importance of continuing in what he had "learned and firmly believed" (v. 14). He reminded Timothy that from childhood Timothy had "known the sacred writings that are able to instruct you for salvation through faith in Christ Jesus" (v. 15). How good it is to be able to look back on a childhood that included loving guidance in spiritual matters! Let us remind ourselves, too, that as we instruct and minister to children today in our church and in our homes that what we do is of eternal importance.

Note, too, the foundation for this instruction: "the sacred writings." Timothy would have understood these "sacred writings" to be what we know as the Old Testament. Our definition of these "sacred writings" would include the New Testament. Verses 16-17 remind us of the significance and power of scripture.

Cell phone users know that they can sometimes improve reception if they'll get close to a window or even get closer to the tower that sends the signal out. When we experience scratchy religion, it's time to turn again to the "sacred writings" and reemphasize the gospel. (Ross West)

THE DEMANDING WIDOW

LUKE 18:1-8

Jesus tells a parable about a remarkable woman who through sheer force of will is able to convince a corrupt judge to give her justice. Why did the incompetent judge do the right thing? Because the widow bothered him. The Greek word here is *pare-cho,* and it means to cause one to have something, either favorable or unfavorable. Another connotation means to show oneself. Regular prayer incorporates both of these qualities. While we

must resist ever drawing a direct cause and effect between petitioning prayer and favorable results (in that we don't always get
the response we want or expect), Jesus is telling us that God
expects to hear from us. Through prayer, we are granted the privilege of an audience with our Creator. Persons who truly believe
that they have this venue to God will not neglect it. Further, we
have an opportunity through regular prayer to show ourselves to
God. Once again we encounter the paradox of God's sovereignty
versus our ability to act. We must take pains not to reduce the
status of God to some cosmic waitperson that brings us what we
ask for. Rather, Jesus is talking about the importance of persistence and conscientious communication with God. If an indifferent judge delivers a woman because of her persistence, how will
a loving God respond to our prayers? Consequently, Jesus invites
us to take ownership of our prayer life. I have heard it said before
that prayer does not change God but rather prayer changes us.
This text actually indicates something different than that. Ongoing dedicated prayer would seem to make inroads into the consciousness of God. While we do not have the power to redefine
God's essence, our prayers may influence God's decisions. God,
with infinite compassion, will not ignore our presence through
prayer. Further, by being persistent in seeking God's attention we
act true to our own nature. God has created us to be God-seek-
ers. When we defy this essential nature and pursue the idols of
self, we fall into despair. For this reason, consistent petition to
God keeps us stretching toward the divine. This prayerful pester-
ing not only can result in a positive response from God but also
keeps us from being distracted by so many other petty pursuits.
In short, striving to reach God makes it easier for us to allow God
to find us.

The idea of presenting oneself to God represents the very best
that we can offer. In the Christian faith, we hold incarnation as a
sacred gift whereby God cared enough to come in person, or in
the flesh. When we make it a priority to show up to God, our
decision has important benefits for our lives.

In addition to petitioning God, we can take inspiration from
the widow in the parable and ask ourselves, "What if we
demanded justice for others the way that the widow demanded
justice for herself?" All too often we rest comfortably upon con-

ventional reasons why true justice cannot happen. Inventory your parish and see what needs are not being met and then brainstorm how your church can meet those needs. Usually, problems settle into an equilibrium that requires a substantial change in some variable. If the education level is low, you can recruit volunteers to tutor. If there are children going to school hungry, your church can provide a school breakfast program. All too often the response of churches is that they would help if they had the money, and then the very same church turns around and raises thousands to invest in brick and mortar. The widow's example prods us to keep people first. (John Fiedler)

OCTOBER 24, 2004

Twenty-first Sunday After Pentecost

Worship Theme: The quality of our prayers offered to our God reveals the character of those who produce the prayers.

Readings: Joel 2:23-32; 2 Timothy 4:6-8, 16-18; Luke 18:9-14

Call to Worship (Psalm 65:1-2*a*, 4-6, 8-9)

Leader: Praise is due to you, O God, in Zion; and to you shall vows be performed, O you who answer prayer!

People: **Happy are those whom you choose and bring near to live in your courts.**

Leader: We shall be satisfied with the goodness of your house, your holy temple.

People: **By awesome deeds you answer us with deliverance, O God of our salvation; You are the hope of all the ends of the earth and of the farthest seas.**

Leader: By your strength you established the mountains; you are girded with might.

People: **Those who live at earth's farthest bounds are awed by your signs; you make the gateways of the morning and the evening shout for joy.**

All: **You visit the earth and water it, you greatly enrich it; the river of God is full of water; you provide the people with grain, for so you have prepared it.**

Pastoral Prayer:

We rejoice in you, Lord of Heaven and Earth. Our assembly sings your praises and shouts thanksgiving to you who has created and is creating. In you the rains fall and the flower blooms. Out of your generous benevolence toward your creation we live in the garden of your keeping. You have asked us to till and keep it, yet it is your handiwork that we extol. You have given us plenty and fed us from your hand. All that you ask of us is that we be our sister and brother's keepers. Is this so much to ask? We fail when we forget that many do not eat and do not thrive. Insofar as it is within our power, help us provide for those who live at the margins of our society. Let us reach out to others in the name of Jesus. Jesus always took time for the children, the aged, the lonely, the hungry, and those trapped in literal or figurative prisons. Can we do less? Let us respond to your grace with gracious action on behalf of those for whom Christ also died. We pray for this strength in Jesus' holy name. Amen. (David Mosser)

SERMON BRIEFS

IN THE BEGINNING, AGAIN AND AGAIN

JOEL 2:23-32

What a time that will be! When God pours out the Spirit on all flesh, it will be a time of spiritual renewal, a time of rejoicing, a time of reversal, a time of reunion and communion, a time of fireworks and smoke—the coming of the kingdom of God.

We pray for that time every Sunday—"Our Father which art in heaven, . . . thy kingdom come. Thy will be done in earth, as it is in heaven"—and wait for that time to come (Matt. 6:9-10 KJV).

The prophets throughout the ages have painted word pictures of the kingdom of God. Joel is no exception. Joel doesn't stop with graphics of death and destruction, but moves on to paint an up-to-date picture of God's kingdom for the people of his time.

According to Joel, the kingdom of God affects the whole of creation. It is a restoration to the way things were in the beginning, back in that first garden. There will be food and wine enough for all. Remember that Adam, because of his sin, was condemned to struggle to get enough to eat, when food had been freely given in the garden. Now, once again, because of God's graciousness, not because of any human effort, everyone shall eat in plenty.

In the kingdom of God, which Joel sees as Israel restored, "My people shall never again be put to shame" (v. 26d). Remember, once again, that garden of beginnings. Adam and Eve were naked, and they were not ashamed. They had no reason to hide from God, until they had sinned. Now God wipes the slate clean, people are freed from the stain of shame and can begin again.

In the kingdom of God, God walks with creation. "You shall know that I am in the midst of Israel" (v. 27a). God walked with Adam and Eve in that early garden. God moved in close relationship with humanity. Now, in salvation, God walks again in the midst of God's people.

In the kingdom of God, there are no distinctions that separate. God's Spirit is poured out on all flesh. Hear that: *all flesh*.

Traditionally, the prophets were wise and old, but Joel reports that God will pour the spirit of prophecy on young men. Traditionally the prophets were male, but Joel reports that God will pour the spirit of prophecy on women. Traditionally young men were the dreamers of the culture and the elders were those who held steadfast to the conservative traditions. But Joel reports that God will cause old men to dream dreams, to "think young" again. Traditionally slaves were not considered worthy of God's concern. But Joel reports that God will pour out the spirit even on those slaves, who were often pagan foreigners.

In the kingdom of God, creation is restored to God's will and God says it is very good.

So that's Joel's time, but what about today? What about now? Didn't Jesus say something about God's kingdom coming here and now? What are the signs we can look for today?

God's kingdom is present today wherever the hungry are fed, wherever abundance is shared, wherever God is praised for providing. God's kingdom is present today wherever those who have known shame are healed and restored: victims of sexual and physical abuse; children who have been bullied and put down; repentant thieves and murderers; and run-of-the-mill sinners like you and me. God's kingdom is present today wherever God's footprints are seen in our society. Wherever outcasts are embraced, conflicts are reconciled, faith in light of crisis is sustained, or pain and suffering are endured with hope, God walks with us. God's kingdom is present today wherever our children lead us in renewing our world; wherever our elders look to the future with hope; wherever men and women dwell and work as equals; and wherever distinctions of class, race, religion, gender, or sexual orientation draw no lines in compassion and caring.

Wherever God's kingdom is present, God is in the process of beginning again and again and again.

And, wherever these things happen, God says it is very good. (Sharee Johnson)

TAKING THE VICTORY LAP

2 TIMOTHY 4:6-8, 16-18

A custom in some racing sports is for the winner to take a victory lap, one more lap around the track in recognition of having finished and won the race. This passage, particularly verses 6-8, depicts Paul taking that victory lap. He could even see out ahead of him an awards ceremony in which the Lord would give him "the crown of righteousness." Picture the Olympic awards ceremony multiplied infinitely in grandeur.

At first glance, it seems as if Paul was boasting of his Christian exploits. Perhaps we can excuse such boasting, given the greatness of the apostle Paul. Actually, however, Paul himself puts these verses in perspective. In 1 Timothy 1:15, Paul referred to himself as the "foremost" of sinners. He also confessed how he had been "a blasphemer, a persecutor, and a man of violence" (1 Tim. 1:13). In our text Paul testifies of how the Lord stood by him and gave him strength and of how the Lord had "rescued" him and would continue to do so (v. 17). If we see Paul appearing to boast as he takes his victory lap in verses 6-8, let us temper that with these confessions of Paul's need and of his reliance on God. We should see Paul running his victory lap not of his own strength but in the strength of God, who had granted mercy to him.

What about the race you are running? Is there a victory lap in your future? According to your current stage of life, you may consider your victory lap to be so far off that it is beyond the horizon. You may be right, but do not forget that life can slip by quickly, even unexpectedly. Or you may see your victory lap off in the distance, either near or far. You may even feel that you are beginning that victory lap right now. Whatever your stage of life, it is important that you begin now for preparing to run that victory lap.

The athletic images that appear throughout Paul's writings indicate that if he was not an athlete himself, he was a fan of athletic events. In 1 Corinthians 9:25-26, Paul provided a vivid image of the necessity of preparation and discipline in the life of the athlete. Athletes do not suddenly begin running the victory lap. If they tried to do so, they would be booed off the track. To run the victory lap, athletes must first run the race. Even before that, they must prepare and discipline themselves as athletes.

This athletic image speaks to our lives as human beings and as Christians. It is true that we can "turn over a new leaf" at any stage of our lives, even in the senior adult years. By God's grace and mercy, we can run the victory lap even though we might get into the race late, very late. Still, people we have known who have lived life this way have generally expressed two main feelings. The first feeling is joy that they at last got their lives on the right track. That feeling of joy is tinged with regret, however, regret that they waited so long and wasted so much of life before they decided to take another, better way.

As with the victorious athlete, Paul's Christian life had not been easy. Holding to his Christian convictions and pursuing his Christian mission had placed him in dangerous and difficult situations. If such has not been our lot, we would do well to ask ourselves whether the Lord has simply allowed us to serve in less dangerous situations or whether we are as faithful to the Lord as the Lord expects. Let us begin preparing now so that we will be ready to take our own victory laps. (Ross West)

CONFESSION LEADS TO EXALTATION

LUKE 18:9-14

As a one-point, short narrative, a parable drives home a specific truth, and this one is no exception. Jesus teaches the disciples (and us) that humility is the way to righteousness. The Pharisee follows the law to the letter and uses his relationship with the law to justify himself. Unfortunately, he is trying to be righteous through his relationship with an inanimate object: the scroll of scriptures. He does not request God's mercy but rather states his case as a self-righteous individual. The tax collector, however, relies completely on God's mercy. This parable of Jesus makes clear that this is what we, too, are called to do.

Yet in order for this process to be authentic for us, we must recognize our own sinfulness. There are many barriers to this: We are easily self-deceived, and we are quick to grant forgiveness to ourselves as we cite extenuating circumstances. It's always interesting to read about a fundamentalist preacher who demands that ministers who experience divorce resign from the ministry—until their own (the fundamentalist preacher's) marriage comes to a screeching halt. Suddenly, they are granted a mandate from the congregation and dispensation from God allowing them to continue despite their divorce.

The goal we should all cherish is going home justified. The Greek word translated as "justified" is *dikaioo* and it means "to render righteous." Why is it so hard for us to grasp that we simply cannot render ourselves righteous? This is the human condition that God sent Christ to rectify. As fallible humans we require the intervention of an agent on our behalf so that we might be rendered righteous. This is the radical gift of grace available to us in Christ. However, good deeds can be an impediment for this grace if we use such deeds to perpetuate a delusion of self-reliance and lack of sin. Authentic faith cannot be used as a lever to view others through a lens of superiority.

Still, in an age where high self-esteem seems to be the Holy Grail of most spiritual pursuits, how can we Christians endorse an attitude of self-flagellation and referencing ourselves as sinners? The answer to this important question is that confession does not demean our self-image. Rather, it solidifies it by providing an accurate understanding of our true nature. Only then do we make the connection regarding our need for God. The tax collector would seem to have little need for God other than to share with the Almighty a glowing progress report.

I recall my first Sunday at my first solo pastoral assignment. After the service, a middle-aged couple waited patiently as the other congregants filed past. When everyone else was gone they announced that they always went to lunch with the pastor and pastor's family. Then with a knowing look, they went on to say that they were "on a higher spiritual plane" than the rest of the congregation. Time revealed that this was hardly the case. Rather, they had a desperate need to appear spiritual and to curry the minister's favor. As we experience Christians who make audacious claims regarding their lofty status before God (or listen to preachers who couch their admonitions in such a way that it is understood that they have already achieved Christian perfection), I am continually amazed at such efforts to turn Christ's message of grace back into law. I find myself wanting to say, "You're right. That faith is certainly biblical all right, but weren't those people called Pharisees?" This parable states clearly that Jesus does not endorse a faith that exalts itself. (John Fiedler)

OCTOBER 31, 2004

Twenty-second Sunday After Pentecost

Worship Theme: No person is beyond the reach of God's gracious hand. Even when we feel near despair or, in our pride, think that we have no need of God, nothing within us or without "will be able to separate us from the love of God in Christ Jesus our Lord" (Rom. 8:39).

Readings: Habakkuk 1:1-4; 2:1-4; 2 Thessalonians 1:1-4, 11-12; Luke 19:1-10

Call to Worship (Psalm 119:137-144)

Leader: You are righteous, O LORD, and your judgments are right.

People: **You have appointed your decrees in righteousness and in all faithfulness.**

Leader: My zeal consumes me because my foes forget your words.

People: **Your promise is well tried, and your servant loves it.**

Leader: I am small and despised, yet I do not forget your precepts.

People: **Your righteousness is an everlasting righteousness, and your law is the truth.**

Leader: Trouble and anguish have come upon me, but your commandments are my delight.

People: **Your decrees are righteous forever; give me understanding that I may live.**

Pastoral Prayer:

In your imaginative grace you conceived us, O Lord. We are your people because you not only created us but also named us at our baptisms. You gave us not only a name but also a task. Our task is to follow the upward call you presented to us in the life, death, and resurrection of Jesus Christ, our Lord and Messiah. When the task becomes heavy, Lord, you bring to our attention that, "my yoke is easy, and my burden is light" (Matt. 11:30). Give us the faith to believe this beautiful promise of Jesus. Help us live under that promise and be covered by your spirit of loving-kindness. When we stumble on the path toward the divine dominion of the heavenly places, you, O God, pick us up. When our integrity fails us, you beckon us once again to walk before you with integrity of heart and uprightness. You summon us, O Lord, to listen to all you have commanded us. Help us turn to scripture and the story of faith when life and its multiplicity of choices befuddle us. Let us stay close to your voice and presence. In Jesus' name we pray. Amen. (David Mosser)

SERMON BRIEFS

FAITH REQUIRED

HABAKKUK 1:1-4; 2:1-4

From Habakkuk to Paul to Martin Luther to Mother Teresa, for all who follow Jesus Christ, faith is the required reality. Apart from faith, as Hebrews 11:6 reminds us, we cannot please God. But what is faith? Dr. R. Maurice Boyd, Pastor of The City Church of New York, reminded me not long ago that faith is not something we acquire, but rather a reality, an attitude God places deep within our lives. Harry Emerson Fosdick was fond of saying "faith is not something you get, but rather something you have."

Now faith is not optimism, a shallow, ephemeral, thin smile we place on all that is gloomy and threatening. Nor is faith "believeism" that conjures up some good feeling about how things could be if only everyone believed in God. For some, faith is nothing more than a slogan when life crumbles around one's feet. What is faith?

In my judgment, faith is a reality within us that enables us to face the fierce and often brutal "slings and arrows" of this life, all the while believing God will bring God's purposes to their full and faithful conclusion. Faith is not fantasizing a better future, but a gift from God to live today into whatever the future may bring.

The prophet Habakkuk was a realist. He began his prophecy, as recorded in the book that bears his name, by complaining! All around him is violence, death, destruction, and injustice. Life, as he sees it, is crumbling under the weight of human folly and self-destruction. Unlike most of us, however, Habakkuk is a realist who dares to believe. In other words, he does not give up on God. Government has a role to play in maintaining civil order; the integrity of the family unit is much of the glue that holds our lives together; friendships give deep meaning to being human, but in all of reality only God can live, move, and be faithful simultaneously. Believing God is present in all of life is bedrock to living by faith.

The first four verses of Habakkuk 2 are profoundly etched in the Hebrew and Christian faiths. Chiseled into the rock of the Protestant Reformation is "the righteous live by their faith." But how? How does one face the challenges of a day's worth of living with faith?

First, and at the very least, we are called to "keep watch!" Faith summons us "to see what [God] will say" to us. Most times, we of faith simply quit looking for God. Either we have "found" God in our theological system and have no need to look elsewhere, or we have relegated God to some safe, predictable place, such as the church, a seminary community, or a prayer group. Faith means to "watch for God!"

Second, we are to look for the vision. As a child, I learned from my mother that when you lose something and can't find it in the place where it ought to be, start looking in places where it ought not to be. The gospel of our Lord Jesus Christ is all about God's transforming vision at work making "all things new."

Our society deeply needs Christian believers to be "salt and light" as mentors to children in the public schools, workers at after-school programs, helpers in soup kitchens, and companions to the elderly. Look for the vision in unexpected places.

Finally, Habakkuk calls us to live "as if" the fulfillment of God's promises has already taken place. To "live by faith" is to live "as if" God's kingdom has already come and God's will is already being done. Imagine what transforming work could happen if we would live by faith "as if" we are forgiven of our sins, "as if" we are reconciled to each other, "as if" we are healed of our painful memories, "as if" all God's people were your sisters and brothers. (Timothy Owings)

GRACE AND PEACE TO YOU

2 THESSALONIANS 1:1-4, 11-12

"Grace to you and peace from God our Father and the Lord Jesus Christ." This is the same manner in which Paul begins several of his letters to the early churches. It is a common greeting for Christians, one the readers of the letter would recognize. They probably even quickly skipped over this part of the greeting just as we would briskly skim over, "So how are things with you? I am doing fine." However, in this letter, the opening sentence should not be skimmed. It offers a word that the church at Thessalonica urgently needs to hear.

Paul, Silvanus, and Timothy, those noted for penning the letter, give thanks to God for the faith of the church, which is growing abundantly. Their love is increasing so much that they are worthy of boasting about it to other churches. Through their persecutions they have been faithful and steadfast. The authors of the letter offer a prayer that God will make the church worthy of "his call" and fulfill works of faith among the members.

No pressure on the church at all! Paul, Silvanus, and Timothy's praises of the church serve as encouragements to continue growing, loving, and being faithful, steadfast, and worthy. What a tall order! This is why the opening statement in this letter to the Thessalonians is more than just a greeting. The church has much to do and a great letter of praise by which they are measured. They need a command of grace and peace. They need to take the time to rest in the comforting arms of the God for whom they are working so intensely. In the midst of their growing, loving, and being faithful throughout persecutions, Paul extends to them a word of peace. They receive grace—soothing words from those who understand their condition better than anyone else could.

This simple introductory statement at the beginning of 2 Thessalonians is a message for us as well. Jesus Christ writes the same letter to each of us. "To my beloved, hard working Vacation Bible School worker; to my dedicated church organist; to my tired friend who always sits on the back row; grace and peace to you, from me."

Unfortunately, we are often too busy to read the letter. We have to go to work to be able to make enough money to tithe our ten percent. We have to make the extra sandwiches in the morning to drop off at the homeless shelter. We have to mow the neighbor's lawn because her husband is sick. We have to visit the new parents in the hospital. Each of these is a noble and worthy task. They are tasks that should be done within the body of Christ, as those within the church at Thessalonica do. But the command for peace and grace comes in at the point when we become so busy with the tasks of the church that we forget to be the church.

Our time should be spent, as in the letter of 2 Thessalonians, loving, growing, and being faithful and steadfast in the love of God. Yet these are tasks, righteous as they are, which take a great deal of time and energy. We are offered a respite in the midst of our busy righteousness. We are offered grace and peace. Notice in the letter that it is not a suggestion; it is a command. "Grace to you and peace from God our Father and the Lord Jesus Christ." It is time to sit, rest, and listen. Grace and peace to you. (Victoria Atkinson White)

COMING DOWN TO SALVATION

LUKE 19:1-10

As I read this passage I can visualize my college-aged daughter as she performed in the preschool musical singing, "Zacchaeus, you come down. 'Cause I'm coming to your house today." What a great surprise for this individual! Zacchaeus was a very resourceful type, able to work his way up to being the head tax collector. He was rich, yet he was also aware that he needed something else in his life. Why else would he go to such extra effort to see Jesus? His "sycamore plan" was a good strategy even more than he could have imagined. Jesus called him by name and announced that he would be staying at his house. This announcement resulted in two immediate responses: the grumbling of the bystanders and the announcement by Zacchaeus that he would donate half of his possessions to the poor.

It is refreshing to be reminded that people grumbled about the decisions that Jesus made as well. One of the real "joy-sucking" dynamics of church is grumbling. If ever there was a brand X alternative to being a person of faith, it was Zacchaeus. Yet Jesus affirmed Zacchaeus! We never can escape the human propensity to compare our blessings with those of another. Grumbling is a tiresome dynamic in the church, yet we can know that even Jesus was not spared the pettiness of daily life.

Still, Jesus had no problem enduring the second-guessing of the bystanders. His choice to choose Zacchaeus yielded immediate results. This diminutive tax collector was needful of a catharsis by which he could reconcile with his self-seeking ways. Jesus called him by name and gave him just such an opportunity. Have you ever noticed what a difference it makes to be able to call a person by his or her name? Naming gives us access to a person in a very profound way. We cannot know how Jesus knew this tax collector's name, yet we see the power of Jesus calling him by name. Zacchaeus was quite literally "up a tree," and Jesus commanded him to come down and be host to the Lord of life.

The narrative culminates in Jesus pronouncing that salvation had come to Zacchaeus. The Greek word translated as "salvation" is *soteria,* and it means "deliverance and preservation." Zacchaeus's deliverance comes as a result of his dramatic response to the call of Jesus in his life. Zacchaeus has a change of heart. While most Christians would be hard-pressed to point to one single encounter as the source of their call, the theme of calling is a vital one. Jesus actively invited persons to a better life. Those of us who would claim to represent the way of Christ can do no less. We must actively invite others to a better life. Many mainline Protestants have so honored the free choice of others that we have virtually abdicated the responsibility of inviting others to Christ. Often we have been so jaded by seeing instances of manipulative or coercive evangelism that we decide not to discuss our faith at all. However, such overreaction is unfortunate. Why? Because responsible, timely inviting can render dramatic results in the lives of persons. In other words, we really can make an important difference, and we must never forget this. When we have the courage to invite the stranger, the homeless person, and the person with different views than our own, we emulate Christ. Picture a society of alienated individuals perched on tree limbs for a better view of what's going on. Such persons are isolated and alienated from the goodness of God's kingdom. You can be a means by which they are called to be a part. You can help ensure that Christ dwells within their home. (John Fiedler)

REFLECTIONS

NOVEMBER

Reflection Verse: *"Though the fig tree does not blossom,*
   and no fruit is on the vines;
though the produce of the olive fails,
   and the fields yield no food;
though the flock is cut off from the fold,
   and there is no herd in the stalls,
yet I will rejoice in the LORD;
   I will exult in the God of my salvation." (Habakkuk 3:17-18)

I am not sure about most people, but occasionally I get a little downcast with a tinge of discouragement near the beginning of November. Maybe this odd characterization of November is because many of my closest friends are preachers. I cannot speak for others, not even for my most familiar colleagues, but I experience November as an austere month for preachers for several reasons.

First, I have noticed in my twenty-five plus years of ministry that I celebrate more services of death and resurrection in November than any other month, with January and February a close second and third respectively. With All Saints' Day as a reminder in November of departed saints whom we revere, the memory of these people often occupies my innermost thoughts.

Second, many churches raise the topic of next year's budget in November. We all know enough church history to know that raising money has never been easy, but this necessity seems especially difficult today.

Third, shorter days signal the end of the old year. In addition, this shortening of days has a debilitating effect on our optimism. All these circumstances can make November slightly gloomy. The prophet Habakkuk prophesied in a gloomy time, and perhaps he is a good voice for us to heed in the starkness of November.

When we hear the name *Habakkuk* pronounced out loud our first inclination is to call a doctor. Who is this prophet with a strange name (which means "to embrace") and what does he have to say to the people of God? Surprisingly for most of us, Habakkuk is a prophet who says much about things to which we can relate. One of the first issues addressed in this prophecy is the issue of God's justice. Sounding much like a psalm of lament, Habakkuk launches his prophetic word: "O LORD, how long shall I cry for help, and you will not listen? Or cry to you 'Violence!' and you will not save?" (Hab. 1:2).

Such questions might reflect all too human doubts about God's readiness to protect God's people. However, another way to understand Habakkuk's words are simply as an honest plea for the Lord to look upon God's people and come to their aid. Few faithful people have not been in circumstances in which they have prayed for God, even begged God, to intervene on their behalf. We all know of situations and times in which we knew we needed divine help, and needed it desperately.

Whether we know we need divine help because of physical infirmities, economic problems, relationship problems, or so called acts of God, we seek a God who too often seems silent. What can we know, and where can we turn for answers?

Among many questions that Habakkuk packs into his brief prophecy, one is plainly the question concerning human suffering. Part of our human predicament in understanding suffering is that we see suffering from an angle that is not always realistic. In order for us to exercise our choice in human free will, God cannot predetermine the outcomes of various human decisions. If God did predetermine every step that we take in life, then why did Jesus teach so much about the importance and qualities of our decisions? Jesus urged people to love rather than hate, to trust God rather than wealth, and to decide to live a godly life rather than one that was strictly self-serving. Even in Jesus' parable of the dishonest steward, a servant whom Jesus lifts up as an example of good faith, the servant says, "I have decided what to do so that, when I am dismissed as manager, people may welcome me into their homes" (Luke 16:4).

Our decisions are important. But our decisions also must be authentic decisions and in fact be free, not simply appear to be free. Therefore, God may know all the possible outcomes of a certain decision or action, but God does not determine what we will do or how we decide. We do that. This is what makes the ethical life possible. It also gives our decisions meaning. Thus our perspective on life is what either gives that life meaning or sinks us into a mire of anxious unknowing.

Our perspective determines our response. Habakkuk prophesied to his people that although God often seemed far away, in reality God still rules over all. If we are to be truly free with respect to the human free will given to us by God, then occasionally we will question God's providential care for us. It is only a natural human response. But even in the darkest of human circumstances, Habakkuk reminds those who have ears to hear of a very important affirmation of faith.

In 2001, Gregory Knox Jones wrote a book entitled *Play the Ball Where the Monkey Drops It*. In it he tells a story about how British golfers in India were constantly bedeviled on a golf course they built in Calcutta, presumably in the 1920s. After inventing a half dozen ways to combat the monkeys who kept picking up the golf balls—sometimes helping the golfer, sometimes hurting the golfer—an ingenious new golf rule emerged: Play the ball where the monkey drops it.

Sometimes the monkey helps you, and sometimes the monkey hurts you. Sometimes you hit a perfect shot, and the monkey carries it into the rough. Sometimes you hit into the rough, and the monkey carries it and places it next to the hole. Either way, you never know how the monkey will affect your shot or your game. Life is like this. But even in the darkest of human circumstances, Habakkuk reminds those who have ears to hear of a very important affirmation of faith. Habakkuk reminds even faithful preachers that, despite outward circumstances of life, God remains in the fabric of our lives—even in the darkest days of November.

"Though the fig tree does not blossom, / and no fruit is on the vines; . . . / yet I will rejoice in the LORD" (Hab. 3:17-18). (David Mosser)

NOVEMBER 7, 2004

Twenty-third Sunday After Pentecost

Worship Theme: Our God is the God of the living. Therefore the life we live for Christ makes all the difference.

Readings: Haggai 1:15*b*–2:9; 2 Thessalonians 2:1-5, 13-17; Luke 20:27-38

Call to Worship (Psalm 145:1-5, 17-21 RSV)

Leader: I will extol thee, my God and King, and bless thy name for ever and ever.

People: **Every day I will bless thee, and praise thy name for ever and ever.**

Leader: Great is the LORD, and greatly to be praised, and his greatness is unsearchable.

People: **One generation shall laud thy works to another, and shall declare thy mighty acts.**

Leader: On the glorious splendor of thy majesty, and on thy wondrous works, I will meditate.

People: **The LORD is just in all his ways, and kind in all his doings.**

Leader: The Lord is near to all who call upon him, to all who call upon him in truth.

People: **He fulfils the desire of all who fear him, he also hears their cry, and saves them.**

Leader: The LORD preserves all who love him. . . .

All: **My mouth will speak the praise of the LORD, and let all flesh bless his holy name for ever and ever.**

Pastoral Prayer:
God of all Benevolence, we search our hearts and minds, and yet your ways are inscrutable to us. Even in our most earnest meditation we still cannot plumb the depths of your magnificent love for us. Help us accept your grace poured into our lives daily. Create in us the desire to live in thanksgiving, knowing that we can never repay your divine generosity. At the same time, remind us of your mandate: food for the hungry and care for the needy. Grant us loving hearts that never begrudge what we share with others. Furnish us eyes that see those in need and hearts that help others retain dignity when we offer of our bounty. Let us share our treasure given us out of your great generosity, O God. Help us understand that our time is a most precious gift. By sharing it with others we please you. In all that we undertake may others see your loving hand in all we do. We pray for this character strength in Christ's sacred name. Amen. (David Mosser)

SERMON BRIEFS

TAKE COURAGE AND WORK

HAGGAI 1:15*b*–2:9

As a nation, we have had four years to determine the direction our country was taking. One day, Tuesday, we voted to influence our future. Of course, in the last year and a half, we have been inundated with campaign speeches, bipartisan rhetoric, idealistic promises, and political ads, to say nothing of the mudslinging and name-calling. The airwaves are restfully quiet and the inaugural balls anticipated while we settle in for another four years. How does it look to you now? Remember four years ago? Al Gore's phone call to concede the race had been made—and rescinded—

and the "official" announcement of the presidential election was postponed until we settled all the court cases and countersuits.

We still postpone, put off, delay important instructions and decisions, just like those exiles who returned home to Jerusalem all those years ago. Procrastination is nondiscriminatory; it plagues all occupations, ages, races, creeds, genders, and ethnic groups.

The exiles had returned to their homeland eighteen years before, with the intention of rebuilding the temple. Then, in chapter one of the book of Haggai, the prophet had reminded these procrastinators that their homes had roofs, their fields were planted, they had food and drink, but God's house still lies in ruin. Haggai invites them to consider if their sparse harvest and meager wages might not be a testimony to God's displeasure.

Through the mouth of Haggai come the words of the Lord of hosts, "Build my house. You have taken care of yourselves long enough, now build my house, or I will call a drought on you and everything you love and are dependent on."

The Israelites then begin work on God's house. Even with the support of the top political and religious leaders like Zerubbabel and Joshua, the work goes slowly. Haggai must again remind them of what the Lord said: take courage, work, and do not fear.

Fear: a debilitating root cause of procrastination. Jane B. Burka and Lenora M. Yuen, authors of *Procrastination: Why You Do It, What to Do About It,* list the reasons we put off tasks: fears of failure, success, judgment, control, separation, and attachment. In building a house for God, don't you know some of these reasons played into their procrastination? They may have thought: Our materials are not as good as the previous ones. What if God didn't like the end product? If God were going to send a drought just because the work went slowly, what would God do if their creation wasn't good enough? Or what if their building had been so good that God expected something even greater this time? Will my family and home do without if I work on this project?

God knew some of their fears, and through Haggai, reminded them not to fear but to take courage and work—get back on task. God will *not* leave them. God's Spirit abides with them, just as it did when they came out of Egypt.

God does not abandon us, but we sometimes abandon God and the tasks God sets before us. Many times we wish we could hear a personal word of prophecy for ourselves, so we would know exactly what to do, what direction to go, or how we are to spend our lives. I wonder if we would be more attentive than those exiles? Procrastination is one of the surest ways to hinder a prophetic word. The second prophetic word came approximately a month after the first, not very long to become discouraged or to procrastinate. Yet even in that short amount of time, God needed to nudge them and remind them to take courage, work, and not be afraid.

What is God telling you to do? It may be to rebuild the temple of the Spirit by losing weight or quitting smoking. Or perhaps, it is to rebuild a relationship by repentance and forgiveness. Or maybe God is asking you to build God's kingdom by not tearing somebody else down with criticism or gossip. Whatever your task, take courage, work, and do not fear, for God's Spirit abides with you. (Raquel Mull)

DECEIVERS IN OUR MIDST

2 THESSALONIANS 2:1-5, 13-17

An enormous mall was just built up the interstate. It has both indoor and outdoor shops. The newspaper claims shoppers are driving from three states away to come and boost the economy in the glitzy and spacious stores. The advertisements are endless on the television stations. If one would only dare to venture through the traffic jams to make it to the parking lot of this new shopping mall, heaven will be within reach. It is supposed to be that good.

The parapets on the tops of the buildings span higher than the surrounding trees, ensuring that the stores are visible from the interstate. The lighting at night gives the impression of a constant carnival in our midst. Movie stars and soap opera divas have been invited to cut the ribbons to open the stores. The designers promised that this shopping complex would reform our city. We would become the envy of the surrounding counties.

To my surprise, when I visited this supposed shopping mecca,

I was gravely disappointed. I found only one store that could not have been found in other malls in the area. Granted, I was amazed at the architecture. The shops were spacious and impressive. The restaurant choices spanned the tasteful ethnicities of the globe. But for the most part, the designers of this mall had created a facade. There was little available to me that I could not have found elsewhere in my town. The only difference was that everything was now available in a new package. I was disappointed. I felt deceived.

In today's passage, Paul and others are writing to the Thessalonians to make them aware of potential deceivers in their midst. Just as the shopping mall boasted of high ceilings, airy aisles, and magnificent window dressings, there are those who will send false impressions to the church of Thessalonica with the intention of deceiving them. The text says this deceit may come in the form of spirit, word, or letter. These methods indicate the articulate planning behind the deceivers. They would use the same means of communication Paul uses to stay in touch with the Thessalonians. How unfortunate, that as the church at Thessalonica would be yearning to hear a word of encouragement and instruction from Paul, they could be reading a similar deceitful letter with the exact opposite kind of instruction. The church must be on guard. They must know who they are, what they believe, and why they are choosing to remain faithful to the traditions set before them. If they can do this, they will know when a deceiver is before them.

Paul, Silvanus, and Timothy worked diligently to set an example for this congregation while they were in their midst. They began a tradition of faithfulness and good work. It is this example that the Thessalonians must now cling to in order to remain faithful stewards of the church. It is a difficult task. Deceivers are cunning, brilliant, and manipulative. They appear to stand for what we want and desire. They appear to be exactly what we have been searching and yearning for. They appear to be authentic messengers of truth. Yet deceivers do not bring the satisfaction or fulfillment that we desire. They bring lies, hurt, and harm.

You may not have a new shopping complex in your midst. But there are certainly ways in which there exists potential for you to be deceived. What are your deceivers? Can you name them?

Naming them enables you to know the power they can have in your life. Paul let the Thessalonians know that they should be aware of possible deceivers in spirit, word, and letter. What form do yours take? (Victoria Atkinson White)

OH, THOSE QUESTIONS

LUKE 20:27-38

The Sadducees just love questions. This is what they are best at, asking questions, and asking questions again and again. In particular, they are good at asking the "trap" question, a question to which there is no good answer. Somehow if they can ask Jesus the question that he cannot answer, or if they can ask Jesus the question to which there is no good answer, or if they can ask Jesus the question whose answer makes him look foolish, then they will have won. Their task is to discredit him by asking questions he cannot answer.

In our lesson the Sadducees begin with questions regarding the resurrection. They are bent on proving that resurrection is a foolish if not impossible idea, therefore they propose the exaggerated "what if" sequence of events in which it is impossible to find a good answer. If Jesus cannot answer the question this must prove that he is a cheap imitation, a false prophet, or worse.

Jesus, of course, is not bound by the Sadducees' way of thinking. He makes fun of their thinking that resurrected life has the same rules as physical life. He chastises their foolish assumption that you would find the same sort of things in the next life that you find in this life. God has a whole different set of rules that are beyond the Sadducees, a set of rules illumined in Jesus. Jesus has come to put humankind in touch with a whole new reality, with different rules and a different way of understanding.

Jesus is not into an "answer game." Jesus is into a "reality game" (a whole new reality). Whose world is this? What is really going on in this world? The answer comes in the resurrection. The resurrection reorders everything.

Jesus is not in the "answer game" in the sense of ask a question and get an answer. Jesus is not in the "answer game" in the sense of people standing around sparring with one another regarding the law in order to work out their salvation. Answers to this type of question do not save us. Christ saves us. The only important questions are "what do you think of Christ?" and "who do you say that I am?"

The Sadducees, who are asking the wrong questions, have the answers to the right questions right there in front of them in Jesus. New life comes not in having the right answers to the wrong questions. New life comes from the right answer to the right question, "Who is this man Jesus?"

Our future hinges on your answer to this question. (Wayne Day)

NOVEMBER 14, 2004

Twenty-fourth Sunday After Pentecost

Worship Theme: As always, false prophets abound. Looming in the air we breath daily are modern predictions of impending doom. Yet, God rules over God's creation. The end of human history only appears as it fits the divine calendar.

Readings: Isaiah 65:17-25; 2 Thessalonians 3:6-13; Luke 21:5-19

Call to Worship (Psalm 98:1-6 RSV)

Leader:	O sing to the LORD a new song, for he has done marvelous things!
People:	**His right hand and his holy arm have gotten him victory.**
Leader:	The LORD has made known his victory, he has revealed his vindication in the sight of the nations.
People:	**He has remembered his steadfast love and faithfulness to the house of Israel. All the ends of the earth have seen the victory of our God.**
Leader:	Make a joyful noise to the LORD, all the earth; break forth into joyous song and sing praises!
People:	**Sing praises to the LORD with the lyre, with the lyre and the sound of melody!**
All:	**With trumpets and the sound of the horn make a joyful noise before the King, the LORD!**

Pastoral Prayer:

O Brilliant God of ages past and God for eons to come, we approach the end of this Christian year. Let us give thanks for the life you have given out of your charitable munificence. We too often feel as if we can never acquire enough. Yet you have displayed in Jesus' life that a person of good will and compassion has everything necessary for an extraordinary life. We need to examine and consider the lives of your saints. They remind us that although often poor in material possessions, they were exceedingly rich toward you. Help us emulate their generosity. Let us do so with gracious giving that lifts our spirits and warms our souls. Allow the apostle Paul's words to ring true when he told his elders to remember the words of the Lord Jesus: "It is more blessed to give than to receive" (Acts 20:35). Comfort us when words of modern and authentic prophets challenge our ways of thinking. Gird us against those false prophets who predict "the day of the Lord," when you alone set the schedule for your divine creation—both its beginning and its end. Create in our hearts a desire to work for your kingdom until that day when you call us home. We pray this as always in the powerful name of Jesus. Amen. (David Mosser)

SERMON BRIEFS

OUT OF ADVERSITY WE RECEIVE OPPORTUNITY

ISAIAH 65:17-25

Anne Frank was a young, Jewish girl living in Amsterdam when the Nazis came to power. She was no longer able to play along the beautiful canal outside her home. She had to go into hiding, never leaving her neighbor's apartment. Friends were rounded up and sent to death camps. Anne lived under constant threat of being discovered. One day she wrote in her diary, "I just heard the church bells ring. I believe they are saying, 'there are better days ahead!' "

This is the message Isaiah shared with the people of Israel. Isaiah writes this passage to a people in exile. For years they have lived in Babylon. They remember Jerusalem in smoke. Nebuchadnezzar tore down the gates to the city, setting it on fire. Nebuchadnezzar put young and old to the sword. Those who survived were forced to march to Babylon while foreigners lived in their homes, enjoying the fruit of their vineyards. Isaiah brought a word of hope to people who had experienced how hard and unfair life can be.

We understand the people of Israel. Life is not always fair. We toil and work, but others get credit. Life hasn't always work out the way we planned, but Isaiah brings a word of hope today. First, a new day is possible! Life can be different. "For, behold, I create new heavens and a new earth" (v. 17 KJV).

Second, Isaiah also relates that we can let go of the past. We can learn from the past, but we will not be imprisoned by it. We do not have to let yesterday's defeats determine tomorrow's dreams. "The former [things] shall not be remembered, nor come into mind" (v. 17 KJV).

Finally, Isaiah reminds his people that it is God who gives us a new day. The good news of Isaiah to the people of Israel will be the good news of Jesus to the world. Death and defeat are not the final words in our lives! Instead, God has the final word, and it is grace. It is out of our darkest nights and most difficult days that God gives us opportunities for a new life.

Dave Thomas was put up for adoption when he was just a baby. His adoptive mother died when he was only five years old. His father was in construction, so the two of them had to hit the road to make a living. By age twelve, Dave was working in a grocery store. At fifteen he was serving specials in a restaurant. The owner became a mentor to Dave. Dave joined the Army, and because of his previous experience, he was able to get a job in food service. When he left the Army he went to work for Kentucky Fried Chicken. Seven years later, when he left Kentucky Fried Chicken, his stock in the company was worth 1.5 million dollars. In 1969 he opened Wendy's. Dave Thomas didn't have a college education or even a high school diploma. Life had been hard, but there had been some wonderful people who had helped him along the way. "It was out of adversity that I got the opportunity to make it," Dave Thomas said. That is the gift God gives to us all. (Robert Long)

WHO DO YOU WANT TO BE?

2 THESSALONIANS 3:6-13

We have all heard the phrase, "Idle hands are the devil's workshop." These words are usually interpreted to mean that when one has little or nothing to do, little or no good will be accomplished. The "devil" takes advantages of such situations so that the little or no work that is being done is done for a bad rather than a good end. Yet in today's text, are the idle hands being accused of doing nothing? Perhaps because they are, in the same sentence, called busybodies, they are rather doing the wrong kind of work.

The authors of this letter to the Thessalonians have set an example for those reading their words from personal experience with the church. They set up a tradition to follow. When Paul, Silvanus, and Timothy were in their company, they modeled a method of behavior of honest and fair compensation for a day's labor, regardless of the fact that they may have been entitled to special privileges because of their religious stature.

At the time this letter was written, the example is obviously not being followed by enough members of the community to be noticed. Those not working for their daily bread are being singled out. Perhaps they believe they have a sense of entitlement, perhaps they feel their work is so important that others should care for their daily needs so they can spend time on more worthy duties. To them, their work is more important than taking care of the simple tasks of provision and daily care. Although they are working, they are busybodies, busy with the wrong kind of work.

What a terrible title: a busybody. It brings up childhood memories of a student who thought the current day's gossip lines were the most important words anyone could utter, even more important than the wisdom the teacher was speaking above the whispers of the busybody. To the busybody, gossip is essential to the outcome of the student's day. If there are great amounts of juicy, detailed gossip, it is a great day. If there is nothing more to talk about than who brought what for lunch, the busybody has a slow day. But the point is that gossip is crucial to the existence of the busybody's role in the classroom, and it consumes his or her ability to listen, participate, and learn in a privileged environment. The busybody students, because they choose to gossip rather than pay attention, loses out on their education.

The same is true in our text. The church at Thessalonica, while it has been persecuted and oppressed at times, is a growing and loving congregation. They know what it means to be perpetuating the work of Christ. They have good examples set before them, yet some of them are choosing to work toward efforts contrary to the work of the church. They are making conscious decisions that their work is more important than the simple tasks of preparing for the day like other Thessalonians are doing.

Are we not guilty of the same? Christ's path for us is simple. Jesus gave us explicit commands of love and service. Jesus continues to give us examples to follow in faithful men and women dedicated to the propagation of the church. Yet, we choose to complicate matters. We choose what is the most important task of the day. We allow our hands to become idle, we let them stray to what we believe are crucial tasks, yet in the bigger picture, we see our reflection as busybodies. Is that who you want to be?

The way of Christ is clear: love and serve. Examples can be found all around us. Those who choose to be an example in the tradition of Christ are on a clearly defined and simple path. Those who choose to be busybodies are so distracted by their idle hands that they miss all of the good things along the journey. Which do you want to be? (Victoria Atkinson White)

GOD'S LOVE NIXES OUR DEAD END

LUKE 21:5-19

There is always a fear that the end of the world is coming and that the end will come not because of something God did but because of something humans did. In the aftermath of September 11, the events in the Middle East convinced many people that the end of the world was indeed near and that everything we knew and loved was about to be destroyed. It appears that for the first time in the twenty-first century human beings have become powerful enough to destroy the world. Ever since "the bomb" became a reality, humanity has lived with the terrible fear that indeed we will destroy the world.

Jesus in Luke 21:5-19 warns that life will not be easy. There will be many times when it seems that the world is coming to an end, and there will be many people who go about announcing that the end of the world is near. In the era of mass communication it is impossible to listen to the radio or watch television without someone proclaiming that the end of the world is near. Every generation has its prophets of doom and certainly in the twenty-first century there have been more and greater reasons to believe that destroying the world is not only possible but probable.

This passage suggests that we need not worry. Yes it is true that trouble may come upon the earth. Humankind may suffer every imaginable hardship and difficulty. However, the good news is that Jesus has already foretold the end. There will be difficulty; there will be trouble; and there will be wars and rumors of wars. However the good news is that for those in "the faith" it has already been disclosed that the last word will not be the destruction of the world—the last word is God's word, and that is always a word of love.

The critical event in human history is not nuclear war, or anthrax, or a meteor destroying the earth. The critical event in human history is the life, death, and resurrection of Jesus. Because of Jesus' life and death and resurrection, we know who is in charge of this universe and who has determined the end. The end is not ours; it is God's.

The struggle between life and death, good and evil, hope and despair has already been decided. It was decided on the cross. Through Jesus the veil has been pulled back, and we have a glimpse of the final chapter that God has already written. The earth is God's, and that includes us. The decisive event of history has already appeared in Jesus. We need not be afraid because the one in charge is a good and loving God who has given his son that we might believe that one thing will survive: God's love.

Our job then is to persevere. This is God's world and not ours. We need not be afraid. (Wayne Day)

NOVEMBER 21, 2004

Christ the King/Reign of Christ Sunday

Worship Theme: The incarnation of God, this Jesus of Nazareth who has been exalted as king by virtue of a crown of thorns and an enthronement on a cross, reigns as God's ironic symbol. The irony is that God's reign begins in power perfected in apparent weakness.

Readings: Jeremiah 23:1-6; Colossians 1:11-20; Luke 23:33-43

Call to Worship (Luke 1:68-79 RSV)

Leader:	Blessed be the Lord God of Israel, for he has visited his people and redeemed his people.
People:	**And has raised up a horn of salvation for us in the house of his servant David, as he spoke by the mouth of his holy prophets from of old, that we should be saved from our enemies, and from the hand of all who hate us;**
Leader:	To perform the mercy promised to our fathers, and to remember his holy covenant, the oath that he swore to our father Abraham, to grant us that we, being delivered from the hand of our enemies, might serve him without fear, in holiness and righteousness before him all the days of our life.
People:	**And you, child, will be called the prophet of the Most High; for you will go before the Lord to prepare his ways, to give knowledge of salvation to his people in the forgiveness of their sins,**

All: Through the tender mercy of our God, when the day shall dawn upon us from on high to give light to those who sit in darkness and in the shadow of death, to guide our feet into the way of peace.

Pastoral Prayer:

Blessed Lord of the Universe, we look back at the good fortune you mercifully bestow upon your people. We are quick to forget the many occasions for which we might give you thanks. Instead we fret about all the things that did not develop for us the way we had planned. We confess, O God, that our field of vision is far too narrow. Help us to see the larger panorama of your providence for us. Give us the heart and will to share your good news to a human race near despair. Inspire in us the spirit of Christ who always opened himself to the needs of others. Allow us to partake more fully in your realm that Christ Jesus inaugurated for your creation by his suffering, death, and resurrection. This Sabbath day make us your people once again. In Jesus' name we pray. Amen. (David Mosser)

SERMON BRIEFS

SO MY SHEEP MAY SAFELY GRAZE

JEREMIAH 23:1-6

Christ the King/Reign of Christ Sunday is sometimes a difficult Sunday for us to observe in the Christian year. Kingship, at best, is a foreign concept to those of us living in the present-day United States. For many people in our churches, it will seem irrelevant to examine Israel's search for an effective king. Yet, the challenge for the preacher is to talk about kingship in such a way that we are challenged to look at society and its leaders, regardless of how the system of government is structured.

In chapter 23, Jeremiah gives a summary judgment of the kings of Israel. Jeremiah offers harsh words for those who have failed to live up to the trust placed upon them as rulers. He writes, "It is you who have scattered my flock, and have driven them away, and you have not attended them. So I will attend to you for your evil doings" (v. 2). God has pronounced that no longer will the kings be absolved from their responsibility, but rather they will be removed so that a new king may be placed in power. "The days are surely coming, says the LORD, when I will raise up for David a righteous Branch, and he shall reign as king and deal wisely, and shall execute justice and righteousness in the land" (v. 5). Jeremiah makes use of an ancient image of kingship when he writes that this new king will be unlike any other, for he will rule as a gentle shepherd.

In order to understand this new notion of kingship, we must look at how this office was understood in biblical times. In *The New Interpreter's Bible*, Patrick D. Miller writes, "The view of kingship here, is rooted in the covenant with David. It assumes and builds upon the responsibility of the king for the maintenance of justice and order in the community, a responsibility that often seemed to get lost in the shuffle of military endeavors, political maneuverings, and economic aggrandizement" (6:739). Miller then goes on to explain that "The Old Testament . . . sets the criterion for determining whether justice is present in the way one treats the weakest members of the community, the powerless and the marginalized, the economically depressed, and the vulnerable" (6:745).

We are here reminded that the biblical criteria for leadership is different from popular notions of what makes a good leader. Jeremiah reminds us that God blesses communities that live within the bounds of justice and righteousness. The true measure of a community and its leaders lies not in how the powerful get along, but rather in how those with the least get along. As Christians, we should heed this alternative call of kingship and leadership. It remains difficult for us in our affluence and comfort to remember those on the margins of society. The words of the prophets once again call God's people to look at how individuals, society at large, and the government relate to those who are oftentimes forgotten. How do the poor, single-parent families, the homeless, or AIDS patients fare in today's world? What about the elderly who cannot afford expensive medications, the dying, and the mentally or physically disabled? Who is rising up and making sure that justice and righteousness prevail in our land? The church is called to be an advocate for these groups and others. In our communities, we are called to exercise the gentle leadership of the shepherd. We are called to exercise a different kind of power, one that seeks after the justice and welfare of all. (Wendy Joyner)

PREACHING HEAVEN'S MUSIC, SINGING HEAVEN'S TRUTH

COLOSSIANS 1:11-20

Dad was a weekend preacher, only he never preached on Colossians. I asked him why. He shook his head and said, "It's beyond me. I don't understand it." I was in seminary at the time, and replied, "You mean it's too cosmic?"

Dad showed great restraint. "What I said is that it is beyond me, and I don't understand it. So I don't preach it." It is not unusual for many preachers to feel that certain texts, themes, or books overmatch them or that they are unequal to preaching that particular sermon. I sometimes describe that feeling in myself as "having the words but not the melody." It's when I can state the idea but can't sing the song, can't find the sermon's true rhythm. Maybe Dad felt that he couldn't read Colossians' music.

All these years later, though, with Dad's preaching long-since silenced by death, I wish he had gotten on friendlier terms with Colossians, because it really is his kind of song, and not least the text for this Christ the King Sunday.

Dad loved nothing better than preaching as he was praying. At least that was the way it seemed to me. He'd start praying, whether before his sermon or after his sermon or at the dinner table the next Tuesday, and pretty soon he was anticipating his sermon or summarizing his sermon or working on his next one.

Our text for the morning is a prayer, but it sounds for all the world like a three-point sermon as the author prays that the Christians in Colossae might be "strong with all the strength that comes from his glorious power"; that they might be "prepared to endure everything with patience"; that they might "joyfully [thank] the Father, who has enabled [us] to share in the inheritance of the saints in the light" (vv. 11-12). It's hard to know where the praying ends and the preaching begins when he writes, "[The Father] has enabled us to share in the inheritance of the saints in the light. He has rescued us from the power of darkness and transferred us into the kingdom of his beloved Son, in whom we have redemption, the forgiveness of sins" (v. 13).

Dad could have preached that prayer, and he could have prayed that sermon.

Dad loved nothing better than to preach after a great old hymn, something rousing and upbeat. Sometimes, if he got "happy," he'd begin the sermon right there, expounding on the hymn itself. "Pay attention to the words," he'd say. "They'll teach you something!"

Part of what we have in our text for today is one of the oldest hymns we know, and rousing besides. And if we pay attention to its words, it too can teach us something, for it is a most comprehensive hymn to Christ.

Christ is the beginning: "He is the image of the invisible God, the firstborn of all creation; for in him all things in heaven and on earth were created. . . . He himself is before all things" (vv. 15-17). Christ is also the end: "Through him God was pleased to reconcile to himself all things, whether on earth or in heaven, by making peace through the blood of his cross" (v. 20). And Christ is all points in between: "in him all the fullness of God was pleased to dwell" (v. 19).

What a hymn! Cosmic, I guess you'd call it, but comforting too, in a way that only the best old hymns can be. For my part I am comforted to know that, although Dad never quite got the tune to Colossians while he was preaching on earth, now in heaven's precincts he sings it by heart. It's no longer beyond him at all, but all around him every eternal moment. (Thomas Steagald)

WHO IS KING?

LUKE 23:33-43

The question of this passage is, "Who is King?" The problem is that the question is not simple. Everyone lives with political realities. Democrats, Republicans, Marxists, Socialists, Communists, and Anarchists each know who is king. Their ideology and the political power that advances that ideology is king.

Ideologies, however, are transient. From time to time ideologies themselves change as do their "true believers," who move from one ideology to the other. One of today's best-selling authors is a prominent spokesperson for conservatism. He announced that he has been duped, denounced his former certainties, and disclosed his new allegiance to liberalism. The question remains, "Who is King?"

Jesus was labeled "King" as a joke. Pilate gave him that name in order to point out just how foolish and irrelevant Jesus was. Since that time almost every generation has wrestled with Jesus' role in their lives and in society.

On Christ the King Sunday the church proclaims boldly who is king. The text suggests that neither the nations nor their rulers are "King." The very act of following Jesus calls into question all political arrangements. "All political arrangements" means even those "enlightened" arrangements we find in the United States.

The text suggests that the question, "Who is King?" is primary. First you answer the question about Jesus and then you move to considering the political arrangement. The political arrangement itself is not God. God is God. The political arrangement is not mandated by Jesus. Jesus is Jesus and cannot be reduced to political structures. Humanity is not the measure of things; God is. We find ourselves in need of "saving," and this "saving" will not come in any political arrangement.

It is a mistake to give the kingdoms of this world our ultimate allegiance. Certainly, Christians have constantly been in conflict with kingdoms of this world that promote slavery, child labor, discrimination, ethnic cleansing, and so on. Placing our ultimate allegiance in political structures spawns disillusionment.

The church believes that the mocking sign above Jesus' head is no joke. The mocking sign above Jesus' head is our contact with what is eternal and everlasting. Jesus *is* King. The church proclaims that "the Word became flesh" (John 1:14) and that in Jesus "all the fullness of God was pleased to dwell" (Col. 1:19).

In Jesus on the cross there is a cosmic realignment of power. It remains a good question, "Who is King?" Are world leaders kings? The text calls out for an answer to the question, "Who is King, and what does that mean?" (Wayne Day)

NOVEMBER 28, 2004

First Sunday of Advent

Worship Theme: Faithful people long for God to teach us God's ways. Someday we humans will learn peace. When God teaches us peace through the agency of the promised Messiah, then salvation becomes a reality, but God alone knows this moment.

Readings: Isaiah 2:1-5; Romans 13:11-14; Matthew 24:36-44

Call to Worship (Psalm 122 RSV)

Leader: I was glad when they said to me, "Let us go to the house of the LORD!"

People: **Our feet have been standing within your gates, O Jerusalem!**

Leader: Jerusalem, built as a city which is bound firmly together,

People: **To which the tribes go up, the tribes of the LORD, as was decreed for Israel, to give thanks to the name of the LORD.**

Leader: There thrones for judgment were set, the thrones of the house of David.

People: **Pray for the peace of Jerusalem! "May they prosper who love you! Peace be within your walls, and security within your towers!"**

Leader: For my brethren and companions' sake I will say, "Peace be within you!"

People: **For the sake of the house of the LORD our God, I will seek your good.**

Pastoral Prayer:

O Lord, we your people cry out with the prophet, " 'Peace, peace,' when there is no peace" (Jer. 8:11). Yet you, O God, hold out this divine possibility to your people. During this time of Advent preparation for the Christ child's birth, make peace our chief concern. Let each of us look deep within and find those things that diminish the peace that we all desire. O Dear Lord, erase the thoughts and resentments we hold against our sisters and brothers. Help us understand that many times it is our ability to forgive others that opens wide the portals of peace. Help us give peace a chance, and may we begin with our own lives. As we await your promised fulfillment of the Messiah's birth, may we study our lives in the light of your holiness. Create within our lives a space where we cultivate the contentment and tranquility that the gospel pledges. As the day's light shortens and the time of darkness lengthens during this Advent season, allow your holy light to illumine our steps. Furnish us that inner radiance that conveys our commitment to Christ and his holy church. This and all things we pray in Jesus' name. Amen. (David Mosser)

SERMON BRIEFS

DO YOU SEE WHAT I SEE?

ISAIAH 2:1-5

Among my friends who refuse to board airplanes is a woman who claims that her fear is based on biblical principles. When asked for clarification, she quotes the verse: "Lo [low] I am with you alway" (Matt. 28:20 KJV), which makes her more comical than commonplace, given that most of our Judeo-Christian ancestors believed that going higher brought God closer. In this regard, mountains were especially important, given their special potential for encountering the divine. Even today, we describe spiritual ecstasy with the phrase "mountaintop experience."

In this passage, however, the "mountain of the Lord" is more likely the elevated plateau in Old Jerusalem equated with the Temple (the "house of the God of Jacob"). This fact means that the hymn "Marching to Zion" is more representative of this text than the Sunday school song of my childhood, "Climb, Climb Up Sunshine Mountain." Clearly, Isaiah envisioned a day when the Temple would be a desirable destination for vast multitudes of people, with the word *highest* having more to do with its prominence than its elevation.

Ironically, the only remnant of the building available for viewing today is a portion of the western ("wailing") wall at the base of the Temple Mount. One need not climb a single stair to reach or touch it. Not that the area lacks the stairs to take one higher. But those stairs lead to a pair of mosques and are climbed primarily by adherents of Islam along with a slew of Western tourists. To whatever degree, there remains a vision of the "holy hill," it is much clouded in the politics of the Middle East, with the words of soldiers and statesmen drowning out those of the prophet.

The beauty of this passage has always had less to do with how the mountain looks than with how the mountain feels. In short, it feels breathtakingly complete and surprisingly secure. All nations will stream to it and, with the aid of the Lord, will learn to get along. God shall judge between them, not in the sense of accepting some and rejecting others, but in the sense of settling the disputes which have historically divided them—so much so that they won't fight anymore.

And what of the weapons that will be rendered unnecessary? They'll become farm implements, that's what. The killing fields will become the planting fields. Where once people bled, future generations will be fed. The capstone of the vision is in the line (omitted here, but appended in Micah):

> But they shall all sit under their own vines and under their
> own fig trees,
> and no one shall make them afraid;
> for the mouth of the LORD of hosts has spoken. (Mic. 4:4)

Unfortunately, this doesn't sound very realistic, either in regard to the killing fields of the Middle East or the killing fields of Detroit, I don't see it happening anytime soon. This doesn't defeat me, although it does depress me. "How long, O Lord?" is not only a biblical cry but the only cry that makes sense. To which I do not automatically yield. The pragmatist in me wants to assess damages, mobilize allies, define strategies, and commence chewing on bite-sized pieces of the dream. It's what I know how to do. It's what the church has always done.

Perhaps this Advent, I need to preach as well as practice, lifting up Isaiah's vision for all to see, marveling at its inevitability every bit as much as its desirability. It may sound crazy, but this is no pipe dream to the prophet. He knows it's going to happen. He can see it, taste it, and even smell it. There is no doubt in his mind it will come to pass. Why? Because it is God's doing, that's why. And God will keep at it, even after you and I have quit on it. For, at the end of the day, the true prophet goes beyond a detailed depiction of what's wrong with us to an imaginative vision of what's right with God. Then the prophet grabs us by the throat—or is it by the heart?—until we see it too.

Without visions, people really do perish. Very few suicides take place when people are in a state of free fall. Rather, people resort to self-destruction after they have bottomed out, looked up, and failed to see a place worth going to or a way to get there. This feature of human life means that when the next Christmas balladeer croons, "Do you see what I see?" that lyric, in addition to being prophetic, may also be a matter of life and death. (William Ritter)

LIVING RIGHT IN THE RIGHT NOW

ROMANS 13:11-14

Six years ago as a college freshman, my son experienced a defining moment in his faith development. He called me at 1:00 A.M. to explain it to me. (Isn't that the hour most college students call home to explain a revelation they have had?) In troubling words, he described how he had taken the wrong direction and indulged in activities in his college life not becoming a Christian. He had been under the false impression that almost everyone went away to college, enjoyed a fun-filled life of reveling, and then graduated, eventually settling down, maturing, and doing the usual things like getting a job, marrying, and establishing a normal life of adulthood. But now he realized he needed to make changes in his life.

He had not planned on God intervening in his plan for a "normal" life. When he would go to bed at night in his cubicle dorm room, he remembered verses of "Amazing Grace" he had learned growing up in church. This song caused him to think of his life's condition. Then he said it came to him that this lifestyle in which he was engaged would not be easy to exit in four years. He recalled acquaintances he had met who had graduated from college, and they were still partying long after college days were behind them. My son felt God speaking to him, seeking him out to end this lifestyle, and make his life count as a Christian. Why wait four years, ruining his college life and running the risk of ruining his entire life? As I, his pastor, listened on the phone, his words were an encouragement to me that he wanted to change the direction of his life.

According to the apostle Paul in Romans 13:11-14, all Christians should imitate the actions that my son took at college: Awake to their condition, assess their lifestyle, and adorn themselves accordingly!

Paul actually compares a believer's awareness to a person waking from sleep. The apostle hints that the day is almost here; time is short. Whether he was referring to the brief time humankind has on the earth to live or whether the second coming of Christ is nearer than some believers understood, he was first warning believers to become prepared to live for Christ while they had the time and opportunity. Hence, he exhorts: Awake!

Second, Paul challenges believers to assess their lifestyle. The Christian who is equipped to live for Christ must put off indecent clothes, that is, clothes worn in the darkness and not appropriate for the Christian servant. Just as my son had to shed those old clothes of partying, so the Christian must put aside revelry, drunkenness, immorality, shamelessness, contention, and envy. Such activities can never equip the believer to achieve the goals of righteousness that Christ has set for his followers. A Christian must constantly assess his or her lifestyle in order to be a devoted follower of Christ.

Finally, Paul declares that once believers have disrobed the sins of the flesh (meant only to gratify the desires of one's human nature), they are ready to adorn themselves properly. They become children of the light. They then adorn themselves with Christ; He is their robe, dressing their lives with every good blessing and meeting every need of their spiritual well-being. The Christian servant is ready to serve when he or she has the proper attire.

These serious words of Paul are full of care for the Christian. Paul admonishes: Awake to the shortness of time you have to live for Christ! Assess your lifestyle in order to put off sin! Adorn yourself with good works that honor the name of Christ and benefit the kingdom of God! A Christian must seek to live a life that does not misjudge the brevity of life or the length of eternity! (Billy Compton)

WHAT TIME IS IT?

MATTHEW 24:36-44

We've all asked that rather innocuous question of someone else, "What time is it?" Typically all we want is a straightforward reply so we can mentally mark what part of the day we're in. It's a throwaway question with a throwaway answer, for as soon as we know it, the answer becomes meaningless, subsumed by the march of minutes into years. To us moderns, time is our servant and we its masters.

Can the witness of faith, however, contribute a renewed understanding of how we relate to God through each day? Today's text stands at the forefront of a host of others that proclaims to a finite creation a message of limited time. That claim may sound simplistic, even passé to our postmodern minds, and to some cultured church ears it may smack of revivalist fantasy. However, I believe we can come to a nuanced understanding of this passage that moves us beyond textual stereotypes to a deeper, more imaginative reality.

As a preacher, I've typically seen people get tied in knots around this text and its apocalyptic nature. Our culture has been inundated with any number of pseudo-scholarly treatises or pulp fiction novels based on the end times. It's easy to succumb to fear-filled images when we look at this passage because we can focus too much on the actions that Jesus describes. What does it mean that our generation will be like Noah's, unaware of the impending flood, living life to its fullest, ignorant of impending doom? What does it mean that two workers in the field will be plowing, sewing, or harvesting, and one will be taken? What does it mean that two women will be grinding meal at the mill or baking bread, and one will be taken? Our sermonic imaginations can take over here, and we can begin inserting parallel images of stockbrokers and soccer moms disappearing in a flash and miss what Christ is trying to tell us.

What is Jesus proclaiming here? These images that Christ uses are literary constructs designed to highlight a truth rather than describe a reality. The truth of this text, indeed it's claim, is twofold: God, not us, is in control of time, and we should always be expecting Christ's return! Jesus' words warn us not to get too comfortable in this world, for God has decided that Jesus' work is unfinished. To see this point, let's engage in a bit of literary exercise. Imagine reading this passage without including verses 37-41. By setting aside those verses for just a moment, there's absolutely no break in thought between what Jesus introduces as the subject of God's time in verse 36 and the beginning of his warning in verse 42. If we add in the images in the intervening verses, they properly serve their function of arresting our attention and pointing to the larger truth of the text.

This Advent, the church can posit a fresh understanding to the world of the nature of time by proclaiming that God is in control of our days, and Christ is coming soon. To those hearers who maintain that time is their servant and that they control their destiny, that's a threatening revelation that subverts their self-understanding. Such a word can bring down kingdoms. To those hearers, however, who because of suffering, injustice, and despair look to God for a new vision of reality, that's a comforting assurance that lifts them up from bondage. Indeed, such a word heralds a new kingdom. Let our prayer be that of the early church, "Come, Lord Jesus!" (Rev. 22:20). (Timothy Mallard)

REFLECTIONS

DECEMBER

Reflection Verse: *"I will draw near to you for judgment; I will be swift to bear witness against the sorcerers, against the adulterers, against those who swear falsely, against those who oppress the hired workers in their wages, the widow and the orphan, against those who thrust aside the alien, and do not fear me, says the LORD of hosts."* (*Malachi 3:5*)

If we look at many of the prophets' messages, and especially this text from Malachi 2:17–3:5, then we may notice that they sound like courtroom scenes. If you want to think of *Law & Order*, or for those of a previous generation, *Perry Mason* or *The Defenders*, then you get the idea. The courtroom clerk reads the indictment, and then the defendant enters a plea. Here, however, no plea is required, for the Divine Judge speaks through the prophet. The people need not make a plea because, before God, they are guilty. We need not hear any other voice after the word from the Lord. Clearly from the text's evidence both the people and their leaders are guilty of cynicism and disbelief.

How do we see their guilt? The prophet exposes the people's guilt by the kinds of statements the leaders of Judah and Jerusalem make and the kinds of questions they ask. They say, "All who do evil are good in the sight of the LORD, and he delights in them" (2:17). They ask, "Where is the God of justice?" God's indictment against the people is that they mock God. Mocking God, of course, is a poor way to curry favor (see Isa. 37:24 and Gal. 6:7).

However, in the face of the indictment from Yahweh, Malachi, the messenger of God, has a remedy to bring the people back to faith. First, God sends a messenger "to prepare the way before" the Lord (3:1). Second, God sends this messenger to be "like a refiner's fire and like fullers' soap; he will sit as a refiner and purifier of silver, and he will purify the descendants of Levi and refine them like gold and silver, until they present offerings to the LORD in righteousness" (3:2-3). Then, and only then, will the people's offerings be pleasing to the Lord. This act is an act of ritual cleansing, and it puts some pressure on us preachers. If we understand ourselves as preachers/priests, then we must necessarily feel some responsibility for our people's spiritual health. Thus, from time to time, all God's people need a ritual of cleansing, even some of God's prophets engaged in this ceremonial cleansing. Perhaps this is a part of our modern call to ministry.

For example in the call of the prophet Isaiah we see a similar ceremonial refining that prepares the prophet Isaiah to speak on the Lord's behalf. Do you remember the scene in the temple in the year King Uzziah died? Isaiah saw the Lord high and lifted up. Of course in the presence of such a grand and glorious vision Isaiah blurts out his confession: "Woe is me! I am lost, for I am a man of unclean lips, and I live among a people of unclean lips; yet my eyes have seen the King, the LORD of hosts!" (Isa. 6:5).

This is yet another circumstance where Yahweh makes ritual preparation to prime the prophet. Then, the prophet speaks a word to prepare the people. This is how the Lord accomplishes Isaiah's ritual cleansing or healing: "Then one of the seraphs flew to me, holding a live coal that had been taken from the altar with a pair of tongs. The seraph touched my mouth with it and said: 'Now that this has touched your lips, your guilt has departed and your sin is blotted out' " (Isa. 6:6-7). At last, after the cleansing, the Lord commissions the prophet Isaiah. The way Isaiah relates the vision is like this: "Then I heard the voice of the Lord saying, 'Whom shall I send, and who will go for us?' And I said, 'Here am I; send me!' " (Isa. 6:8).

Rituals are an important element in making promises and keeping covenants. We have what I would call the ritual of friendship in our church. Near the beginning of worship we turn to our friends or our church's guests and we exchange words of welcome and hospitality. Some churches even "pass the peace" in which people turn and embrace one another and say, "The peace of the Lord be with you." The ritual response is "And also with you." However, in our church, we do not want to press our luck, so we feel good if we can get people to give at least a ritual

"How're y'all doing this morning?" This ritual of friendship conveys goodwill and good faith to those who worship with us.

Our society engages in many kinds of rituals. Each ritual reveals our good faith and best intentions toward others. Some of these rituals include singing our national anthem prior to sporting events, shaking hands with people we meet, or giving and receiving rings during a wedding covenant ceremony. These rituals indicate our willingness to live in love and charity with one another. They show respect for our nation, our fellow citizens, or people with whom we make sacred promises.

After God sends his messenger, Malachi, and the prophet becomes like a refiner's fire or like fullers' soap, then and only then will God cleanse the priests. Then and only then, will these priests receive the "offerings to the LORD in righteousness." Then, and only then, will the people's offerings please the Lord. This act of offering concludes the function of ritual cleansing.

Subsequent to these acts of ritual cleansing, the Lord "will draw near to you for judgment; I will be swift to bear witness against the sorcerers, against the adulterers, against those who swear falsely, against those who oppress the hired workers in their wages, the widow and the orphan, against those who thrust aside the alien, and do not fear me, says the LORD of hosts" (v. 5).

In the prophets' understanding of God, how people live and treat one another reflects their belief and covenant with God. We act on what we believe. Therefore if one shows good faith toward God, then one likewise shows good faith toward his or her sisters and brothers. To engage in sorcery; adultery; false witness; and oppression of workers, widows, and orphans shows bad faith. Plainly, the wages of bad faith, at least according to Malachi, will be a swift bearing of witness against these who show bad faith.

Simply put, those who show good faith toward God will "fear the Lord." This term "fear of the Lord" means that we respect God and God's Word among God's people. People who show justice and equity toward God's children are people who fear the Lord.

For pastors who assume the mantle of leadership in their local church and who function as leaders from the pulpit, the example and challenge that Malachi issues is daunting. We love our people. To throw their sin back into any congregation's teeth is, at best, easier said than done. Yet, as an old-time preacher once put it: "God created us for something much grander than to be left to our own sinful devices." (David Mosser)

DECEMBER 5, 2004

Second Sunday of Advent

Worship Theme: From something as dead and dormant as the stump of Jesse, God brings forth new growth. John the Baptizer announces the time to repent and that the kingdom of heaven has come near. Our salvation stands in this promise of hope.

Readings: Isaiah 11:1-10; Romans 15:4-13; Matthew 3:1-12

Call to Worship (Psalm 72:1-7, 18-19)

Leader: Give the king your justice, O God, and your righteousness to a king's son.

People: **May he judge your people with righteousness, and your poor with justice.**

Leader: May the mountains yield prosperity for the people, and the hills, in righteousness.

People: **May he defend the cause of the poor of the people, give deliverance to the needy, and crush the oppressor.**

Leader: May he live while the sun endures, and as long as the moon, throughout all generations. May he be like rain that falls on the mown grass, like showers that water the earth.

People: **In his days may righteousness flourish and peace abound, until the moon is no more.**

All: **Blessed be the LORD, the God of Israel, who alone does wondrous things. Blessed be his**

glorious name forever; may his glory fill the whole earth. Amen and Amen.

Pastoral Prayer:

On this holy day, O God of Ages Past and Hope for Years to Come, let us celebrate the promise that only you can give. In the former days, O God, your promise propelled the people of Israel through the desert and through times of tribal turmoil. By your promises Israel both thrived and suffered under the monarchy. The Assyrians and Babylonians drove first Israel and then Judah into exile. Yet, during these times of trial, your people regarded your promise as from on high. You announced to your people that you would always be their God and that they would always be your people. We now are spiritual heirs of this lasting legacy. Help us claim our divine inheritance and celebrate that great cloud of witnesses that surround us and encourage our faith journey. In every thought, word, or deed that we perform, let your promise, recalled by the preachers who baptized us, ring as true for us now as when they first laid their hands upon our heads. These preachers blessed us with the Holy Spirit and called on Jesus' name. Let this blessing guide all that we are on our way to becoming disciples. In Jesus' name we pray. Amen. (David Mosser)

SERMON BRIEFS

THE FAMILY TREE AND THE PEACEABLE KINGDOM

ISAIAH 11:1-10

Duke's Will Willimon, who hangs out with hundreds of identity-seeking college students, never tires of admonishing them to "remember who you are." Which, after a night of heavy imbibing, is harder than it seems. But Dr. Willimon's larger concern is that his students "remember who your people are" (it's a Southern thing) and "remember what your baptism says about who you are" (it's a Christian thing). My mother used to say something similar every time I ventured forth from the house. But to cover her bets, she inserted iron-on nametags in my shorts, meaning that my identity was never farther away than my underwear.

In this Sunday's slice of Scripture, Isaiah is talking about a messianic king—a coming king, an ideal king, God's ideal king, possibly even a Jesus-like king—and employs an incredibly visual metaphor to answer the questions: Where will he come from, and who are his people? He will come from an old tree stump, and Jesse will be traceable in his genealogy.

The "stump," of course, recalls the forest-leveling indignation of the Lord of hosts (Isa. 10:24-34). The "shoot" suggests that, where the Lord is concerned, indignation shall never completely destroy anything (especially hope) or anybody (especially Israel). Where God is involved, life is as insistent as restoration is inevitable. I have seen burned-over forests pockmarked with hints of green. And I have seen dandelions not only find but create cracks in the asphalt. But the prophet's point has less to do with nature's resiliency than with God's resourcefulness. Where God has a will, there's a way.

Jesse, of course, is the father of David. Which may or may not suggest that dormant monarchies are able to be resuscitated. Is the Davidic line, by inference, the cut-down stump? Or is the image more poetic than literal? I'll vote for the former. But we can arm wrestle next week in Bible study. Suffice it to say that Israel shall not lack for leadership forever and that when God's leader emerges, both gifts and genetics will be favorable. In short, God's king will have it all.

To the six gifts of the spirit (wisdom, understanding, counsel, might, knowledge and fear of the Lord), the Greek translator adds "piety." Better still, this ideal king will tip the scales so that justice rolls in the direction of those who need it, rather than into the backyards of those who can afford it. That's because he will be a "good eyes" ruler who will see through appearances and render justice conversant with his discernment. Which is good news for those of us who sense that "things are not always as they seem."

Then unfolds this wonderful vision of reconciled zoology: wolves and lambs sharing a condo; leopards and baby goats sharing a bunk; lions taking lunch breaks with oxen; cows and bears listening to Mozart in meadows; complete with toddlers teasing poisonous snakes with no fear of injury.

It's a wonderful image, one we'd almost rather paint than preach. Yet few of us rush down to the zoo, Bible in hand, and unlock all the cages. Or, as Woody Allen once put it: "The lion and lamb may lie down together, but the lamb won't get much sleep."

Is the point that a truly God-redeemed world will erase dangerous distinctions common to the natural order? Hardly. Is the point that those who are childlike in their innocence before God will be able to handle venomous snakes as evidence of their faithfulness? Only if they worship within five miles of an emergency room. Is the point that Isaiah's messianic king predicts Jesus Christ some seven hundred years before the fact? Only in the sense that Isaiah's vision probably framed Israel's expectation for an eventual King of Kings. As messianic measurements go, clearly, Jesus fits the suit. But as a vision for what God desires from all who rule, there's a certain universality to both the qualifications and the job description. Jesus may have been the "true fit," but hopefully not the last fit.

As for this business of the peaceable animals, I watch them eat each other weekly on the Discovery Channel. What is harder to take is seeing the same behavior, depicted with the same regularity, on CNN. This means that creation may best be healed from the top down, rather than the bottom up. Humans before hippopotamuses. This message will preach as Isaiah ably demonstrates. (William Ritter)

A PRAYER FILLED WITH HOPE

ROMANS 15:4-13

The apostle Paul offers a prayer for new believers in Christ in Romans 15:4-13. His petition focuses on bountiful hope for Christ's followers. He knows these fledglings in the faith have no clear point of reference from which to make decisions about their Christian lives. They need his teaching directives. They need reminding that Jesus Christ is their role model. Facing new issues each day, they have few past experiences with which to compare their new lifestyle. Paul then prays for them to know and understand the way that is opening up for their guidance. Already, Paul has experienced divisive factions and jealous strife among members of the church in Rome. As a result, Paul's prayer is genuine and needful for these new believers.

Paul could easily be praying that same prayer for believers in the twenty-first century. He would not be surprised to find out that Christians continue to have a problem with the same areas in Christian living he addressed in his prayer. Paul himself understood the sin nature that worked against him in serving Jesus Christ his Lord. Thus, his prayer was voiced for the Roman Christians and for all of us who overhear scripture today. Paul prays three specific requests: He asks for them to be encouraged through the Word of God, to be strengthened by cooperation with fellow believers, and to be empowered with the Holy Spirit.

First, believers are to be encouraged through the Word of God. Paul's studies and experiences caused him to become an expert on understanding the meaning of the Scriptures. He was equipped to relate its significance to everyday discipleship in living out his faith. Paul's faith was a living faith and the Word to him was life, the very fiber of his belief system. Paul based his life on the truth that a Savior had come who would change the old system from only a certain few being allowed into the kingdom of God to a new system proclaimed within John 3:16 (KJV), "whosoever believeth in him." Paul could not keep quiet that the old law had changed to all who would receive Christ as Savior, and a new covenant had been established. He knew and believed a floodgate of forgiveness had opened for the Jew and the Gentile to come to God. What hope! What a blessing! This treasure, this pearl of great price found in the scripture is there for encouragement to the believer. Once you were nobody, but now you are somebody in the Lord. Once you were far away in your sin and death, but now you have been brought near to salvation, forgiveness, and eternal life. Hope thou in God! You have encouragement from the living Word of God!

Next, Paul prayed for believers to be strengthened by cooperation. One must understand that singing, "We are one in the bond of love," is only a "feel-good" hymn if followers of Christ are not accepting of one another as Christ accepts the sinner. Paul knew a person's entire perspective must change in order to cultivate a cooperative work in the body of Christ. The supreme example has been set; the servant model is in place. There will be no barrier too high or any argument too hopeless that believers cannot work through when we imitate Jesus' example. When Christians come together in love for the Savior and with a heart to praise and glorify Christ, a unity prevails which empowers the work of God in the world. Unity in the church will not rest on pettiness, selfishness, jealousy, or pride. Members of the body must give up their expectation of receiving recognition and continual affirmation while performing ministry. Such immature expectations do not foster cooperation and unity, only a divisive spirit. Praise God, Paul points out to Christians to look to Jesus for the most appropriate model of cooperation! The strength of the body is that it has been called to cooperate, "We are labourers together with God" (1 Cor. 3:9 KJV).

Finally, Paul prays believers will be empowered with the Holy Spirit. These Christians will never be fulfilled or live the overcoming Christian life without this empowerment. Paul knew already that most Christians know much more than they will ever accomplish in their Christian experience. What a shame when the Holy Spirit of God stands ready to equip believers for every good work! Paul testified that "when" the spirit comes, not "if," that Jesus' followers will be empowered. Believers abuse and misuse the Holy Spirit by simply ignoring it. The renowned H. G. Wells declared that a person needs power to make "the secret splendour of our intentions" into actual facts. The Holy Spirit gives that power to Christians. Paul knew that by ourselves we can do nothing; but with God all things are possible (Mark 10:27).

Paul's prayer is for believers to overflow with hope. With encouragement from the Scriptures, cooperation with fellow believers, and empowerment by the Holy Spirit, Paul's prayer will be answered! (Billy Compton)

STAYING FOCUSED

MATTHEW 3:1-12

John the Baptist is not the kind of person most of us expect to meet at church. His appearance and demeanor shock us. The word he proclaims seems confrontational, even frightening. Yet John is the herald of Christ, and his word guides us on the Second Sunday of Advent.

In a culture of timid religion, John stands as a reminder that the Advent of Christ will forever set a dividing line in history. A new day is dawning and in its light neutrality is not possible. No longer is God just a concept to be taken or left as one may choose. God is about to break into history in a decisive, unique way, and all must respond.

In the aftermath of the September 11, 2001, terrorist attacks on the United States, the nation listened carefully and hungrily for words from our leaders. In one of his speeches to the nations of the world, President Bush said there could be no option of neutrality in response to the attack on the United States. Bluntly, Bush spoke to world leaders and said, "Either you are for us or against us." A line had been drawn and the president was determined to force nations to be clear about where they stood in relation to that line.

John is not a nationalist or a militarist. Nevertheless, he draws a clear line on history's ground and says that neutrality is not an option in light of the one who is coming. We are "either for him or against him." This is the judgment we must live with.

In some ways John's proclamation of the coming of Christ is so confrontational that it hardly seems like gospel (good news) language. John's imagery is frightening as he speaks of the "wrath to come," and of the "ax lying at the root of trees," and of being "cut down and thrown into the fire." John is insistent that the coming of Christ will require a decision from all people for all time.

In a multiple-choice world where absolutes are difficult to find and where relativity is the order of the day, John's proclamation seems strangely out of place. Yet his word can have a settling influence on our lives. If we take John seriously we find ourselves becoming focused. We begin to live lives of intentionality. We "repent," which is to say, we choose to walk in a certain direction, to be defined by a certain ethic, to be shaped by a particular narrative. No longer are we people in the grips of constantly shifting cultural styles; we have become centered and have discovered a new energy which comes as the result of passionate commitment.

John's proclamation on this second Sunday of Advent really is an invitation of good news: We are being challenged to stand with others in history who experienced compelling calls that made all the difference in their lives. Hearing, really hearing, John's message leads us to declarations not unlike that of the great church reformer, Martin Luther, who declared, "Here I stand, so help me God!" as he insisted on a new way of understanding the way God works in our lives.

Those who live with such conviction are the blessed ones. Every moment is defined by their expectation and conviction. May it be for us in the Advent Season that we are people of such conviction, for we know, as Jesus has told us, "The kingdom of God has come near" (Luke 10:11). Nothing, absolutely nothing, will ever be the same again in the light of this proclamation. (Chris Andrews)

DECEMBER 12, 2004

Third Sunday of Advent

Worship Theme: Paul writes "faith, hope, and love abide" (1 Cor. 13:13). For those lost in the desolation of life, Christ's birth offers those in the bleakest circumstances fresh hope. The coming of the Lord is near.

Readings: Isaiah 35:1-10; James 5:7-10; Matthew 11:2-11

Call to Worship (Luke 1:47-55)

> *Leader:* My spirit rejoices in God my Savior, for he has looked with favor on the lowliness of his servant.

> ***People:*** **Surely, from now on all generations will call me blessed; for the Mighty One has done great things for me, and holy is his name.**

> *Leader:* His mercy is for those who fear him from generation to generation.

> ***People:*** **He has shown strength with his arm; he has scattered the proud in the thoughts of their hearts.**

> *Leader:* He has brought down the powerful from their thrones, and lifted up the lowly; he has filled the hungry with good things, and sent the rich away empty.

> *All:* **He has helped his servant Israel, in remembrance of his mercy, according to the promise he made to our ancestors, to Abraham and to his descendants forever.**

Pastoral Prayer:

O God of all Human Consolation, again we congregate to hear the good news of our salvation. During our hours of hopelessness, you alone assure us that all things are possible through your providential word of promise. In your power and compassion, O God, we see the possibility of blessing in all things. Too often life crushes the hope in the best of us. We read in scripture that even an imprisoned John second-guessed the arrival of the promised one. Yet, you continue to put forward your grace and mercy despite our anxious need for divine reassurance. Help us decide to put our faith and trust in you Lord. We have failed to live out of the fullness of your promise, and yet it is the basis for all our hope. Remind us to provide for those in need, for an active faith supplies for us a measure of the confidence we seek. During this holy season of Advent, make real to us the profound relationship and covenant you make with us in your Messiah. May Jesus guide, guard, and protect us as we come to the fullness of faith. In Jesus' holy and sanctified name we pray. Amen. (David Mosser)

SERMON BRIEFS

THE HIGHWAY

ISAIAH 35:1-10

In Michigan's Upper Peninsula, where relatively few people live, the joke is that there are only two seasons: winter and poor sledding. Closer to Detroit, where I live, there are still only two seasons: winter and road construction. Somebody must be paying taxes, given that road crews snarl traffic on every road I travel. The phrase, "You can't get there from here," may have been the punch line of an old joke, but it becomes reality every summer.

We Americans take highways and thoroughfares for granted. Anybody can go anywhere, often at great speed. We claim it as our right. This means that potholes, traffic snarls, and "under construction" signs are viewed as demonic nuisances, meant to curb our mobility and thwart our free will. Has not God decreed that we should be able to get from point A to point B in a matter of minutes?

Ten years ago, I traveled to Costa Rica with a mission work team. While this was neither our first trip nor our last, it was, far and away, the most difficult. Our charge was to build a church in a jungle clearing for a congregation that would access it only by river—which meant that we were able to reach the work site only by boat. Everything we needed had to be floated across by dugout canoe. This method worked fine, once we reached the launch area.

The road to the river, however, proved the greater obstacle. Rains had rutted the road in some parts and washed it away in others. At one impasse, we had to unload the entire bus, cut down several small saplings and build a new roadbed. Then we pushed the bus beyond the point of difficulty before reloading and reboarding. Eventually we arrived and built a church. None of us, however, claimed that getting there was half the fun.

In the text before us, the people of Israel are given a trio of promises. The first concerns the blossoming desert. The second concerns the firming of feeble knees (so as to enable the disabled to leap, even as the deaf hear and the voiceless sing). The third promise addresses a highway that shall be called "The Way of Holiness." People shall travel it freely and fearlessly. No one shall stop them, neither shall ravenous beasts devour them. The passage concludes with a glorious vision of returnees, with gladness in their hearts and songs on their lips. People are coming home.

Home from where? Home from exile. Home from oppression. Home from hiding. Home from "the far country." Home from separation from a loved land, a loved people, and a loved God. And, glory be, they don't even have to push the bus. Of all the images in chapter 35 of Isaiah, the "promised highway" is the most magnificent. In a world where all of us have been slowed to a crawl or gridlocked into inactivity, a free and fluid passage is as good as it gets.

But there is something else to consider. The same highway that takes us toward God brings God toward us. The plaintive chant at the beginning of *Godspell* suggests that the "way prepared" is the way of the Lord. And the last time I sang the recitative that launches Handel's *Messiah,* the lyric ends: "Prepare . . . in the desert a highway for our God."

God moves, too. Not just "hither and yon," but here and now. This is Advent. We talk about God drawing nigh and "pitching his tent among us." According to divine reasoning, if we won't move, God will.

When I was a youngster, I used to go to sleepovers at the homes of my friends. We'd all sack out on the living room floor, but we seldom went to sleep. In fact, whenever one of our number threatened to doze off, someone else would tell a joke, shine a flashlight, or make some noise. With each passing hour, we got sillier and louder. That is, until we aroused the ire of our host's father. We always knew we'd gone too far when, from the landing of the stairway, we heard the thunderous threat: "Don't make me come down there!" We were never quite sure what would happen if we did but were seldom of a mind to try. The father's descent was something to be feared.

Not so in the Bible. God's descent is to be welcomed, even embraced. God will come wherever "here" is. The direction of God's movement is irrelevant. So, too, the means of approach. All I know is that, as an image, the stairway doesn't cut it. But a highway does. Quite nicely, in fact. (William Ritter)

CALL WAITING

JAMES 5:7-10

In his early career the most important things to Richard Pryor were fame, money, and success. Then one day he was critically burned in an accident. Doctors didn't know if he would live or die. Day by day his life hung in the balance. He did recover, and his first public appearance was on *The Tonight Show* with Johnny Carson. "What pulled you through those dark nights?" Carson asked. Richard Pryor said, "I was so critically ill all I could think of was to call on God. I didn't call on the Bank of America a single time. All I could do was call on God." The good news is when we call, God promises to listen. And God not only listens but also works in our lives.

James was writing to the early church. The letter assumes an understanding of Christianity on the reader's part and appears to have been written around the end of the first century. The early church believed the return of Christ was imminent. When the end came God would interrupt history and set everything right. Now as the years passed, Christians asked, "When will Jesus come? When will God intervene in the world?"

To the early church, James had two messages: First, be patient. Trust God's promises. While you are waiting, prepare your hearts; don't be grumbling with one another. Let this be a time of sowing seeds of love and encouragement for one another. Second, the farmer must be patient for the fruits of the earth. When the farmer looks at his field each day, it appears nothing is happening. You can't see crops growing, but they are. Slowly, unperceived, they are growing each day. It is only over a period of time that you see the change.

Patience is a word we don't like to hear. We want results now. Although we don't always see, God moves in our lives and in the world. Sometimes it seems imperceptible, but it is happening. Trust that God will help us see the world through new eyes.

It was in England on Christmas Eve, 1642 that the wife of a farmer went into labor. She didn't have the child until Christmas morning, giving birth to a little boy. The family was very poor. The father (who died before the boy was born) was illiterate, but the little boy had a thirst for learning. By the time he was twenty-three he had developed the elements of differential calculus. Not long after that he invented the reflecting telescope. When he was forty-five years old he produced *Principia Mathematica*, a paper that discussed the universal principle of gravity.

His name was Isaac Newton, and he was born on Christmas Day. We often think of Isaac Newton sitting under an apple tree, getting hit in the head, and saying, "Wow, gravity, what a neat discovery." But there isn't a single thing that Isaac Newton discovered that hadn't existed since the start of time. Isaac Newton saw things in a new way. His vision changed the world forever. That's what Christmas is all about. It's about seeing God's love in a new way that will change our world forever. (Robert Long)

TAKING FAITH TO THE EXTREME

MATTHEW 11:2-11

In America, we've been awash in images of "extreme" life the past few years. Arising from the Post-Boomer generations (Generations X and Y), young folk between the ages of (roughly) seventeen to thirty-five have invented radical soft drinks, dangerous sports, and even life-threatening vacations. Of course the underlying message of such daredevil living is that we should experience all that the world has to offer and do it on the edge of social acceptability. In that kind of light, not surprisingly, many young people look at the Christian faith as too boring or passé to be really challenging. However, if such people could talk to John, I think he'd tell them they weren't even close to realizing what the faith entails.

Chapter 11 in Matthew's Gospel marks a turning point in Jesus' ministry, one from which more and more conflict with religious authorities will ensue. John is now in prison at Herod's command, most probably at the fortress at Machaerus on the eastern side of the Dead Sea (Robert H. Mounce, *Matthew: A Good News Commentary* [San Francisco: HarperCollins, 1985], p. 101). While it may be problematic to analyze John's emotional state during this crisis, it seems safe to say that his imprisonment has prompted an agonizing descent into despair. Our image of John up to this point has been one of a humbly assured yet confrontational herald. Here, however, Matthew expands our perspective of John. The public mission of being God's witness to the Christ has given way to the private confusion of a man facing execution for his faith, summed up in his desperate question, "Are you the one who is to come, or are we to wait for another?" (v. 3).

For us, is this not a more accurate picture of what the Christian faith entails than a modern stereotype? In the face of crisis, like marbles falling onto a tile floor, our doubts can pour forth in whispered, pleading questions that some could construe as heretical. John's kingdom function was to prophetically call the world to repentance in advance of the coming Messiah. That's what he did in his life. However, what he did with his life remains instructive for us as well. For John's life is also prophetic, in that

411

it illustrates the pattern that every Christian must ultimately be willing to emulate: Our faith in this world-reconstructing Christ might cost us everything.

However, more than just John's life is patterned here. In response to John's question, Jesus offers what must have been a comforting answer back through the messengers. Alluding to several passages from Isaiah (29:18-19; 35:5-6; 61:1), Jesus draws on words he used when he first began his public ministry (cf. Luke 4:17-21) to assure John that the waiting is over, the Messiah is indeed here! Moreover, Jesus goes on to extol John's commitment to him, while yet framing John's ministry as only the introduction to the kingdom of heaven now at hand. By his loving reassurance to John, Jesus is patterning for all believers the corollary to the crisis of faith, and that is the abiding presence of Christ to those who are called to account for their beliefs. In a world in which Christians must live and yet change, often at great risk, this is indeed good news during Advent. For some in the pews whose lives seem bland and devoid of challenge, Jesus' words to John might sound like an unfamiliar yet enticing song that calls for renewed commitment. For those who don't yet know Christ and may think the faith of little consequence, John's "extreme" faith might challenge their assumptions. Oh how radical God can be! (Timothy Mallard)

DECEMBER 19, 2004

Fourth Sunday of Advent

Worship Theme: From cradle to grave, from manger to cross, Jesus represents the most intimate portrait of God that humans can ever grasp. In Jesus we receive our call to be the people of God. By the child's name, "Emmanuel," we know that God is indeed with us.

Readings: Isaiah 7:10-16; Romans 1:1-7; Matthew 1:18-25

Call to Worship (Psalm 80:1-4, 7, 17-19 RSV)

Leader:	Give ear, O Shepherd of Israel, thou who leadest Joseph like a flock! Thou who art enthroned upon the cherubim, shine forth before Ephraim and Benjamin and Manasseh!
People:	**Stir up thy might, and come to save us!**
Leader:	Restore us, O God; let thy face shine, that we may be saved!
People:	**O Lord God of hosts, how long wilt thou be angry with thy people's prayers?**
Leader:	Restore us, O God of hosts; let thy face shine, that we may be saved.
People:	**But let thy hand be upon the man of thy right hand, the son of man whom thou hast made strong for thyself.**
Leader:	Then we will never turn back from thee; give us life, and we will call on thy name.

All: **Restore us, O LORD God of host! let thy face shine, that we may be saved.**

Pastoral Prayer:

As we approach this most mysterious and frequently emotionally satisfying season of the Christian year, O Lord, the strangeness of it all strikes us once again. We read about the angel's announcement to Joseph in a dream, how an infant will be born through the agency of the Holy Spirit. We read that this child will save all people from their sins. Help us draw near this mystery of faith and the message of Messiah with childlike wonder and anticipation. Let us not forget the joy we had as children when Christmas approached. It enthralled us. As the gospel story of John, Mary, Joseph, and others rouses us, create in us a longing for the hope that this story creates. Help us imagine the advent of a better world. Almighty God, let us too dream divine dreams that help us envision a peace that passes all our human understanding. When we reflect upon all you have done for us, O Lord, it humbles us before you. We thank you for the gift of salvation through the birth of this Christ child. We pledge ourselves to you by living lives worthy of the gospel's promise. Amen. (David Mosser)

SERMON BRIEFS

LEARNING TO SEE

ISAIAH 7:10-16

What would you do if you were told you were going blind? When Lisa Fittipaldi got that news, she decided to become an artist. She had been a CPA, traveling extensively and observing the cultures and customs of people around the world. When she was told she would never see color again, she started to paint. She is a completely self-taught watercolor and oil artist. How she paints is a mystery to her and everyone else, but she is being heralded as a genius and prodigy. Her paintings are collected extensively in Europe, South America, and the United States. Lisa says she now sees more clearly with her mind than she did with her eyes. She says when she lost her sight she gained a new vision.

It is God who comes into our darkest nights to give us a new vision. So often the vision God gives is very different from anything we could ever imagine. We must keep our minds open to God's leading so we don't miss the unexpected answers that come.

Ahaz was the young king of Judah when he was faced with a terrible crisis. Rezin, the king of Aram, and Pekah, the king of Israel, joined forces to wage war against Jerusalem. It would be known as the Syro-Ephraimite War (2 Kings 16:1-20).

Isaiah told Ahaz he had nothing to fear and that God would strengthen Judah against her enemies. But Ahaz wasn't so sure. Rather than trusting God to strengthen Judah, he decided to trust Tiglath-Pileser, king of Assyria. Ahaz sent great treasures from the temple and his own house to the King of Assyria asking him to fight against Judah's enemies. Isaiah said the answer is not in the help of Assyria but in the help of the Lord. The Lord will give you a sign. A young woman will conceive and bear a son and shall call his name Immanuel, which means God with us. But Ahaz was sure the Assyrians were the answer; he couldn't glimpse a new vision. He couldn't see that God would provide a different possibility.

It would be seven hundred years later, to people oppressed by Rome, that God would send the same message. A young woman will conceive and bear a son and his name shall be called Immanuel, God with us. Jesus was a surprise, not the expected answer; a Messiah who would talk of love, forgiveness, and peace instead of hate, retaliation, and war. We still struggle with openness to God's surprises and answers different from what we expect.

Dr. Marvin Pope was the world's foremost scholar on Ugaritics. Ugarit was a Syrian city founded eight thousand years ago. After the Jews were captured by the Babylonians, they went to Ugarit to translate their scriptures. So how do you decide to become a scholar in Ugaritics? For Dr. Pope it happened in college. When he signed up for his classes a clerk transposed two of the class numbers. When he showed up for his first day of class the professor came in and wrote on the board "Hebrew 101." Marvin Pope didn't want Hebrew 101, but he was such a shy person he couldn't bring himself to walk out in front of the professor. He decided he would sit through the one class. When the hour was over, the professor had him. Hebrew seemed so fascinating. He changed his major to Hebrew and became an archeologist studying at Ugarit. Dr. Pope says his whole life changed because of two transposed numbers. It was an answer to prayer, but it certainly wasn't what he expected. (Robert Long)

CHRIST: SEED OF DAVID AND HOPE OF ALL PEOPLE

ROMANS 1:1-7

Paul's letter to Rome is his greatest exposition of the gospel of Christ, a gospel that extends the hope of salvation to all persons. When Paul wrote these words, neither he nor any other church leaders, including Peter or James, had ever been to Rome. Paul did eventually preach in Rome (Acts 28), perhaps even to Caesar himself. The church located in the city was probably established either by believers who had been to Jerusalem for Pentecost or by travelers who had heard the gospel in other places and brought it to Rome with them. Priscilla and Aquila (Acts 18:2) were good examples of the latter group.

Especially at this season of the year some might tend to see the Lord only as the Babe of Bethlehem. Christmas cards, lawn decorations, and church pageants feature God arriving on the human scene as a tiny baby boy. Paul's lofty teaching in Romans focuses our eyes not only on the birth of the promised seed of David, but also on the crucified, risen, and coming Son of God, bringing hope to all.

In this passage from Romans, Paul reaffirmed that this Christ was the child of promise, prophesied by the prophets in the Holy Scriptures. The Old Testament constantly testifies to this truth. The first hint came in the Garden of Eden when God said to Satan, "I will put enmity between thee and the woman, and between thy seed and her seed; it shall bruise thy head, and thou shalt bruise his heel" (Gen. 3:15).

Forty years after Israel's deliverance from Egypt, Isaiah

promised a deliverer. "Behold, a virgin shall conceive, and bear a son, and shall call his name Immanuel" (7:14). Further, according to Isaiah, this Son would be a suffering servant, bearing our griefs and carrying our sorrows (42:1-4; 52:13-15). This promised one's coming would be during the dark night of the soul for the Jewish people, the period of Roman rule.

The fulfillment of the promise so clear in scripture came in the birth of Jesus who "was made of the seed of David according to the flesh" (Rom. 1:3 KJV). The angelic message was clear to Mary: 'Thou shalt conceive in thy womb, and bring forth a son. . . . He shall be great . . . the Son of the Highest. . . . Of his kingdom there shall be no end" (Luke 1:31-33 KJV). The same clarity is seen in the angel's message to Joseph, "Thou shalt call his name Jesus: for he shall save his people from their sins" (Matt. 1:21).

The authentication of this promise came when Jesus was "declared to be the Son of God with power . . . by the resurrection from the dead" (Rom. 1:4 KJV). On the night of the Savior's birth, the stars shone brightly down on a manger scene. On Easter morning, resurrection morning, the "bright and morning star" gave new hope to all people. Death no longer had its sting, nor the grave its victory (1 Cor. 15:55).

As a result of receiving this grace and peace from God through Jesus Christ, we have been called of God; we have become God's beloved; and we are saints. Thanks be to God for his gifts to us this Christmastime!

As we share gifts with one another, let us also thank God for his unspeakable gift to each of us. Let us never forget that the greatest gift we can give anyone is the knowledge of the Christ who freely gave himself for each of us in order that we might have hope, not for this world alone, but for all eternity! (Jerry Gunnells)

HOW THE BIRTH OF JESUS CAME ABOUT

MATTHEW 1:18-25

We enjoy knowing exact details about how something happened. Graphic, even lurid, details are preferable. We have it all in the story of how the birth of Jesus came about.

417

The Gospels of Mark and John start with a full-grown Jesus. It is the Gospels of Matthew and Luke that give us the enchanting and anecdotal material about the birth of Jesus that we love so much.

Both Matthew and Luke supply genealogy of Jesus. Luke's genealogical account is completely male and goes back to Adam. While Matthew only goes back to Abraham, he includes four women in Jesus' lineage. This is strange considering the attitudes toward women in that time. Stranger still is the backgrounds and reputations of these women. Tamar was a seducer, Rahab, a prostitute, and Bathsheba (referred to as "Uriah's wife") an adulteress. Ruth did not have a dark side to her reputation, but like the other three, she was not Jewish. She was a Moabite, an alien and hated people. To the Jews, four more unlikely candidates could not be found for the genealogy of Jesus. Perhaps this suggests something of the manner in which the ministry of Jesus will topple so many barriers. With this unusual genealogical introduction, we come now to the specifics of how Jesus' birth came about. In our generation, this would be tabloid material.

It was discovered that Mary, who was betrothed to Joseph, was pregnant. What happened? Mary said this child was by the action of the Holy Spirit. The response of Joseph, family, and friends was about the same as it would be today: "Yeah, right!"

Marriage customs of that day were somewhat different than they are today. There were three steps to full marriage. There was engagement, which was usually arranged by parents or matchmakers, while the couple were children. Next was betrothal, which was the acceptance by the couple of the arrangements made for them when they were children. This stage in the process lasted for a year. During this time they were legally recognized as husband and wife, but did not have the specific rights of intimacy as husband and wife. The third step was the marriage.

The discovery of Mary's pregnancy was during the betrothal— before marriage. It does not take much of an imagination to realize the seriousness of the situation. According to Matthew, Mary knew the proper explanation of her pregnancy, but Joseph does not yet know. This is a big problem!

Who else knew or would soon know of Mary's condition? Had

they talked about it at the beauty parlor, the well, the grocery store, or the synagogue? It was bound to become public knowledge sooner or later. Joseph, her betrothed husband, had to make a decision. He could not ignore the problem. He had two choices: Death or divorce. He could report her to the synagogue and see her stoned to death (Deuteronomy 22), or Joseph could divorce Mary. (Betrothal was legally binding, but could be terminated by divorce.)

Joseph had every right to be angry and hurt at what was an obvious betrayal. He would be within his rights to follow harsh legal procedures. But, because Joseph is a righteous man, he does not want to expose Mary to public disgrace. He makes up his mind to quietly divorce her. This is the most caring thing he can do under the circumstance of his knowledge at this point. The character of Joseph begins to come into focus.

The scene changes. Joseph goes to bed with his mind settled on divorce. Then he has a dream in which an angel of the Lord appears to him. The angel tells Joseph not to be afraid to take Mary as his wife because the child she is carrying is from the Holy Spirit. The angel further informs Joseph that the child is a son and that Joseph is to give the child the name "Jesus, for he will save his people from their sins."

Joseph is obedient to this heavenly message. He takes Mary as his wife. Joseph names the child Jesus. By naming the child, he adopted Jesus into the lineage of David. Joseph goes beyond the angel's command. He abstains from sexual relations with Mary until the child is born. Matthew makes it clear that Joseph is not the biological father of Jesus, but implies that after Jesus' birth Mary and Joseph developed normal marital relations. One may properly draw the conclusion that the "brothers and sisters" of Jesus in Matthew 13:55-56 are, in fact, the sons and daughters of Mary and Joseph.

It would be difficult to maintain the idea of the "perpetual virginity" of Mary from this passage. It appears that Mary and Joseph became parents of a normal family where there were brothers and sisters. Jesus would have grown up in a normal Jewish family atmosphere. This understanding is reinforced in the account we have of Jesus when he was twelve years old in Luke 2:41-52.

The seamy beginning of the story of how Jesus' birth came about resolves itself satisfactorily primarily because Joseph is a good and loving person. His propensity to do what was right was reinforced by his obedience to the angel of the Lord. Joseph is usually overshadowed by the attention we give to Mary. But Joseph is the unsung hero of the story. His sense of justice, his caring heart, and his spiritual discernment make him a leading character in this divine drama. When it becomes clear to Joseph what should be done, he does it.

The life of Joseph drifts into mystery. After the Lukan account of the Jerusalem trip when Jesus was twelve years old, we can only assume that much of the early instruction of Jesus came from this righteous man who risked ridicule in order to be just and obedient. (Thomas Lane Butts)

DECEMBER 26, 2004

First Sunday After Christmas Day

Worship Theme: Like Jesus' ancestors, Jesus too descends into Egypt. By this Egyptian journey, God saves the Holy Family from Herod's aggression. Through the incarnation God stoops to approach humanity in a human form. God's act of incarnation raises us toward becoming that for which God initially created us.

Readings: Isaiah 63:7-9; Hebrews 2:10-18; Matthew 2:13-23

Call to Worship (Psalm 148:1-2, 11-14)

Leader:	Praise the LORD! Praise the LORD from the heavens; praise him in the heights!
People:	**Praise him, all his angels; praise him, all his host!**
Leader:	Kings of the earth and all peoples, princes and all rulers of the earth!
People:	**Young men and women alike, old and young together!**
Leader:	Let them praise the name of the LORD, for his name alone is exalted; his glory is above earth and heaven.
People:	**He has raised up a horn for his people, praise for all his faithful, for the people of Israel who are close to him. Praise the LORD!**

Pastoral Prayer:

Today is a day of looking forward as we stand on the cusp of a new year. For what the old year brought us, O God, we thank you. Within this year's days, weeks, and months we have experienced many occasions for spreading the good news of Jesus Christ. As we look forward to more occasions to share the gospel with a wounded and divided world, make us strong in conviction and stout of heart. Lord, we praise you for the gift of newness and the manifold opportunities it affords. The Resurrection propels our faith, just as the Resurrection occasions our faith. Paul reminds us that, "Christ was raised from the dead by the glory of the Father, so we too might walk in newness of life" (Rom. 6:4). The new year, with all its potential for goodness, presents itself now to us. May we live thankfully as we sojourn the frontiers of a new year with assurance. Bless our lives in the shadow of your presence. We pray this in the fervent hope that Jesus will abide with us in the future as he has in our past. In Jesus' name we offer our every prayer. Amen. (David Mosser)

SERMON BRIEFS

REMEMBER!

ISAIAH 63:7-9

Christmas is over. John and Jane Doe slowly emerge from the rubble of unwrapped gifts and detritus of leftover food. It is time to get back to normal living. Or is it? The preaching task is to share the ongoing story of God's incarnate love. Coming as it does a week after Christmas, this passage presents the reader with a set of interesting choices. In its original setting, this text is a part of a communal lament. The relationship between God and the people is endangered by their forgetfulness. In the context of the lectionary reading on the First Sunday after Christmas Day, the prophet's words are place alongside the joy of the Savior's birth. While these two positions may appear at odds with each other, in actuality they work together to strengthen the faithful.

Facing the inevitable tendency to experience a letdown after the celebration of Christmas, we are afforded the opportunity to worship in heartfelt thankfulness and deep praise. We remember in order to recommit ourselves. Thus the passage urges our attention not on ourselves, but on what God has done, is doing, and will do. The Christmas proclamation of God's redeeming presence is with us still.

Remembrance is a treasure that keeps alive our present hope and reconnects us to God's ongoing redemptive love. Often we see the hand of God best through a rearview mirror. The text focuses our attention on God's "gracious deeds." The prophet's heart overflows in praise and gratitude.

> I will recount the gracious deeds of the LORD,
>   the praiseworthy acts of the LORD,
> because of all that the LORD has done for us. (v. 7*abc*)

The remembrance to which the passage calls us is about far more than simply the mental process of recalling what God has done. Praise is tied to grace. Indeed, the two can hardly be separated. The prophet's opening words of praise lead directly to the remembrance of God's gracious action. "He has shown them according to his mercy, / according to the abundance of his steadfast love" (v. 7*ef*). The claim of verse 8—"surely they are my people,"—comes with an expectation—"children who will not deal falsely." Verse 9 reinforces the theme of grace and offers an opportunity to tie the passage to the Christmas experience. "It was no messenger or angel / but his presence that saved them." A messenger may come for a short period of time, deliver the message, and then leave. God comes to stay. The closing phrase focuses us again on God's mighty acts: "He lifted them up and carried them all the days of old" (v. 9*d*).

The rhythm of this text fits nicely with the celebration of Christmas. Faithful preaching begins in praise. It moves on to stress God's gracious action in remembrance of the past and points to the future. We are to exercise caution to avoid falling into the trap of using this Sunday as a mere encouragement not to forget Christmas and try harder to be good. Throughout its majestic verses, the stress is constantly on God. "In his love and in his pity he redeemed them" (v. 9*c*).

In Dickens's *A Christmas Carol*, it is the "Ghost of Christmas Past" who first awakens in Scrooge an awareness of the joy of Christmas. For Christians, it is the remembrance of God's mighty deeds of grace and mercy that awaken in us the confidence of

God's ongoing grace and future salvation. We remember in order to reenact and recommit ourselves to God's gracious ongoing action of salvation on our behalf. (Mike Lowry)

HE UNDERSTANDS

HEBREWS 2:10-18

When my friend James was about ten years old, he had to go to the hospital for an operation. Have you ever been in the hospital? Well, James was scared. I tried to make him feel better, but I don't think I did. I had never been in the hospital for an operation, so I really didn't understand all he was feeling, his fear.

But I will never forget another friend from school, Charles. Charles came to see James the day of the operation. Charles had undergone the same operation last year. He told my friend that he would be okay, that he would be sore for a time but the doctors and nurses would take really good care of him. "Besides," he said, "they give you ice cream afterwards, all the ice cream you want." No one loved ice cream more than James! So Charles really helped him feel better. Sure enough, James came through the operation just fine. I remember seeing Charles and James in that hospital room eating ice cream together.

Why was Charles able to help James in a different way than I was? Charles had been there, hadn't he? He had been through the operation. He was able to understand what James was going through. James knew this, and it really made a difference.

I listened quietly as a woman told me about the results of her biopsy. She had cancer. Although I very much felt her pain, I could not tell her I really understood. So what I did was bring her and another woman in the community together who had been through the same thing years ago. They became the best of friends. She really did understand and that made all the difference.

That's a lesson I have learned and used as a pastor many times. There are many things persons in my congregation go through that I can not really understand. I give them my support, my presence, my prayers. But one of the best things I can often do for them is to get someone who has been where they are to minister to them.

In our Bible lesson for today, it tells us that Jesus is the same way. Jesus became one of us, a real person. He went through all the problems and troubles we face, and more. The author of Hebrews writes, "Because he himself was tested by what he suffered, he is able to help those who are being tested" (v. 18). In other words, Jesus understands. This passage from Hebrews tells us that Jesus is the one who has been there! He did not live in an ivory tower. He did not choose to stay above and over everything. To the contrary, Jesus "in every respect" became as we are, even to the experience of death, so that we might know that Jesus understands and can help us. He knows how we feel. When we are afraid, when we are sick, or when we feel lost, Jesus understands. He's been there, he's experienced it, just like Charles and Jesus can help us. All we have to do is talk to him, pray to him, tell him how we feel, trust him to help us no matter what. Jesus will, for he understands and loves us.

Prayer: Jesus, you understand, don't you? You know all we feel and all we will ever feel. You came to show us and tell us that God is with us and loves us, that God will never leave us. We believe you. We trust you. We know you understand. Amen. (Bass Mitchell)

CONFRONTING EVIL

MATTHEW 2:13-23

We moderns are distinctly uncomfortable in addressing the issue of evil in our world. Our nonconfrontational culture and faith have bred a slow blindness to an acknowledgment that evil is real, actively seeking to fight God's kingdom in any way it can. Consequently, we also don't see that our human sin is an expression of that tangible evil. Even when facing such heinous acts as the terrorist attacks of September 11, 2001, in time we have retreated into a comfortable amnesia. In essence, we've become so accustomed to sin that we're numb to it. Karl Menninger, the late American psychiatrist, prophetically asked:

425

Is no one any longer guilty of anything? Guilty perhaps of a sin that could be repented and repaired or atoned for? Is it only that someone may be stupid or sick or criminal—or asleep? Wrong things are being done, we know; tares are being sown in the wheat field at night. But is no one responsible, no one answerable for these acts? Anxiety and depression we all acknowledge, and even vague guilt feelings; but has no one committed any sins? (Karl Menninger, *Whatever Became of Sin?* New York: Hawthorne Books, 1973)

Despite our not wanting to see, evil and sin are present not only in our lives but also in our biblical texts. Take today's Christmas message. There are no two ways around it: Matthew portrays God and Satan as being locked in spiritual combat. Ironically harkening back to Pharaoh's slaughter of all Hebrew boys at Moses' birth (Exod. 1:22), the demons marshal themselves in an all-out attack to quash this holy baby whom they know will ultimately do them in. In Matthew's distinct and consistent cosmology, Herod the Great, although a human figure, is clearly an agent of Satan in his bid to crush the infant God. So vile was Herod that he murdered his favorite wife, her family, and his own eldest son, prompting the Roman Emperor Augustus to comment that it would be "safer to be Herod's pig (*hus* in Greek) than his son (*huios*)" (Robert H. Mounce, *Matthew: A Good News Commentary* [San Francisco: Harper & Row, 1985], p. 7). In the face of such a determined effort, we might despair and conclude that all is lost, that the little child stands no chance against a vengeful and vile king, that God might just not win this one. However, there's a tension in this story that we should never lose because that tension fuels the plot and teaches us something in the process.

Just when we think that things can't really be different from what we see, God surprises us in this story. In Matthew's view, not only are evil and sin real forces in this world working at the behest of Satan, but Jesus' power and status as the Son of God are fully active in this fight even at his birth. Moreover, the fight's not even a fair one. For where Herod can only try to catch up with the baby and dust off past schemes of wrong, God is always out front forging new ways for the Christ child and his family to safely live and grow. In fact, God wins this battle by moving the Holy Family back to Egypt. God knows that although Satan has now reworked Pharaoh's treachery, he'll never think to search for Jesus back in the desert. In essence, God doesn't ignore evil but outwits it, outplans it, and outmaneuvers it. That's a message of hope for us today that we only gain once we pay attention to the reality of evil in this world. For only by acknowledging that can we also become surprised and emboldened witnesses to God's power working through the birth of Jesus. (Timothy Mallard)

BENEDICTIONS

Advent Season

Take the good news of the gospel with you as you depart the house of God. God's blessing, Son, and Holy Spirit, permeate your life and your work. Celebrate with joy God's coming to earth to reveal the fullness of God's love and mercy, today and forever. Amen.

Live in the bounty of God's good grace. Remember that God's compassion surrounds you in the revelation of Creator, Redeemer, and Sustainer. Depart with the love of God in your heart and mind and soul. Give God your strength and the world your witness. Amen.

We are God's people. May God's Spirit of holiness and righteousness enter your every thought and act as we depart to serve the risen Lord. Go in thanksgiving and serve with joy. Amen.

> O sing to the LORD a new song;
>   sing to the LORD, all the earth.
> Sing to the LORD, bless his name;
>   tell of his salvation from day to day. (Ps. 96:1-2)

Today is the Lord's day. Be re-created in God's image and have the mind of Christ in you. Amen.

Christmas Season

We have witnessed God's care and loving-kindness for God's people in the story of Jesus. Take the love of Christ with you into the world and spread the joy of the good news far and wide. Broadcast the gospel in the name of God, the Son, and Holy Spirit all your days. Amen.

"The LORD sits enthroned as king forever.
May the LORD give strength to his people!
May the LORD bless his people with peace." (Ps. 29:10*b*-11)
Depart the household of faith and spread scripture holiness throughout the land. Claim the promise of the gospel for your life and your kindred. Amen.

Season After Epiphany

The light of Christ is upon us and around us and within us. Take this light and live by it all your days. Let the glow of love illuminate a path for others in a darkened world. Let the light of Jesus Christ be a beacon to a people shrouded in darkness. Celebrate the joy of God's light. Amen.

"May the LORD, the God of your ancestors, increase you a thousand times more and bless you, as he has promised you" (Deut. 1:11). Claim God's magnificent promise and walk in God's assurance in each and every day. Live your life in the fullness of God's glory, Son, and Holy Spirit. Amen.

"May the LORD reward you for your deeds, and may you have a full reward from the LORD, the God of Israel, under whose wings you have come for refuge" (Ruth 2:12). From the confidence in God's care and protection, speak the word of truth boldly and care for God's creation gently. Amen.

In the waters of Jesus' baptism and by that same water that covered your sin, decide today again whom you will serve. The Lord gives a great divine pledge. Declare this pledge as God's own faithful guarantee and live under the shelter of the Almighty, Creator, Redeemer, and Sustainer. Amen.

Season of Lent

May the LORD give you increase,
 both you and your children.
May you be blessed by the LORD,
 who made heaven and earth.
The heavens are the LORD's heavens,
 but the earth he has given to human beings. (Ps. 115:14-16)

Go forward now and become the holy and sanctified people of God. Amen.

"May the God of peace himself sanctify you entirely; and may your spirit and soul and body be kept sound and blameless at the coming of our Lord Jesus Christ" (1 Thess. 5:23). Amen.

Go into the world with the confidence that the One who sent Jesus as our Messiah and provides the Holy Spirit as our Advocate will also abide with us to the end of our days. Depart as disciples and serve a world in need. Amen.

> But [God's servant] was wounded for our transgressions,
>   crushed for our iniquities
> upon him was the punishment that made us whole,
>   and by his bruises we are healed. (Isa. 53:5)

Therefore, God has redeemed his people to be a sign of redemption for all humankind. Amen.

Season of Easter

We sing, "Christ the Lord Is Risen Today." Let us now go forth into our world with the confidence and assurance of faith. In Christ, God defeats the last enemy and gives us life. Depart with the joy of life in your heart and the song of Christ on your lips. Amen.

God, the Son, and Holy Spirit bless, preserve, and keep you; the Lord's favor be upon you; the Lord's grace surround you today, tomorrow, and forever. Amen.

"The grace of the Lord Jesus be with you" (1 Cor. 16:23). Amen.

The good news of the gospel of Jesus Christ surround you. The creative force of God the Divine Potter form you. The sweet fellowship of the Holy Spirit embrace you now and forever. Amen.

Season After Pentecost

May the Spirit of God Almighty guard and guide your steps. In God's wisdom and teaching is life for God's people. Go forth as those who learn of God and teach God's wisdom to others in all you say and do. Amen.

"You [O God] are a hiding place for me;
    you preserve me from trouble;
    you surround me with glad cries of deliverance." (Ps. 32:7)
Let the Lord's goodness encircle you for all your many long days of life. Amen.

"Bless God and acknowledge him in the presence of all the living for the good things he has done for you. Bless and sing praise to his name. With fitting honor declare to all people the deeds of God. Do not be slow to acknowledge him" (Tob. 12:6).

"May the God of hope fill you with all joy and peace in believing, so that you may abound in hope by the power of the Holy Spirit" (Rom. 15:13).

Other Occasions
Remember the risen Christ's word to Christ's Holy Church: "Because you have kept my word of patient endurance, I will keep you from the hour of trial" (Rev. 3:10). Remember Christ is our abiding presence. This we pray in the name of the Creator, Redeemer, and Sustainer—God in three persons, blessed trinity. Amen.

As we depart this hour of worship O Lord, give us a sustaining vision of how the world might be. Grant us fulfillment in the holy words spoken and sung in our holy worship. Give us the will and courage to follow your beckoning today and forever. In the name of the Father, Son, and Holy Spirit. Amen.

(David Mosser)

TEXT GUIDE*

THE REVISED COMMON LECTIONARY (2004—YEAR C)

Sunday	First Lesson	Psalm	Second Lesson	Gospel Lesson
1/4/04	Eccl. 3:1-13	Ps. 8	Rev. 21:1-6a	Matt. 25:31-46
1/11/04	Isa. 43:1-7	Ps. 29	Acts 8:14-17	Luke 3:15-17, 21-22
1/18/04	Isa. 62:1-5	Ps. 36:5-10	1 Cor. 12:1-11	John 2:1-11
1/25/04	Neh. 8:1-3, 5-6, 8-10	Ps. 19	1 Cor. 12:12-31a	Luke 4:14-21
2/1/04	Jer. 1:4-10	Ps. 71:1-6	1 Cor. 13:1-13	Luke 4:21-30
2/8/04	Isa. 6:1-8 (9-13)	Ps. 138	1 Cor. 15:1-11	Luke 5:1-11
2/15/04	Jer. 17:5-10	Ps. 1	1 Cor. 15:12-20	Luke 6:17-26
2/22/04	Exod. 34:29-35	Ps. 99	2 Cor. 3:12–4:2	Luke 9:28-36 (37-43)
2/29/04	Deut. 26:1-11	Ps. 91:1-2, 9-16	Rom 10:8b-13	Luke 4:1-13
3/7/04	Gen. 15:1-12, 17-18	Ps. 27	Phil. 3:17–4:1	Luke 13:31-35
3/14/04	Isa. 55:1-9	Ps. 63:1-8	1 Cor. 10:1-13	Luke 13:1-9
3/21/04	Josh. 5:9-12	Ps. 32	2 Cor. 5:16-21	Luke 15:1-3, 11b-32
3/28/04	Isa. 43:16-21	Ps. 126	Phil. 3:4b-14	John 12:1-8
4/4/04	Isa. 50:4-9a	Ps. 31:9-16	Phil. 2:5-11	Luke 22:14–23:56
4/11/04	Acts 10:34-43	Ps. 118:1-2, 14-24	1 Cor. 15:19-26	Luke 24:1-12
4/18/04	Acts 5:27-32	Ps. 150	Rev. 1:4-8	John 20:19-31
4/25/04	Acts 9:1-6 (7-20)	Ps. 30	Rev. 5:11-14	John 21:1-19
5/2/04	Acts 9:36-43	Ps. 23	Rev. 7:9-17	John 10:22-30
5/9/04	Acts 11:1-18	Ps. 148	Rev. 21:1-6	John 13:31-35
5/16/04	Acts 16:9-15	Ps. 67	Rev. 21:10, 22–22:5	John 14:23-29

*This guide represents one possible selection of lessons and psalms from the lectionary. For a complete listing see *The Revised Common Lectionary*.

432

Sunday	First Lesson	Psalm	Second Lesson	Gospel Lesson
5/23/04	Acts 16:16-34	Ps. 97	Rev. 22:12-14, 16-17, 20-21	John 17:20-26
5/30/04	Acts 2:1-21	Ps. 104:24-34, 35b	Rom. 8:14-17	John 14:8-17 (25-27)
6/6/04	Prov. 8:1-4, 22-31	Ps. 8	Rom. 5:1-5	John 16:12-15
6/13/04	1 Kgs 21:1-10, (11-14) 15-21a	Ps. 5:1-8	Gal. 2:15-21	Luke 7:36–8:3
6/20/04	1 Kgs. 19:1-4, (5-7) 8-15a	Ps. 42	Gal. 3:23-29	Luke 8:26-39
6/27/04	2 Kgs. 2:1-2, 6-14	Ps. 77:1-2, 11-20	Gal. 5:1, 13-25	Luke 9:51-62
7/04/04	2 Kgs. 5:1-14	Ps. 30	Gal. 6:(1-6), 7-16	Luke 10:1-11, 16-20
7/11/04	Amos 7:7-17	Ps. 82	Col. 1:1-14	Luke 10:25-37
7/18/04	Amos 8:1-12	Ps. 52	Col. 1:15-28	Luke 10:38-42
7/25/04	Hos. 1:2-10	Ps. 85	Col. 2:6-15 (16-19)	Luke 11:1-13
8/1/04	Hos. 11:1-11	Ps. 107:1-9, 43	Col. 3:1-11	Luke 12:13-21
8/8/04	Isa. 1:1, 10-20	Ps. 50:1-8, 22-23	Heb. 11:1-3, 8-16	Luke 12:32-40
8/15/04	Isa. 5:1-7	Ps. 80:1-2, 8-19	Heb. 11:29–12:2	Luke 12:49-56
8/22/04	Jer. 1:4-10	Ps. 71:1-6	Heb. 12:18-29	Luke 13:10-17
8/29/04	Jer. 2:4-13	Ps. 81:1, 10-16	Heb. 13:1-8, 15-16	Luke 14:1, 7-14
9/5/04	Jer. 18:1-11	Ps. 139:1-6, 13-18	Phil. 1-21	Luke 14:25-33
9/12/04	Jer. 4:11-12, 22-28	Ps. 14	1 Tim. 1:12-17	Luke 15:1-10
9/19/04	Jer. 8:18–9:1	Ps. 79:1-9	1 Tim. 2:1-7	Luke 16:1-13
9/26/04	Jer. 32:1-3a, 6-15	Ps. 91:1-6, 14-16	1 Tim. 6:6-19	Luke 16:19-31
10/3/04	Lam. 1:1-6	Ps. 137	2 Tim. 1:1-14	Luke 17:5-10
10/10/04	Jer. 29:1, 4-7	Ps. 66:1-12	2 Tim. 2:8-15	Luke 17:11-19

*This guide represents one possible selection of lessons and psalms from the lectionary. For a complete listing see *The Revised Common Lectionary.*

Sunday	First Lesson	Psalm	Second Lesson	Gospel Lesson
10/17/04	Jer. 31:27-34	Ps. 119:97-104	2 Tim. 3:14–4:5	Luke 18:1-8
10/24/04	Joel 2:23-32	Ps. 65	2 Tim. 4:6-8, 16-18	Luke 18:9-14
10/31/04	Hab. 1:1-4; 2.1-4	Ps. 119:137-144	2 Thess. 1:1-4, 11-12	Luke 19:1-10
11/7/04	Hag. 1:15*b*–2:9	Ps. 145:1-5, 17-21	2 Thess. 2:1-5, 13-17	Luke 20:27-38
11/14/04	Isa. 65:17-25	Ps. 98	2 Thess. 3:6-13	Luke 21:5-19
11/21/04	Jer. 23:1-6	Luke 1:68-79	Col. 1:11-20	Luke 23:33-43
11/28/04	Isa. 2:1-5	Ps. 122	Rom. 13:11-14	Matt. 24:36-44
12/5/04	Isa. 11:1-10	Ps. 72:1-7, 18-19	Rom. 15:4-13	Matt. 3:1-12
12/12/04	Isa. 35:1-10	Luke 1:47-55	James 5:7-10	Matt. 11:2-11
12/19/04	Isa. 7:10-16	Ps. 80:1-7, 17-19	Rom. 1:1-7	Matt. 1:18-25
12/26/04	Isa. 63:7-9	Ps. 148:1-2, 11-14	Heb. 2:10-18	Matt. 2:13-23

*This guide represents one possible selection of lessons and psalms from the lectionary. For a complete listing see *The Revised Common Lectionary.*

CONTRIBUTORS

Tracey Allred
Central Baptist Church
1500 Courthouse
Richmond, VA 23236

Chris Andrews
First United Methodist Church
930 North Boulevard
Baton Rouge, LA 70802-5728

Bob Buchanan
Parkway Baptist Church
5975 State Bridge Road
Duluth, GA 30097

Thomas Lane Butts
First United Methodist Church
324 Pineville Road
Monroeville, AL 36460

Gary Carver
First Baptist Church of
    Chattanooga
401 Gateway Avenue
Chattanooga, TN 37402-1504

Michael Childress
St. Andrews United Church of
    Christ
2608 Browns Lane
Louisville, KY 40220

Billy Compton
Severns Valley Baptist Church
P.O. Box 130
Elizabethtown, KY 42702

Wayne Day
First United Methodist Church
800 West Fifth Street
Fort Worth, TX 76102-3599

John Fiedler
First United Methodist Church
1928 Ross Avenue
Dallas, TX 75201-3282

Travis Franklin
The Methodist Children's Home
1111 Herring Avenue
Waco, TX 76708

Jerry Gunnells
1205 Dominion Drive, E.
Mobile, AL 36695

Tracy Hartman
Baptist Theological Seminary
3400 Brook Road
Richmond, VA 23227

Don Holladay
Eastern New Mexico University
P. O. Box 2054
Portales, NM 88130

Bob Holloway
First United Methodist Church
313 N. Center
Arlington, TX 76011

Karen Hudson
5709 Drayton Drive
Glen Allen, VA 23060-6381

Jim Jackson
Chapelwood United Methodist
  Church
11140 Greebay Drive
Houston, TX 77024

Laura Jernigan
1776 Stonecliff Court
Decatur, GA 30033

Sharee Johnson
Fairbury-Endicott United
  Methodist Church
605 E. Street
Fairbury, NE 68352

Wendy Joyner
Fellowship Baptist Church
P.O. Box 1122
Americus, GA 31709

Gary Kindley
First United Methodist Church
5601 Pleasant Run Road
Colleyville, TX 76034

Hugh Litchfield
6012 Currituck Road
Kitty Hawk, NC 27948

Robert Long
St. Luke's United Methodist
  Church
222 NW 15th Street
Oklahoma City, OK 73103-3598

Mike Lowry
University United Methodist
  Church
5084 DeZavala Road
San Antonio, TX 78249

Timothy Mallard
7045 Ashleigh Manor Court
Alexandria, VA 22315

John Mathis
High Hills Baptist Church
211 S. Halifax Road
Jarratt, VA 23867

Bass Mitchell
Route 2 Box 68
Hot Springs, VA 24445

Lance Moore
First United Methodist Church
324 Pineville Road
Monroeville, AL 36460

David Mosser
First United Methodist Church
P.O. Box 88
Graham, TX 76450

Raquel Mull
2220 Utah, NE
Albuquerque, NM 87110

Timothy Owings
First Baptist Church
P.O. Box 14489
Augusta, GA 30919

Bill Ritter
First United Methodist Church
1589 W. Maple Road
Birmingham, MI 48008

Carl Schenck
Manchester United Methodist
  Church
129 Woods Mill Road
Manchester, MO 63011-4339

Mary Scifres
3810 67th Avenue Court, NW
Gig Harbor, WA 98335

Thomas Steagald
Marshville United Methodist
    Church
P.O. Box 427
Marshville, NC 28103

Tim Walker
First United Methodist Church
422 Church Street
Grapevine, TX 76051

Ross West
Positive Difference
    Communications
100 Martha Drive
Rome, GA 30165-4138

Mark White
302 North Estes Drive
Chapel Hill, NC 27514

Victoria Atkinson White
302 North Estes Drive
Chapel Hill, NC 27514

Ryan Wilson
First Baptist Church
P.O. Box 828
Columbus, GA 31902-0828

Philip Wise
First Baptist Church
P.O. Box 2025
Dothan, AL 36302

Sandy Wylie
P.O. Box 986
McAlester, OK 74502

INDEX

OLD TESTAMENT

NEW TESTAMENT